OXFORD ENGLISH MONOGRAPHS

MILTON AND THE INEFFABLE

NOAM REISNER

OXFORD
UNIVERSITY PRESS

OXFORD
UNIVERSITY PRESS

Great Clarendon Street, Oxford OX2 6DP

Oxford University Press is a department of the University of Oxford.
It furthers the University's objective of excellence in research, scholarship,
and education by publishing worldwide in

Oxford New York

Auckland Cape Town Dar es Salaam Hong Kong Karachi
Kuala Lumpur Madrid Melbourne Mexico City Nairobi
New Delhi Shanghai Taipei Toronto

With offices in

Argentina Austria Brazil Chile Czech Republic France Greece
Guatemala Hungary Italy Japan Poland Portugal Singapore
South Korea Switzerland Thailand Turkey Ukraine Vietnam

Oxford is a registered trade mark of Oxford University Press
in the UK and in certain other countries

Published in the United States
by Oxford University Press Inc., New York

British Library Cataloguing in Publication Data
Data available

Library of Congress Cataloging in Publication Data
Data available

Library of Congress Control Number: 2009935891

Typeset by SPI Publisher Services, Pondicherry, India
Printed in Great Britain
on acid-free paper by the
MPG Books Group, Bodmin and King's Lynn

ISBN 978-0-19-957262-5

1 3 5 7 9 10 8 6 4 2

To my parents

Contents

Acknowledgements

This book has its remote origins in my doctoral thesis (Lady Margaret Hall, Oxford, 2005), and although what remains of the original thesis is only faintly shadowed in the present monograph my enduring debt of gratitude remains as clear as ever to my doctoral supervisors, John Carey and Robin Robbins. Professors Carey and Robbins oversaw with great care my original doctoral research and followed and supported my work throughout my graduate studies at Oxford. They have been and remain exemplary teachers. John Carey especially always came to my rescue when I most needed his advice, always asked the right questions, and was abundantly generous with his time, wisdom, and profound learning far, far beyond the call of duty. I would not have been in a position to publish this book were it not for his warm and steadfast support, and for that my gratitude to him is truly ineffable. Tom Weinandy supervised with commendable patience the theological and philosophical aspects of the original thesis (which now survives as some of the material in Chapters 1 and 2), and Peter Hawkins, at the time a visiting fellow at Lady Margaret Hall, generously commented on the penultimate draft. The task of transforming the original thesis into a publishable monograph has been a particularly challenging one as well, and I would like to thank my examiners, Colin Burrow and the late, great A. D. Nuttall, one of my most inspiring teachers, for their invaluable comments and criticism on route to publication. Colin Burrow also reviewed the monograph's penultimate revised typescript, and I thank him for his many helpful suggestions for improvement and warm encouragement throughout the arduous revision process. I would also like to thank the anonymous readers for Oxford University Press for their wealth of constructive and very timely criticism and Jacqueline Baker, my editor at the Press, for her outstanding professionalism as she calmly guided this book through many drafts with a steady hand.

Crucially, I was able to complete new research and undertake the revision work suggested by my examiners and readers in a relatively short space of time, and this would not have been possible were it not for St Anne's College electing me in 2006 for a Plumer Research

Fellowship. I would like to thank, therefore, the governing body of St Anne's College, my many friends and colleagues there, and especially some of my former students (my 'fit audience...though few'), for providing me with the perfect scholastic setting for my work and for making my stay there a joyful and memorable one. Many friends and colleagues, both at St Anne's and elsewhere, also helped in a variety of ways during the writing process, and so I would like to extend my warmest thanks (in alphabetical order) to Paul Fiddes, Chanita Good-blatt, Siân Grønlie, Freya Johnston, Alexis Kirschbaum, Anne Mullen, Ann Pasternak-Slater, Dawn Phillips, Matthew Reynolds, Nat Stein, Kathryn Sutherland, Bharat Tandon, Olivier Tonneau, Shira Wolosky, and Shirley Sharon–Zisser—their friendship has made this book much better than it would have been without it. Ann Pasternak-Slater, Alexis Kirschbuam, and Olivier Tonneau also helpfully commented on parts of my typescript in progress, and I thank them for their numerous suggestions and for challenging me when I thought I knew better. Naturally, however, I alone remain accountable for whatever infelicities and faults inevitably remain. Finally, on a more personal note, I would like to thank my parents, without whose loving support and enthusiastic encouragement a choice of academic career in English literature would not have been possible. In so many ways this book is indebted, and therefore dedicated, to them. And last but always first in my mind, I proclaim my undying debt of gratitude to my partner-in-life, Meirav, for her love, patience, and unconditional support in all that I do. I thank her for reminding me daily that there is a life to be lived beyond the covers of books, and for putting up with all things ineffable more than most people would have endured.

A small section of Chapter 3 has appeared before (in a much less developed form) as 'The Prophet's Conundrum: Poetic Soaring in Milton's "Nativity Ode" and "The Passion"', *Philological Quarterly*, 83 (2004), 371–88, and I thank the editor of *PQ* for giving me permission to reproduce this material.

List of Abbreviations

CM	Blackwell's *A Companion to Milton*, ed. Thomas N. Corns
CCM	*Cambridge Companion to Milton*, 2nd edn., ed. Dennis R. Danielson
CHB	*Cambridge History of the Bible*, ed. P. R. Ackroyd *et al.*
CHRP	*The Cambridge History of Renaissance Philosophy*, ed. Charles B. Schmitt and Quentin Skinner
CCW	The Columbia edition of *The Complete Works of John Milton*, gen. ed. Frank Allen Patterson
CSP	*Milton: Complete Shorter Poems*, 2nd edn., ed. John Carey
ODNB	*Oxford Dictionary of National Biography*
Poems 1645	1645 edition of *Poems of Mr. John Milton Both English and Latin Compos'd at several times*
YCP	The Yale edition of the *Complete Prose Works of John Milton*
Anglia	*Beiblatt zur Anglia*
C&L	*Christianity and Literature*
Cithara-	*Cithara: Essays in the Judeo-Christian Tradition*
CI	*Critical Inquiry*
CL	*Comparative Literature*
CLS	*Comparative Literature Studies*
CQ	*Cambridge Quarterly*
E&S	*Essays & Studies*
ELH	*A Journal of English Literary History*
ELN	*English Language Notes*
EC	*Essays in Criticism*
GHJ	*George Herbert Journal*
JMRS	*Journal of Medieval and Renaissance Studies*
LT	*Literature & Theology*
MA	*Medium Aevum*

MQ	*Milton Quarterly*
MS	*Milton Studies*
MLR	*Modern Language Review*
MPH	*Modern Philology*
Mosaic	*Mosaic: A Journal for the Interdisciplinary Study of Literature*
NM	*Neuphilologische Mitteilungen*
NQ	*Notes & Queries*
PQ	*Philological Quarterly*
PT	*Poetics Today*
PMLA	*Publications of the Modern Languages Association*
RP	*Renaissance Papers*
RQ	*Renaissance Quarterly*
RS	*Renaissance Studies*
SC	*The Seventeenth Century*
SEL	*Studies in English Literature, 1500–1900*
SPH	*Studies in Philology*
TLS	*Times Literary Supplement*
TSLL	*Texas Studies in Literature and Language*
UTQ	*University of Toronto Quarterly*
YR	*Yale Review*

Note to the reader

References to both primary and secondary sources will be given as short titles in the footnotes; full references for all cited and consulted sources are gathered into the Bibliography at the end of the book, which is divided according to primary and secondary sources. Where I have consulted only one essay from a collection I will list the individual essay rather than the collection. All quotations from contemporary sources retain where possible the original spelling, punctuation, capitalization, and italics, but the use of 'v' and 'u', 'f' and 's', 'i' and 'j' has been modernized. With the exception of short phrases or passages where the exact wording and syntax of the original language is germane to my immediate argument, texts not originally in English have been quoted in an English translation. Except for a few passages in Hebrew where the translation is my own, the majority of translations have been taken from published academic sources. For classical texts in Greek and Latin and their translations I have relied heavily on the Loeb Classical Library. Transliteration of Greek and Hebrew words follows standardized conventions. Unless otherwise noted, all quotations from the English Bible are from the Authorised Version. All references to Milton's poetry are to John Carey, *Milton: Complete Shorter Poems* (2nd edn.), and Alastair Fowler, *Milton: Paradise Lost* (2nd edn.). All translations of Milton's Latin poems are John Carey's and are from his edition.

Introduction

SI ILLUD EST INEFFABILE QUOD DICI NON POTEST, NON EST INEFFABILE QUOD VEL INEFFABILE DICI POTEST.

If what cannot be spoken is unspeakable, then it is not unspeakable, because it can actually be said to be unspeakable.

(Augustine, *De Doctrina Christiana*)

Wenn man sich nicht bemüht das Unaussprechliche auszusprechen, so geht nichts verloren. Sondern das Unaussprechliche ist,—unausspre-chlich—in dem Ausgesprochenen enthalten!

If only you do not try to utter what is unutterable then *nothing* gets lost. But the unutterable will be—unutterably—*contained* in what has been uttered!

(Ludwig Wittgenstein, Letter to Paul Engelmann, 9. 4.1917)

> *Words, after speech, reach*
> *Into the silence. Only by the form, the pattern,*
> *Can words or music reach*
> *The stillness, as a Chinese jar still*
> *Moves perpetually in its stillness.*

(T. S. Eliot, 'Burnt Norton')

Confronting the inexpressible and the unsayable is a commonplace of human experience. Every day of our lives we experience those moments when language fails us; when ideas, emotions, or mental images—those things which fall under the nebulous category of meaning—are mis-transmitted, misinterpreted, or simply passed over in silence in the processes of human communication. Finding the words to describe an idea, an image, or an emotion is not only the greatest obstacle to human language but also the greatest challenge for its art. Like any other pervasive phenomenon of human experience, the ineffable has long played a major role in both Western and Eastern philosophies and theologies and the literary discourses which have arisen and continue to arise from within and without, against and about, these traditions.[1] As I will argue in this study, the struggle with ineffability in many ways defines Milton's triumphs as a poet and goes to the heart of the central critical debates to engage his readers over the centuries and decades. Granted, such a declaration sounds positively trivial when we consider the ubiquitous nature of ineffability as silent presence in all human affairs: might we not say the same of any other poet or artist? Indeed we may, and many critics have done so in relation to numerous other authors and thinkers, ranging in time and cultural contexts from Dante to Paul Celan. It is not only the concept of the ineffable as such, however, which attracts the critic's interest in any given author's treatment of this concept, but rather the uniqueness of the personal, cultural, intellectual, and historical moment which shape a given poet's understanding and literary engagement with the ineffable, whether it is conceived, as in Milton's case, within Christian Neoplatonic traditions of religious and metaphysical ineffability, or in other overlapping configurations.

It is clear, then, that in talking about Milton and the ineffable I need to define the exact terms I am concerned with as precisely as possible, as well as the intellectual-historical forces which shaped those terms. Depending on how we understand the relationship between language, meaning, and the world around us, the 'ineffable', as a concept, can mean many things. Our modern, post-Freudian understanding of the term is primarily psychoanalytical. Certain experiences, particularly those associated with intense emotions such as love, terror, or religious ecstasy, do not lend themselves to literal description. Such experiences belong to conceptualizations that often slip into metaphors that signify, or ineffably point to, what Lacan for example terms 'the real'. Like Roman Jakobson, Lacan uses metaphor in the sense of the structure of substitution (as distinct from metonymical displacement), not as a

---

[1] Scharfstein, *Ineffability*, discusses at length the many conceptual links and echoes between formulations of apophasis in Western and Eastern religions and philosophies. See also the essays by D. G. Jones, Harold F. Coward, Joseph Epes Brown, and David W. Atkinson in Blodgett and Coward, *Silence, the Word and the Sacred*.

formal instance of language; the unconscious, in other words, is not a text in which there are metaphorical expressions but a locus in which some representations (or memory-traces) are not allowed by the pleasure principle to be translated into conscious representations and hence are substituted by something else. The ineffable 'real' for Lacan is that which exceeds words (the signifier, the symbolic), and needs to be excluded from the symbolic so that signification might become possible. As one of the English translator of Lacan's *Écrits* explains, the 'real' is used in Lacan's system adjectivally to describe 'the ineliminable residue of all articulation, the foreclosed element, which may be approached, but never grasped: the umbilical cord of the symbolic'.[2] Alternatively, there is the deconstructive, competing Derridean understanding of 'ineffability' as the negative non-presence, or the absence of meaningful transcendental constructs in the endless play of signifiers upon other signifiers. Derrida's ineffable is that which extends beyond the text and beyond the range of what is capable of being processed by the structures that produce textual meaning. The famous statement from *Of Grammatology*, 'il n'y a pas de hors-texte',[3] registers Derrida's sober recognition that in matters of signification only the text matters, and that anything thought to exist *outside* the text is a virtual projection made from within it.

None of these modern (or post-modern) definitions, however, would have necessarily made any obvious sense to Milton, who believed resolutely in the immutable truth of the Bible and the existence of God, and who worshipped at Plato's logocentric altar. Milton could never conceive of ineffability outside Christian logocentric discourse and the transcendental, hyperbolic order on which it depends. Peter Hawkins and Anne Schotter, co-editors of *Ineffability: Naming the Unnamable from Dante to Beckett* (New York, 1984), provide a very plausible distinction between modern and pre-modern notions of ineffability in their introduction:

If the ineffable is that about which nothing truly can be said, perhaps (to borrow a line from Wallace Stevens's 'Snowman') we can differentiate between

---

[2] *Écrits: A Selection*, trans. A. Sheridan, p. x.
[3] 'There is nothing outside of the text.' French original embedded in the English translation, Spivak, *Of Grammatology*, 158.

'the nothing that is not there and the nothing that is'—between what we may call a 'negative' ineffable and a 'positive' one. Although it has many secular manifestations, the latter is most fundamentally a religious notion, one which acknowledges the great gulf fixed between the divine and what human beings can think or say about divinity.[4]

Although very useful as a starting point, the implied distinction here between a 'negative' and a 'positive' ineffable along the lines of religious belief and modern secularism can be misleading. For the pseudo-Dionysius and his Christian Neoplatonic heirs, for example, what would be meant by 'positive' in this sense already contains its own dialectic of negative–positive expression, since negation leads the mind up a ladder of mystical ascent towards an ineffable understanding of that which is absolutely positive, or deemed existent. Similarly, although ostensibly worlds apart, Lacan's theory of the ineffable, for all its impact on secular post-modernism, is profoundly 'positive' since Lacan's 'real' is precisely what *is* (at least until Lacan's later teaching) outside the text, or manifest in the text in the holes in sense. For Derrida, on the other hand, what is outside the text is neither negative, nor positive, but simply absent—it lacks ontology in any sense whatsoever. It is true that a number of scholars and critics have attempted to show in recent decades that Derrida's theory of deconstruction actually rhymes with negative theology in significant ways. John Caputo, for example, in his influential *The Prayers and Tears of Jacques Derrida*, asserts that negative theology, like deconstruction, 'is a deeply affirmative irruption . . . a passion for the impossible, for trespassing and transgression'.[5] However, as Shira Wolosky clarifies in her rebuttal of Caputo and those who would seek to rescue Derrida 'not from, but for theology', 'Derrida does not contest [the] mutual implication of negative and positive theology. Indeed, he explores it, but in doing so he questions the escape of negative theology from ontology. Negation does not in itself guarantee such an escape, does not necessarily deontologize theological structures.'[6] Rather, the un-utterable *telos* of negative theology for Derrida is not 'existent', but

[4] Hawkins and Schotter, *Ineffability*, 1–2.
[5] Caputo, *The Prayers and Tears of Jacques Derrida*, 27.
[6] Wolosky, 'On Derrida's "How To Avoid Speaking: Denials"', 264.

merely a self-emptying discourse which testifies to what it cannot say—a postscript, as it were, to eviscerated presence.[7]

The crux of this unfolding paradox rests in the idea of an ontological presence which is accepted, as a matter of religious faith, to be radically ineffable. Hawkins and Schotter's use of the term 'positive ineffable' to describe the solemn silence which ensues in the presence of 'an over-plus of being' derives from Rudolf Otto's canonical essay, *The Idea of the Holy*. In it, Otto memorably supplies a series of elegantly argued (though not infallible) terms to account for the various psychological elements of religious experience. Of particular influence is Otto's discussion of the 'numinous' and its attendant religious feeling of the '*mysterium tremendum*'. According to Otto's formulation, the 'tremor' or 'fear' a religious mystery excites can manifest itself in a variety of ways, but always in the presence 'of that which is a *mystery* inexpressible and above all creatures . . . the term does not define the [mysterious] object more positively in its qualitative character. But though what is enunciated in the word is negative, what is meant is something absolutely and intensely positive'.[8] Or, to cite Derrida's inverted atheist point of view, 'if there is a work of negativity in discourse and predication, it will produce divinity'.[9] The distinction between a 'positive' and a 'negative' ineffable, therefore, *is* helpful as a starting point to clarify the terms with which this study is most concerned. To the extent to which the 'positive' ineffable is associated with belief in a transcendental reality that may be deemed existent, and the 'negative' ineffable with the denial of such reality, it could be argued that this study is mostly concerned with religious notions of 'positive' ineffability as opposed to secular, predominantly modern, 'negative' ones. My use of the term 'ineffable', therefore, is confined to its religious theist uses which, while in themselves potentially having recourse either to positive or negative expression, ultimately proceed from the axiomatic assumption that God exists and that his existence is something about which nothing can be said using ordinary language, except through negation. After all, while there are many subtle

---

[7] For further reflections on this difficult idea see Franke, *On What Cannot Be Said*, i. 446.

[8] Otto, *The Idea of the Holy*, 12–13 (italics original to the text).

[9] Derrida, 'How To Avoid Speaking: Denials', trans. K. Frieden, in Budick and Iser, *Languages of the Unsayable*, 4–70, at p. 6.

and unsettling manifestations of 'negative' ineffability in Milton's work, as we shall see, none of these negative irruptions can be rightly identified, for example, with Nietzsche's outright contempt for the limits of human speech,[10] or, for that matter, with the disembodied voice of, say, Beckett's *The Unnameable*.[11]

However, the question of whether or not it is at all possible to say anything meaningful in 'ordinary' language about that which is existent yet ineffable asks finally what an 'extra-ordinary' use of language might be; and, more critical to this study, did Milton find a way to talk about the ineffable without *actually* talking about it. A common trope of traditional apophatic theology (that is, negative theology which moves away from speech and is therefore, using the Greek term, *apo-phatic*) is to pretend to be talking 'about' the ineffable God while actually talking around the subject, because to really talk about God as he is in himself— that is, not about how he might appear to us, but how he really is—would be, of course, impossible: God as he is in himself is designated only by deep, meaningful silence.[12] There are, however, many ways

---

[10] In *Twilight of the Idols* Nietzsche writes: 'Our true experiences are not garrulous. They could not communicate themselves if they wanted to: they lack words. We have already grown beyond whatever we have words for. In all talking there lies a grain of contempt. Speech, it seems was devised only for the average, medium, communicable. The speaker has already *vulgarized* himself by speaking' (*Twilight of the Idols and The Anti-Christ*, trans. R. J. Hollingdale, 94). It should be noted that for Nietzsche any notion of an abstract, metaphysical 'experience' of a good God within the context of Christian theology is inevitably an absurd corruption of the 'God type' which, if anything, must be beyond good and evil if it is to hold any relevance to 'actuality' (ibid. 138–40). The only 'true' experiences for Nietzsche are those of total and unrestrained life and it is this sort of experience which language, with its bondage to logical representational systems and ideologies, has long lost the ability to articulate. Clearly, this type of a 'negative' ineffable is very different from one which holds that the transcendentally existent can only been expressed negatively.

[11] For a good reflection on the presence of ineffability in Beckett as it relates to Wittgenstein's *Tractatus* see Bruce Kawin, 'On Not Having the Last Word: Beckett, Wittgenstein, and the Limits of Language', in Hawkins and Schotter, *Ineffability*, 189–201. See also Kane, *The Language of Silence*, ch. 5, and Wolosky, *Language Mysticism*, 91–134.

[12] For a discussion of the 'about'/about distinction in the context of ineffable mystery see Cooper, *The Measure of Things*, 285–9. Cooper argues that mystics do not necessarily violate the ineffable by speaking 'about' it because in fact they only ever talk about their *experience* of failing to talk about it. He then qualifies this, however, by also pointing out that mystical utterances are not necessarily descriptive or assertive in the first place. This would fit with Denys Turner's seminal re-evaluation of mystical theology in *The Darkness of God*, where he shows that all ancient and medieval mystical writings in the

of talking *around* a subject and they do not all involve the more familiar gesture of humbly falling silent. My main argument is this: Milton engages with a rich apophatic tradition which tells him quite precisely what can and cannot be said about that which is traditionally considered ineffable, and he nevertheless tries to find creative ways to talk not just around the subject, but around the problem of ineffability altogether. In his classic book *Beginnings: Intention and Method*, Edward Said remarks, almost in passing, that to read *Paradise Lost* 'is to be convinced, in Ruskin's phrase, of the idea of power: by its sheer duration and presence, and by its capacity for making sense despite the absence [of a lost Paradise] at its center, Milton's verse seems to have overpowered the void within his epic.'[13] Said's 'void' in this case is not the shifting void of deconstruction—at least not intentionally—but the void left behind when fallen, logocentric man is divorced from the infinite beatitudes of divine ontology and is left only with its remote dream. The most challenging aspect of my argument, therefore, is to explore how Milton's verse indeed *seems* to 'overpower' the void of ineffability at the centre of his major poetry without actually doing so. Milton, I argue, only ever wants to be *seen* to say the unsayable without *actually* saying it, and without once sacrificing either intelligibility *or* the sense of mystery which authorizes such intelligibility. This surely sounds impossible, but it is precisely out of the sheer impossibility of these propositions that Milton's poetry assumes its shape and power.

One potential approach to this study could have been to engage with Milton's poetry and implicit metaphysical ideas directly with little by way of exordium or prolegomenon. Milton, however, wrote his poetry at a crucial juncture in Western intellectual history, when central theological, metaphysical, and literary concerns were being reshaped and refocused with astonishing force. As a teleological poet, Milton struggled within and against a large variety of interrelated religious, philosophical, and literary traditions even as he mapped his unique

Western tradition are, in essence, non-experiential to begin with. As Turner elucidates, apophatic theology does not in itself constitute a spiritual 'experience' but is rather a *critique* from within normative language-driven piety *of* that piety. According to Turner, therefore, thinkers like Rudolph Otto misread the apophatic tradition by seeking to fill its perceived experiential vacuum with 'the plenum of the psychologistic' (Turner, *The Darkness of God*, 259).

[13] Said, *Beginnings*, 280.

vision of the world, its origins, and his own place within it. The idea of
the ineffable, which can be glossed as a proper concern for the limits of
speech when confronted by the unsayable that nevertheless needs to be
said, is silently present in all of the intellectual traditions which shaped
Milton's poetics. C. A. Patrides once noted that Milton 'used traditional
ideas in such a way that they were transformed into seeming novel-
ties';[14] this is also true of Milton's treatment of traditional apophatic
imagery and concepts, except that in this case there is nothing 'seeming'
about the resulting novelty. I will argue that Milton's approach to the
very notion of ineffability was uniquely novel for its time. Milton was
responding in his art to a crisis about ineffable presence and mystery in
both Reformation thought and Christian humanism and was forced to
reposition his poetic voice within the apophatic tradition in ways which
radically challenged its conventional literary decorum and semiotic
codes. To focus only on Milton's poetry, therefore, would have left
half the story untold, and the story of ineffability—notwithstanding all
the paradoxes involved—needs to be told if Milton's initial defiance
of sacred silence and final surrender to its interior promptings is to be
placed in its suitable historical and intellectual context.

The first two chapters provide the necessary historical and intellectual
background for my ensuing analysis of Milton's treatment of the
ineffable in his poetry. I do not claim in these two chapters to outline
an exhaustive historical survey of philosophical and theological traditions concerned with the problems of ineffability; such an attempt far
exceeds the scope of this study and in any case would have detracted
from the literary focus on Milton's poetry.[15] Rather, I have chosen to
highlight important intellectual milestones in Western thought that are
most relevant to understanding Milton's subsequent literary engagement with ineffable presence in the context of Christian Platonic

---

[14] Patrides, *Milton and the Christian Tradition*, 5.
[15] For reasons of scope and argumentative focus, several key thinkers and contributors
to the idea of ineffability in Western religion, philosophy, and literature before Milton
are conspicuously absent from my survey: Eriugena, Meister Eckhart, Dante, and
Wycliffe are the most glaring omissions, though their absence was deemed necessary to
make room for thinkers more relevant to my immediate argument about Milton. For a
comprehensive survey of the apophatic tradition from Plato to Derrida in all its aspects
see the introduction and critical essays in William Franke's impressive two-volume
anthology, *On What Cannot Be Said: Apophatic Discourses in Philosophy, Religion,
Literature and the Arts*.

humanism and Reformation theology. The first chapter examines a number of key stages in the development of speculative ideas about the ineffable, from the Exodus account of Moses's prophetic appointment by the burning bush, through Greek and early Christian philosophical reflections on the *logos*, to late medieval philosophical theology and its attempts to formulate a semiotics and grammar for and about divine ontology.

Following chronologically from the first chapter, the second chapter explores the radical changes in the intellectual presence of ineffability in Western thought following the rise of humanism and the impact of religious reform. It seeks to demonstrate how the notion of the ineffable ceases in the period to be merely speculative and, in the processes of Renaissance and Reformation, becomes a temporal source for profound individual empowerment but also religious anxiety and intellectual dissent. I develop my argument here in stages by surveying and analysing the permutations of thinking about ineffability in the Renaissance Neoplatonic philosophy of man, in the philological practices of Erasmian humanism, and in Reformation debates about the use of signs and metaphors in the operation of the *logos* in scripture and sacrament. The final section focuses specifically on the English Reformed landscape, and sets the scene for the analysis of Milton's early poetry by considering the impact of these ideas on some of Milton's godly contemporaries and the emerging English Protestant preoccupation with the motions of interior sacredness, holy silence, and the language of election. The overriding narrative of the first two chapters, therefore, is one of continual struggle against silence, whether in metaphysical speculations about divine ontology, or an active, socially responsible religious life which seeks to engage with God's revealed word and its promise of redemption for the fallen world. The second chapter in particular thus aims to highlight emerging Protestant anxieties about the inevitable dislocation of the ineffable in Reformed discourse, while looking ahead to Milton's consequent attempt to emancipate this idea from the clutches of emerging orthodoxies on either side of the Reformation divide.

The purpose of the first two chapters is not to reconstruct a teleological blueprint of specific textual sources which Milton may have read and therefore drew on in his thinking about the ineffable, but to establish a sufficiently detailed context for an examination of the ways in which a man of Milton's learning and religious-political disposition would have responded to this idea and its underlying literary implications in seventeenth-century England. Although I frame the problem of ineffability in broadly speaking historical terms of 'Renaissance' and 'Reformation', my subsequent critical approach to Milton's poetry is not in the least 'historicist'. My focus is on Milton's intellectual engagement with an abstract philosophical-theological, and finally literary, problem which, although having inevitable political and historical implications in some narrow contexts, ultimately yields its literary significance in a broader, speculative discussion about the limits of language and representation. Be that as it may, I am well aware that the claim to novelty in Milton studies is a notoriously difficult one, and I make no such claim in what follows beyond offering a fresh perspective from which to re-examine a familiar subject. Milton's struggle with the ineffable, especially in *Paradise Lost*, is hardly a new topic for the critic. His theories of accommodation and biblical hermeneutics, as well as his idiosyncratic brand of Reformed theology have all been analysed in minute detail. The theme has also been more glancingly touched upon by the countless critics who have analysed Milton's elevated style, his view and use of language, his love of music and use of musical metaphors, and the structure, symbolism, and argument of *Paradise Lost*. Other contextual studies, especially those by William Kerrigan, Joseph Wittreich, and Michael Lieb, have established the importance of prophecy, the visionary, the sacral, and the numinous in Milton's poetry, not to mention his intellectual indebtedness to a seemingly never-ending catalogue of religious, philosophical, and occult ideas.[16] The reader will note, however, that I call this study *Milton and the Ineffable* and not, for example, *Milton and the Ineffable God*. Although much of the ineffable character of Milton's poetry derives from the intrinsically numinous character of his subject, I am not directly concerned in this study with the numinous *per se*, but with the formal problems of ineffability such a numinous presence poses to a devout thinker who wishes to compose poetry about and around its experience. In other words, if Michael Lieb analyses at length Milton's 'poetics of deity',[17] I wish to complement that analysis with an examination of Milton's 'poetics of ineffability',

---

[16] The list of the studies I have in mind here is too long to include in a footnote; I refer to each of them at the appropriate places in this study.
[17] Lieb, *Theological Milton*, 127.

which is not quite the same thing. Lieb's study offers a primarily theological analysis of Milton's poetic imagery of God and of the discursive relationship between theological and poetic vocabularies in Milton's imagination; my study seeks to analyse the crisis of mimesis in relation to apophatic discourse which Milton inherits from the humanist-Protestant traditions and attempts to resolve creatively *in* his poetry and theological thinking. The precise objective of the first two chapters' selective history of the ineffable, therefore, is to demonstrate that by the time Milton enters this history, the theological and philosophical assumptions associated with the idea of ineffability were unsettled by intellectual and religious conflict. As I will show in my ensuing analysis of Milton's poetry, such unsettling of the intellectual assumptions about the ineffability of transcendental subject-matter allowed him finally to accommodate the elusive presence of the numinous in his art in ways which set his mature poetry apart from traditional formulations of ineffable rapture in Judaeo-Christian theology and mysticism before his time.

After a brief reconsideration of Milton's well-documented impatience with, or even fear of, ineffable mystery in more general terms, I begin my analysis of Milton's poetry in the third chapter by examining the shape and development of his prophetic and pastoral voices in *Poems 1645*. I focus in particular on the elusive presence of ineffable mystery and rapture in the 'Nativity Ode', 'The Passion', 'At a Solemn Music', *A Masque*, 'Lycidas', and 'Epitaphium Damonis', in the order they appear in the volume. I explore the difficulty Milton faced as a young devout Protestant, still unsure of his own radical ideas, in resolving the conceptual contradiction between his religious belief in the power and perspicuity of words, and his desire to capture that which is beyond words in rapturous poetic flight. I argue that Milton of the 1620s to 1640s sought to create an imaginary and ultimately unstable space where the vatic poet briefly sheds his shackles of sin and begins to soar beyond the reach of human language.

I continue to pursue this theme in the fourth chapter, in my analysis of *Paradise Lost*, where I examine the dislocation and elaborate diffusion of ineffable presences in the monist materialist universe of the poem. Beginning with the famous invocation to holy light in the opening of Book III, I analyse the various poetic gestures Milton uses to assert his putative ability to say the unsayable while simultaneously allowing the poetic imagery and tone of the invocation to suggest that such feats are merely imagined and are not in fact available to the humbly fallen, though inspired, poet. This naturally raises important questions about the precise function of metaphor and allegory in the poem. While the inspired poet allegedly accommodates hidden vistas to his fallen readers using analogies and metaphors, the evoked universe of the poem consists only of luminous matter and literal truths. The materialism of the universe in the poem and of the poetry itself, I argue, is a metaphorical consequence of Milton's attempt to contend with the imperatives and limitation of ineffability. The result is a contradictory but poetically powerful theory of monist accommodation which allows Milton to preclude ineffability and deny that accommodation need ever take place where he is concerned, even as he reintroduces a sense of ineffable loss and mystery on the level of poetic feeling by pointing out that, where the fallen reader is concerned, the resulting vision of Heaven and a lost Paradise is distinctly accommodated. This leads to a more detailed analysis of what I term ineffable 'speech effects' in the poem, where Milton first deploys and then subverts apophatic imagery in the process of evoking the otherworldly and indeed alien character of divine, angelic, demonic, and prelapsarian speech. Such growing dissonance between what words literally and plainly say and their aural and affective impact, I argue, conditions the reader of the poem to believe that what should be understood literally in the poem, especially when God speaks, is in fact *radically* ineffable. This strategy finally allows Milton to invest the objectified *idea* of the ineffable—deployed in the poem adjectively as an attribute of divine effluence—with an ethical dimension, where speechlessness can become a form of absolute punishment when the fallen creature is ejected from God's kingly presence. This idea links up with the poem's sustained meditation on the ineffable encounter with the divine as an interiorized spiritual experience, where God's creatures, whether they are fallen angels or fallen man, must contend with the emerging silence that is the consequence of divine loss. Such an experience can only confirm the irredeemable devils in their sinfulness and state of divine privation, but for Adam and Eve it signals the path for repentance and ultimate redemption.

This naturally leads then into the fifth and final chapter, in which I turn to the 1671 volume of *Paradise Regained* and *Samson Agonistes.* Here I analyse the crisis of apophatic discourse at the heart of the poet's subjectivity, when modes of spiritual interiority surrender to ineffable silence at the expense of voice and meaning. Whereas in his early poetry and *Paradise Lost* Milton tries to find the words or poetic imagery with which to capture the presence of the ineffable without once falling silent, I argue that *Paradise Regained* and *Samson Agonistes* are reflective and meta-poetic in that they explore the potential failure or success of this process for the vatic-sacral poet contemplating redemption for humanity. In these two oddly comparable poems about the merits and limits of individual Christian heroism, Milton finally confronts the ineffable mystery at the heart of the Protestant election and regeneration narrative. In doing so he offers his readers seemingly two very different, yet in fact congruent, didactic, and intensely dialectical reflections on the nature of interior holiness and what it takes to secure salvation and redemption for the individual, if not for his nation.

1

Silence and presence: ineffability in ancient and medieval Western thought

THE PROPHET'S HEAVY TONGUE

The story of ineffability in Western thought must begin, if anywhere, with the Hebrew Bible and its portrayal of a mysterious, omnipotent paternal deity. The God portrayed in the Bible, enigmatically alluded to as Yahweh, is a deity of radical contradictions. On the one hand the Bible portrays Yahweh as a being infinitely beyond the comprehension of man, but on the other hand as susceptible to a wide range of distinctly human emotions, such as deep paternal care, anger, and even petulance. This profound paradox lies at the devotional core of Jewish and Christian notions of deity, even though the implications of this paradox for either religion are significantly different. St Augustine expresses the typical view of this paradox from the Christian perspective: 'the Divine Being is beyond words and cannot be spoken of in any way without recourse to expressions of time and place.'[1] However, since God, according to prevailing monotheistic orthodoxies, deeply cares for his creation, he remains profoundly immanent within it. As Augustine immediately qualifies the statement I have just quoted: 'whereas God is before all time and all place, nevertheless the one who made us is nearer to us than many things which have been made.'[2] At the very heart of this complex relationship with the hidden God stands the Hebrew Bible, or *Tanakh*. According to tradition, the *Tanakh* more generally,

---

[1] Hammond, *The Literal Meaning of Genesis*, i. 166–7.
[2] Ibid.

but the Pentateuch especially, is an infallible record of God's perceived immanence within the created order. Significantly, the human–divine relationship established in the Book of Genesis and then enacted throughout the *Tanakh* is predicated not on image, but on sound. The Word, the creative utterance of God, is that which fills the meaningless void with substance, with *meaning*, and which ultimately places man, God's creature, at the centre of this *meaning-full* creation as lord of all that he surveys: God names Adam, and Adam names the animals. Consequently, the Hebrew God of the Bible is almost never seen, but often heard, his favourite form of communication with his chosen creatures requiring some form of verbal accommodation.

This basic paradoxical attitude towards the sacredness of Scripture traces its roots to the very beginnings of the rabbinical movement and the shift in ancient Judaism from aural to textual sacredness.[3] As Walter Ong explains: 'The word of God centered in the Hebrew and Christian heritage... came to man at a strategic point in history, which is to say... at a strategic point in the development of the human psyche, when the oral-aural world was being reshaped toward visualism by the force of alphabetic writing.'[4] Thus, as Ong intimates, the ancient shift within Judaism towards textual sacredness operated fully within the mystical context of the oral-aural sensorium, where the written word was seen to flow from the power of God's spoken Word, not to resist it. Any attempt to understand the idea of the ineffable within the context of Judaeo-Christian theology and mysticism (as opposed to merely Jewish theology), therefore, must begin with the Torah, or the earliest written record of the divine utterance from its traditional point of view as a text dictated to Moses by angels during the theophany at Mount Sinai, when God came to Moses on the mountain 'in a thick cloud' (Exod. 19: 9) and spoke to him 'by a voice' (Exod. 19: 19). Especially revealing in this context is the story of Moses himself, and the account of his momentous prophetic appointment by the burning bush in Exodus 3–4.

The philosophical and theological crux of this familiar story comes at the first, and in some respects last, moment in recorded Jewish and

[3] See Fishbane, *Biblical Interpretation in Ancient Israel*, 1–23; and Kugel and Greer, *Early Biblical Interpretation*.

[4] Ong, *The Presence of the Word*, 189.

Christian traditions in which Abraham's God lets his mask of ineffable mystery drop:

And Moses said unto God, Behold, *when* I come unto the children of Israel, and shall say unto them, the God of your fathers hath sent me unto you; and they shall say to me, What *is* his name? What shall I say unto them? And God said unto Moses, I AM THAT I AM: and he said, Thus shalt thou say unto the children of Israel, I AM hath sent me unto you. And God said moreover unto Moses, Thus shalt thou say unto the children of Israel, The Lord God of your fathers, the God of Abraham, the God of Isaac, and the God of Jacob, hath sent me unto you: this *is* my name for ever, and this *is* my memorial unto all generations. (Exod. 3: 13–16)

In this single, much-cited, and much-debated passage of Scripture is embedded the conceptual germ of the entire tradition of the ineffable that would exert its influence on Western thought for over three millennia. What the various faiths and key religious thinkers (including Milton) have made of this passage over the centuries will become relevant later in my argument; for now, let us consider the simple facts. The first name God volunteers is ultimately unintelligible: 'I AM THAT I AM' is not a name at all, but a kind of ingenuous metaphysical deflection. It is God's way of saying to Moses, 'it is not for the creature to name his Creator'. Since, however, God foreknows that Moses cannot just simply walk up to his people and say 'I AM has sent me', he provides him with a gloss on the 'I AM' name—with a name by association: 'thou shalt say . . . The Lord God of your Fathers, the God of Abraham, the God of Isaac, and the God of Jacob,' and so on. Moreover, God pronounces this simpler, longer, and more reductive name to be his 'name for ever, and this *is* my memorial unto all generations'.

Many Jewish and Christian thinkers attempted over the centuries to solve the riddle of the name 'I AM THAT I AM' (usually with spectacularly absurd results). But, according to orthodox Judaism at least, the obscure divine name is a kind of metaphysical riddle that was never meant to be contemplated rationally, let alone solved. Although not everyone today is convinced of this, it seems likely, as the Exodus reference to 'I AM' indicates, that the Hebrew letters also designating the name YHWH (יהוה) make up a pun on the verb 'to be', HYH (היה). Whether this is true or not, it seems clear enough that the name 'I AM THAT I AM' signifies that God, as he relates to himself as subject, verb, and object, is indivisible, perfect, and eternal in his immutable oneness. God is, quite simply, that which *is*. Nevertheless, the actual mystery of the nameless God whose only available 'name' is 'I AM' cannot be penetrated, let alone spoken of, and so God provides Moses with another name, or rather with the names of the three flesh-and-blood patriarchs who have borne witness to his majestic divinity in the past: he is the God of Abraham, Isaac, and Jacob, whose name is Israel. God's two-layered response to Moses thus delineates the semantic and epistemological boundaries of the human–divine relationship: God may be in some measure known and spoken of, but only using the terms supplied by his revealed relationship with his chosen creatures.

Moses, however, is still uncertain, because a mere name is not enough. Now that Moses has a name for God, he wants visible concrete signs of his own vested power as God's agent. With keen insight into human nature, Moses knows that his people might not be able to make the necessary leap of faith in recognizing his prophetic office. God acquiesces and imbues Moses's staff with magical power: 'That they may believe that the Lord God of their fathers... hath appeared unto thee' (Exod. 4: 5). However, Moses is still reluctant. He can now tell his people who has sent him, and he can even demonstrate his newfound divine powers, but he cannot, for the life of him, understand *why* God has chosen him:

And Moses said unto the Lord, O my Lord, I *am* not eloquent, neither heretofore, nor since thou hast spoken unto thy servant: but I *am* slow of speech, and of a slow tongue. And the Lord said unto him, Who hath made man's mouth? or who maketh the dumb, or deaf, or the seeing, or the blind? have not I the Lord? Now therefore go, and I will be with thy mouth, and teach thee what thou shalt say. And he said, O my Lord, send, I pray thee, by the hand *of him whom* thou wilt send. And the anger of the Lord was kindled against Moses, and he said, *Is* not Aaron the Levite thy brother? I know that he can speak well... And thou shalt speak unto him, and put words in his mouth: and I will be with thy mouth, and with his mouth, and will teach you what ye shall do. And he shall be thy spokesman unto the people: and he shall be, *even* he shall be to thee instead of a mouth, and thou shalt be to him instead of God. (Exod. 4: 11–16)

In this crucial passage, here rendered in the English of the Authorised Version, Moses appears to have said to God, by his own admission, that rhetorical eloquence must be necessary when communicating God's message to his people—eloquence which he lacks. God loses patience with the doubting Moses and reminds him of his earlier promise, 'I will be with you', which now God explains was meant quite literally in the sense that God will speak *for* Moses. Moses, a simple man of no eloquence, still refuses to accept his role as an inspired orator, and an impatient God capitulates and nominates Aaron, Moses's apparently far more eloquent brother, as an intermediary between Moses and the people.

The only problem with this interpretation of the story—for this is what the English AV translation amounts to—is that it is only one possible interpretation. According to an ancient Midrashic tradition, in referring to his 'slow tongue' Moses was not professing to lack rhetorical ability but pointing to an actual speech-impediment. The *Greater Midrash* on the Book of Exodus, *Midrash Shmot*, explains that Moses was a stutterer. The exegetical crux here is in the Hebrew words, literally rendered, 'I am heavy of tongue and heavy of speech'. As both the Geneva and AV translators correctly assumed, the Hebrew for 'heavy' (*kaved*) can be rendered as 'slow' in the context of eloquence. However, a 'heavy tongue' is also an ancient coinage in Hebrew which denotes not merely ineloquence, but far more commonly some sort of physical speech-impediment. According to a fable recorded in the *Midrash Shmot* as a gloss on these verses, when Moses was a baby the angel Gabriel forced a burning coal into his mouth in order to save him from imminent execution at the hands of Pharaoh's magicians, inadvertently maiming his tongue in the process.[5] The seventeenth-century English translators of the AV felt no doubt 'inspired' in translating this passage as they did, since the virtues of a plain discourse free from the guiles of elaborate rhetoric were particularly appealing to their Protestant imagination. Borrowing the terms supplied by the earlier English translation in the Geneva Bible, the AV translators no doubt found the idea that Moses was incapable of rhetorical manipulation uniquely powerful and pleasing. For the ancient rabbis, however, the notion that Moses lacked rhetorical ability was unthinkable. The emphasis in the Midrash, rather, is metaphysical: to be able to conduct unmediated discourse with God, a prophet of Moses's stature could not be allowed to profane himself in the use of lapsarian speech. In the Midrashic fable the angel Gabriel descends from Heaven not only to save the life of the baby Moses, but also to brand him physically as a prophet-to-be, purging in the process

---

[5] See the Appendix for the full version of this fable.

the physical organ that was to come in touch with the divine. The fable amounts, in fact, to a form of teleological exegesis which inscribes Isaiah's so-called 'vision of glory', with its familiar image of the burning coal, into the earlier Mosaic myth.[6] This idea is not confined to early Jewish myth; one need only glance at comparable traditions in Greek mythology to note the ubiquitous appeal of this prophetic motif. According to one such tradition, Tiresias the seer was said to have been blinded upon catching a glimpse of the naked goddess Athena bathing. This comparable myth places an extraordinarily literal turn on the idea of the denuded deity whose unmediated presence can potentially destroy or seriously maim the offending mortal's senses. Just as Tiresias had to be blind in order to see into the future, Moses had to be all-but mute in order to speak with God.

The entire episode of the burning bush begins to emerge, therefore, as a powerful aetiological myth aimed at delineating the semantic and epistemological boundaries between God and man, Creator and creature. It points towards a sharp dichotomy between words and their objects of representation, and the inevitable sense of transgression and threat of destruction that always looms over those who attempt to contain in words a transcendental object that cannot be circumscribed within the finite realms of empiricism and semantic description. Traditionally mythologized in images of blinding light or fire, the reference to this threat or prohibition can be traced through all world religions.[7] It is strongly implicit in the burning bush itself from which Moses averts his eyes, 'for he was afraid to look upon God' (Exod. 3: 6). We encounter it again in the ancient story of Semele, who is consumed in flames once she is tricked by Hera to look upon the brilliance of the denuded Zeus. It re-emerges in the glory of the light of God which blinds the converted Paul (Acts 22: 11), and it can also be traced in the emanation of the second hypostasis from the supreme One of Neoplatonism, portrayed as the brilliant light radiating from the eternal and changeless sun (Plotinus,

---

[6] 'Then flew one of the seraphims unto me, having a live coal in his hands, *which* he had taken with the tongs from off the alter: And he laid *it* upon my mouth, and said, Lo, this hath touched thy lips; and thine iniquity is taken away, and thy sin purged' (Isa. 6: 6–7).

[7] The 'Light Stream' is one of the most pervasive religious motifs to be isolated by the endeavours of the 'history of religions' (*Religionsgeschichte*). See briefly Goodenough, *By Light, Light*, 11–23.

Enneads 5.1.6). Ultimately, however, as the emphasis on Moses's heavy tongue indicates, this is primarily a semantic prohibition. In Judaism, of course, the very utterance of the name of Yahweh in profane speech is held to be deeply transgressive. According to this fundamental Jewish prohibition, to pronounce the name of Yahweh with unhallowed lips is to ontologically profane the very idea of God's sacred otherness. To portray God or to speak God's sacred name is to transgress the Fourth Commandment of the Decalogue; a prohibition already alluded to in God's dire warning to the Israelites at the Sinai theophany that they may not go 'up into the mount, or touch the border of it: whosoever toucheth the mount shall be surely put to death' (Exod. 19: 12). The uncompromising nature of this prohibition is famously captured in Uzzah's grim story recorded in 2 Samuel 6: 6–7. The story recounts how David and his court attempt to bring the Ark of the Covenant up to Jerusalem with song and dance: 'And when they came to Nachon's threshingfloor, Uzzah put forth *his hand* to the ark of God, and took of *it*; for the oxen shook it. And the anger of the Lord was kindled against Uzzah; and God smote him there for *his* error; and there he died by the ark of God.' Even well-meaning and inadvertent profanation, in this case of the Ark of the Covenant which is the cultic focal point of God's immanence in the created world, results in swift and fatal divine retribution. The point of this difficult episode is not God's unreasonable anger against Uzzah, who was merely trying to stop the Ark from falling off the cart, but the absoluteness of the divide or veiling between profane and sacred, fallen world and sacred divine presence: Uzzah's unclean lapsarian hands are far more offensive to God than the dirt on 'Nachon's threshingfloor'. The Hebrew Bible allows for no movement across this divide; it is only in the deepest silence, when the world stands still, that God's immanence in the created and now fallen world can be glimpsed fleetingly. This was Elijah's experience when, like Moses, he was called before God at Horeb but found him neither in earth, wind, or fire, nor indeed in the created world and its elements at all, but only in the stillness and ontological silence of what is described in the original Hebrew as *kol dmama daka*, which ought to be properly translated as the 'faint sound of silence' (translated in the AV rather freely as 'still small voice'[8]): 'And, behold,

---

[8] The AV's translation is also retained in the Revised Standard English Bible, and is partly based on the Geneva Bible's 'stil and soft voyce'. The Hebrew homonym *kol* may

the Lord passed by, and a great and strong wind rent the mountains, and brake in pieces the rocks before the Lord; *but* the Lord *was* not in the wind: and after the wind an earthquake; *but* the Lord *was* not in the earthquake: And after the earthquake a fire; *but* the Lord *was* not in the fire: and after the fire a still small voice' (1 Kgs 19: 11–12). In such transcendental structures of radical difference the idea of the ineffable itself—of a speaking silence, or a still voice—becomes an intellectual and mythological burning coal. It constitutes a palpable presence of enticing threat which ultimately attracts rather than deters those whom we may term in the broadest sense as 'mystics' to somehow touch the untouchable, and speak the unspeakable. Christians, of course, will pin their hope of mystical ascent on the radical unveiling implied in the miracle of the Incarnation, but in order to talk about this miracle they would first need to borrow a crucial semantic-epistemological term, not from the Hebrew Bible, but from Greek philosophy.

PLATO AND ARISTOTLE

Long before it was hijacked by Christian theology, one of the most enduring intellectual legacies of Greek philosophy to Western thought is the semantic-epistemological concept of the *logos* (speech/utterance, but also thought/reason), and the fundamental idea that spoken words have some referential relationship to the tangible and intelligible objects that make up our world and our life experiences within it. When Derrida attacked and deconstructed the so-called 'logocentrism' implied

---

indeed be translated as 'voice', but in this context the grammar suggests that it denotes 'sound' in a more abstract sense. Moreover, the AV's choice of 'still' to render the word *dmama* is too weak. *Dmama* in Hebrew unequivocally means 'absolute silence', while the adjective *daka* (lit. 'thin' or 'faint') describes here the silence, not the sound. The confusion is understandable, however, because the homonym *kol* does mean 'voice' in the next verse, when God actually speaks to Elijah. This would explain why even some rabbinical interpretations stretch the syntax of the original Hebrew to accommodate a reading of the first *kol* as 'voice', and then claim that the verse indicates that God's way with his creatures is gentle as a whisper. Some modern English versions, however, have attempted to rectify the AV's translation but with even more perplexing results. The New English Bible's 'a low murmuring sound' translates *kol* correctly but then renders *dmama*, inexplicably, as 'murmuring'. Still, this is nothing compared to the Jerusalem Bible's far-fetched 'sound of a gentle breeze', no doubt intended to facilitate the predetermined gloss: 'signifies that God is a spirit [i.e. *ruakh*—wind, but also spirit].'

in the linguistic theory of Edmund Husserl, the real target of his attack was not of course Husserl but Plato, for whom *logos* is both an analytical 'account' of a concept (*Theaetetus* 206c2–210a9) and/or (depending on whether one has a unitarian or revisionist view of the chronology of Plato's dialogues) a divine rational ordering principle of the cosmos (*Timaeus*). Seeking to deconstruct the myth of metaphysical transcendence, and by implication all theories of referential semantics (if not all hope of rational enquiry), Derrida writes in 'Genesis and Structure': '*Logos is nothing* outside history and Being, since it is discourse, infinite discursiveness and not an actual infinity, and since it is meaning… Inversely, no history as self-tradition and no Being could have meaning without the *logos* which is *the* meaning which projects and proffers itself.'[9] As Derrida intimates, it is virtually impossible to exorcize the ghost of the Greek *logos* from modern notions of meaning. The Greek idea of the *logos* permeates (some would say contaminates) all Western intellectual engagement with what Derrida labels as 'transcendental structures'. The writings of Platonic and especially Neoplatonic philosophy greatly influenced the development of ancient and medieval Christian apophatic mysticism, and function as the primary intellectual vehicles to shape the engagement with the notion of ineffability in religion and philosophy within the Christian Platonic tradition.

In Plato's *Timaeus*, the eponymous interlocutor famously says, 'now to discover the Maker and Father of this Universe were a task indeed; and having discovered Him, to declare Him unto all men were a thing impossible'.[10] This famous Platonic maxim, often cited by Church Fathers from Clement onwards, expresses the central Platonic precept that human language is fundamentally unreliable in matters of rational enquiry. Plato is not merely saying in the *Timaeus* that the demiurge is by nature ineffable, but that trying to discover who and what the demiurge is cannot be helped by a referential, that is, logocentric, linguistic description. In the *Cratylus*, for example, Plato argues that language signifies 'things' arbitrarily and is therefore an unreliable dialectical tool. In this dialogue Socrates' rejection of the mimetic function of language and his ironic dismissal of etymology as a reliable epistemological tool sound curiously modern (or even post-modern).

---

[9] *Writing and Difference*, 209.
[10] 28C; Bury, *Timaeus, Critias, Cleitophon, Menexenus, Epistles*, 51.

This is especially true of the statement Plato puts in Socrates' mouth, that 'both convention and custom must contribute something towards the indication of our meaning when we speak'.[11] However, while it may be tempting to see here Plato's Socrates articulating anachronistically something like modern theories of relational semantics, it is important to note that the view that names (and hence words more generally) signify things arbitrarily according to custom and convention moves Socrates altogether to mistrust the relevance of linguistic signification to the practice of dialectics:

I myself prefer the theory that names are, so far as is possible, like the thing named; but really this attractive force of likeness is, as Hermogenes says, a poor thing, and we are compelled to employ in addition this commonplace expedient, convention, to establish the correctness of names. Probably language would be, within the bounds of possibility, most excellent when all its terms, or as many as possible, were based on likeness, that is to say, were appropriate, and most deficient under opposite conditions.[12]

However, since language, according to Plato, *does* apparently function under the 'opposite conditions', it is inherently and inevitably 'most deficient' (the adjective here is *aischista*, ἄισχιστα, which can also be translated as 'marred' or 'deformed').

Most modern readers who take comfort in a notion of meaning, or sense rather, constituted by the perpetual flux of relational semantics would revel in the fact that Socrates' argument forces Cratylus to concede the entire argument, by retreating into the famous trope common to most referential semantic theories that 'the power which gave the first names to things is more than human, and therefore the names must necessarily be correct'.[13] While Plato clearly scorned this view, he nevertheless found the threat of Heracleitian flux (or can we say Saussurian flux?) also deeply irrational:

Now whether this is the nature of things, or the doctrine of Heracleitus and many others is true, is another question; but surely no man of sense can put himself and his soul under the control of names, and trust in names and their makers to the point of affirming that he knows anything; nor will he condemn

---

[11] 435B; Fowler, *Cratylus, Parmenides, Greater Hippias, Lesser Hippias*, 173.

[12] 435C–D; Fowler (Loeb edn.), 175.

[13] 438C; ibid. 183.

himself and all things and say that there is no health in them, but that all things are flowing like leaky pots, or believe that all things are just like people afflicted with catarrh, flowing and running all the time.[14]

Because Plato's starting premiss in the *Cratylus* and the early Socratic dialogues before it (as well as in the later *Timaeus*) is that our unexamined conception and semantic definition of object *x* (whether tangible or intelligible) derives from our imperfect memory of an ideal Form (*eidos*) or Idea which is a special and unambiguous, imperceptible but intelligible, example of object *x*, he would have held in equal scorn modern theories of relational semantics.[15] Instead, believing as he did that the universe holds some hidden order and structure of ultimate truth which the pursuit of philosophy can illuminate, he concluded that the presence of ineffability in human discourse recommends the pursuit of truth through rational dialectics over and above the imperfections of language. As Platonists, to answer the Socratic question 'what is *x*?' we must submit the truth or falsity of certain statements about '*x*' to close dialectical scrutiny, instead of merely deferring to a system of mimetic referential signification, which, as the *Cratylus* demonstrates, is mostly arbitrary and if pursued can only end in a retreat into a metaphysical primary cause of meaning. That this Socratic method almost always ends in suspended *aporia* is itself a fitting critique of the limitations of any philosophical account (*logos*) which depends on words to communicate knowledge: the most that such an account can produce is an understanding that certain definitions of object *x* are false or inadequate, but never what *x* really *is*; in the *Theaetetus*, for example, Socrates and his interlocutors even fail to give a satisfactory account of the 'account' (*logos*) itself. Therefore, whether it is the ineffable nature of the Ideas (*Meno, Phaedo*), of the demiurge of the cosmos (*Timaeus*), or indeed of the One of the first hypothesis of the *Parmenides* which can only admit rational enquiry in negative terms, ineffability for Plato stimulates rather than defeats rational enquiry. It stimulates a rational enquiry of the universe through pure reason, over and above our empirical sense

---

[14] 440C–D; ibid. 191.
[15] For Plato the form of *X* is 'the thing that is *x* itself'. See Bostock, 'Plato on Understanding Language', in Everson, *Companion to Ancient Thought*, 3: *Language*, 10–27, at 13.

perceptions of the world and the language we use to make sense of that world, and it is this promise of rational revelation, so to speak, which fundamentally shaped the religious impulse of Western metaphysical thought.

After Plato, Platonic ideas about the function of the *logos* in relation to the transcendent continued to evolve within the so-called Middle Platonic movement up to the great reshaping of Platonism in the Porphyrian *Enneads* of Plotinus during the second century AD.[16] However, while Plato may well have articulated the importance of mastering dialectics where linguistic interrogation could not penetrate, Greek philosophers outside the Platonic school, most prominently Aristotle, were not as methodologically concerned as the Platonists with the place of transcendental ineffability in their systems. Aristotle's epistemological interrogation of universals (as opposed to Plato's Ideas), however, results in a rhetorical style where transcendence is already written into its epistemological terminology: universals are not transcendental concepts in an ontological sense, but they are transcendentally abstract by definition in that they transcend particulars. This might explain why it was Aristotle and not Plato who, strangely enough, ultimately bequeathed to the Western world what is the definitive discussion of an ineffable God within the context of pagan Greek philosophy. In an attempt to give an anti-Platonic example of an abstract deity that defies even the most rigorous rational interrogation, Aristotle discusses in Book XII of the *Metaphysics* the abstract God of Greek philosophy as a perfect self-thinking thought; that is, as an uninterrupted, eternally reflexive pure act of intellection. For Aristotle, God as *primum mobile* is pure 'actuality' (*energeia*, alternatively discussed elsewhere in the *Metaphysics* as *entelecheia*), the efficient and primary cause of the universe and an immutable and immaterial intellectual as well as moral principle: 'Moreover, life belongs to God. For the

---

[16] Transcendental Platonism continued to flourish in the works of Platonists and Neopythagoreans (who argued that Plato 'Platonized' the ideas of Pythagoras), from Speusippus (*c.*407–339 BC) and his successor as head of the academy Xenocrates, through Antiochus of Ascelon (whose thought was virtually indistinguishable from Stoicism, *c.*130–69/8 BC), the Alexandrian Eudorus (fl. *c.*25 BC), to the Neopythagorean Moderatus of Gades (*c.* AD 50–100) and Numenius (2nd cent. AD, the most intriguing of the Middle Platonists, who knew the Hebrew Bible and had considerable influence on Plotinus and Origen). See Dillon, *The Middle Platonists*, 11–38, 52–135, 344–83.

actuality of thought is life, and God is that actuality; and the essential quality of God is life most good and eternal. We hold, then, that God is a living being, eternal, most good; and therefore life and continuous eternal existence belong to God; for that is what God is.'[17] However, Aristotle's God is clearly not transcendental in the Platonic, and certainly not in the Judaeo-Christian, sense of the term. For Aristotle, the Prime Mover stands at the apex of a finite order, and is transcendental only in the sense of being far removed from the cognitive reach of human reason and linguistic description, but not in the sense of transcending the finite order itself. On the contrary, God for Aristotle is an integral part of the finite order, an abstract principle of being from which all thought and life emanates. There is no point in worshipping or revering such a passive 'God', and there is certainly no point in attempting to interrogate rationally an entity so profoundly elevated beyond the existence of mankind. Because Aristotle rejects the Platonic idealism associated with the theory of Forms, and in particular the Platonic theory of the soul's possible recollection of such Forms, there is therefore no discussion of ineffability *per se* in the Aristotelian system. However, Aristotle and most of the other Hellenistic philosophers outside Platonism *were* concerned to varying degrees with the way language operates, and in this respect some of the theories advanced by the Peripatetics or the Stoics did eventually find their way into monotheistic discussions of the ineffable in medieval times. Although, for example, the semantic analysis of true or false propositions contained in Aristotle's *De Interpretatione* has nothing to do with the felt presence of the ineffable in human speech, its famous opening passage, as we shall see later, did suggest a philosophical space that would allow medieval Jewish and Christian thinkers such as Rabbi Moses Maimonides and Aquinas to accommodate transcendental ineffability within the Aristotelian system.

PHILO AND CLEMENT

Philo of Alexandria (*c.*20 BC–AD 50) was the first monotheistic exegete to give the thought of Plato in general, and the *Timaeus* in particular, a

---

[17] 12.7.9; Tredennick, *Metaphysics*, vi. 151.

pre-eminent place in his theological system.[18] Philo is especially important for my eventual discussion of Milton because of his ardent Platonic
belief that some aspects of the ineffable, unnameable God *can* be known
through an introspective contemplation of the 'Divine Logos' and its
immanent energies (or action) within the created, finite order. Philo's
preoccupation with the ineffable, like Plato's, is primarily epistemological. His use of the term 'Divine Logos' is probably inspired by the
Timaeus which talks of a 'λόγος . . . θεοῦ' (38C, *logos theoū*). In Philo,
however, the term is extraordinarily complex and difficult to define
because he deploys it in many different, overlapping contexts. Broadly
speaking, it is simultaneously consistent with the divine presence of
God in the universe, with the instrument of God's creation, and with
the divine part of man's soul and mind wherein the 'Divine Logos' may
operate to bring man closer to a knowledge of God.[19] Speaking about
the 'Divine Logos' in his book *On the Cherubim*, Philo states:

> It comes from a voice in my own soul, which oftentimes is god-possessed and
> divines where it does not know. This thought I will record in words if I can. The
> voice told me that while God is indeed one, His highest and chiefest powers are
> two, even goodness and sovereignty. Through His goodness He begat all that is,
> through His sovereignty He rules what He has begotten. And in the midst
> between the two there is a third which unites them, Reason ['*logos*'], for it is
> through reason that God is both *ruler* and *good*.[20]

The triangular relationship established in this passage between God as
pure *logos*, God as 'ruler' (*archonta*, ἄρχοντα), and God as 'the good'
(*agathon*, ἀγαθόν), is central to Philo's philosophical and crucially
scriptural approach towards the ineffable. That God is absolutely ineffable and unnameable, and mostly unknowable is an axiom for Philo
based on proof of Scripture, particularly Exodus 3: 14. The Septuagint's
translation of God's words to Moses, 'I Am that I Am', 'ἐγώ εἰμι ὁ ὤν',
is taken by Philo to mean 'my nature is to be, not to be spoken'.[21] The

---

[18] See Runia, *Philo of Alexandria and the 'Timaeus' of Plato*; also more generally,
Goodenough, *By Light, Light* and *An Introduction to Philo Judaeus*; Sandmel, *Philo of
Alexandria: An Introduction*; Berchman, *From Philo to Origen.*
[19] Runia, *Philo of Alexandria and the 'Timaeus' of Plato*, 446–56, and Goodenough,
An Introduction to Philo, 100–11.
[20] *De Cherubim* 9; *Philo* (Loeb edn.), ii. 24–5 (my emphasis).
[21] *De Mutatione Nominum*, 2.12; *Philo* (Loeb edn.) v. 147.

divine attributes of goodness and sovereignty, therefore, relate to two of God's most commonly effable biblical names, 'God' and 'Lord', as opposed to the one 'true' name, Yahweh, which is traditionally unspeakable. The two effable names point not to God's ineffable being, but to his perceptible activity in the universe as the good creator, 'θεός' (*theos*, 'God'), and as the ruler of his good creation, 'κύριος' (*kurios*, 'Lord'). God as total being, 'τὸ ὄν' (*to-on*), is beyond the semantic realms of Scripture itself and, as God's 'true' biblical name of Yahweh suggests, is not only ineffable but also unknowable in essence.[22]

In this triangular structure of exegesis, where the base of the triangle is grounded in the biblical text while its apex, the 'Divine Logos', floats in the transcendental realm of the ineffable, we begin to see the first major difference between the Platonic and Philonian notions of wisdom (*sophia*). For Philo, the mystery of God's wisdom is encrypted in what he believes to be the inspired writings of Moses. However, the notion of a sacred text that operates differently from profane speech forces Philo to depart from Plato's anti-Cratylian scepticism. Philo elevates the sacred language of Scripture beyond the profane arbitrariness of Plato's *Cratylus* into a realm of allegorical plenitude. For all intents and purposes, Scripture for Philo is precisely the 'excellent speech' or 'language' Plato is willing to consider, assuming that the terms of the language 'προσήκουσιν' ('are appropriate'); that is, that they correspond by divine design to total logocentric reality. This makes perfect sense for Philo, whose conviction that the wisdom of Moses antedates and foreshadows that of Plato allowed him to champion the view that hidden Mosaic wisdom can be extracted from the Hebrew Bible through allegorical and inspired etymological methods. Once extracted, distilled Mosaic wisdom is comparable for Philo with that of Plato, whose teachings provide the dedicated religious philosopher with the appropriate dialectical tools with which to grasp the truth and rational beauty of God's encrypted scriptural wisdom.

---

[22] Sandmel, *Philo of* Alexandria, 92. To this day it is common practice among Jews when reading the Bible to substitute the words 'God' or 'Lord' for Yahweh. It is important to note, moreover, that the Septuagint translators could not supply a suitable Greek alternative for the Hebrew 'Yahweh', and so used instead the title 'κύριος' (*kurios*, 'Lord').

The biblical text becomes in this context the speech-bound key that allows Philo to unlock God's wisdom and ascend through the workings of the 'Divine Logos' towards the ineffable *to on* standing at the apex of his exegetical triangle. Significantly, Philo often discusses the intellectual and spiritual movement along this triangle in allegorical terms as an inward journey from the Aaronic institutions of the priesthood and the Law into the ineffable Mosaic mysteries, symbolized by the Temple's inner sanctum and the Ark within it. For Philo, this is a necessary transition from the lesser divine mysteries of the outer Temple to the greater, fundamentally ineffable mysteries of Moses, where all that is hidden is revealed, where signs and things cohere, and where God is revealed as the absolute Platonic *to on* which is self-contained, eternal, and transcends being and multiplicity. To loiter in the Temple's allegorical outer court under the rod of Aaron where the 'Existent' can only be perceived through its multiple actions in the created world is to be consigned to God's 'minor rites' and thus to a 'second-best voyage':

So the central Being with each of His potencies as His squire presents to the mind which has vision the appearance sometimes of one, sometimes of three: of one, when that mind is highly purified and, passing beyond not merely the multiplicity of other numbers, but even the dyad which is next to the unit, presses on to the ideal form which is free from mixture and complexity, and being self-contained needs nothing more; of three, when, as yet uninitiated into the highest mysteries, it is still a votary only of the minor rites and unable to apprehend the Existent alone by Itself and apart from all else, but only through Its actions, as either creative or ruling. This is they say, a 'second best voyage'; yet all the same there is in it an element of a way of thinking such as God approves.[23]

In terms of scriptural exegesis, then, the trappings of Aaron's 'minor rites' represent the novice exegete's initial encounter with the literal biblical text whose hidden 'Mosaic' meaning remains locked behind symbols relating to the multiple aspects of God's revealed action in the created world. In this symbolic realm God is either a ruler or creator, but never as he *is*; he is indeed a number of things but never the One. In a move which will later become the guiding principle of Milton's monism as well, Philo resolves the problem of how the One can

---

[23] *De Abrahami*, 24; *Philo* (Loeb edn.), vi. 62–5.

manifest multiplicity by latching onto precisely the idea of the 'Divine Logos'—the utterance of God—as the agency of his action; God as he in himself does not act except through the operation of the *logos* as it manifests itself in creation.[24]

To pass, therefore, beyond a rudimentary or literal understanding of the biblical text is to purify one's mind in sympathy with divine reason, or the *logos*, and walk hand in hand with Moses into an intimate knowledge of the ineffable *to on* that lies beyond language. What is especially significant for the literary tradition of the ineffable in Western thought is that Philo often describes the movement from the symbolic institutions of Aaron's priesthood and the Law to the ineffability of the Mosaic mystery as an exegetical process of metaphorical unveiling, where the initiate moves from the equivocal speech of Aaron to the univocal mind of the stuttering Moses.[25] This idea is grounded, moreover, in a potent structural allegory which reads the dialectic of the Aaron–Moses mysteries into the Tabernacle's architectural features and the symbolism of Aaron's breastplate described in Exodus 25–8.[26] This allegorical structure, which will become important to most Christian thinkers, including Milton, allows Philo to portray Aaron, the bearer of the High Priest's rod, as the purveyor of external 'minor rites' of religious ritual which lend themselves to normative linguistic description. This, says Philo, is the *outer* court of the Temple. Philo allegorically portrays Moses, on the other hand, as the guardian of the Temple's sacred and forbidden interior, the *sanctum sanctorum* and resting-place of the Ark of the Covenant and the Ten Commandments. The movement from empirical fact to mystery, or from a world of words to the silence of the ineffable, is also a move inwards from outer finite space into an introspective realm of infinity. This peculiarly Alexandrian Judaeo-Hellenistic belief in the rational aspects of what is in fact a wholly mystical mode of scriptural revelation will echo down the ages in both Judaism and Christianity, at first eliciting great support, but

---

[24] See Broek, *Studies in Gnosticism and Alexandrian Christianity*, 121.

[25] Goodenough, *By Light, Light*, 96–120. It is important to note that the 'Philonian Mystery' theory advanced by Goodenough, which argues that Philo was prescribing in code a set of mystical keys for a faith more in tune with Orphism than with orthodox Judaism, has never won wide acceptance among Philonian scholars. See Runia, *Exegesis and Philosophy*, 50–1 and Sandmel, *Philo of* Alexandria, 140–7.

[26] *De Vita Mosis*, 2.77–108, 136–40, *Philo* (Loeb edn.), vi.

eventually encountering much resistance from the emerging agnostic Jewish and Christian orthodoxies, until its ultimate revival in Christian Reformation thought.

Certainly in the first three centuries AD the call to contemplate God philosophically helped shape a Christian faith eager to assert its intellectual validity; but this was not achieved without controversy. If man's rational and revelatory relationship to God is as Philo the Jew envisions it, how can that vision be reconciled with the implications and promises of the Christian belief in the Incarnation? It is an established fact, for example, that esoteric apocalyptic doctrines taught in Pharisaic circles during the Second Temple period inspired the famous account of Paul—a converted Pharisee—of his rapture to the third Paradise.[27] Paul's Moses-like account of his ecstatic mystical experience in which he enjoyed an unmediated audible revelation of God, described negatively as hearing 'unutterable words' (ἄρρητα ῥήματα), is a key text in the history of Christian mysticism. Compounded, however, with the enduring Pauline emphasis on charity and faith, and the exhortation to the Colossians to abandon empty philosophy in Colossians 2: 8,[28] Paul's mystical message is deliberately and emphatically agnostic, as is that of traditional Jewish Throne-Mysticism by which it is informed.

This was indeed the basis for the strict anti-intellectual stance taken, for example, by the early Latin Father Tertullian, who strongly rejected any attempt to intellectualize (if not Hellenize) the Christian faith. When Tertullian was moved to write about the unfathomable idea of God dying on the cross, he famously cried out: 'It is utterly believable,

---

[27] Such apocalyptic doctrines developed within the wider theosophical context of 'Throne-Mysticism', which was popular at the time among Jews, Gnostics, and Hermetics. See Scholem, *Major Trends in Jewish Mysticism*, 44. For a lucid account of the Pauline 2 Corinthians passage and its relationship to contemporary Jewish apocalyptic writing see Scholem's *Jewish Gnosticism, Merkabah Mysticism, and Talmudic Tradition*, 14–20.

[28] 'Be on your guard; let no one capture your minds with hollow and delusive speculations, based on traditions of human teaching and centred on the elemental spirits of the universe and not on Christ.' I have preferred here the translation of the Revised English Bible. The early Christian Platonists Justin and Clement interpreted this Pauline injunction as a warning against such materialist and/or pantheist philosophies as Epicureanism and Stoicism, but not against Platonism, which was highly congenial to Christianity on account of its overt theism.

because it is absurd.'[29] As Henry Chadwick explains, in this statement
Tertullian was reacting to a climate in early Christianity that was profoundly intellectual and intimately dependent on Greek philosophy and
Hellenistic modes of thought.[30] But just as there were Christian thinkers eager to jettison all forms of *gnosis* from the Christian faith, there
were also thinkers who sought to redeem *gnosis* in the face of the
emerging Gnostic crisis.[31] While early Judaeo-Christian thinkers generally agreed on the paradoxical reasons for God being simultaneously
transcendental and immanent, ineffable and yet in some measure
knowable, many diverged on the consequent questions arising from
this paradox: (1) how does one attain knowledge of that which is
ineffable; and (2) what kind of concepts should be used when describing
such knowledge? Several centuries later, St Augustine would provide a
thoroughly intellectual and rational exposition of the Pauline emphasis
on faith, but prior to him there were Christian thinkers who had
nothing but sympathy for the Philonian vision of rational Platonic
revelation.

Clement of Alexandria (*c.*150–*c.*215), who was deeply influenced by
his Jewish compatriot, is a prime example of the attempt made by some
early Hellenistic Christians to accommodate the idea of *gnosis* within
the promises of the Christian Gospel.[32] In his attempt to defend Christianity against such pagans as Celsus, who argued that Christianity was a
religion for the ignorant, 'aimed at entrapping illiterates, women and
slaves',[33] Clement drew on Middle Platonism and Philo to demonstrate
Christianity's similar call for rational deification through a philosophical contemplation of God. Clement's ultimate philosophical goal was to
demonstrate that Christianity is the perfect and final fulfilment of both

---

[29] The full quotation runs: 'crucifixus est dei filius: non pudet, quia pudendum est.
et mortuus est dei filius: prorsus credibile est, quia ineptum est. et sepultus resurrexit:
certum est, quia impossibile.' Evans, *De Carne Christi*, 5.

[30] Chadwick, *Early Christian Thought and the Classical Tradition*, 1–8.

[31] By *gnosis* I do not mean the Gnostic theosophy, but neutrally, as Justin and
Clement salvaged the term in reference to the possible *gnosis*, or 'knowledge' of the
divine through a rational, *gnostic* process. See Chadwick, ibid. and Lilla, *Clement of
Alexandria*, 142–88.

[32] For Philo's influence on the early Greek Fathers and Clement especially see
Louth, *The Origins of the Christian Mystical Tradition*, and McGinn, *The Foundations
of Mysticism*, vol. 1.

[33] Chadwick, *Early Christian Thought and the Classical Tradition*, 34.

the Hebrew Bible and Greek philosophy. Given Christ's promise in the so-called Fifth Beatitude of a personal vision of God (the *visio Dei*) to those of 'pure heart' (Matt. 5: 8), it is, as McGinn points out, 'difficult to fault the educated Greek Christians who from the second century sought to understand Christ's promise of "seeing God" in terms of the Platonic traditions of contemplative *theoria*.[34] Continuing the trend set by Plato and introduced into monotheist theology by Philo, Clement also believed that because God is ineffable, only dialectic and the pursuit of philosophy could show the way towards divine revelation. In this unique context of dialectical revelation the Incarnation does not stand as a unique event in which the previously accommodated Word, or *logos*, of the Hebrew Law becomes flesh and thus readily accessible to all men. Instead, Clement envisions the Incarnation as a repeat event in which the same degree of revelation granted to Moses on Mount Sinai is reintroduced into a backsliding world to reassert God's immanence in the created order in the most radical of ways—by becoming flesh.[35]

For Clement, the Incarnated Christ is (as he would be for all subsequent Christian thinkers with an eye towards Platonism) Philo's Aaron and Moses coexisting in one body—the Incarnated *logos* paradoxically and unfathomably uttering unutterable wisdom for all eternity. In his effort to demonstrate the intellectual profundity of Christianity, Clement could not make do with a simple doctrine of faith in the revealed truth of the gospels. Instead, faith (πίστις) provides the framework within which a believer may assent to the first ontological proposition, or the divine axiom of God's being and creation, thereby facilitating in a rather circular process the ascent of reason towards the divine nature.[36] The belief that the Christian philosopher could move beyond the literal words of Scripture into the hidden wisdom of God in turn leads Clement to consider the epistemological relationship between that which is ineffable and that which is unknowable. If one cannot talk about God, then the hope of knowing some aspects of God must be passed in silence, and silence is the last thing the early Christian apologists could acquiesce to. Clement is arguably the earliest Christian

---

[34] McGinn, *The Foundations of Mysticism*, i. 68.
[35] Chadwick, *Early Christian Thought and the Classical Tradition*, 50.
[36] Lilla, *Clement of Alexandria*, 118–42.

thinker, therefore, to retreat into the '*via negativa*' of Plato's *Parmenides* in order to explain the semantic limitations of a discourse about God, but in doing so he came dangerously close to denying the very rational basis of his theology.

Because Clement strongly believes, like Philo before him, that some aspects of God's immanence may be knowable through his visible action in the universe, his was not strictly speaking a negative theology. But Clement's rational pursuit of what we may call, anachronistically, a kataphatic theology (one which moves towards speech and is hence affirmative and not negative) exposes a disabling paradox in the rational attempts to assert a kataphatic or positivist approach to God. Later theologians in the West, most prominently St Augustine, would respond to this paradox by accommodating the rational gaps of the kataphatic within the economy of faith and the evolving creeds. Clement, however, can only invoke paradox. The following long passage from Clement's *Stromateis* 5 captures perfectly the sense of paradox attached to the idea of divine inscrutability and ineffability in Western traditions, and the metaphorical language such paradox generates:

And John the apostle says: 'No man hath seen God at any time. The only begotten God, who is in the bosom of the Father, He hath declared Him'— calling invisibility and ineffableness the bosom of God. Hence some have called it the Depth, as containing and embosoming all things, inaccessible and boundless. This discourse respecting God is most difficult to handle. For since the first principle of everything is difficult to find out, the absolutely first and oldest principle, which is the cause of all other things being and having been, is difficult to exhibit. For how can that be expressed which is neither genus, nor difference, nor species, nor individual, nor number; nay more, is neither an event, nor that to which an event happens? No one can rightly express Him wholly, for on account of His greatness He is ranked as the All, and is the Father of the universe. Nor are any parts to be predicated of Him. For the One is indivisible; wherefore also it is infinite, not considered with reference to inscrutability, but with reference to its being without form and name. And if we name it, we do not do so properly, terming it either the One, or the Good, or Mind, or Absolute Being, or Father, or God, or Creator, or Lord. We speak not as supplying His name; but for want, we use good names, in order that the mind may have these as points of support, so as not to err in other respects. For each one by itself does not express God; but all together are indicative of the power of the Omnipotent... It remains that we understand, then, the Unknown, by divine grace, and by the word alone that proceeds from Him.[37]

At first glance this passage appears to express the rational Philonian idea that only pure logic can possibly triumph where profane human discourse and language fail. However, the farther Clement retreats down the *via negativa* the greater the distance between his fideist assertions and rational yearnings. The conclusion of the passage, 'it remains that we understand, then, the Unknown, by divine grace, and by the word alone that proceeds from Him' (λείπεται δὴ θεία χάριτι καὶ μόνῳ τῷ παρ᾽ αὐτοῦ λόγῳ τὸ ἄγνωστον νοεῖν)[38], though predictable, is nonetheless peculiar in the Clementian context, for in order to understand ('νοεῖν'), as it now emerges, one has to rely not only on the operation of the 'Divine Logos', but also on the instrument of 'divine grace' ('θεία χάριτι'). If our rational capacity to understand is inherently deficient and dependent on the grace of God, Clement seems to concede, or at least to imply, that the terms in which we think are no more valid than the lapsarian terms in which we speak. It is true that Clement held with Philo that the appropriateness of the words supplied by the Bible which allow us to know certain aspects of God—the 'good names' (ὀνόμασι καλοῖς) as Clement calls them—is guaranteed by the sacredness of the text which sanctions its allegorical interpretation. But Clement's need to accommodate the Christian belief in the Incarnation within the Philonian rational landscape ultimately forces him to invoke paradox. His Christian reshaping of Philonian thought thus exposes the most obvious chink in the rational armour of early Judaeo-Christian Platonists: to talk rationally about an immaterial, infinite, and ultimately ineffable God one must participate in an ill-defined, ultimately irrational, process of divine revelation. The paradoxical problem of course is that the more God reveals the more inscrutable his nature becomes. Since, moreover, rational thinking is predicated upon, and invariably impeded by, the lapsarian semantics which sustain the dialectical process, the most a rational enquiry of God can produce is a concession that at some point reason must be suspended. In the final analysis, therefore, the crux of the intellectual dispute between Tertullian and the likes of Clement was

---

[37] Wilson, *The Miscellanies: The Writings of Clement of Alexandria*, ii. 267–8.
[38] Boulluec, *Les Stromates*, v. 160.

simply that Tertullian is willing to suspend reason sooner rather than later. After all—and this is a problem which, as we shall see, resurfaces again in Reformation theology—if superimposed grace is the be all and end all of divine revelation, rational enquiry in the revelatory process becomes a futile or even hubristic gesture. The Reformers of the sixteenth century would indeed respond to this anomaly by redefining the precise role of human reasoning in the revelatory process, and their prime model for doing so was the towering figure of St Augustine.

PLOTINUS AND AUGUSTINE

Keeping Philo and Clement in mind, it is appropriate to veer for a moment from the evolving mystical theologies of the early Judaeo-Christian Hellenists of Alexandria, and return to the fold of contemporary paganism. In other words, this is as good a place as any to stop and consider, if very briefly, the philosophical mysticism of Plotinus (AD 205–70). It would be impossible to do even remote justice to the complex thought of Plotinus in the scope of one chapter, let alone a few paragraphs. Nevertheless, it is at least possible to indicate the important Plotinian contribution to the discussion of the ineffable by extracting one or two key themes from Tractate 5.3 of the *Enneads* that are in indirect dialogue with the themes I have drawn out so far from Plato, Philo, and Clement, and which will make the important transition to Augustine more coherent.

Porphyry's *Enneads*, a systematization of the teachings of Plotinus, is an abiding landmark in the formation of mystical apophatic theology, setting out in great detail, and even greater confusion, the complex relationship between the contemplative self and what Plotinus defines as the three transcendental degrees of reality, or hypostases: the transcendental One, the Intellectual-Principle or mind, and the All-Soul.[39] Tractate 5.3 on 'The Knowing Hypostases and the Transcendent' (the title is Porphyry's) deals with the question of self-knowledge as it relates to the movement and emanation between the three hypostases. Of

---

[39] In my discussion of Neoplatonism I have chosen to abide by the terms supplied by MacKenna for the specific Plotinian usage of such broad Greek terms as 'νοῦς' (mind) and 'ψυχή' (soul). See MacKenna, *Enneads*, pp. xxiv–xxx.

particular importance is the emphasis on the potential of the self to come into the presence of the primary hypostasis of the One through an act of reflexive intellectual thought, as it is mirrored in the second Plotinian hypostasis of the Intellectual-Principle ('*νοῦς*'), and its opera- tion on the higher rational Leading-Principle of the third hypostasis, the All-Soul ('*ψυχή*'), 'concentrated in contemplation of its superior'.[40] In describing the various intellectual motions between the three hypos- tases, Plotinus offers an enduring formula which accommodates, or is seen to accommodate, rational ascendance within a transcendental structure without ever having to suspend rational enquiry in the face of revelatory assertions.

At the heart of Plotinus' formula for attaining cognition of the divine One presented in Tractate 5.3 is the belief that self-knowledge, in the strictest formal sense of knowledge of oneself, from oneself, as one indivisible unity, is synonymous with knowledge of the One. Such knowledge, moreover, is made possible precisely where negative terms such as 'unintelligent intelligence' can no longer be logically admitted:

The Soul therefore (to attain self-knowledge) has only to set this image (that is to say, its highest phase) alongside the veritable Intellectual-Principle which we have found to be identical with the truths constituting the objects of intellec- tion, the world of Primals and Reality: for this Intellectual-Principle, by very definition, cannot be outside of itself, the Intellectual Reality: self-gathered and unalloyed, it is Intellectual-Principle through all the range of its being—*for unintelligent intelligence is not possible*—and thus it possesses of necessity self- knowing, as a being immanent to itself and one having for function and essence to be purely and solely Intellectual-Principle.[41]

Moreover, such self-knowledge for Plotinus 'is not merely plausible but inevitable',[42] given that the Intellectual-Principle which emanates from the One, and simultaneously partakes both of the One and also of the aspiring part of the All-Soul, by definition yearns to return to the One,

---

[40] Ibid., p. xxviii.
[41] Ibid. 387–8 (my emphasis). I have preferred here the English translation of MacKenna over that of Armstrong's Loeb edition for its terminological sensitivity (despite its over-embellishments).
[42] 5.3.6; MacKenna, *Enneads*, 388.

taking the soul, as it were, along with it. The act of reflexive contemplation guarantees knowledge of God through a process of mystical mimesis whereby, reflecting upon itself, the Intellect transports itself into the
ineffable plateau where predicative syntax collapses and the distinction
between subject, act, and object ceases to exist. In seeing itself, the
Intellect is both seen and seeing, and therein, according to Plotinus, is
the primal emanation of the indivisible One, manifesting itself in the
Intellectual-Principle. The Soul, according to Plotinus, although it has
no vision of its own, can share in this process by attaching its contemplative higher part to the higher Intellectual-Principle.

   The Plotinian process of ascent through an act of introspective
intellection that 'carries over' the soul into a likeness of the One is
nevertheless imperfect, and very hard to attain even under the best of
contemplative circumstances. The concluding tractate of the *Enneads*,
Tractate 6.9, reiterates in ringing tones the inevitable gap between our
incessant desire to apprehend the One, and our limited or fleeting
ability finally to do so. The process of ascent is presented as a passing
beyond the act of knowledge into the presence of the Divine Unity
(6.9.3). Knowledge of the One, even through the process of self-knowledge, is not knowledge at all, we now learn, but a 'presence overpassing
all knowledge'.[43] This 'presence' (*parousia*, παρουσία), moreover, fills
the soul with dread and forces it to flee back to the 'solid ground' of
empiricism:

> The soul or mind reaching towards the formless finds itself incompetent to
> grasp where nothing bounds it or to take impression where the impinging
> reality is diffuse; in sheer dread of holding to nothingness, it slips away. The
> state is painful; often it seeks relief by retreating from all this vagueness to the
> region of the sense, there to rest as on solid ground, just as the sight distressed
> by the minute rests with pleasure on the bold.[44]

According to Plotinus, therefore, to attain divine proximity with the
One may only be possible fleetingly in a moment of intense introspective contemplation that is itself ineffable, wherein the sublime presence
of the One God linguistically translates into silence, or the complete
absence of predication. This is not the same as the modern notion of
ineffability where silence is understood negatively as the meaningless

---

[43] 6.9.4; MacKenna, *Enneads*, 617.   [44] Ibid.

void left vacant when language falls silent, ceasing to generate sense. In Plotinus, silence signifies divine oneness, where the semantic relationship between subject, predicate, and object collapses into a single ineffable presence.

The idea of silence as divine presence, which also emerges as a key religious element in the *Corpus Hermeticum*, is the inevitable silence which ensues, as Hawkins and Schotter put it, in the face of an 'overplus of being'. The author of the first treatise in the *Corpus Hermeticum* sings praises to the transcendental God, concluding with the plea: 'Accept pure offerings of speech from a soul and heart uplifted to thee, Thou of whom no words can tell, no tongue can speak, whom silence only can declare.'[45] It is this overplus which forced succeeding Neoplatonists such as Iamblichus (*c*. AD 245–*c*.325) and finally Proclus (410/12–485) paradoxically to retreat into the practices of ritualistic theurgy in order to fulfil the elusive Plotinian vision of divine knowledge. As abstract philosophy devolved into inscrutable syncretic magical rituals, it is little wonder that a serious Christian thinker such as Augustine would find it relatively easy to demolish Plotinian claims for mystical self-sufficiency.[46] Although the Plotinian quest for the knowledge of the One through a process of introspective intellection proved to be a major source of inspiration for Augustine, Porphyry's (234–*c*.305) anti-Christian polemics, compounded with his inclination towards the efficacy of theurgical practices in *De Regressu Animae* (now lost),[47] drove Augustine vigorously to rethink the influence of Platonism on Christian thought and its implications in his own theological treatment of presence, silence, and the ineffable.

---

[45] Scott, *Hermetica*, i. 131.

[46] See Turcan, *The Cults of the Roman Empire*, 266–79. Turcan provides a helpful overview of the sacramental diffusion of Neoplatonism within occult theurgical mysteries based on Neoplatonic readings of such theosophical texts as the *Corpus Hermeticum*, *Orphic Hymns*, and the *Chaldaean Oracles*.

[47] We can only assume what Porphyry's lost treatise *On the Ascent of the Soul* contained, based on Augustine's constant references to it in his attacks on Porphyry's sympathy for theurgy, particularly in *De Civitate Dei*, 10.9. Augustine gives the name of the treatise in 10.24. In Porphyry's defence it must be pointed out, on the basis of his surviving work, that although he believed the follower of Plotinian ascension ought to seek some sacramental initiation into the divine process, he was nevertheless somewhat sceptical of the merits of theurgy. The first exponent of theurgy in the Neoplatonic context was actually Iamblichus, in his treatise *The Mysteries of Egypt*.

Whereas Fathers like Tertullian clamoured against any attempt to over-intellectualize the Christian mysteries, demanding a strict adherence to the truths of the gospels based on faith alone, St Augustine (354–430) invests the traditionally fideist, anti-intellectual stance with profound intellectual substance. In his exegetical preaching manual, *De Doctrina Christiana*, Augustine expounds on his somewhat unremarkable, yet highly influential, semiotic theory. In the introductory chapters he stops to consider the limitations of language in relation to the ineffable God, and in the process delivers a powerful rational blow to such Neoplatonists as Porphyry (and by extension, Plotinus), indirectly critiquing his Greek gnostic predecessors as well:

Have I spoken something, have I uttered something, worthy of God? No, I feel that all I have done is to wish to speak; if I did say something, it is not what I wanted to say. How do I know this? Simply because God is unspeakable. But what I have spoken would not have been spoken if it were unspeakable. For this reason God should not even be called unspeakable, because even when this word is spoken, something is spoken. There is a kind of conflict between words here: if what cannot be spoken is unspeakable, then it is not unspeakable, because it can actually be said to be unspeakable. It is better to evade this verbal conflict silently than to quell it disputatiously. Yet although nothing can be spoken in a way worthy of God, he has sanctioned the homage of the human voice, and chosen that we should derive pleasure from our words in praise of him. Hence the fact that he is called God: he himself is not truly known by the sound of these two syllables (*deus*), yet when the sound strikes the ear it leads all users of the Latin language to think of a supremely excellent and immortal being.[48]

Initially, it seems, Augustine recommends here avoiding the disconcerting paradoxes of ineffability altogether. The desire to talk about that which is ineffable results in a 'battle' or 'conflict of words' (*pugna verborum*), both on the literal level of semantic paradox, but also on a profound intellectual and, one presumes, spiritual level. This conflict, moreover, is one which is 'better to evade . . . silently than to quell . . . disputatiously' ('silentio cavenda potius quam voce pacanda est'). Unlike the silence of Plotinian *parousia* which is the fleeting reward of a possible process of intense introspective intellection (and which is quite distinct from the Christian-biblical notion of *parousia* as the advent of Christ's royal presence, or Second Coming), Augustine points to the efficacy of silence as an axiomatic theological starting point; indeed, it gives Augustine's theology its ultimate sense of direction. But whereas many of the pagan Neoplatonists looked to the theosophy of the *Chaldaean Oracles* and its related theurgical rites to seek sacramental initiation into the divine presence, Augustine seizes on the notion of ineffable silence to recommend prayer and the affective adoration of the Incarnated Christ who is the one and only true mediator between mankind and the ineffable God (*De Civitate Dei* 10.32). Consequently, the specific type of silence Augustine recommends to his Christian student in the above passage is not the silence of the human voice altogether, but the silence of futile rational analysis and philosophical disputation.

In contrast with the early Greek gnostics, Augustine held that faith in the Incarnated Christ and the institution of his Church was sufficient to secure salvation. This is not to say that having secured salvation a Christian should not attempt to contemplate rationally the profounder mysteries of God. After all, this is precisely what Augustine attempts to do in *The Trinity* (*De Trinitate*): 'to account for the one and only and true God being a trinity, and for the rightness of saying, believing, understanding that the Father and the Son and Holy Spirit are one and the same substance or essence.'[49] Since, however, 'it is difficult to contemplate and have full knowledge of God's substance', Augustine emphasizes that 'it is necessary for our minds to be purified before that inexpressible reality can be inexpressibly seen . . . In order to make us fit and capable of grasping it, we are led along more endurable routes, nurtured on faith as long as we have not yet been endowed with that necessary purification.'[50] Indeed, the very opening sentence of *De Trinitate* functions as a type of rational waiver, expressly establishing the precedence of faith over reason: 'The reader of these reflections of mine on the Trinity should bear in mind that my pen is on the watch against the sophistries of those who scorn the starting-point of faith, and allow themselves to be deceived through an unseasonable and misguided

---

[49] *De Trinitate*, 1.1.4; Hill, *The Trinity*, 67.
[50] 1.1.3; Hill, *The Trinity*, 66.

love of reason.'[51] Expounding Augustine's noetic quest for God, Étienne Gilson identifies five philosophical steps in the Augustinian corpus, of which faith is always the first.[52] But as the few excerpts from the
opening of *De Trinitate* show, and Gilson clarifies, there is nothing
irrational about the Augustinian notion of faith: 'even though belief
takes the place of a direct knowledge which is lacking, there is nothing
unreasonable about it. It is based entirely on the credibility of certain
testimony, and consequently its value is in proportion to the value of the
rational investigation to which we have submitted that testimony.'[53]

At the heart of Augustine's argument with the Neoplatonists memorably documented in Book X of *De Civitate Dei*, therefore, is not so
much the question of how to conduct a rational enquiry into the nature
of God, as how to secure the divine route along which the soul may ascend
towards such rational illumination. Augustine had tremendous respect for
Plotinus, 'that great Platonist' (*ille magnus Platonicus*),[54] whose writings
Augustine tells us in the *Confessions* (7.9), he had read in Latin (most likely
in Victorinus' Latin selection). Augustine was sympathetic to the Plotinian
vision, complementary to that of the Bible, of a fundamentally good
supreme being from whom all life emanates, and to whom the rational
soul forever aspires in the intelligible light of its supreme Creator. But
these points of agreement only aggravated Augustine's antipathy towards
Platonic rational self-sufficiency and the Neoplatonic rejection of Original
Sin. The merit of Platonism or Neoplatonism was in its ability to convey
philosophically, and with the greatest of intellectual integrity, the beauty
and transcendence of the One God, but it did not offer any viable route
towards divine ascension.[55] Had they recognized their sinful, lapsarian
natures, so Augustine argues, had they worshiped God and embraced
Christ the Mediator, the Platonists would have sought redemption rather

---

[51] 1.1.1; Hill, *The Trinity*, 65.

[52] The four other successive steps, according to Gilson, are: 'rational evidence', 'the
soul and life', 'sense knowledge', and 'rational knowledge'. See Gilson, *The Christian
Philosophy of Saint Augustine*, 25–112.

[53] Ibid. 28.

[54] *De Civitate Dei*, 10.2; Weisen, *The City of God*, iii. 257.

[55] See R. Russell, 'The Role of Neoplatonism in St. Augustine's *De Civitate Dei*', in
Blumenthal and Markus, *Neoplatonism and Early Christian Thought*, 161–70.

than ascension, and their philosophizing would not have 'become futile in their thinking'.[56]

Consequently, Augustine advocated not only introspective worship through prayer and mystical contemplation (of which the account of the Ostia vision in *Confessions* 7.10 is a perennial model), but also visible worship through sacramental ritual. Here perhaps is the most important and most enduring Augustinian contribution to the idea of the ineffable in the West—the idea that all human beings, regardless of their intellectual alacrity, can partake of the ineffable Godhead and the invisible reality of Christ's mystical Church through the metaphors of ritual enshrined within the earthly Church and the celebration of ineffable mystery in its sacraments:

> As for those who think that these visible sacrifices are appropriately offered to other gods, but that God, inasmuch as he is invisible, greater and better, should receive invisible, greater and better sacrifices, for instance the due oblation of a pure heart and a good will, they are surely unaware that these visible sacrifices are symbols of the invisible, just as spoken words are symbols of the realities to which they refer. Therefore, just as in prayer and praise we address to him words that have a meaning and offer him in our hearts the actual things which this meaning represents, so in sacrifice let us be aware that visible sacrifice should be offered to none other than to him whose invisible sacrifice we ourselves ought to be in our hearts.[57]

Sacraments are symbols, just as words are. As with the words of Scripture, what determines the unique sacramental efficacy of such symbols is their divine referent. Crucially for the Western intellectual engagement with the ineffable, Augustine responds to the sacramental shortcomings of Neoplatonism by relocating the silence of the ineffable from a paradoxically unsustainable environment of dialectical disputation—as it is problematically in Clement's writings—into the *a priori* ineffable act of participating in a sacramental ritual. Furthermore, by employing such distinctive semiotic terms as 'sign' and 'symbol', Augustine effectively marries the sacramental tradition with the religious belief in the power of some words, or some unique verbal constructs,

---

[56] *De Civitate Dei*, 10.3; Weisen, *City of God*, iii. 261.
[57] *De Civitate Dei*, 10.19; Weisen, *City of* God, iii. 339.

not only to refer to a hidden transcendental reality, but also to evoke its numinous presence.

GREGORY OF NYSSA AND THE PSEUDO-DIONYSIUS

While the institution of the sacraments, and in particular the Eucharist, celebrated the ineffable character of the Christian mysteries within the symbolic rituals of the Church, active intellectual contemplation of the ineffable Godhead continued to flourish within the growing ascetic movements of monasticism. The solitary desert experience of the ascetic hermit seeking divine illumination through contemplative ascension was relocated to that of the cell, as monasteries gradually became the new strongholds of Christian wisdom. In the Greek East the evolving monastic mysticism of such luminaries as Gregory of Nyssa (*c.*330–*c.*395) and the mysterious pseudo-Dionysius (*c.*500) continued to explore the complex noetic quest for God in the spirit of their Greek predecessors. However, as McGinn explains, 'in the wake of the Arian controversy, the major doctrinal dispute of the fourth century, the Greek fathers were forced to examine the doctrine of God with more care and in greater depth than had hitherto been the case'.[58] Revisiting the Platonic texts with renewed energy and focus, Gregory of Nyssa, the younger brother of Basil, the great anti-Arian bishop, returned to the questions of *gnosis* and *theoria* (i.e. 'knowledge' and 'contemplation' of the *visio Dei* as promised to those of pure heart in the Fifth Beatitude) with an eye towards readdressing some of the most vexed paradoxes concerning the ineffable qualities of the divine presence.

In his *Life of Moses or Concerning Perfection in Virtue* Gregory echoes Philo in venerating the speech-impeded Moses as the ideal model for the ascetic enjoying unmediated communion with a God who is mysteriously present and yet altogether hidden. Picking up, for example, the traditional episode of the burning bush as an exemplum of the ascetic's unmediated encounter with God, Gregory insists in time-honoured Platonic tradition that only knowledge of true being is knowledge at

---

[58] McGinn, *Foundation of Mysticism*, i. 140.

all. According to Gregory, such truth of being, 'which was then manifested by the ineffable and mysterious illumination which came to Moses, is God',[59] and can be arrived at by ascetically emulating the life of Moses (2.26). Although he would not systematize the process of negative ascension to the degree of the pseudo-Dionysius, Gregory is seminal in his advocacy, based on Philippians 3: 13 ('Brethren, I count not myself to have apprehended: but this one thing I do, forgetting those things which are behind, and reaching forth unto those things which are before'), of *epektasis*, or 'the endless pursuit of the inexhaustible divine nature',[60] and the consequent negative Plotinian recasting of the idea of silent divine presence. Jaroslav Pelikan has shown that the point of the apophatic impulse in Gregory's teachings, and the Cappadocian thinkers more generally, is to remedy the potential chill an apophatic discourse might otherwise bring to dogmatic reflection about God's mysteries: if you insist too strongly that nothing positive about God can be said, then you run the risk of suggesting that there is no point in even thinking about God.[61] Apophasis, however, allows the believer to recognize the transcendence of God from a position of knowledge, not ignorance. Such transcendence, argues Pelikan, does identify 'God as the point "beyond" which it was impossible for human understanding to go, but not as the point "to" which it was impossible for human understanding to go'.[62] By resubmitting to Neoplatonic scrutiny the questions of God's infinite, immutable, and ultimately ineffable nature as being beyond being, Gregory arrives at a deliberately paradoxical negative conception of God's ineffable presence in which, to be able to talk about such presence, the mystic must use negative language to trace the contours of its hidden aspects. However, these intellectual contours, as it were, cannot be communicated without affirming something, which in turn produces the obsession of the negativists with rhetorical paradox.

At the outset of his treatise on *Mystical Theology* pseudo-Dionysius the Areopagite (Denys) exhorts: 'Think not that affirmations and denials are opposed but rather that, long before, is that—which is itself

---

[59] Malherbe and Ferguson, *The Life of Moses*, 59.
[60] McGinn, *Foundation of Mysticism*, i. 141.
[61] Pelikan, *Christianity and Classical Culture*, ch. 13.
[62] Ibid. 201.

beyond all position and denial—beyond privation.'[63] That which is
ineffable cannot admit strictly negative or positive statements, but only
the paradox of coexisting negative affirmation, or affirmative negation.
Denys' approach to the presence of the numinous centres on the
dynamic movement between two theologies, one which is positive and
is grounded on what can be said about God based on his revealed
and accommodated nature in Scripture, and one which is negative
and focuses on God's hidden, strictly ineffable nature. The positive or
symbolic theology is *kata-phatic*, moving towards speech, and the
negative is *apo-phatic*, moving away from speech towards a resounding
and meaningful silence. Denys discusses the former kataphatic theology
in his book on the *Divine Names* and the latter apophatic or negative
theology, as well as the movement between the two, in his book *Mystical
Theology*. In chapter 3 of the latter treatise he explains the movement
from the kataphatic to the apophatic in the following terms: 'The higher
we ascend the more our language becomes restricted by the more
synoptic view of what is intelligible. Now, however, that we are to
enter the darkness beyond the intellect, you will find not a brief
discourse but a complete absence of discourse and intelligibility.'[64]
According to Denys, therefore, a mystic finally ascends towards God
at the point where the two theologies meet. The notion that the
Dionysian mystical formula gives birth to a strictly negative theology
is erroneous. The Dionysian stress on the double movement of regres-
sion and ascension, epitomized by the two theologies, captures the
monotheist premiss, championed by Philo, that on the one hand God
as total being is unknowable, but on the other hand God the Creator, as
manifested through his 'energies', may be knowable through his divine
names as they appear in Scripture. In other words, the mystic can only
safely ascend towards the negative by placing his feet firmly on the
positive. The road of negation (*via negativa*) does not offer a mystical
formula which guarantees a spiritual, religious experience of what Otto
would discuss as the *mysterium tremendum*, but is a way for the mystic to
register in language an irruption of ineffable, divine presence which is
nevertheless *contained*, negatively, in what *can* be said using positive
affirmations. In terms of the literary tradition of the ineffable, the

[63] 1.1.2; Jones, *The Divine Names and Mystical Theology*, 212.
[64] 1033B–C; Jones, *Divine* Names, 217.

abiding legacy of the *Corpus Areopagiticum* lies, therefore, not in its elusive spirituality, but in its constant radical exploration of the ineffable boundaries of language, where the countless neologisms, and the constant use of parallelism, antithesis, and endless layers of *paradoxia* kataphatically trace the dazzling contours of that which is apophatic and invisible, present and yet hidden.

MAIMONIDES AND AQUINAS

So far I have focused on transcendental notions of ineffability as they relate to strictly metaphysical questions of divine ontology and epistemology. Although, as we shall see in the next chapter, the presence of ineffability continued to flourish in the writings of various medieval and Renaissance theologians and philosophers within the parameters of a broadly Platonic mystical theology, by the time of the sixth century and the writings of Denys the general theological framework for such ideas was well in place. However, there is an inherent risk in marginalizing the important semiotic contributions of later medieval peripatetism to the intellectual tradition of the ineffable. Contrary to popular belief, the considerable achievements of medieval scholasticism were not casually overthrown and relegated to oblivion by the anti-scholasticism of the humanists. In fact the opposite is true; many of the humanist philosophers who later sought to re-establish the importance of Platonic teachings did so not at the expense of medieval Aristotelianism, but in a sincere effort to highlight the agreement between Plato's and Aristotle's teachings.[65]

As the works of Aristotle were slowly being recovered, first in the Greek East during the sixth century, and later in the Latin West beginning from the ninth century, heightened interest in the application and development of peripatetic logic saw the emergence of elaborate epistemological theory, drawn along the lines of Aristotelian psychology and logic. In the wake of the peripatetic revival within the Muslim world and that of scholastic Christendom, a whole range of semantic and cognitive solutions for the problems of ineffability begin to emerge.

---

[65] On the subject of the Aristotelian–Platonic controversy of later medieval and early humanist thought see *CHRP* 558–84.

While the great Muslim philosophers Ibn Sina (Avicenna, 1135–1204) and Ibn Rushd (Averroes, 1126–98) paved the way for the first theological systematization of Aristotelian philosophy, the most radical exploration of the role of faith, reason, and language in religious experience can be found in *The Guide for the Perplexed*, the landmark philosophical handbook by Rabbi Moses Maimonides (1138–1204). Written *c*.1190 in transliterated Arabic (using Hebrew characters), the *Dalalat ha'irin*, soon thereafter translated into Hebrew as *More Nebukhim*, is today as widely read and influential as it was when Thomas Aquinas (*c*.1225–74) pored over its contents in the later Latin translation of the Hebrew version (*Doctor dubiorum, c*.1220). Aquinas owed a profound intellectual debt to Maimonides, especially on questions relating to revelation and the application of Aristotelian logic to the philosophical problems of creation and the divine names.[66] However, in order to extrapolate from the mesh of peripatetic arguments both thinkers' key ideas on the ineffable it is necessary to emphasize straight away the fundamental and rather obvious differences between their views.

In the opening passage of *De Interpretatione* Aristotle asserts:

Words spoken are symbols or signs of affections or impressions of the soul; written words are the signs of words spoken. As writing, so also is speech not the same for all races of men. But the mental affections themselves, of which these words are primarily signs, are the same for the whole of mankind, as are also the objects of which those affections are representation or likenesses, images, copies.[67]

Although Aristotle's use in this context of the word *pathemata*, usually translated as 'affections or impressions', is still debated, it probably means simply 'thoughts'. In any case, the statement becomes crucial in the Middle Ages as a starting point for the scholastics' attempts to explain how human language operates in relation to the ineffable Godhead. Because, as Anselm of Canterbury (1033–1109) famously puts it, God is an absolute *maximum* 'than which nothing greater can be thought', and because 'than which nothing greater can be thought' necessarily exists outside the mind, God for Anselm (1) must necessarily exist, and (2) is

---

[66] See D. Burrell, 'Aquinas and Islamic and Jewish Thinkers', in Kretzmann and Stump, *The Cambridge Companion to Aquinas*, 70–82. See also Burrell, *Knowing the Unknowable God*.

[67] *De Interpretatione*, 1; Cooke, *Aristotle*, i. 115.

radically ineffable on Aristotle's terms, because whatever 'affections or impressions' he produces in our mind concerning his being cannot adequately represent the total ineffable reality of the *maximum* which is God. Anselm's famous 'ontological argument' for the existence of God as set out in chapters 2 and 3 of his *Proslogion* is not original in its definition, but is highly original in its argumentative method, because it proceeds logically from the axiomatic belief in the existence of God as an objective reality accepted as an article of faith. Like Augustine before him and Aquinas after him, Anselm uses logic to set out what his faith compels him to understand, not to prove logically what then must be accepted by faith.[68]

In his *Guide* Maimonides similarly sets out to explain logically the role of faith and rational enquiry in the process of divine revelation, but in the context of the Judaic dispensation which lacks, of course, the fundamental Christian belief in the Incarnation and all that it entails in semantic terms. Coming to discuss the nature of faith, for example, Maimonides explains to his student Joseph that a truly profound faith occurs not when man merely states 'I believe that God exists', but only when man rationally accepts the concept of God imprinted in his mind as a truthful image of that which exists outside his mind. In the process of this reasoning, Maimonides directly attacks Christianity:

When reading my present treatise, bear in mind that by 'faith' we do not understand merely that which is uttered with the lips, but also that which is apprehended by the soul, the conviction that the object [of belief] is exactly as it is apprehended... If... you have a desire to rise to a higher state, viz., that of reflection, and truly to hold the conviction that God is One and possesses true unity, without admitting plurality or divisibility in any sense whatever, you must understand that God has no essential attribute in any form or in any sense whatever, and that the rejection of corporeality implies the rejection of essential attributes. Those who believe that God is One, and that He has many attributes, declare the unity with their lips, and assume plurality in their thoughts. This is like the doctrines of the Christians, who say that He is one and He is three, and the three are one... For belief is only possible *after* the apprehension of a thing; it consists in the conviction that the thing apprehended has its existence beyond the mind [in reality] exactly as it is conceived in the mind.[69]

---

[68] See Luscombe, *Medieval Thought*, 43–6.

[69] 1.50 (my emphasis). Translated from the original transliterated Arabic by Friedlander, *The Guide for the Perplexed*, 67–8.

This passage, which serves as a prologue for the controversial and apophatically radical sections on the 'attributes of God', proceeds from the empirical Aristotelian premiss, common both to Maimonides and Aquinas, that language, and hence rational analysis, can only negotiate the objects of cognition which lie within the realms of human experience. Since God clearly exists beyond the realms of human experience, both Maimonides and Aquinas were forced to rethink the nature of God's immanence and whether or not it is possible to predicate anything of God using human language. For his part, Maimonides held that since it is impossible to predicate any statement about God as he is in himself, only the rational negation of God's attributes, including such fundamental attributes as 'existence', could open up the road for sound faith. Maimonides' position is apophatic in the extreme. He radically suggests not only that God is totally unknowable, but also that God is completely detached, philosophically at least, from the world of his creation. This radical stance appears to undermine theories of divine immanence and problematically to suggest, as Leaman argues, that 'the idea of God possessing an attitude of care and concern for 'his' creatures so prevalent in the liturgy of both Islam and Judaism is accordingly inappropriate and empty'.[70] However, by logically stripping away from God all erroneous semantic attributions and predications Maimonides is in effect establishing the rational parameters for his student's faith. It is beyond the scope of this study to enter into a complex philosophical discussion about the various contradictions and logical loopholes in this sort of argument. What is significant for my own purposes is Maimonides' implied theory of meaning and his view that the use of religious language is completely equivocal, not univocal.

Maimonides is not saying that God has no existence *per se*, but that he does not exist in the semantic sense in which we tend to use such terms. Such words as 'life', 'existence', 'power', 'will', and so on are equivocal—some of them, like *ruakh* (spirit/wind/breath) even homonyms—and represent, according to Maimonides, the greatest danger to persons of lax intellectual powers, constantly and inevitably reducing all religious uses of language, and hence God, into the profane realm of literal speech. In fact, Maimonides devotes the first forty-five chapters of the *Guide* to root

---

[70] Leaman, *Moses Maimonides*, 26.

out the blight of literalism when encountering in the exegetical process various scriptural equivocal terms, or 'names', associated with God's immanence in the created world, such as '*zelem*' ('image' or 'figure'), '*makom*' ('place'), '*adam*' ('man'), or '*kisse*' ('chair' or 'throne'), to name just a few. Only the Tetragrammaton, according to Maimonides, is the one true, univocal name of God, and is in itself indecipherable and incomprehensible (1.62). Reflecting in the manner of Philo on Exodus 3:14 (*ahyeh asher ahyeh*), Maimonides argues that the name 'I AM THAT I AM' is a gloss on the Tetragrammaton, signifying perfect eternity where both subject and predicate are identical (1.63). All other 'names', or the various appellations used to describe God in the Bible, are mere words that conform to the lapsarian malady of equivocation, made sacred only by the overall context of their inspired transmission through Moses. The conceit that God is corporeal, or is a trinity, or partakes of any apparently human attribute is an error, therefore, which results, according to Maimonides, from an uninspired, literal misinterpretation of Scripture. God's ineffable nature can only be conveyed through the use of metaphor, or synecdoche rather, and this in turn reflects on the lapsarian nature of human language which can only speak of the ineffable by displacing the conventional meaning of symbols—by engaging in meta-phoric activity. While this idea echoes the type of semantic reflection we find in Denys' *Divine Names*, in Maimonides' *Guide* it receives an evolved Aristotelian, anti-Platonic slant which distinguishes between the words we can utter, the thoughts which our words attempt to convey, and the actual reality to which our thoughts correspond. Maimonides' anti-Platonism not only eschews the Christian-Platonic semantic idea of the hypostatic *logos*, but the very possibility of transcendence inscribed in the idea of hypostasis itself. Created man, bound to the epistemological constraints of grammar and language, can never assimilate himself, mystically or otherwise, into the radical otherness of God whose immanence manifests itself in the very difference of language, not in its negation.[71]

---

[71] See e.g. Shira Wolosky's reading of Gershom Scholem's 'The Name of God and the Linguistic Theory of the Kabbalah' in relation to Derridean deconstruction: 'Linguistic differentiation . . . is not opposed against divine ultimacy but rather manifests it, both as creation and as figure' ('On Derrida's "How to Avoid Speaking: Denials"', 273).

For his part, Aquinas responds to Maimonides on two successive levels. Initially he argues with Maimonides whether or not we can predicate certain statements of God, and he then follows that argument with the semantic explanation of how we *can* make certain affirmative statements about God, imperfect though these may be, without introducing multiplicity into God's perfect oneness. In both these arguments the opening passage of Aristotle's *De Interpretatione* looms large, and in both instances Aquinas modifies Aristotle to accommodate not only the transcendental, but also, more importantly perhaps, the Incarnational. Citing, for example, Maimonides' negative assertion that with a statement such as 'God is good' one is not affirming anything, but rather denying something of God, Aquinas retorts that something affirmative is stated, but imperfectly:

This is not what people want to say when they talk about God. When a man speaks of the 'living God' he does not simply want to say that God is the cause of our life, or that he differs from a lifeless body. So we must find some other solution to the problem. We shall suggest that such words do say what God is; they are predicated of him in the category of substance, but fail to represent adequately what he is. The reason for this is that we speak of God as we know him, and since we know him from creatures we can only speak of him as they represent him.[72]

Aquinas is suggesting, therefore, that words can signify imperfectly and still affirm something about their object of reference. While this would not seem such a strange idea for those of us who live in the post-Saussurian age, at the time of Aquinas this was a revolutionary idea. Up to a point, Aquinas sides with Maimonides' view that the words we use to speak of God are equivocal, 'non sunt synonyma' (1a.13.5), but he differs from Maimonides in his view on how such equivocal language operates, since for Aquinas, as for all Christians, the promise of the Incarnation inscribes the very idea of a transcendental exchange into linguistic difference. Siding, in effect, with the earlier view maintained by the Muslim Averroes, that words spoken of God 'signify what is one from many different points of view',[73] Aquinas arrives at his important idea that religious language (the use of 'divine names') operates neither univocally nor equivocally, but 'analogically'. According to Aquinas,

----

[72] 1a.13.2; McCabe, *Summa Theologiae*, iii. 55.
[73] 1a.13.5; McCabe, *Summa Theologiae*, iii. 61.

God is a pure act (*actus purus*) of being, and insofar as man is God's creature, we are all then an act of God. But since only God is the fullness of being, man, who is himself only an action of God, can only predicate analogically of what the divine being may be like. Therefore, when Aquinas says 'we speak of God as we know him' his meaning is that we can only discuss God in analogical terms predicated on human experience, which while accurate to a certain limited degree are nonetheless imperfect. Judging from human examples of goodness, for example, we can predicate of God either that he is good in an adjectival sense, or that his existence is synonymous with the actual noun 'good', but since both terms are analogical such description remains imperfect and we can never truly grasp *the* good that is God.

As Burrell explains, Aquinas's method 'is rather a shorthand way of establishing a set of grammatical priorities designed to locate the subject matter as precisely as possible... Where less patient thinkers would invoke paradox, Aquinas is committed to using every resource available to state clearly what can be stated.'[74] Consequently, when Aquinas turns to respond to antitrinitarian arguments under Question no. 36, he can confidently insist on a methodology in which 'for the true meaning of language we need to take into account not merely what is signified but also the mode of signifying'.[75] This crucial Modistic distinction between the various *modi significandi* in turn allows Aquinas to distinguish between substantive and adjectival signification in relation to the Triune God, refuting, as it were, the type of objections advanced by Maimonides against any triadic references to God which introduce plurality into the divine One. Differentiating between the noun 'God' and the adjective we may attach to God, 'having divinity', Aquinas explains:

The name 'God' does signify 'having divinity', but the two expressions differ in their way of signifying: 'God' as a noun; 'having divinity', as an adjective. Accordingly whereas there are three having divinity, that still does not entail there being three Gods... Each distinct language has its proper idiom. Thus, even as Greek uses the expression 'three hypostases', because of the plurality of supposits in God, so too Hebrew uses the plural form, *Elohim*. Latin does not use the plurals, 'Gods' or 'substances', however, lest plurality be associated with God's substance.[76]

---

[74] Burrell, *Aquinas: God and Action*, 5–6.
[75] 1a.39.5; McCabe, *Summa Theologiae*, vii. 121.
[76] 1a. 39.3; McCabe, *Summa* Theologiae, vii. 111.

It should be noted, however, that the intended swipe at Jewish anti-trinitarianism in the reference to the plural of *Elohim* was one Maimonides is fully alert to in the *Guide*, where he explains that *Elohim* is an equivocal name which only refers to God metaphorically in the same way one would reverence a king by addressing him in the plural. Reading *Elohim* univocally as 'many gods' is precisely the type of literal misinterpretation Maimonides is eager to root out. Nevertheless, Aquinas shrewdly deploys the logical permutations of semantic theory not only to affirm something about God, but also to demonstrate the semantic logic of the Trinity and even the process of symbolic transubstantiation in the sacraments (3a.60). Crucially for the Christian tradition of the ineffable, Aquinas's method of analogical predication and imperfect signification offered to literary as well as philosophical posterity an enduring dialectical *via media* between the polarities of total negative *aphairesis* (literally 'a taking away') on the one hand, and total univocal literalness on the other.

The thinkers surveyed in this chapter continually addressed themselves to three speculative questions about divine ontology and epistemology— Why is God ineffable? How can we know that which is ineffable? And finally, what terms can we use when describing our limited knowledge of that which is ineffable? However, at the time of Aquinas few medieval thinkers questioned the philological integrity of the scholastic Latin used to articulate such complex theological and philosophical pronouncements, or the authority of pope and councils to canonize the doctrines issuing from the Sorbonne. After all, medieval Latin was not only the language of monastic intellectuals but also the language of Church liturgy and, most importantly, it was in the medieval West the official language of Scripture. That Jerome's Vulgate was so called because it too had ultimately supplanted what was once a mere 'vulgar' translation (that is, a translation whose aims were primarily spiritual and not literary, and therefore *ad usum vulgi*),[77] and that Latin was also inevitably

---

[77] At the time of Jerome the so-called *editio vulgata* was in fact the popular title of what we now term the *vetus Latina* or 'Old Latin' version, which Augustine was still using and which Jerome's piecemeal revisions and translations aimed to replace. The earliest use of 'Vulgate' to describe Jerome's Bible can be traced to the thirteenth century, and was only made universally current at the Council of Trent. *See CHB* i. 518.

subject to the subtle corruption of time and custom were unavailable perspectives in the Western medieval world, where Greek scholarship was nonexistent and Latin the only available language with which to establish the necessary semantic boundaries between sacred and profane.[78] All this, however, was about to change. The gradual rise of humanism in Western Europe during the fourteenth and fifteenth centuries, and the subsequent, if not consequent, ecclesiastical schisms and doctrinal controversies that rent Western Christendom changed forever the way in which central intellectual concepts such as the ineffable were understood and negotiated.

[78] See Muller and Taylor, *A Chrestomathy of Vulgar Latin*, 1–18; and Reynolds, *Medieval Reading*, 45–73.

2

The power and illusion of words: renegotiating ineffable presence in the advent of humanism and reform

Competing approaches about how to address the problem of ineffability in religious and philosophical discourse can be found at the heart of much Renaissance thought and theological polemic. It was especially the rise of what we now think of as 'humanism', and the advent of the printing-press, rapidly enlisted in its service, which ultimately exposed the spiritual and intellectual bankruptcy of overly speculative scholastic contemplation and the decrepitude of its philological apparatus. In this respect, the sort of impact humanist thinkers made on the conceptual fortunes of the ineffable as an idea can be divided into two distinct spheres of activity. The first activity involved the Italian Neoplatonists of the Florentine Academy, who sought to recover and then develop Platonic thought in the process of sketching a synthesized Christian theosophy. The other, quite distinct, humanist activity involved those biblical scholars and philologists who sought to apply their considerable philological skills, first to patristic and finally to biblical texts in an attempt to restore the sacred textual record to its pristine form. Although both spheres of activity have at their heart a shared humanist respect for the original Greek of their respective texts (Plato's dialogues and the *Hermetica* on one hand, the New Testament on the other), in terms of the ineffable the two enterprises could not have had a more different outcome. For their part, the efforts of late-medieval and Renaissance Neoplatonists ultimately gave birth to the Renaissance concept of man as a being of limitless potential, a 'microcosm' at the centre of God's creation. The parallel efforts of humanist biblical scholars, however, profoundly unsettled the sacred fixity of God's

Word and ultimately, though indirectly, contributed to the Reformation crisis and the evolution of a Christocentric view of man that emphasized man's salvific dependency on grace. The world into which Milton was born and in which he was educated was shaped by these two divergent spheres of early humanist activity, and in his poetry he embodied the emerging dichotomy between them.

THE DIGNITY OF MAN AND THE RENAISSANCE CONCEPT OF POETIC THEOLOGY

At the height of the Italian Renaissance, Count Giovanni Pico della Mirandola (1463–94) recorded in his short philosophical treatise, *De Ente et Uno* (*On Being and the One*), the following standard apophatic reflection on the participial quality of the divine names:

These names, being, true, one, good, mean something concrete, and, as it were, participated. Hence we say that God is above being, above true, above one, above good, since he is existence itself, truth itself, unity itself, goodness itself. But we are still in light. God, however, has established his dwelling in darkness. Therefore we have not yet reached God. For until we also understand and comprehend what we say about God, we are said to remain in light, and what we say and feel about God is as inferior as the capacity of our intellect is inferior to his infinite divinity. Let us rise to the fourth step and enter into the light of ignorance, and blinded by the darkness of divine splendour let us cry out with the Prophet, 'I have become weak in thy courts, O Lord,' finally saying only this about God, that he is unintelligibly and ineffably above everything most perfect which we can either speak or conceive of him.[1]

When read against the literature surveyed in the previous chapter, there is nothing about this passage which seems original. Pico, who was by all accounts a highly imaginative thinker, was never the most original philosopher; he inherited his Neoplatonism and passion for the occult texts of the *prisci theologi* from his mentor, the great Florentine Platonist Marsilio Ficino, who was in turn deeply influenced by the mystical Neoplatonism of Nicholas Cusanus and ultimately the pseudo-Dionysius.

---

[1] *On the Dignity of Man, On Being and the One, Heptaplus,* trans. Wallis, Miller, and Carmichael, 49–50.

Pico in particular was fond of quoting from the *Corpus Areopagiticum*: the passage just cited from Pico's *De Ente et Uno* actually introduces a long quotation from Denys' *Mystical Theology*; and in his kabbalistic commentary on Genesis, the *Heptaplus*, Pico uses countless quotations from Denys' *Celestial Hierarchies* to prop up his mystical exegesis. But Pico's dependency on the mystical tenets of Denys is not slavish. There is in Pico's appeal to the tropes of apophatic mysticism a change in focus and an energy which is very much a symptom of what we now think of as a 'Renaissance' or 'humanist' world-view. To get a better sense of how this 'Renaissance' energy, or dynamism, evolved we have to go back several decades and consider the ground-breaking mysticism of Nicholas Cusanus (1401–64).

Charles H. Lohr helpfully divides the history of Renaissance metaphysics into two phases. The second, more familiar phase begins with the efforts of the Florentine Academy and Ficino's monumental translation into Latin of the *Corpus Hermeticum* (*The Pimander* and *Asclepius*) and Plato's dialogues, followed by his two widely read and influential treatises *De Religione Christiana* and the *Theologia Platonica de Immortalitate Animorum*. The first phase, however, has a far more complex genesis and begins, if anywhere, with the *Ars generalis* of the medieval philosopher and lay missionary Ramon Lull (*c*.1233–*c*.1315), the reintroduction of Plato into Western Christendom through the teachings and commentaries of Pletho, and the celebrated *De Docta Ignorantia* (*Of Learned Ignorance*) of Nicholas of Cusa (Cusanus).[2] Lull's teachings and the work of Pletho helped to enshrine a new spirit of anthropocentric universality which slowly began to take root in Western Europe in the late fourteenth and early fifteenth centuries, largely prompted by the economic and political imperatives of trade with the Greek East and Muslim nations. Indeed, it was in Italy, and the Venetian Republic in particular, that, as Lohr puts it, 'out of the need to formulate a conception of knowledge which transcended the differences between Greek, Latin, and the vernaculars, between East and West, was born a new vision of man himself'.[3] Today we identify this new vision of man mostly with the seminal scholarly achievements of Petrarch, who echoed in his *De Vita*

[2] C. H. Lohr, 'Metaphysics', *CHRP* 537–84. See also Moore, *The Infinite*, 45–55.
[3] Lohr, 'Metaphysics', 547.

Solitaria the spirit of Lull's natural theology when he exhorted all men of learning to turn their mind inwardly, for 'only in the solitude and *silentium* of a mind turned upon itself away from worldly distractions could man find that divine link which united all men and committed them to the service of their kind'.[4] What is remarkable about this sentiment is not its call for introspection as such, but the belief that in discovering his divinity man could better himself both as a divinely speculative creature and as a socially responsible one. For humanists like Petrarch and his Italian disciples, metaphysics could be brought to bear on ethics and politics: by ascending mystically towards God through introspection, man ultimately illuminates himself and his endless potential for self-perfection as a moral, creative human being acting within human society to better the species.

It is in this context that the future cardinal and bishop of Brixen, Nicholas Cusanus, then a young student of canon law at Padua, probably came across the works of Lull and began his lifelong interest in Byzantine culture and Greek philosophy outside the Aristotelianism of the schools. As Cusanus' career developed he cultivated his interests into a profound knowledge of Plato, Philo, Proclus, and the pseudo-Dionysius. He used his familiarity with both worlds—the scholasticism of the Latin West and the mystical theosophies of the Greek East—to form his own synthesized mystical theology which, as the title of his most famous theological work indicates, centred on the paradoxical idea of 'learned ignorance'.[5] The principles of negative theology are already contained in the idea of learned ignorance: the only learning that is really possible for man is that which admits its own ignorance in the face of a God whom Cusanus describes, using Anselm's 'that which nothing greater can be thought', as a 'simple' or 'absolute' *maximum.* At the heart of Cusanus' theory of learned ignorance is the axiom that 'a finite intellect . . . cannot by any means of comparison reach the absolute truth of things',[6] and this later accounts for the way in which Cusanus accommodates the pseudo-Dionysian principles of negative theology into his system. Because Cusanus develops a theory of the 'absolute'

---

[4] Quoted by C. Vasoli in 'The Renaissance Concept of Philosophy', *CHRP* 62.
[5] Lohr, 'Metaphysics', 548–58; See also Moore, *The Infinite*, 55-6; Wind, *Pagan Mysteries in the Renaissance*, 220–5.
[6] 1.3; G. Heron, trans., *Of Learned Ignorance*, 11.

maximum which is from the outset beyond any measure of 'more' or 'less', and is therefore indistinguishable even from the absolute *minimum* (because if the absolute *maximum* admits no degrees of 'more' or 'less' it cannot be distinguished from the *minimum*, 1.5), he rejected the Thomist idea of analogy. According to Cusanus, our relationship to God as the 'absolute *maximum*' 'is like that of a polygon to a circle' where 'no multiplication, even if it were infinite, of its angles will make the polygon equal the circle'.[7] Consequently, the very idea of predicating something of God analogically from our knowledge of creatures, even if it is deemed to be imperfect, becomes in this context meaningless because there is no point in setting up an analogical scheme where one of the terms making up the scheme—God in this case—is logically unique and utterly transcendental.

It is at this point of logical crisis that Cusanus begins to develop his unique mystical approach by reconsidering the pseudo-Dionysian dynamism between affirmative kataphatic theology and negative apophatic theology. Like Maimonides, whom Cusanus cites as an authority on this view, Cusanus dismisses the names men use for God to be no names at all, but anthropomorphic expressions of a particular attribute of God as perceived through his immanence in the created world. For Cusanus, however, such naming of God is not analogical in any way but merely an exercise in metaphorical circumlocution performed by someone forever falling short of his meaning, even as he draws ever closer towards it. Cusanus follows Maimonides here in asserting that even the one real name of God recorded in Scripture, the Tetragrammaton, is only a 'name' in the negative sense that it is itself something which is 'ineffable and above our understanding'.[8] Metaphors, in other words, can say nothing about the 'absolute maximum', not even by way of analogy, because God as 'absolute maximum' is beyond any form of distinction whatsoever, and words which operate referentially by distinguishing one thing from another (for this was the basic semiotic assumption at the time) simply can never be used to say *anything* about God:

Sacred ignorance has taught us that God is ineffable, because He is infinitely greater than anything that words can express. So true is this that it is by the process

---

[7] 1.3; G. Heron, trans., *Of Learned Ignorance.*
[8] 1.24; Heron, *Of Learned Ignorance*, 54.

of elimination and the use of negative propositions that we come nearer the truth about Him . . . From this it is clear how in theology negative propositions are true and affirmative ones inadequate; and that of the negative ones those are truer which eliminate greater imperfections from the infinitely Perfect.[9]

However, whereas Denys rests on articulating the paradoxes of negative affirmation and affirmative negation, Cusanus situates these paradoxes within a wider theology that constitutes, as Cassirer puts it, 'a new point of departure in [Western] religion'.[10] As Cassirer explains, Cusanus takes the inadequate symbol and endows it with 'new content and value', where it can be conceded 'that all names, in so far as they proceed from a genuine religious conviction and are conscious of their limited and mediate capacity, may be assured of a certain relationship to the divine'.[11] Whereas a similar optimism in the much earlier mysticism of Denys fixes its gaze, transcendentally, on the 'hidden face of God', the Catholic Cusanus draws from the force of that vision a deliberately anti-scholastic defence of healthy religious heterodoxy which focuses at once on the self and its place in the world. The tenets of Cusanus' 'learned ignorance' open up the path to faith in a way which celebrates rather than stifles man's divine inheritance at the centre of creation, because man, for Cusanus, is a microcosm, or a 'world in miniature',[12] a finite being forever embraced by the infinite. As Lohr clarifies, man is a microcosm for Cusanus, 'not because he comprises in himself all the different degrees of reality and thus is subject to all its conflicting forces, but rather because—situated at the centre of creation, at the horizon of time and eternity—he unites in himself the lowest level of intellectual reality and the highest reach of sensible nature and is thus a bond which holds creation together'.[13] Moreover, because man is the microcosmic polygon within a circle whose centre is everywhere and circumference nowhere (to use the famous Hermetic metaphor also used by Cusanus), 'the centre and the circumference [of the world] are identical',[14] and man may, under the 'perfect' mystical conditions effectively become a

---

[9] Heron, *Of Learned Ignorance*, 60–1.
[10] Cassirer, *The Platonic Renaissance in England*, 14.
[11] Ibid.
[12] 3.3; Heron, *Of Learned Ignorance*, 135.
[13] Lohr, *CHRP* 553.
[14] 2.11; Heron, *Of Learned Ignorance*, 107.

'contracted' *maximum* at one with the Creator. Ultimately, Cusanus clarifies that no mere man could ever really achieve such radical, thinly disguised Neoplatonic apotheosis whereby assuming all features of the *maximum*, albeit in a contracted form, 'this man assuredly would so be man as to be God, would be so God as to be man, the perfection of all things and in all things holding the primacy'.[15] Only Jesus, the incarnated Son of God is the 'maximally perfect man' (*maxime perfectus homo*),[16] who is, in Cusanus' philosophical terminology, a 'perfect human nature, which now subsists by the subsistence of the Word, [and] does not in any way exceed the bounds of its species, since it is finite nature [i.e. human nature] at the peak point of perfection'.[17] It is only through faith in Christ that the Christian mystic may, by degrees, enjoy a revelation of divine truths. However, whereas Mainonides, the Averroists, and Aquinas clearly distinguish between the realms of rational reasoning and revelation, Cusanus' philosophical musings are already revelatory in that they are expressions of a paradoxically non-rational reasoning that relies on metaphor rather than logic to convey the force of its truth.

This last point is especially evident in Cusanus' concluding encomium of the 'mysteries of faith' as the driving energy behind his theological reflections. In a succession of ever-more absurd mixed metaphors, Cusanus likens Christ to a 'mountain...which our animal nature is forbidden to touch'. The 'mountain' next becomes itself a metaphor for 'that very darkness...in which He is pleased to dwell for the sake of all those who live a life of the spirit'. However, we soon learn that those mystics who rise above the empirical world by clinging to faith are then admitted into the 'interior' of the 'mountain', where one hears 'interiorly...the voices and the thunder and the dread signs of His majesty'. This, finally, metaphorically translates into the Christ-God's 'incorruptible footprints', which are then interpreted as the moment when 'hearing the voice not of mortal creatures but of God Himself in His

[15] 3.3; Heron, *Of Learned Ignorance*, 135.

[16] 3.4; Heron, *Of Learned Ignorance*, 141; *Opera*, i. 132.

[17] 3.5. The phrase 'subsists by the subsistence of the Word' is a curious interpolation here by Heron, but it follows from the context of Cusanus' previous discussion of Jesus as the Word. The Latin here merely reads: 'quoniam humanitas perfectissima sursum suppositata, cum sit terminalis contracta praecisio, naturae illius penitus speciem non exit', *Opera*, i. 133.

holy organs and in the words of His prophets and saints, we come, as in a cloud of more transparent quality, to perceive Him more clearly'.[18] The elaborate use of metaphor in this sequence is itself indicative of the 'blurred clarity', as it were, of Cusanus' notion of the *visio Dei*. The tenor of these metaphors—mountain, darkness, thunder, footprints— simultaneously eschews and authorizes the use of such inadequate and deliberately mixed metaphors, where darkness can be a mountain and sound leaves footprints, precisely because God is at once all of these things and none of them. Whatever is stated, the presence of the ineffable grows stronger with each successive utterance. At least, such is the elusive promise of the *visio Dei* Cusanus holds before us.

In the Introduction I proposed that mystics can actually talk 'about' or around the ineffable without actually talking about it by using negative similes and metaphors. As philosopher David E. Cooper has shown in *The Measure of Things*, the ways in which language behaves when confronted by what Rudolph Otto described as the 'numinous' received fuller treatment in Heidegger, who maintained that the 'language of mystery' performs a number of speech acts that are not necessarily assertive or descriptive, but which may attune or intimate an ineffable presence.[19] To a limited extent, Cusanus' use of metaphor fits this idea. There is, indeed, nothing inherently descriptive or representational about Cusanus' understanding of metaphorical language when used in this way to 'describe' the indescribable, since it cannot be deemed either 'more' or 'less', 'negative' or 'positive'. Nevertheless, one cannot even intimate the ineffable or gesture to it in speech without at least uttering something, if not about it then at least directed at it. It is interesting in this context that Cusanus draws a distinction between written and spoken language. Written language, he says, 'is but speech that has been given permanent shape'.[20] God, of course, is beyond any notion of 'shape' and therefore cannot be written about, but does this mean then that there *can* be some way of actually speaking about God, even if this 'about' is entirely non-representational? Cusanus hints that the answer is possibly yes, but warns that 'if these revelations came to be

---

[18] 3.11; Heron, *Of Learned Ignorance*, 161–2.
[19] Cooper, *The Measure of Things*, 286–95.
[20] 3.11; Heron, *Of Learned Ignorance*, 162. A more literal translation would be: 'speech is given shape through writing.'

told, unutterable things would be framed in human speech, things beyond all hearing would fall upon human ears'.[21] But it would be possible to say something. That 'something' is bound to be, as Wittgenstein would say, 'nonsense', but the utterance of such nonsense would manifest what cannot be said.

I base this comparison with Wittgenstein on his enigmatic remark in the *Tractatus* that 'what *can* be shown, *cannot* be said'.[22] At the risk of oversimplifying a profound philosophical idea, Wittgenstein's 'say–show' distinction proposes that that which can only be shown, the logical form of propositions, is already present in what *can* be said: 'propositions cannot represent logical form: it is mirrored in them. What finds its reflection in language, language cannot represent.'[23] What can only be shown shows itself, or is reflected in what we *can* say logically. Or, to put it more precisely, what can be shown is what makes it possible for us to grasp the sense of propositions, without having their sense explained to us, and it is for this reason that Wittgenstein finally concludes the *Tractatus* with the famous aphorism: 'What we cannot speak about we must pass over in silence.'[24] However, in order to understand the conceit of Christian mystics such as Cusanus and the theories of negative theology more generally, we need to take Wittgenstein's idea and wilfully misread it. We must assent to the logocentric axiom of Christian theology and so take the 'say–show' distinction to mean that that which can only be said and that which can only be shown constitute two *distinct* categories of meaning or 'sense'. We need to locate the ineffability of divine alterity strictly in what can be shown, not what can be said, and then separate the two so that what can be shown is not manifested in what can be said but precisely in what Wittgenstein would construe as the incomprehensible realm of nonsense and silence. Cusanus, for example, everywhere assents to the idea that by trying to say the unsayable we produce nonsense, but he firmly believes that precisely by abandoning the realms of logical sense we effectively show or intimate an unsayable presence without

---

[21] 3.11; Heron, *Of Learned Ignorance*, 162. A more literal translation would be: 'speech is given shape through writing.'

[22] Wittgenstein, *Tractatus Logico-Philosophicus*, 4.1212 (trans. Pears and McGuinness, 31).

[23] Ibid. 4.121 (31).   [24] Ibid. 7 (89).

actually saying it; that is, he locates the ineffable itself *in* nonsense or at the point in which normative language breaks down.[25]

This, in essence, is the core belief which drives all discussion of radical *aphaeresis* in relation to the hidden God within a logocentric Neoplatonic-Christian context, and which helps explain therefore Cusanus' most enduring contribution to what begins to emerge in the Renaissance as a preoccupation with a form of transcendental *poetics* rather than *theology*. It is helpful at this point to bring in Edgar Wind, who reminds us that Cusanus engages in his complementary treatise, *De Visio Dei*, in a form of metaphysical *serio ludere*: 'In order to guide the mind towards the hidden God, Cusanus invented experiments in metaphor, semi-magical exercises which would solemnly entertain and astonish the beholder. These serious games (*serio ludere*) consisted in finding within common experience an unusual object endowed with the kind of contradictory attributes which are difficult to imagine united in the deity.'[26] I understand Wind's 'semi-magical' to mean not that such 'serious (literary) games' ingeniously pretend to say the unsayable—that is a given—but that it is a mode of literary expression which naturally flows from the Renaissance mystic's belief that there must be something more to man, as Shakespeare's Hamlet says, than this 'quintessence of dust'. What has occurred here is a shift in emphasis: whereas mystics in the earlier Neoplatonic tradition were concerned strictly with defining the ineffable parameters of an absolute reality which transcends the finite order, Nicholas Cusanus and his Renaissance heirs draw inspiration from their own belief that transcendence is already programmed into their own finite human nature. A. W. Moore calls this the fantasy of infinity—the desire, especially acute in the

---

[25] For the Wittgenstein of the *Tractatus* this idea is naturally false, since 'nonsense' does not constitute its own privileged sense which is somehow ineffable, but is merely the consequence of attempting to explain propositions or prove them without understanding how their logical form actually communicates 'sensibly'. For the early Wittgenstein it is the logical form of propositions which is ineffable, not something transcendentally *other* than language (like God) which a nonsensical expression can somehow point to. In this way, Wittgenstein is not denying that God exists or invalidating mystical experiences, but merely narrowing the scope of philosophical-logical discourse to the realms of propositional sense: God may very well exist, but his existence is something about which philosophy can and should have nothing to say.
[26] Wind, *Pagan Mysteries*, 222.

Renaissance, to aspire towards the infinite and to be effectively 'all there is'.[27]

A typical Renaissance expression of this fantasy can be found in Ficino's exordium to his monumental *Platonic Theology*:

It seems therefore to follow of necessity that once our souls leave this prison, some other light awaits them. Our human minds, 'immured in darkness and a sightless dungeon,' may look in vain for that light, and we are often driven to doubt our own divine provenance. But I pray that as heavenly souls longing with desire for our heavenly home we may cast off the bonds of our terrestrial chains; cast them off as swiftly as possible, so that, uplifted on Platonic wings and with God as our guide, we may fly unhindered to our ethereal abode, where we will straightaway look with joy on the excellence of our own human nature.[28]

Ficino expresses here his yearning for infinity in the language of a poet, talking of 'wings', 'chains', and an 'ethereal abode' to evoke man's sense of entrapment in his finite, mortal form. Reluctant perhaps to rely on his own rather pedestrian powers of poetic suggestion, he turns to Virgil for support, quoting *Aeneid* 6.734: 'immured in darkness and a sightless dungeon' (*clausae tenebris et carcere caeco*). The quotation from Book VI of the *Aeneid*, however, does not simply provide Ficino with a convenient metaphor likening the body to a 'sightless dungeon'. It expands literarily the evocative power of Ficino's conceit by simultaneously conjuring the Pythagorean philosophy of Anchises' lecture on the soul, as well as the oppressive, chthonic setting of Hades where the shade of Anchises lectures his son. The Virgilian citation triggers a series of literary ripples that spread from Virgil's Hades to the evocative torments of Dante's *Inferno*, conjuring in the process a poetic image of mortality so frightening that any man would indeed wish to escape it. As Moore explains, the inherent paradox of such yearning—and necessarily of its poetic vocabulary—is that 'we are tempted, so far as is compatible with our knowing that this is impossible, to proceed as if our representations constituted reality, and to treat conditions of their existence, such as our knowing how to produce them, as conditions of reality itself'.[29] The embedded quotation from Virgil is a wonderful illustration of this

---

[27] Moore, *Points of View*, 259–66.
[28] 1.1.1; Hankins and Allen, *Platonic Theology*, i. 15.
[29] Moore, *Points of View*, 260.

paradox. Ficino borrows from Virgil the metaphor of a 'sightless dungeon' to describe the condition of the soul's entrapment, and it is this poetic conceit which constitutes Ficino's reality as he perceives it. However, Ficino equally treats the conditions of how such a conceit came about—the God-given poetic imagination of Virgil—as itself a condition of this presupposed reality, namely that man may imaginatively create in the first place representations which constitute such a reality.

Many more examples of this paradox can be found in Renaissance philosophical writings, but none perhaps as spectacular as those found in the writings of the Italian Renaissance's most ambitious fantasist—Pico della Mirandola. It should be clearer now that when Pico cries out in his *De Ente et Uno*: 'Let us rise to the fourth step and enter into the light of ignorance', he is not merely prescribing in the spirit of Denys a system for mystical contemplation in four steps, but is in fact encouraging his fellow initiates, in the spirit of Cusanus and Ficino, to rediscover something hidden about themselves. He declares this much at the outset of his *Oration on the Dignity of Man*: 'Let a certain holy ambition invade the mind, so that we may not be content with mean things but may aspire to the highest things and strive with all our forces to attain them: for if we will to, we can.'[30] Pico's position in this celebrated text should not be confused with modern philosophical theories of absolute freedom or solipsism. Human nature for Pico objectively contains within it and holds in tension the angelic nature (identified with reason and the soul) and animalistic nature (identified with appetite and the body). Through his intellect man knows and comprehends the microcosmic duality of his nature and so has a choice of either pursuing philosophy and becoming one with the angels, or relinquishing his divine birthright and becoming a slave to sensual appetite. Pico's metaphysical ambition in the *Oratio* thus underlines the force of his oratorical conviction as a poet-philosopher who is caught up in his own mythology of the Orphic seer. Like Ficino before him, Pico was deeply inspired by the alleged antiquity of the occult texts attributed to the so-called *prisici theologi*, Hermes Trismegistus, Orpheus, and Zoroaster. In the *Oratio* he cites a mélange of Christian, Jewish-kabbalistic, and pagan Neoplatonic and Hermetic 'authorities'

---

[30] *On the Dignity of Man*, 7.

in his advocacy of a synthesized 'ancient wisdom' that deliberately blurs the distinctions between theology, philosophy, and inspired poetry. He seems to have been especially fascinated with what he perceived to be the pristine wisdom contained poetically within the *Orphic Hymns*, which we now know to be a collection of mostly late Hellenistic theogonies attributed in antiquity to the mythical poet-theologian Orpheus (cited by Ficino as one of the *prisci theologi*) and preserved today mostly in fragments within Neoplatonic writings. Like Proclus, Iamblichus, and other Neoplatonists before him, Pico believed that the pagan myths recounted within the Orphic texts were in fact complicated metaphors for a hidden, transcendental reality. 'Orpheus', he argues, 'covered the mysteries of his doctrines with the wrappings of fables, and disguised them with a poetic garment, so that whoever reads his hymns may believe there is nothing underneath but tales and the purest nonsense.'[31] Pico proceeds in this passage to stress his own monumental achievement in digging out, as he says, 'the hidden meanings of a secret philosophy from the calculated meshes of riddles and from hiding-places in fables'.[32] What these precise hidden meanings might have contained is anybody's guess—Pico had planned to record his insights into the *Orphic Hymns* in a treatise which he was going to name suggestively *Poetic Theology*, but the treatise either was never written or has not survived.[33]

However, the notion of a 'poetic theology' remains a very powerful one and can go a long way towards illuminating the method of Pico's mystical approach. It is not simply that the blurring of boundaries between pagan poetry and theological dogma results in one becoming the other in the superficial sense that Pico would now use a rich, poetic language to outline religious truths. We must always remember that Pico held a generally low opinion of the poet's art *per se*. Outside the *Orphic Hymns* and revered poems such as Homer's *Odyssey* (cited in the *Oratio* as another 'sacred' text), Pico had very little patience for poetry that was not in some way directly amenable to an allegorical reading along Christian-Neoplatonic lines. In his *De Rerum Praenotione*, for

---

[31] *On the Dignity of Man*, 7. 33.   [32] Ibid.
[33] For speculation as to what the treatise might have contained see Wind, *Pagan Mysteries*, 17–25.

example, he condemns much of pagan poetry as 'detestable' and argues that 'most poets mixed into their verses the greatest wickedness and impurities, which are not only not to be touched by a Christian but are to be utterly expelled by him'.[34] After all, reasons Pico, Plato was clearly in the right when he banished the misleading and beguiling poets from his Republic. The emphasis in the idea of a 'poetic theology', however, is not on the actual creation of poetic verses, but on the adjectival use of the word 'poetic' to signify a theological activity that is imaginatively engaged in the active *re-creation* of divine truths. The corollary of this idea lies in the original Greek word for 'poet', ποιητής (*poiētes*), which derives from the verb ποιέω ('to make', 'produce', 'create'), and ultimately denotes a 'craftsman', someone who creates rather than writes poetic verses.[35] Moreover, we may recall that Plato's *Timaeus* describes the demiurge as the 'maker' (ποιητὴν, *poiētēn*) of the universe, and Pico, following most of his contemporaries, would have readily understood this to mean that God is in a profound theological sense *the* ultimate 'poet', and his language of creation *the* language of divine 'poetry'. This was the basic principle behind medieval and Renaissance theories of musical world harmony (*harmonia mundi*) and the numerology associated with the *ars aeterna* of creation as emanating from the poetic mind of God and manifested in all created nature. And insofar as artists—both poets and painters—were believed to be imitating nature, art in general was seen to be imitating patterns derived from the mind of God, if not even imitating God's very methods of creation.[36]

It is in this borrowed Platonic sense that Pico probably thought of himself as a poet when he eventually turned his hand to actual neo-Latin poetry in his *Hymn to Christ* and *Heroic Hymns* (which Milton knew and possibly drew on for his 'Nativity Ode'[37]). But outside these rather laboured, neoclassical poems, a good example of Pico's 'poetic' mode of

---

[34] Quoted in Weinberg, *A History of Literary Criticism in the Italian Renaissance*, i. 255.

[35] This is echoed in Latin as well, where the common coinage is 'versum facere' and not 'versum scribere'.

[36] For a comprehensive survey of these ideas in relation to Renaissance Neoplatonism and later to Milton see Røstvig, 'Ars Aeterna', and the essays in Fowler, *Silent Poetry*. For theories of *harmonia mundi* see Spitzer, *Classical and Christian Ideas of World Harmony*.

[37] For the possible influence of Pico's *Hymn to Christ* on Milton's 'Nativity Ode' see Feinstein, 'On the Hymns of John Milton and Gian Francesco Pico'.

religious expression can be found in the prose exordium of the *Oratio*. In one of the *Oratio*'s most famous passages—often cited for its Renaissance platitudes about the anthropocentric view of creation—Pico rewrites Genesis by imagining a fictional conversation between God and the newly created Adam:

Therefore He took up man, a work of indeterminate form; and, placing him at the midpoint of the world, He spoke to him as follows: 'We have given to thee, Adam, no fixed seat, no form of thy very own, no gift peculiarly thine, that thou mayest feel as thine own, have as thine own, possess thine own the seat, the form, the gifts which thou thyself shalt desire. A limited nature in other creatures is confined within the laws written down by Us. In conformity with thy free judgement, in whose hands I have placed thee, thou art confined by no bounds; and thou wilt fix limits of nature for thyself. I have placed thee at the center of the world, that from there thou mayest more conveniently look around and see whatsoever is in the world. Neither heavenly nor earthly, neither mortal nor immortal have We made thee. Thou, like a judge appointed for being honorable, art the molder and maker of thyself; thou mayest sculpt thyself into whatever shape thou dost prefer. Thou canst grow downward into the lower natures which are brutes. Thou canst again grow upward from thy soul's reason into the higher natures which are divine.'[38]

Countless scholars cite this speech as a typical expression of the Renaissance philosophy of man, but few seem to be troubled by the fact that Pico is effectively assuming in this passage a radically transcendental point of view by presuming to talk for God. To most modern readers the literary strategy of using God to put across a philosophical point is neither unusual nor necessarily radical; we see it for what it is: an innocent fiction. But Pico, like Milton after him, is hardly innocent of the underlying claims to 'prophetic' authority such strategy makes. In both Pico and Milton this gesture exploits its intended audience's susceptibility to a biblical discourse which requires the reader willingly to suspend his disbelief (or rather, to willingly engage in religious belief) when faced with the notion of divinely appointed authors eavesdropping on God's conversations with himself and a select number of his creatures. The similarities between Pico and Milton on this point end here, however, most obviously because the Catholic Pico is not attempting

[38] *On the Dignity of Man*, 4–5.

a theodicy. Nevertheless, it is hard to tell what the 'venerable fathers' of the papal curia to whom Pico addressed the *Oratio*—all men conditioned to believe in the credible testimony of prophecy—made of Pico's speaking God. Whatever they thought about it, we do know that Pope Innocent VIII found some of Pico's *900 Conclusions*, which the *Oratio* was meant to introduce, demonstrably heretical and that Pico had to escape to France to avoid facing a heresy trial. It is easy to see why the pope and his 'venerable' advisors found the general tenor of Pico's thesis objectionable: the suggestion that occult pagan mysticism and Jewish kabbala could reveal hidden truths about the Christian faith which are not already available in the gospels was simply unthinkable for them. However, one wonders if the battle was not already lost, subliminally, when Pico's God made his 'innocent' cameo appearance in the *Oratio*.

Pico's attempt to exploit the conventions of prophecy by projecting his philosophy onto God results in circular meta-textuality. God delivers a sermon on Pico's personal sense of self-worth as philosopher and Orphic orator, but it is Pico himself who, as author of this dialogue, provides the example of a man who is at the 'center of the world' and who, 'confined by no bounds', 'sculpts' himself into 'whatever shape' he wishes—in this case the 'shape' of God speaking to Adam. Sensing that he may have overstepped his bounds, however, Pico immediately follows this feat of inspired ventriloquism by reverting to the human point of view with a humble, and very shrill, cry of thanks: 'O great liberality of God the Father! O great and wonderful happiness of man! It is given him to have that which he chooses and to be that which he wills.'[39] This radical change in tone and perspective, from the transcendental to the merely human, betrays a certain unease, and captures the essence of Pico's philosophy, which for all its optimism about the power of man to will himself into the divine mind is forever haunted by the many imperfections of man's fallible nature. Nevertheless, Pico's ability to vacillate imaginatively between the human and divine perspectives as if the two were naturally available to him is his major contribution to the Renaissance reinterpretation of the inspired *vates* as someone who, as Philip Sidney would later put it, goes 'hand in hand with nature, not

---

[39] Ibid. 5.

enclosed within the narrow warrant of her gifts, but freely ranging only within in the zodiac of his own wit'.[40]

It is true, of course, that Sidney's later statement is much more radical than Pico's implicit idea of a poetic theology, not least because the Protestant Sidney is reacting as a poet to the cultural and theological pressures of Edward VI's uncompromising legacy of Calvinist iconoclasm.[41] Nevertheless, the profound sympathy between Pico's philosophy and Sidney's radical view of the creative powers of the poetic imagination as limitless and morally free 'another nature' can be traced easily enough. Sidney's interest in religious Hermetism, his acquaintance with the English astrologer and magician John Dee, and later with the flamboyant Giordano Bruno (who visited England to much fanfare in 1583), are all well documented.[42] Bruno and Dee were both creatures of a Renaissance tradition fascinated by occult mysticism; a tradition which begins, indirectly and ironically enough, with the dynamic mysticism and tolerant religiosity of the devout Catholic cardinal, Nicholas Cusanus. It is certainly ironic that Cusanus' religious open-mindedness nurtured and inspired a movement of mystical occultism which, though religious in tenor, increasingly departed from any meaningful association with orthodox Christianity, whether Catholic or Reformed. In England, at any rate, the imported brand of Italian and Erasmian humanism cultivated by More and Colet was to develop hand in hand with institutional religion, which meant eventually that the imported Hermetic optimism of the Florentine Academy had to contend with the powerful advent of Calvinism and its diametrically opposed view of man as a wretched, sinful being with absolutely no independent capacity for good outside the workings of grace. This looming conflict contextualizes, moreover, Frances Yates's important observation that, 'if there was any interest in [Hermetism] in [Elizabethan] England, it was not in officially established circles in Church and University, but in private circles, such as Sir Philip Sidney's group of courtiers studying number in the three worlds with John Dee, or in survivals of the More–Colet

---

[40] *The Defence of Poesie*, in *Sir Philip Sidney: A Critical Edition of the Major Works*, ed. Katherine Duncan-Jones (Oxford, 1989), 216.

[41] See MacCulloch, *Tudor Church Militant*, 157–222. Professor MacCulloch provides what is still one of the best accounts of the Edwardian legacies of reform during Elizabeth's reign.

[42] See Yates, *Giordano Bruno and the Hermetic Tradition*.

tradition'.[43] It is a telling fact that Renaissance philosophers of Pico's and Bruno's persuasion had long since become what we would now describe as 'poets' rather than theologians or philosophers. There is a sense in which the true English heirs of Cusanus, Ficino, Pico, and Bruno are not men like Sir Thomas Browne and the Cambridge Platonists, but poets such as Sidney and Spenser, and in a more complicated way, as we shall see, Milton as well.[44]

ERASMUS AND THE PRACTICES OF INSPIRED PHILOLOGY

The humanist view that the Bible is pre-eminently a sublime, if somewhat inelegant, literary text was maintained as early as Petrarch. It was only much later, however, when philologists such as Traversari, Manetti, and Valla applied their considerable erudition to patristic and then biblical texts, that humanist biblical scholarship took on a life of its own.[45] The first aspect of Scripture to come under intense philological scrutiny was the general linguistic integrity of the Vulgate translation and the myths surrounding its inspired authorship by Jerome. By the fifteenth century the Vulgate text was confusedly diffused through countless corrupt and derivative manuscripts containing various assimilations of the 'Old Latin' versions and Jerome's translations and revisions.[46] Valla's *Collatio novi testamenti*, an extensive Latin commentary on the Greek New Testament, and Manetti's unrelated project to produce a fresh Latin translation of the Greek New Testament, both exposed the textual reality of a Vulgate text corrupted by centuries of transmission at the hands of semi-literate copyists. Using a now-unknown and

---

[43] Ibid. 208. See also Cassirer, *Platonic Renaissance in England*, 8–24.

[44] For a good discussion of the intellectual links between Sidney, Spenser, and Milton within the framework of Neoplatonic poetical theory see S. K. Heninger, Jr., 'Sidney and Milton: The Poet as Maker', in Wittreich, *Milton and the Line of Vision*, 57–95.

[45] For a detailed survey of the efforts of each of these early humanists see Bentley, *Humanists and Holy Writ*, 32–69.

[46] Until the Council of Trent canonized and sealed an approved Vulgate text, retroactively declared to be the inspired translation of St Jerome, the textual history of the Latin Vulgate was a mind-boggling amalgam of imperfect transmission and assimilation. See R. Lowe, 'The Medieval History of the Latin Vulgate', *CHB* ii. 102–54.

probably unreliable set of Greek manuscripts as his proof texts, Valla
nonetheless questioned the homogeneity of the Latin Vulgate, and was
one of the first Western thinkers to insist on the importance of mastering Greek before any serious New Testament scholarship could be
attempted. Although the revolutionary work of the Italian humanists
was only known in limited, albeit highly influential circles, the need to
readdress the translation and transmission of the Scriptures had become
a matter of spiritual as much as pedagogical urgency. In Spain, for
example, the collaboration of converted Jews and Christian humanist
theologians between 1514 and 1517 saw the production of the first
polyglot edition of the complete Bible, the *Complutum Polyglot*, which
printed the original Hebrew alongside the Septuagint Greek and the
Vulgate Latin for the Old Testament, and the original Greek alongside
fresh Latin translations for the New Testament. The philological triumph of the magisterial parallel-text presentation of the *Complutum
Polyglot* vindicated the essential role of the *studia humanitatis* in
cultivating the necessary philological skills for the literary scrutiny of
biblical texts. Despite being overshadowed, partly no doubt for controversial reasons, by the publication of Erasmus's *Novum Instrumentum* in
1516, the *Complutum* inspired countless similar scholarly enterprises for
over two centuries after its final publication in 1522.[47]

However, right from the outset it became apparent that too close a
philological scrutiny of the biblical text might undermine doctrine.[48]
The humanist revolution of biblical scholarship profoundly impacted
on the sacred efficacy of the language of Scripture. It had effectively
relocated the ineffable moment of spiritual contact with the Word of
God from the act of passively hearing or pronouncing the biblical words
to the fully subjective moment of internalizing and making sense of the
biblical message and declaring it. In the eyes of the humanists, however,
such an act of interpretative reading did not require a profound knowledge of metaphysical philosophy and theology. All that they required
was that the text itself would be as true as humanly possible to the sense
of the original divine dictation. Controversy was inevitable. When

---

[47] Bentley, *Humanists and Holy Writ*, 70–112.
[48] See e.g. the controversy surrounding the so-called 'Johannine Comma', ibid. 44,
95–7; see also A. Hamilton, 'Humanists and the Bible', in Kraye, *The Cambridge
Companion to Renaissance Humanism*, 108.

Desiderius Erasmus (1466/9–1536), arguably the greatest humanist biblical scholar of his time, produced his audacious *Novum Instrumentum* in 1516—a scholarly edition of the Greek New Testament with an embedded Latin translation—there was outrage literally from the first sentence of the Johannine Prologue. To the horror of Catholics across Europe not sympathetic to the humanist enterprise, Erasmus had dared to correct Jerome's 'In principio erat *verbum*' ('In the beginning was the word') into 'In principio erat *sermo*' ('In the beginning was the utterance/speech'). Erasmus' New Testament caused uproar; from England to Spain, incensed and terrified theologians poured invective from pulpit and printing-press on Erasmus's blasphemous innovation. Encouraged, however, by many of his enthusiastic humanist colleagues, Erasmus did not falter in the face of criticism, but went on to prepare a revised and much-augmented edition of the *Instrumentum*, which he published three years later in 1519 and renamed *Novum Testamentum*. This was no longer simply an annotated edition of the Greek New Testament with an embedded Latin translation, but an entirely new Latin translation with a parallel Greek text meant altogether to replace the Vulgate.

The so-called '*sermo*' controversy surrounding the two editions of Erasmus' New Testament is a centre-piece of the general humanist challenge to the sacredness imposed by the Church on Jerome's Vulgate specifically, and on the language of Scripture in general. Erasmus questioned the use of the word '*verbum*' as a fitting translation for the homonym '*logos*' of the Johannine prologue on the basis of apt grammatical usage: quite simply, if the Evangelist wanted to say 'word', he would have written '*lexis*', not '*logos*'. This is not to say that Erasmus was insensitive to the theological implications of his substitution of '*sermo*' for '*verbum*'. Far from it—the various grammatical denotations of the word '*sermo*' (speech, utterance, colloquy) represented for Erasmus the true nature of theological activity. Such an activity in his eyes called for the imitation and participation in the active life of the Incarnated *logos* through prayer, pious living, and a literary pursuit of what has come to be known as 'Christian humanism', described by Erasmus throughout his earlier *Enchiridion militis Christiani* as his *philosophia Christiana*. The use of '*verbum*'—'word'—was too grammatically narrow and spiritually dead to represent fully the wider theological connotations of *logos*. For Erasmus, the wider connotations of the word *logos* suggested

the spiritual marriage of prayer and knowledge, described jointly in the
Enchiridion as the 'Christian armament' (*armatura Christiana*) with
which a pious Christian ought to arm himself against Satan, the soul's
deadliest enemy. Prayer and knowledge are in turn concerned only
with, and flow from, the recorded scriptural words of God, and so
true theological activity (*Theos-legein*) must in turn concentrate only
on the pure and unmediated teachings of Christ as they are recorded in
Scripture. Scripture was originally recorded in Greek, and since Erasmus
believed that Christ, the Incarnated *logos*, or utterance of God, 'has
subjected himself not only to the laws of the flesh, but of grammar
also',[49] the importance of scrupulous philological scrutiny of the original grammar of the biblical text, stripped of scholastic sophistries,
becomes nothing less than a meditation on spiritual and religious
grammar. Erasmus' emerging ideals of active Christian humanism and
lay devotion are indeed typical of the internalized spirituality that
characterized the late medieval lay religious movement of 'The Brotherhood of Common Life' under whose wing Erasmus received his
formative education. The predominance of the Brotherhood's educational programme in the Low Countries and Germany, and in particular its emphasis on lay spirituality, popularly known as the *devotio
moderna*, went a long way in shaping the common intellectual ground
and consequent ideological affinities between such rival theologians as
Erasmus and Luther, and offers a tantalizing link between both of these
thinkers and the German mystic Nicholas Cusanus.[50] As Brian Cummings argues, what was at stake for men like Erasmus and Luther was
nothing less than the 'reordering of the mind of Europe' and the
complete reformation of Christian readership.'[51]

Even though he did not intend to do so, therefore, Erasmus ended up
challenging much more than linguistic usage. He had upset the very
notion of the one hypostatic Word, and by implication the seemingly
unassailable one-word-one-thing semiotic paradigm which Jerome's
reified *verbum* enshrined. Indeed, fuelling much of the anxiety felt in
orthodox circles over the use of the word *sermo* was a growing trepidation

---

[49] O'Rourke, Boyle, *Erasmus on Language and Method in Theology*, 8–9.
[50] See Oberman, *Forerunners of the Reformation*, 7–9; McGrath, *Intellectual Origins*,
14–15.
[51] Cummings, *The Literary Culture of the Reformation*, 104–11.

that the whole received structure of referential meaning was implicitly under attack. Richard Waswo has shown that thinkers as diverse as Valla and Luther all contributed to a fundamental 'semantic shift' in the way in which language and meaning were seen to operate in the period. This implicit shift from the received Platonic orthodoxy of referential semantics to a pre-modern view of language as a utilitarian function of relational linguistic usage radically aggravated traditional anxiety about the presence of the ineffable in the desire to explicate and generate meaning. To demonstrate this, it is useful to pick up Waswo's claim that despite various intimations of relational emancipation, the Renaissance semantic shift could not have been fully realized: 'If we pay most attention to what Renaissance writers say about language, we are likely to dismiss it as jejune and simplistic cliché. If, on the other hand, we pay most attention to what they do with language, we may attribute to them theoretical positions that they had not in fact intended.'[52] Whenever Renaissance thinkers came dangerously close to undermining the secure foundation of referential reality entirely, they always somehow retreated from making the ultimate relational intellectual leap. This was not a matter of choice as much as an intellectual impasse. Even so, many Renaissance thinkers who engaged on some level with linguistic theory or practice were trapped in a paradox wherein what they say is often at odds with the ways in which they say it.

To demonstrate the strength of Waswo's observation and its relevance to Erasmus' unsettling of the idea of the ineffable, we need only consider the literary principle governing Erasmus' *Paraphrase of John*. Viewed dryly, the content of the *Paraphrase* amounts to little more than a pastiche of familiar metaphysical and theological ideas, borrowed primarily from Denys, Chrysostom, Anselm, Aquinas, and Nicholas Cusanus, moulded to reflect Erasmus' own brand of Christian philological theology. The general idea is a familiar one: God as he is in himself is unknowable and ineffable, but he may be known in a circumscribed manner through the Son, the Incarnated *logos*. But whereas Cusanus emphasizes the need to cling in faith to Christ, the perfect man, as a model of pious living, Erasmus emphasizes rather the literary embodiment of Christ in Scripture as the speech of God (*logos–sermo*) made

---

[52] Waswo, *Language and Meaning in the Renaissance*, 80.

flesh, that is, made into fallen human language, and the salvific burden
this places on the need rightly to read and understand the sacred written
record that is Christ:

> [God] did not reveal everything even through the Holy Spirit, but only those
> things that made for the persuasiveness of the gospel teaching and for the
> salvation of the human race. For since the nature of divine things is incompre-
> hensible to even the loftiest human or angelic minds, while the proclamation of
> the gospel concerns all mortals equally, the heavenly Father has disclosed to us
> through his Son only so much of divine matters as he has wished to be sufficient
> for salvation. And so it is a mark of a dangerous recklessness to assert anything
> about the nature of God beyond what Christ himself or the Holy Spirit has
> disclosed to us.[53]

To attempt to know God speculatively outside the salvific remit of the
logos is 'reckless', therefore, and leads to the greater danger of a perverse
or unnatural discourse. Erasmus sees the presence of ineffability, therefore, as threatening and inimical to a theology dependent on unimpeded speech, because 'to speak of things that cannot be set out in words is
madness; to define them is sacrilege'.[54] The limits of what language can
and cannot say thus become for Erasmus also the limits of theology. But
even as this view of theology narrows its metaphysical scope, it sharpens
its sense of religious feeling and the importance of what *can* be said. In
a revealing moment Erasmus repeats one of his own favourite *Adagia*:
'Speech is truly the mirror of the heart, which cannot be seen with
the body's eyes.'[55] For Erasmus the classical rhetorician, speech which is
plain and full of authority in its unerring righteousness reveals the essence
of the speaker and binds people to it. This is how the *logos*, or divine speech
of God, through the agency of Christ, transmits those hidden divine truths
relevant to salvation straight to the hearts of believers.

Unlike the future Reformers, however, Erasmus is not willing to
make the next obvious leap and announce that the Bible is plainly literal
in matters necessary for salvation. On the contrary, Erasmus is at pains
to justify the spiritual merit of his philological erudition and to present
his methods of exegesis as a kind of spiritual Rosetta Stone. The method
of the paraphrase eloquently captures the dynamic energy of Erasmus'
philological theology, but by applying these principles to the text of

---

[53] *Works*, xlvi. 15.   [54] Ibid. 13.   [55] Ibid. 16.

St John's Gospel in making its sense 'clearer' Erasmus is forced to concede a lexical fluidity in the biblical text which radically destabilizes that text's claim to a fixed divine truth. Ironically, Erasmus's attempts in the *Paraphrase* to place prudent metaphysical limits on what the discourse of the *logos* can tell a literarily informed Christian reader falter exactly at the point where the interpretative 'latitude' of the paraphrase, to borrow a term from Dryden, is at its most expansive. Dryden, a poet who was at his best when translating the poetic genius of others, defines the act of paraphrasing as a 'translation with latitude, where the author is kept in view by the translator, so as never to be lost, but his words are not so strictly followed as his sense, and that too is admitted to be amplified, but not altered'.[56] This process of 'amplification' is central to Erasmus' *Paraphrase*, but since the ultimate 'meaning' of Scripture is ineffably extrinsic to the sacred text we must accept as a matter of faith that Erasmus' *Paraphrase* really does stop at 'amplification' and is not in fact re-creating the text's meaning. Keenly aware of the dangerous ground he was treading, Erasmus anticipates this criticism and hastens to point out in the dedicatory letter to the *Paraphrase* the many shortcomings of the paraphrase method (not least the loss of the apostle's taut Greek rhetorical style). However, since, as he argues, 'no Gospel has given rise to more numerous or more difficult problems concerning faith', largely due to the 'obscurity' of the Evangelist's language and the 'highly figurative and obscure' words placed by the Evangelist in the mouth of Jesus, he was determined to apply cultivated precepts of humanist scriptural philology to expound this 'difficult' text. Moreover: 'there were those further problems in which this activity [i.e. paraphrasing] is specially involved: almost all of the language which the Evangelist puts into the mouth of the Lord Jesus is highly figurative and obscure. If one makes these figures clear in the paraphrase, there is no connection with the answers given to him by men who had failed to understand what he said.'[57] Erasmus senses here a potential problem that risks wrecking the entire pedagogical point of his *Paraphrase*. As A. D. Nuttall points out in his critical reading of St John's Gospel, the gaps in Jesus' '(non)answers' to very straightforward questions put to him are an exercise in deliberate transcendence which points not to Nietzschian

---

[56] *Preface to Ovid's Epistles*, in Walker, *John Dryden: The Major Works*, 160.
[57] *Works*, xlvi. 3.

'anti-nature', as in most examples of modernist discontinuous dialogue, but to divine 'super-nature'.[58] What Nuttall does not say (because he has no cause to) is that this 'super-nature' and the silent gaps which point to it in St John's Gospel are radically and purposefully ineffable. In Erasmus' case, the traditional demarcation of an ineffable boundary, so profoundly beyond the reach of any rational or linguistic faculty, is radically at odds with the active amplification (if not re-creation) of meaning at the heart of the paraphrast's technique. Losing the ineffable gaps of Jesus' transcendental obscurity in the Gospel text might seem a small price to pay for the clarity of religious feeling, but it was a price which in hindsight Catholic orthodoxy simply could not afford to pay.

Be that as it may, Erasmus did not set about deliberately to unsettle the orthodox establishment (beyond, of course, the occasional joke at the expense of faculty theologians and corrupt monks). For all its future influence and canonical status, the satirical masterpiece that is *The Praise of Folly* was meant initially as a private discourse among discerning humanist friends, and the tone of astonished outrage that characterizes the many defences Erasmus habitually rushed to the printing-presses in response to the many attacks directed at his philological theology indicates that he never thought of himself as standing on the wrong side of orthodox Catholic doctrine. Inevitably, however, philological scrutiny opens up any text—and especially one with such a long history of transmission as the Bible—in ways which fundamentally undermine its claims for fixed sacred reference. If words have no real meaning beyond their immediate context of use, as in part implicitly suggested by the '*sermo*' controversy, then the ineffable signifies nothing more than a disabling silence beyond expression where one finds not God but only, as Erasmus would say, sacrilegious madness. This distinctly negative, if not modern, view of the ineffable could never have been fully arrived at in the age of Erasmus, just as the 'semantic shift' presupposing it could not have been fully realized. Its menacing shadow, however, was deeply felt and caused great distress. As the conceptual parameters of the ineffable in religious and metaphysical discourse were being redefined and renegotiated, this growing conflict about how to tackle the problems of ineffability in one's personal

---

[58] Nuttall, *Overheard by God*, 133.

expression of faith was getting out of hand. Erasmus and Thomas More would soon be fighting a new battle, defending orthodox doctrine against Luther in the wake of the great sixteenth-century schism, and what McGrath has called the 'productive misunderstanding' between Erasmus and Luther in the years leading up to Luther's break with Rome.[59] Erasmus' linguistic splitting of hairs would soon seem a pedantic trifle compared to the great ecclesiastical and doctrinal reforms advocated by Luther, Zwingli, and Calvin. As an idea, however, the ineffable was now irrecoverably catapulted from the serene medieval solitude of mystical contemplation and metaphysical speculation to the acrimonious realms of religious polemic. The humanist philologists thoroughly undermined the ability of the Catholic Church to exercise its authority as the exclusive mediator between fallen man and the ineffable God. From this vantage-point, the movement from the philological methods underlying Erasmus's *Novum Instrumentum* to Luther's Ninety-five Theses on the abuse of indulgences seems strangely logical.

REFORMATION THOUGHT AND THE DISLOCATION OF THE INEFFABLE

The relationship between the rise of humanism and the Reformation is as elusively complex as it is irrefutably intimate.[60] As suggested above, it is possible to see the humanists' indirect attack on the fixity of the Word and its place in the Catholic Church's metaphysical structures of intercession to have prepared the intellectual ground for more sweeping reform. Shortly before 25 September 1522, Martin Luther's German New Testament issued from the printing press. It is significant that Luther used Erasmus' Greek edition as his copy text.[61] Luther was patently inspired by Erasmus' informed challenge to stale orthodoxy, as well as by his admirable erudition, and just like Erasmus before him,

---

[59] McGrath, *Intellectual Origins*, 59.
[60] See ibid. 34–66, McGrath, *Reformation Thought*, 57–60; and also Levi, *Renaissance and Reformation*, 259 ff.
[61] See E. W. Gritsch, 'Luther as Bible translator', in McKim, *The Cambridge Companion to Martin Luther*, 62–72.

Luther soon found himself defending his translation from outraged Roman Catholics who accused him of doing violence to the immutable Word of God. The first edition of the so-called 'September Bible' did not name the translator, printer, or date of publication, but the 'heretic' Luther's anonymity as the translator was not a well-guarded secret. By September 1534, when the first complete High German Luther Bible was published, its reviled translator was already at the centre of heated controversy, not only with Catholics but with fellow Reformers as well.

Conflict, indeed, lies at the heart of Luther's religious sensibility. For Luther, God and man have been divorced by sin. The ineffable attributes of Luther's *deus nudus* ('naked God', i.e. naked from his Word), are absolute and utterly terrifying, as is the futility of any scholastic contemplation of his ineffable nature. God is absolutely free in his wrath, justice, and boundless mercy, but man is corrupted by Original Sin and can achieve nothing without the superimposed grace of God. Theology for Luther should only concern itself with the justification of sinful man. Only through the reliable promise of salvation given to man through the Word made flesh, the divine grammar of creation and salvation, does man attain the necessary faith in Christ who alone at the end of time will bring together the justified man and the 'absolute' God in the light of glory. In his commentary on Psalm 51: 1, 'Have mercy upon me, O God, according to thy lovingkindness: according unto the multitude of thy tender mercies blot out my transgressions' (AV), Luther writes:

The people of Israel did not have a God who was viewed 'absolutely', to use the expression, the way the inexperienced monks rise into heaven with their speculations and think about God as He is in Himself. From this absolute God everyone should flee who does not want to perish, because human nature and the absolute God...are the bitterest enemies...We must take hold of this God, not naked but clothed and revealed in His Word; otherwise certain despair will crush us.[62]

Where Erasmus saw in the silence of the ineffable only madness and sacrilege, Luther sees in it also devastating despair, because not being able to speak at one with God's Word becomes a mark of some men's

[62] *Works*, xii. 312.

irredeemable reprobation.[63] For Luther and the Reformers, God's active Word, alive in the good words of the Gospel, is utterly effable and human, as he is human who was made flesh.

Moreover, precisely because of the *logos* abasing itself in fallen flesh, its scriptural record was seen to be necessarily subject to the indeterminacy of fallible linguistic signification. Luther saw in the Bible a divine–human text that is efficaciously open either to the erroneous or inspired translation and interpretation of individual readers. The grammatical sense of the *logos* has to be followed according to usage, and Luther understood 'usage' to be a conjoined function of both faith in that which is transcendental and above the ken of man, and historical experience within the world as it is reflected in the Bible and explained by it. In his lecture on Galatians 3: 10—'For as many as are of the works of the law are under the curse: for it is written, Cursed *is* every one that continueth not in all things which are written in the book of the law to do them' (AV)—Luther states:

> When you read in Scripture... about the patriarchs, prophets, and kings that they worked righteousness, raised the dead, conquered kingdoms, etc., you should remember that these and similar statements are to be explained according to a new and theological grammar... For reason should first be illumined by faith before it works. Once a true idea and knowledge of God is held as right reason, then the work attributed to faith is later attributed to works, but only on account of the faith.[64]

Luther's 'new and theological grammar' of salvation elides the dichotomy inherent in pre-Reformation Christianity between an act of faith as such and a Christian act of, say, charity. Faith for Luther is not merely speculative, but a kind of work; indeed, faith *is* work. This 'new and theological grammar', as Luther calls it, not only 'guarantees' the 'truth' which a Christian might glean from the Bible, but also generates the intimately personal 'truth' of Justification which enables a Reformed Christian (at least in theory) righteously to experience, immediately and

---

[63] See Oswald Bayer, 'Luther as Interpreter of Holy Scripture', trans. M. Mattes, in McKim, *Cambridge Companion to Martin Luther*, 73–85: 'The humanity of the person consists [for Luther] in that he or she is addressed [by God] and therefore can hear, answer, and even speak himself or herself' (p. 81).

[64] *Works*, xxvi. 267–8.

historically, the predestined unfolding of time as proclaimed in evangelical testimony and Old Testament prophecy.

For Luther, the authority of Scripture derives from the Word of God
himself, dictated to the inspired prophets and apostles and accommodated to their lapsarian comprehension. Uniquely, however, Luther
took special comfort in the 'humanness' of Scripture and the ability of
the righteous reader to partake of the same accommodated inspiration
the apostles had enjoyed. As theological historian J. K. S. Reid explains:
'the instrument is distinguished from the agent employing the instrument, and qualities of the one need not be attributed to the other.
Hence Luther freely admits human characteristics and even imperfections in Scripture. For him the incarnation provides the clue, and the
humanness of Jesus is a real parallel to the humanness of Holy Scripture.'[65] Crucially for his resulting theory of sacramental consubstantiation, Luther continually emphasizes the double efficacy and sympathetic
relationship of Spirit (faith) and Word (scripture), never privileging one
over the other. Beginning with Luther, therefore, Reformed debates
about the authority of Scripture tended to relocate that authority, and
consequently the ineffable barrier of its language, from text to reader.
But if we were to try and characterize the evolution of the ineffable as
a semantic and philosophical idea in the wake of the Lutheran Reformation we ought not to talk of its relocation so much as of its violent
dislocation. 'Relocation' suggests a benign act of transference which
hardly characterizes the unpredictable nature of Luther's impact on the
idea of ineffability in subsequent Reformed discourse; 'dislocation', on
the other hand, captures the discomfort and unease such an unsettling
would cause. The Reforming imperative to revivify the ministry of the
Word in the Church and to subordinate the ministry of the sacraments
to its preaching introduced a great deal of confusion and debate as to
when exactly in the religious experience the use of language finally gives
way to mystery and silence. To put it another way, the Reformers
appeared to have been confused as to when in the devotional process
the believing self ends and God's promise begins, so that the presence
of the ineffable, though still felt, gradually became something quite
unnatural to Reformed theological sensibilities. Following Luther's

---

[65] Reid, *The Authority of Scripture*, 68.

ideological break with Rome, the idea of the ineffable was thus thrown into a peculiar intellectual limbo. Suddenly it seemed that, despite all their efforts to preclude the ineffable, the *Deus absconditus* of the emerging Protestant faith became even more radically ineffable than he was for Catholic mystics, because his ineffability was not merely a metaphysical attribute but an actual threat to salvation. Paradoxically, and perhaps fittingly, for Luther the *idea* of the ineffable becomes itself ineffable—he will not openly discuss it, but its silent presence oppresses his religious vision to the point where he must act to save himself rather than merely rest in speculation. The core Reformation principles of *sola fides, sola scriptura* become in this context a survival mechanism which demands that Christians read the Bible and read it right, because otherwise there is only the silence of madness, despair, and ultimate reprobation.

Subsequent Reformers on both sides of the emerging doctrinal divide between the Lutheran and Swiss camps continued to develop the cardinal Protestant principle of *sola scriptura* along the lines of the Lutheran dialectic between Word and Spirit. Melanchthon's celebrated *Loci Communes*, for example, offers what is still the most lucid account of the Reformed attitude towards the complex dialectics of faith and Scripture in the process of Justification.[66] However, it was over the interpretation of the Lord's Supper and by implication the efficacy of signs that the German and Swiss Reformations entered into an acrimonious dispute amongst themselves which directly bears on the emerging Protestant impasse on ineffability. The Eucharistic controversy, which began with Luther's increasingly outspoken attacks on Zwingli's sacramental theology, put a final stamp of anxiety on any conceivable attempt by Protestant thinkers to re-create, approximate, or represent in language the presence of the numinous. Despite Melanchthon's failed attempt to effect Eucharistic unity within the Reformers' ranks in drafting the Concord of Wittenberg in 1536, the notorious Marburg Colloquy seven years earlier (1529) had exposed just how unstable the idea of sacramental signification had become following the open challenge to Roman orthodoxy.

Prompted by their respective political backers, Martin Bucer and Melanchthon convened the Marburg Colloquy in order to smooth out the two camps' emerging Eucharistic differences and to form a united

---

[66] See Pauck, *Loci Communes*, 91–2.

Reformed front in the face of mounting Roman opposition. At the time, the doctrinal differences between the various Reformed camps were seen to be negotiable and reasonably bridgeable in the face of the common enemy. During the colloquy, on the basis of John 6: 27 ('Labour not for the meat which perisheth, but for that meat which endureth unto everlasting life, which the Son of man shall give unto thee: for him hath God the Father sealed'), Zwingli insisted that the sacrament of eating the Lord's Supper serves merely to seal the communicant's faith in what the bread and wine symbolize spiritually. Zwingli then quickly lost his temper when Luther refused to concede a trope where, on the basis of Scripture, he claimed none was admissible. One can only imagine the frustration of such moderates as Melanchthon and Bucer when the colloquy devolved into an embarrassing affair of theological and personal mud-slinging. Rather than smoothing out the Eucharistic differences, the Marburg Colloquy threw them into sharp relief.

Luther and Zwingli's dispute was centred on the question of Christ's 'real presence' in the Host. They could not agree on where to locate Christ's real divine presence in the sacramental ritual and what is the relationship of such presence (however it is defined) to the signs of the sacrament relating to it. For his part, Zwingli argued that Christ's real presence during the Lord's Supper was to be found not in the symbolical objects of the bread and wine but in the community of worshippers coming together to celebrate the Lord's Supper in memorial thanksgiving. For Zwingli, the bread and wine are not efficacious in themselves, but are metaphorical objects which underpin the spiritual process of consuming, as it were, and interiorizing Christ. Zwingli treated the doctrine of the Eucharist in many places in his work, but his most eloquent exposition of what has come to be known, slightly misleadingly, as 'sacramental memorialism'[67] remains his German treatise *On the Lord's Supper* published in Zurich in 1526. In it, he writes:

[67] The term sacramental 'memorialism' (as opposed to sacramental 'parallelism', and 'instrumentalism') was first coined by B. Gerrish in 'The Lord's Supper in the Reformed Confessions' (1966), repr. in id., *The Old Protestantism and the New*, 118–30. See also Gerrish, *Grace and Gratitude*, 167. The term should not be misunderstood, however, to mean that Zwingli's insistence on the symbolical or representational qualities of the Lord's Supper obviates the notion of Real Presence, but rather that his 'memorialism' locates that presence in the very act of memory itself and in the shared experience of a congregation which comes together to share in that memorial celebration.

the saying: 'This is my body,' cannot be taken literally, otherwise we tear his flesh with our teeth in the very same way as it was pierced by the nails and the spear.[68]

It has already become clear enough that in this context the word 'is' cannot be taken literally. Hence it follows that it must be taken metaphorically or figuratively.[69]

Hence it follows once again that the bread is the body in the sense that it signifies the body, for by it we are reminded of the body, the body itself not being present.[70]

For Zwingli and the emerging Swiss Reformed orthodoxy, the Lord's Supper was a joyful commemorative event in which the workings of faith endow the symbols of bread and wine with special reverential significance, drawing the faithful inwardly, away from the symbols of the flesh, into a memorial thanksgiving for Christ's Passion. As he goes on to say in the same treatise: 'the very body of Christ sits at the right hand of the Father, but the sacrament, that is, the sign of that sacred and living body is now eaten by us in Christian fellowship in thanksgiving and remembrance that his body was slain for us.'[71]

Luther, on the other hand, maintained in his several attacks on Zwingli and the 'fanatics' as he called them—attacks which culminated in his combative *Confession Concerning Christ's Supper* (published a year before the Marburg Colloquy)—that Christ, whose body has 'a three-fold existence', is simultaneously present both in the Host as well as transcendentally in Heaven, the ascent towards the latter through faith securing the former's spiritual as well as 'real' consumption: 'You must place [the third, "uncircumscribed", existence of Christ], which constitutes him one person with God, far, far beyond things created, as far as God transcends them; and on the other hand, place it as deep in and as near to all created things as God is in them. For he is one indivisible person with God, and wherever God is, he must be also, otherwise our faith is false.'[72] For Luther, to understand the copula 'is' in the words 'this is my body' as 'signifies' undermines the unity of the Trinity, the immutable truth of Scripture, and its acting out of the gospel promises

---

[68] Bromiley, *Zwingli and Bullinger*, 222.   [69] Ibid. 225.
[70] Ibid. 229.
[71] Ibid. 234.
[72] *Confession Concerning Christ's Supper*, *Works*, xxxvii. 223.

of the Incarnation: 'Whenever or wherever I can say of Christ's body, "This is Christ's body given for us," then it must be visible, because it was given for us in no other manner than visibly. If it is not visibly present, it is not there at all.'[73] Luther's consubstantive sacramental theology is a direct product of his radically literal theory of biblical hermeneutics, where what God says *must* be accepted at face value because it was meant to instruct the rational human mind in matters of salvation without any ambiguity, and was not to be subjected to human imagination and the realms of metaphor. To argue that Jesus did not mean to say what he did say, except as some elaborate and mysterious metaphor, reopens a semantic back-door to the ineffable which Luther quite understandingly had to close if he was to maintain the fundamental assumptions of his Reformed theology.

The impact of this controversy on the way in which the language of sacrament and mystery was seen to operate was profound. At the heart of the Reformers' Eucharistic controversy was a fundamental, if abstract, battle for the presence of ineffability in the religious life: Luther's great 'hermeneutical discovery' about what Bayer calls God's 'speech-act of promise' entails that 'the linguistic sign is itself the reality, that it represents not an absent but a present reality'.[74] God's words for Luther establish a relationship between man and God in a way which authorizes the words of the Word not merely to signify but to effect. As one scholar recently put it: 'God's words [for Luther] were not to be bent to human imagination, human tradition, human sensibilities... For all their difficulty, their impenetrability, these words were fixed—sufficient, essential, determinative, and absolute.'[75] This entrenched view of God's words as something solid one can cling to for dear life instantly collapses any distinction between the four traditional methods of biblical exegesis (historical-literal, allegorical, tropological-moral, anagogical) and annihilates any scope for metaphor in its advocacy of only one possible reading—the literal. When Zwingli and the memorialists reacted against Luther's consubstantive Eucharistic theology, they were really defending what they perceived as the unavoidable place of metaphorical language in religious worship, and the need to

---

[73] Ibid. xxxvii. 178.
[74] Bayer, 'Luther as Interpreter', 76.
[75] Wandel, *The Eucharist in the Reformation*, 95.

accommodate the ineffable gaps of language in such a way as to render them conducive to religious experience, not inimical to it. It may be argued that, in their own way, Zwingli and his followers instinctively understood what Luther simply suppressed: that, to borrow the words of Wittgenstein, 'the inexpressible (what I find enigmatic & cannot express) perhaps provides the background, against which whatever I was able to express acquires meaning'.[76] On Wittgenstein's (rather mysterious) terms, one could argue that Luther's consubstantive semantics sheds such a bright light on the 'inexpressible background' against which what could be expressed derives its meaning that that potential meaning quite literally gets lost. It is all very well to argue that God's words are *things* in a broadly spiritual sense (whatever that might mean to a given individual), but such an assertion prompts the further question of the relationship between God's speech as recorded in Scripture and scripturally 'authorized' human speech. Luther's point is precisely that because man is a sinful creature only the scriptural speech of God can offer any criterion for 'truth', but this leaves unanswered how lapsarian man can abandon metaphor and begin to understand words which do not represent but simply *are.* This, then, is the ultimate impasse of Reformation thought on the ineffable—the need to speak away the ineffable only succeeds in dislocating its presence from its 'natural' place in metaphysical ontology and epistemology to the utilitarian operations of a referential language which is anything but referential. A 'justified' reader may understand what the Bible says to them, but they can never rightly communicate what they understand without some loss of meaning because even Luther understands that words, sadly, are simply words, vainly struggling after things.

Granted, Luther conceived his theology in the context of an impassioned, even visceral, attack on what he perceived to be the abuses and absurdities of Catholic doctrine, and as a consequence he never fully addressed the paradoxical implications of his own theology when reflected upon in a broader, systemic view. Not so with the dogmatic Calvin. For Calvin, whose *Institutes* serve as an index of Swiss Reformed thought and stand at the heart of the emerging 'Calvinist' orthodoxy of

[76] *Culture and Value*, trans. P. Winch, 23e.

the Genevan faith, the Lord's Supper is a 'spiritual banquet' (*spirituale epulum*), made up of 'visible signs best adapted to our small capacity'.[77] Calvin's view of the Lord's Supper accords with his widely influential hermeneutical theories. The Triune God, for Calvin, is a transcendental signified that generates his own diverse signs. These signs, moreover, are especially designed to lead the reader of the Bible into one particular vision or secret of God's awesome divinity. At the same time, however, according to Calvin, one cannot unlock these special signs through any actively rational semantic analysis, allegorical or otherwise, but only by recognizing the irresistible operation of grace on the elect soul through one's faith in God.[78] As with Luther, the spoken Word (*logos*) thus becomes paramount. According to Calvin, one is continually regenerated and raised from sin through the audible assimilation of the Word into one's sinful soul by hearing and participating in the preaching of the Word, which is at once readily intelligible in plain Scripture and yet at the same time eternally mysterious.[79] For Calvin, the miracle of the Incarnation thus affirms the divine gulf between lapsarian man and his Creator, and this gulf can only be bridged by God's infinite mercy and his willingness to abase himself grammatically for humanity's sake in the words whose flesh he is.

Like the signs of the sacraments, therefore, the spoken words of God as recorded in Scripture are signs for Calvin that have a numinous veil attached to them. This veil allows God to bring his hidden presence into the lapsarian world of sin without somehow compromising his awesome and ineffable divinity:

---

[77] McNeil (ed.), *Institutes of the Christian Religion*, 4.17; trans. F. L. Battles, ii. 1361.

[78] This idea flows from Calvin's related theory of revelation in nature: God reveals himself in creation which is now tainted by the Fall, so that all men have a natural knowledge of God. This knowledge, however, because tainted by sin, is imperfect and cannot promote salvation, and can only serve to make man inexcusable if he refuses to worship God. Only through the Word of God may the elect be confirmed in grace. For a discussion of Calvin's theory of nature and revelation see Partee, *Calvin and Classical Philosophy*, 42–50.

[79] *Institutes*, 1.6.2 ('For by his Word, God rendered faith unambiguous forever, a faith that should be superior to all opinion'); 3.2.6 (the Word is like 'a mirror in which faith my contemplate God'); 4.3.3 (preaching the Word 'is the administration of the Spirit and of righteousness and of eternal life); 4.8.7 ('when the Wisdom of God was at length revealed in the flesh, that Wisdom heartily declared to us all that can be comprehended and ought to be to be pondered concerning the Heavenly Father by the human mind').

Scripture, gathering up the otherwise confused knowledge of God in our minds, having dispersed our dullness, clearly shows us the true God. This, therefore, is a special gift, where God, to instruct the Church, not merely uses mute teachers but also opens his own most hallowed lips. Not only does he teach the elect to look upon a god, but also shows himself as the God upon whom they are to look.[80]

It is Plato inverted. If we may use a philosophical mixed metaphor, the Incarnation deliberately brought the Idea of God crashing down to earth, giving all men the opportunity to gaze into its mysteries, perhaps even to grasp the ineffable contours of its divine form. Thus, according to Calvin, in reading the Scriptures, hearing sermons, and participating in the Lord's Supper elect Christian believers gain relief from sin, not by passing through the numinous veil in some mystical manner, but by finding comfort in God's hidden presence and swaddling their sinful souls in the mysterious folds of his words which have the numinous and inexpressible already attached to them.

Unlike Luther, the more systematic Calvin is openly concerned about the dangers of radical literalness in the exegetical process. For Calvin there is nothing inherently noble or edifying about human speech in a collective sense—one is either damned or elect, and how one speaks does not bear on this beyond the superficial sense that reprobate sinners are prone to lying and other profane misuses of language. In this system metaphor and allegory are seen as inevitable symptoms of an ailing, fallen world where the *numen* must struggle under the tyranny of the sign, and it is necessary therefore to make allowances for sinful man's rational dependency on metaphor. It is a common misconception that Calvin rejects out of hand the use of allegory and analogy in exegesis. Metaphor, and especially allegorical metaphor, is a necessary evil for Calvin, providing, of course, that Christians are constantly reminded that it *is* evil. Calvin defends the use of figurative expressions in the interpretation of Scripture on this very basis, but his defence is expressed in such equivocal terms as to warn against the very thing he is defending. As Calvin quips, 'concerning God we should speak with less conscientiousness than we should think, since whatever by ourselves we think concerning him is foolish, and whatever we speak, absurd'.[81]

---

[80] *Institutes*, 1.6.1 (McNeill, i. 70).
[81] *Institutes*, 1.13.3 (McNeill, i. 124).

In the majority of cases, however, Calvin exhorts Christians to avoid allegory in scriptural exegesis, because the very presence of allegory, or rather the allegorical instinct, distorts the Scriptures' 'literal' meaning and generates ineffable mystery.[82] As Gordon Teskey puts it, allegory 'draws on the power' of the narrative it has to 'repress', and it is from this very struggle between 'static ideas and dynamic agents, that the sense of pervading mystery is created'.[83] Teskey is discussing in this case the transformation of the pagan gods in late antiquity into allegorical agents, but the same principle applies, if from an inverted perspective, to the Reformers' Platonic God. Especially revealing here is the idea of creating a sense of mystery. The sense of mystery produced by the allegorical vehicle is nothing like the ineffable presence of Neoplatonic mysticism, but a manufactured presence, a silent gap between agency and meaning which attaches itself as a veil to words. On these grounds precisely Calvin explains that the sacrament of the Lord's Supper seals the elect in faith because it has the Word of God attached to it, while the Roman Catholic belief in the mystery of transubstantiation is as a 'crude imagination' which operates on the absurd allegorical assumption that the fixed essence of Christ can inhere in the mutable substance of the Host: 'it is not possible for the human mind, leaping the infinite spaces, to reach beyond heaven itself to Christ. What nature denied to them [Roman Catholics] they tried to correct by a more harmful remedy, so that remaining in earth we may need no heavenly nearness of Christ. Here, then, is the necessity that compelled them to transmute Christ's body.'[84]

However, if Calvin is ambivalent about the numinous 'veils' which attach themselves to the symbols of the sacraments specifically, and scriptural language more generally, it is because he perceives the necessity of such veiling as both an inevitable symptom of fallen human nature as well as an important stop against reckless speculation. Here follows a crucial warning to those who (allegedly like the future Milton) would presume to break through the semantic veil of the biblical text

---

[82] See *Institutes* 3.4.4–5 (the Levitical priesthood was bound to allegories, Christ releases us from allegory); 4.16.15–16 (God's promise to the elect to be fulfilled not allegorically but literally).

[83] Teskey, *Allegory and Violence*, 33.

[84] *Institutes*, 4.17.15 (McNeil, ii. 1377).

and use anthropomorphism and anthropopathy to drag God down from his heavenly seat into the mire of human discourse. In his highly polemical commentary on Hebrews 1: 3, Calvin resurrects Aquinas in offering the analogical model for the way in which lapsarian languages may express the ineffable, but whereas Aquinas only states that an analogical predication of God is imperfect, Calvin stresses that such predication is moreover 'improper': 'In matters so great and so profound nothing can be said except by way of analogy taken from creaturely things... We must allow that there is a measure of impropriety in what is taken from earthly things and applied to the hidden majesty of God.'[85] Like Cusanus before him, Calvin too expresses unease about the analogical model, but seems to be resigned to its 'improper' inevitability in human discourse. Unlike the Catholic mystic, Calvin cannot reject the scholastic analogical model and embrace the silence of God's ineffable presence. Instead, Calvin turns the illogicality of the analogical model to his advantage: it proves his point that fallen man is indeed an 'improper' or 'unsuitable' creature to worship in words and deeds the hidden God. As Professor R. S. Wallace importantly reminds us, 'in making our judgement about Calvin's doctrine of Scripture we must... give full weight to his frequent assertion that, even though there is much that is divine and heavenly about the book, its form at times is of the earth, very earthly.'[86]

Sacraments, therefore, true to the signs which sustain them, cease to mediate in the Calvinist system—they accommodate.[87] Calvin, however, forcefully establishes the idea of accommodation—of a God willing to lower himself so the elect may begin to rise—within the evangelical tradition. He arrives at a typically paradoxical conception of religious semantics where the more religiously intense the application of 'ordinary' metaphorical language in attempting to unveil the hidden God, the more impenetrable the veil enfolding God's Word becomes. This may sound quite similar to the paradoxes of pseudo-Dionysian mystical theology, but the emphasis could not be more different: the

---

[85] *Calvin's Commentaries*, trans. W. B. Johnston, v. 7.
[86] Wallace, *Calvin's Doctrine of the Word and Sacraments*, 113.
[87] In developing Augustine's doctrine of accommodation Calvin was greatly indebted to the theology of Erasmian humanism and a long patristic tradition. See McGrath, *Intellectual Origins*, 56–7.

silence of Denys's *parousia*—an admission into God's ineffable majestic presence—gives way in the doctrine of Calvin and the emerging practices of the Genevan faith to the audible words of a sermon, tirelessly filling the numinous space of silent meaning with reverberating chatter. Driven by the deep-seated anxiety that results from the confused dislocation of the ineffable in the new sermonic activities of preaching and prophesying the audible Word, Calvin transforms the highly charged conflict of his day about the ineffable into resoundingly effable doctrine, not so much of the Word (*verbum*), as of the sermon (*sermo*). Rather than avoiding the semiotic crisis implicit in Luther's teachings, Calvin turns the problem of ineffable dislocation into the very essence of the Reformed Christian's religious activity, where the struggle against silence through the workings of grace becomes a struggle for salvation.

GODLY SILENCE AND THE 'LANGUAGE OF CANAAN'

From the moment Luther burned the condemnatory papal bull in the square of Wittenberg, any attempt to re-engage with metaphysical or intrinsically ineffable subject-matter would henceforth seek to distance itself from, if not actively to confront, opposing intellectual forces. Contending with the Counter Reformation dogmatism that issued from Trent, Calvin's brand of darkly paradoxical systematic theology fed on this sense of struggle. In the prevailing climate of religious reform and counter-reform, sixteenth-century theologians found that it was no longer possible, as Augustine exhorted, 'to evade this verbal conflict silently [rather] than to quell it disputatiously'. In England, Tyndale breathed new life into the Wycliffite project of translating the Bible into English. His efforts, in their turn, elicited from Sir Thomas More a calculated vernacular defence of orthodoxy that was anxious to set itself apart from the overt 'scripturalism' of its heretic other.[88] Subsequent decades of religious and political upheaval saw the demise of both Tyndale and More, Calvinism's iconoclastic rise to power, and its bloody overthrow by the Marian faith and its institution of counter-reform.

---

[88] Mueller, *Native Tongue and the Word*, 177–225.

With the accession of Elizabeth I the pluralism that characterized her fragile religious settlement—embodied in the often ambiguous and even contradictory Thirty-Nine Articles issued in 1563—saw the growth of radically disparate approaches to the problems posed by the ineffability of divine subject-matter. Whereas mainstream English Protestants in the Genevan tradition were finding it increasingly difficult to accommodate their ingrained anxieties about the presence of ineffability in their narratives of election and salvation, Roman Catholics, as well as a growing number of English ceremonialists, demonstrably revelled in it, and, in accordance with the sharp dichotomy between spoken words and written text, maintained that the sacramental core of religious experience was fundamentally ineffable, and therefore more amenable to non-verbal representations. The ineffable character of religious worship which Hooker defended, and such 'avant-garde' Arminian conformists as John Buckeridge (Laud's tutor at St John's) and Lancelot Andrewes practised and preached,[89] became such an eyesore to the Puritans of the 1630s when Laud sought to enforce it on a national scale because it blatantly sought to reintroduce a profoundly numinous, potentially idolatrous, character into religious worship. The taking of the Eucharist in high ceremonial fashion, the railing-off of an altar-wise communion table, the beauty of stained-glass windows, or the sublime music of church choirs all suggested that in religious worship bare words are not enough. In *Of the Laws of Ecclesiastical Polity*, for example, Hooker sets out what would become in future years the Anglican standard, in stating:

Words, both because they are common, and do not so strongly move the fancy of man, are for the most part slightly heard: and therefore with singular wisdom it hath been provided, that the deeds of men which are made in the presence of witnesses should pass not only with words, but also with certain sensible

---

[89] The term 'avant-garde' was first applied to Andrewes' High Churchmanship and implicit Arminian leanings by Peter Lake, 'Lancelot Andrewes, John Buckeridge, and Avant-Garde Conformity at the Court of James I'. Lake's reading builds on Nicholas Tyacke's seminal revaluation of early modern religious and political English history in *Anti-Calvinists*, which presents the later Jacobean Andrewes as a figurehead for an emerging Arminian, anti-Calvinist faction in James' court (pp. 103, 113–14, 166–7). More recently, however, Cummings, *The Literary Culture of the Reformation*, 308–18, has slightly complicated the 'anti-Calvinist' tag by reminding us how notoriously reluctant Andrewes was to openly concede his radical theological positions. It should be noted, however, that Tyacke anticipates Cummings' point and already responds to it convincingly in 'Lancelot Andrewes and the Myth of Anglicanism'.

actions, the memory thereof is far more easy and durable than the memory of speech can be.[90]

For the more orthodox English Protestants, on the other hand, such thinking risked overwhelming the privileged words of God with silence and rapture. Instead, they believed that preaching the Word was not merely enough but entirely sufficient in terms of its salvific efficacy. To suggest otherwise was to mount an attack not just on the salvific exclusivity of the sermon, but on the fullness and perfection of the Word itself.

The sufficiency and perfection of God's Word is reiterated again and again, for example, in the voluminous writings of Bishop William Perkins (1558–1602), one of Calvin's most prolific heirs in the English language, and the so-called patriarch of English doctrinal Puritanism.[91] In *An Exposition of the Symbole, or Creed of the Apostles* (1595), to cite one of many other possible examples, Perkins instructs the uneducated English layperson in definitive Genevan doctrine when he describes the Bible in the following terms:

these are not onely the pure *word of God*, but also the *Scripture of God*: because not only the matter of them; but the whole disposition thereof, with the style and the phrase was set downe by the immediate inspiration of the holy Ghost. And the authority of these books is *divine*, that is, absolute and soveraigne. And they are of sufficient credit in and by themselves, needing not the testimony of any creature; not subject to the censure either of man or Angels; binding the

---

[90] 4.1.3; *The Works of... Mr. Richard Hooker*, i. 419.

[91] Patrick Collinson describes Perkins as 'the prince of puritan theologians and the most eagerly read' (*The Elizabethan Puritan Movement*, 125). Perkins, a grudgingly conformist bishop, can only be described as a 'Puritan', however, in a broad, doctrinal sense (see Michael Jinkins, *ODNB*; Kendall, *Calvin and English Calvinism to 1649*, 51–78; and Spinks, *Two Faces of Elizabethan Anglican Theology*, ch. 1). Consequently, I distinguish here and throughout between 'doctrinal' and 'political' Puritanism. By 'doctrinal Puritanism' I refer to the belief, generally current among both conformist as well as radical English Calvinists, in supralapsarianism, double predestination, and either sacramental memorialism or sacramental parallelism in the administering of Baptism and the Lord's Supper. This excludes 'political Puritanism', which would refer in this case to the wide range of temporal Puritan concerns that preoccupied many of the radical and nonconformist English Protestants, namely radical Sabbatarianism, rejection of the Book of Common Prayer and fixed forms of worship, the Presbyterian rejection of episcopacy, and a militant commitment to fight alongside continental Protestants against Catholic aggression.

consciences of all men at all times, and being the onely foundation of our faith, and the rule and canon of all truth.[92]

Perkins's use of the word 'pure' to describe the scriptural Word of God is pregnant with meaning. It is 'pure' both in the sense of standing on its own without the further need of any gloss, but also in the sense of being perfect, entire, and unmediated. In his widely read and influential preaching manual, *The Arte of Prophecying*, originally published in Latin in 1592 as *Prophetica, sive De Sacra et Unica Ratione Concionandi Tractatus*,[93] Perkins indeed states that the 'perfection of the Word' consists in its 'sufficiency' and 'purity', while 'the sufficiency is that, whereby the word of God is complete, that nothing may bee either put to it, or taken from it, which appertaineth to the proper end thereof... The purity thereof is, whereby it remaineth entire in it selfe, voide of deceit and errour'.[94] Going on to denounce the Catholic (but in fact patristic) fourfold method for the interpretation of Scripture (literal, allegorical, tropological-moral, and anagogical), Perkins unequivocally asserts: '*There is one onley sense, and the same is the literall*.'[95] Problematically, however, Perkins's use of the word 'literal' (as in Luther's and Calvin's use of the term before him) is itself broadly figurative. Rather than excluding the fourfold method of exegesis, Perkins's 'literal' subsumes all four into a single operation of inspired interpretative reading which can yield only one ultimate meaning. Perkins's one 'literal' sense is not to be found, therefore, on the level of the text (the Bible, after all, is plainly not literal in all places), but in the overall application of what is widely discussed in English Reformed discourse as the 'analogy of faith'. Perkins describes the 'analogy of faith' as 'a certaine *abridgement* or *summe* of the Scriptures, collected out of most manifest and familiar places. The parts thereof

---

[92] *Works*, i. 122.

[93] The treatise was translated into English by one Thomas Tuke and published in 1607, several years after Perkins' death, as *The Arte of Prophecying, or a treatise concerning the sacred and onely true manner and methode of preaching*. The English translation went through numerous editions either independently or as a fixed component in Perkins' collected works. The treatise also enjoyed a great vogue on the Continent through a Dutch translation which went through two editions in 1606 and 1609. I have chosen to cite the English version of the text since this was the version that most seventeenth-century readers knew and drew on.

[94] *Works*, ii. 646.

[95] Ibid. 651 (italics original to the text).

are two: the first concerneth faith, which is handled in the Apostles Creed. The second concerneth charity or love, which is explicated in the ten Commandements.'[96] Or as Perkins succinctly states a few lines earlier, 'the supreme and absolute meane of interpretation, is the Scripture itself'.[97] This highlights the paramount principle of Reformed exegesis which views the right interpretation of Scripture as a gathering of 'most manifest and familiar places', where the justified reader uses those parts of the Bible which are 'Analogicall and plaine' to shed light on those parts, or places, which are 'Crypticall and darke'[98]: 'the collation or comparing of places together, is that whereby places are set like parallels one beside another, that the meaning of them may more evidently appeare.'[99] Plain or 'Analogicall places' (i.e. places which readily yield their 'literal' meaning through the analogy of faith), moreover, are often viewed as necessary for salvation, while 'Crypticall and dark' passages are often viewed as indifferent, especially if their inherent ambiguities might potentially undermine doctrine. The only salvific criterion, therefore, for interpreting the words of the Word are the *words* themselves, and it is in this circular sense that Perkins and his Puritan heirs think of the Bible as being somehow absolutely 'literal'.

This idea is also clearly set out in *The Marrow of Sacred Divinity* (1623, 1627, English translation 1643), William Ames's equally influential treatise of Ramist systematic theology:

20. Also the will of God is revealed in that manner in the Scriptures, that although, the things themselves are for the most part hard to be conceived, yet the manner of delivering and explaining them, especially in those things which are necessary, is cleere and perspicuous. 21. Hence the Scriptures need not especially in necessaries, any such explication whereby light may be brought to it from something else: but they give light to themselves, which is diligently to be drawne out by men, and to be communicated to others according to their calling. 22. Hence also there is onely one sence of one place of Scripture: because otherwise the sence of the Scripture should be not onely not cleere and certaine, but none at all: for that wich doth not signifie one thing, signifieth certainly nothing.[100]

---

[96] *Works*, ii. 651.   [97] Ibid.
[98] Ibid. 654.   [99] Ibid. 652.
[100] *The Marrow of Sacred Divinity*, 170–1.

Ames's uncompromising phrase, 'that wich doth not signifie one thing, signifieth certainly nothing' (*quod enim non unum significat, nihil significat certo*[101]), betrays the implicit fear of semiotic nihilism which permeates the Protestant-Calvinist encounter with God's words and the ineffable presence attached to them. The concept of semiotic and finally spiritual literalness which the Reformers yoke onto the Platonic paradigm which stipulates that one word signifies one thing sets up an unforgiving system of inspired exegesis where there is either full disclosure of meaning, or simply nothing—the ultimate silence of reprobation. True to its roots in Renaissance Neoplatonism, the emphasis in this sort of theology is anthropocentric, but in defiance of Ficino, Pico, and their humanist followers, it emphasizes rather man's corrupted inheritance at the heart of a fallen world, not his angelic ability to will himself out of such a predicament. If lapsarian man lacks the rational capacity to understand the semiotic and hence salvific clarity of the Bible, it is not because the figurative text is obscure, but because the individual reader's mind is obscured by sin and is in need of grace to see the literal truth through the dark glass of figurative expression.

The ineffable, or rather the moment of ineffable surrender before the mysteries of God, is not done away with in this unforgiving scheme; it is interiorized and relegated to the mysterious operation of the Holy Ghost or Spirit. Perkins is especially influential in the English Protestant tradition for his ardent belief, reiterated throughout his writings, that when an elect reader immerses himself in the biblical text he is taken over by the Holy Ghost, or Spirit, who alone can persuade the elect of Christ that the Scriptures are the true, unadulterated Word of God:

And there are verie strong proofes, which shew that she [the Canonical Scripture] is the word of God, and no other besides. Of these proofs one doth make a man certainly to know the same, the other doth but declare or testifie it. Of the former kinde there is only one, namely, the inward testimony of the Holy Ghost speaking in the Scriptures, and not only telling a man within his heart, but also effectually perswading him, that these books of the Scripture are the word of God ... The manner of perswading is on this wise: the Elect having the Spirit of God, doe first discerne the voice of Christ speaking in the Scriptures. Moreover, that voice which they doe discerne, they doe approve: and that

---

[101] *Medulla S.S. Theologiae ex Sacris Literis*, 181–2.

which they doe approve they doe believe. Lastly, believing, they are (as it were) sealed with the seale of the Spirit.[102]

As we have seen with Luther and Calvin, the attempt to deny the impact of ineffable presence on Reformed speech-acts only succeeds in dislocating such presence from its traditional place in the unmediated encounter with the ineffable Godhead, to the mediated, interiorized encounter with God's 'perfect' words. Only through the operation of the 'Holy Spirit' the elect may 'discerne the voice of Christ speaking in the Scriptures', and it is in this radically ineffable moment of inspiration where the truly sacramental core of Reformation theology is finally to be found.

Although this sacramental core is fundamentally ineffable, it never-theless produces and authorizes the Puritan obsession with 'godly' speech, which can never be seen to fall short of its meaning. Silence and the threat of misinterpretation continually threaten the salvific integrity of 'godly' speech, so that what remains unsaid becomes just as important as what *is* said. In his short treatise against blasphemy and lying, *A Direction for the Governement of the Tongue according to Gods word* (1593), Perkins once again strikes the definitive Protestant tone when he discusses the importance of 'godly silence':

Wise and godly silence is as excellent a vertue as holy speech: for he knoweth not how to speake which knoweth not how to hold his tongue: the rule of our silence must bee the law of God. By means of which, wise consideration must bee had, whether the thing which wee have in minde bee for Gods glory, and our neighbours good: which done, wee are answerably to speake or to bee silent.[103]

While the Reformed Christian's devotional experience is centred on actively participating and speaking with God's Word, it also includes the important proviso that the scope of such discourse must always confine itself to the Word of God as it is recorded in Scripture, and should have nothing to do with that which lies either profanely below it (or outside of it) or transcendentally above it. The hidden ways of God, the operation of miracles and prodigies, and the realms of mysticism and abstruse theological speculations must remain forever hidden in darkness and silence, or as Perkins says in his final and grim warning: 'all unseemely matters, al things unknowne, things which concern us not,

---

[102] *Works*, ii. 649.   [103] Ibid. i. 450.

things above our reach, are in silence to be buried.'[104] The realm of human experience is dominated, according to this general Calvinist-Bezan belief, by the example and saving power of the God-man Christ and the words of Scripture whose fulfilment he is. The truly ineffable God, Luther's absolutely transcendental *Deus nudus*, has nothing to do with lapsarian man, a depraved and sinful creature. Outside the scope of human knowledge, or Scripture, everything is thus ineffable and unspeakable; within it, however, nothing ought to be ineffable *if* one is numbered among the elect, for the Word was made flesh to dwell among men, some of whom have been preordained to enjoy its saving power while many others are excluded and shut out from its light. Not being able to rightly articulate the 'literal' sense of the Word thus becomes in this context a sign of interior imperfection—of either outright reprobation or a state of grace not yet fulfilled.

Most English Protestants in the Perkins tradition often cryptically allude to this mysterious, covenantal bond with the Word as being eloquent in 'the language of Canaan'. Mason Lawance argues that this ubiquitous Puritan phrase refers 'to the prophetic and metaphorical language used by God's chosen people when they talk of the kingdom of God and its realization in the last days',[105] but this is too narrow and too precise a definition. The phrase 'language of Canaan' was not confined to millenarian discourse, but denoted far more commonly the interior and paradoxically silent discourse of the Reformed heart in its striving for justification by faith. Here, for example, is the nonconformist minister Richard Baxter (1615–91) in his *The saints everlasting rest* (1650):

Surely, if we can get into the Holy of Holies, and bring thence the Name and Image of God, and get it closed up in our hearts: this would enable us to work wonders; every duty we performed would be a wonder, and they that heard, would be ready to say, Never man spake as this man speaketh. The Spirit would possess us, as those flaming tongues, and make us every one to speak, (not in the variety of the confounded Languagues, but) in the primitive pure Language of *Canaan*, the wonderful Works of God. We should then be in every duty, whether Prayer, Exhortation, or brotherly reproof, as *Paul* was at *Athens*, his Spirit . . . was stirred within him; and should be ready to say, as *Jeremy* did, *Jer.*

---

[104] *Works*, 451.
[105] Lowance, *The Language of Canaan*, p. vii.

20.9. *His word was in my heart, as a burning fire shut up in my bones; and I was weary with forbearing, and I could not stay.*[106]

Strikingly, Baxter explicitly associates in this passage the inner working of the 'language of Canaan' with the interiorizing of God's ontological immanence in the shrine, or 'Holy of Holies' and the gift of inspired speech alluded to in the miracle of Pentecost (Acts 2: 3–4), where God's ineffable 'Name and Image' are inscribed not in normal, post-Babel language, but in the 'primitive pure' language of grace that is the 'Language of *Canaan*'. Such sacred, or pure, meta-language liberates fallen man from the rhetorical and ideological snares of elaborate rhetoric and is seen to offer the Protestant everyman, regardless of his actual literacy, a viable route into the mysteries of grace. It is, indeed, the spiritual language of sacred interiority so often celebrated, for example, in George Herbert's poetry which Baxter lauded as 'Heart-work and Heaven-work'.[107]

Once again, however, it is Perkins who provides the most lucid account (relatively speaking, of course) of what the 'language of Canaan' is and how it operates. At the outset of *Governement of the Tongue*, Perkins states: 'The governement of the Tongue is a vertue pertaining to the holy usage of the Tongue according to GODS Word... and for the well ordering of it, two things are requisite: a pure heart, and skill in the language of Canaan.'[108] The 'pure heart' alludes, of course, to the Fifth Beatitude and the promise of the *visio Dei*. Perkins, however, wrenches this idea from its usual place in Christian apophatic mysticism and redeploys it in an evangelical context. In a system of belief where external behaviour is often understood to reflect an interior state of either predetermined holiness or damnation, if one's speech was foul it

---

[106] Baxter, *The saints everlasting rest, or, A treatise of the blessed state of the saints in their enjoyment of God in glory wherein is shewed its excellency and certainty, the misery of those that lose it, the way to attain it, and assurance of it, and how to live in the continual delightful forecasts of it and now published by Richard Baxter*, 621–2.

[107] Quoted in Patrides, *George Herbert: The Critical Heritage*, 137. See esp. Herbert's 'Sion', where Solomon's temple is reconstituted in the poet's groaning heart. Herbert, however, is typically uncertain about his ability to merit the gift of grace implied by such sacred interiorizing, since the presence of sin risks contaminating the new interior 'structure' of groans: 'And now thy Architecture meets with sin; | For all thy frame and fabric is within... All Solomon's sea of brass and world of stone | Is not so dear to thee as one good groan' (11–12; 17–18).

[108] *Works*, i. 440.

followed that one's heart was demonstrably foul as well. Turning to the metaphor of the fountain, Perkins states: 'if the fountaine be defiled the streams that issue thence cannot be cleane.'[109] Moreover, a 'pure heart' presupposes eloquence in the 'language of Canaan'. Anticipating the confusion such a mysterious phrase may cause, Perkins then explains:

The *language of Canaan* is, whereby a man endued with the spirit of adoption, unfainedly calleth upon the name of God in Christ, and so consequently doth as it were, familiarly talke and speake with God. This language must needs be learned, that the tongue may be well grounded. For man must first be able to talke with God, before hee can bee able wisely to talke with man. For this cause when men are to have communication one with another, they are first of all to be carefull that they often make their prayers to God that he would guide and blesse them in their speeches.[110]

The 'language of Canaan' is a typological metaphor, where 'language', with its obvious double gloss in the Genesis story of Babel and the Pentecost miracle of Acts 2, is married to the term 'Canaan', glossed through multiple Genesis accounts as the land promised by God to the seed of Abraham. The 'analogy of faith' then makes it possible to apply this phrase to the life of a Reformed Christian who ought to understand the phrase as signifying the spiritual plateau where the elect person in a state of covenantal grace may, as Perkins says, 'familiarly' talk and speak, as it were, with God. 'Talk', 'speak', 'language', and even 'skill' should not be taken 'properly' therefore, but rather as metaphors that bespeak a discursive intimacy between creature and Creator that is 'familiar' and therefore not subject to the pitfalls of post-Babel human languages and ineffability. The 'language of Canaan' is the spiritual idea from which the use of any language must flow for it to be registered as 'godly', but more importantly it yields the basic hermeneutical principle which allows all devout Protestants to project through their scripturally grounded 'godly' speech their unerring conviction in the complete perspicuity and spiritual literality of their religious discourse.

The purpose of the necessarily brief and condensed intellectual survey in this and the previous chapter was to provide a detailed enough context for my ensuing analysis of Milton's poetics of ineffability. Milton's

---

[109] Ibid.   [110] Ibid.

place in the intellectual traditions I have outlined so far is not, however, merely one of casual indebtedness to a miscellany of textual sources and religious ideas. It is not simply a matter of tracing, say, Milton's use of light or darkness metaphors to Denys' mystical theology, or to Luther-an-Calvinist discussions about the hidden God. Rather, the aim was to establish the necessary background to show that when Milton confronts in his poetry the problems of ineffability, he engages with an ongoing narrative about silence and ineffable mystery which in many ways forms the intellectual framework within which he continually shapes and reshapes his poetic vision in deep awareness of these often dichotomized traditions and their vocabularies. The mystical apophatic strain of the Platonic tradition, from Plato and the early Greek Christian mystics to Cusanus and the Italian Neoplatonists, gave intellectual impetus to Milton's poetic attempts to assert vatic authority in terms of inspired soaring and privileged vision. At the same time, however, his spiritual and intellectual indebtedness to the scriptural tradition of the Nameless God at the heart of the Reformation movement, as elucidated and developed from Calvin and Beza to Perkins and Ames, forced him to explore also the more threatening implications of hermeneutical silence in the salvific processes of rightly reading and interiorizing the fixed meanings of inspired texts. From the free paraphrase of Psalm 114 to *Paradise Regained,* the presence of the ineffable insinuates itself into Milton's poetry as both the catalyst and check for his poetic creativity, where the fear of silence and ineffable mystery on the one hand, and the yearning to lose himself and his readers in unspeakable rapture on the other, become a struggle for poetic self-determination and finally redemption.

3

Milton's *Poems 1645*: the problem with soaring

When it came to confronting the ineffable, the young Milton inherited an intellectual tradition that was divided against itself. The optimistic humanism of the Italian Neoplatonists and their English heirs in the More–Colet tradition found its most eloquent expression in the highly creative poetry of Sidney and Spenser, which glorified the role of the inspired poet as a divine maker who can shadow ineffable truths in poetic metaphor. The Calvinist–Perkinsian tradition, on the other hand, emphasized instead fallen man's abject dependency on irresistible grace and highlighted the threat of attempting to say the unsayable beyond the salvific remit of the Word. As a young man, Milton seemed to have been either unwilling or unable to resolve this difficult contradiction. His education at the hand of private tutors such as the Puritan Thomas Young, and then later at St Paul's and Christ's College, Cambridge, introduced him to Ramist logic and Calvin's school of irresistible grace (as well as to Arminian notions of prevenient grace), but also exposed him to the beauty of orchestral and choir music, the riches of classical literature, and the arts of rhetorical disputation. With the exception of translations and paraphrases of the Psalms, often set to music, poetry in this educational scheme was a morally and spiritually suspect art. Even Sidney, a Protestant poet unashamed of his belief in the morally virtuous qualities of inspired poets, could not help but register the worrying fear that the demiurgic poet's 'erected wit' must always contend with the debilitating effects of the Fall on man's 'infected will'.[1] The Hermetic

---

[1] See the *Defence of Poesie*: 'our erected wit maketh us know what perfection is, and yet our infected will keepeth us from reaching unto it' (ed. Duncan-Jones, p. 217). For a good, if brief, discussion of this tension in Sidney's *Defence* see Cummings, *Literary Culture of the Reformation*, 264–70. For a more general discussion of the 'Will' in the

impulse of poetic flight, even when tempered by morally congenial Neo-platonic concerns for 'truth', 'hidden wisdom', and 'transcendental beauty', presupposes a degree of uninhibited creativity that most Protestants (never mind hard-line Calvinists) viewed as dangerously presumptuous. Indeed, the notion of a *poetic theology* of the kind developed by Pico and celebrated by Sidney was anathema to the average English Calvinist. Perkins, again, expresses the typical Puritan sentiment when, in *Government of the Tongue*—the same treatise in which he celebrates the virtues of 'holy silence'—he also condemns 'ballads, bookes of love, all idle discourses and histories [as] nothing else but enticements and baits unto manifold sinnes, fitter for *Sodom* and *Gomorrah*, then for Gods Church'.[2] Perkins would have found the Picoesque notion of a 'poetic' theology equally abhorrent because the impulse to characterize any theological activity as 'poetic' questioned the rationally literal imperatives of biblical revelation. The type of spiritual anxiety stirred up by the dislocation of the ineffable in Reformed religious discourse would, therefore, force Milton constantly to rethink not only his metaphysical beliefs and theology but also the very meaning of what it is to be a rational human being at the centre (or margins) of God's creation, endowed as he believed with the quasi-mystical, but truly divine gift of poetic utterance. At the spiritual core of this Calvinist–Hermetic dichotomy, which is central to Milton's poetry and which, as we have seen, animates much of English Protestant humanism in general, is the question of ineffable mystery, its place in the devout Christian's religious life, and the sort of religious discourses it can and should inspire.

FEAR OF MYSTERY

Before anything else can be said about young Milton's attitudes to ineffable religious mysteries, it is important to address a familiar biographical

---

clash between Reformation theology and humanism and how this impacted on Milton's thinking on this subject see Reid, *The Humanism of Milton's 'Paradise Lost'*, ch. 1. While Reid's argument that Erasmian humanism lacks the meaningful seriousness of Luther's engagement with Pauline theology is reductive, his summary of the basic dichotomy between evangelical Protestantism and neoclassical religious humanism is very useful. So is Reid's ensuing analysis which shows how Milton 'straddle[s] this line between humanism and the Christian, especially Protestant, study of the will' (p. 20) in *Paradise Lost*.

[2] Perkins, *Works*, i. 450.

question: how orthodox or radical was the young Protestant Milton?
Although the younger Milton of the 1620s to 1640s continually engages
in a spiritual-political dialogue with the High Calvinist mainstream and
ideologically flirts with the 'godly' radicals on its fringes, his proper place
within these milieus is notoriously difficult to determine and is still
debated.[3] The early biographical record is inconclusive. Although, as
Lewalski puts it, Milton 'was reared in a bourgeois Puritan milieu that
fostered in him...a commitment to reformist, militant Protestantism',[4]
he also grew up in a highly cultured household where he was exposed to
music and learnt to play the organ and bass viol; he went on to attend with
his parents a Laudian chapel during the Hammersmith years, and wrote
two aristocratic entertainments in the distinctly royalist masque genre
with the possible intention of courting patronage.[5] Indeed, looking
ahead to *Paradise Lost* we can conclude that, regardless of the sort of
youth Milton's parents and early tutors had hoped to mould, the finished
article would later transgress all bounds of Calvinist decency by daring to
plumb the depths of divine mysteries in his mature poetry and prose. This
was not so much a declared theological ambition as the calling of a deeply
rational aesthetic impulse.

The ever-rationalist Milton, we are often told, was indeed 'impatient'
with mystery, which as a committed Protestant he tended to associate
with the threat of Catholic idolatry.[6] In *Areopagitica*, for example,
Milton blames the tyranny of censorship on Roman Catholic 'Antic-
hristian malice and mystery', which were meant, he argues, to 'extin-
guish, if it were possible, the light of the Reformation, and to settle

---

[3] For Milton's early ambivalence towards the radicals see Loewenstein, '"Fair offspring nurs't in princely Lore"', and more recently, 'Toleration and the Specter of Heresy
in Milton's England', in Achinstein and Sauer, *Milton and Toleration*, 45–71. See also
Hill, *Milton and the English Revolution*, ch. 8; Lewalski, 'How Radical Was the Young
Milton?', in Dobranski and Rumrich, *Milton and Heresy*, 49–67.

[4] Lewalski, *The Life of John Milton*, 1.

[5] See ibid. 54–6, 76–81. While it is true, as is often mentioned, that Milton invested
his Ludlow *Masque* with implicitly anti-Laudian 'Puritan' themes which seek to purge
this courtly genre from its association with decadent, even pagan, allegorical entertainments at court, the gesture is one of subversive conformity, not radical iconoclasm. For
the alleged 'Puritanism' of Milton's masque see McGuire, *Milton's Puritan Masque*.

[6] For some typical expressions of this truism see Frye, *Five Essays on Milton's Epics*, 59;
S. M. Fallon, '"Elect above the rest": Theology as Self-presentation in Milton', in
Dobranski and Rumrich, *Milton and Heresy*, 93–116, at 93, reprinted and developed
in greater detail in *Milton's Peculiar Grace*, ch. 7.

falshood'.[7] However, it is never quite clear how Milton's impatience with mystery manifests in his early poems, and what are its implications for his evolving engagement with ineffably mysterious divine presence in his more solemn early poetic experiments on religious and theological themes. Notwithstanding Milton's eventual quarrel with Calvin on the doctrines of irresistible grace and predestination, and his adoption at various stages in his life of a number of minority beliefs within the wider context of Reformation theology, it is important to appreciate that such departures were always made within the wider context of Reformed discourse: Arminianism, after all, is a debate within and about Calvinism—it is not divorced from it. John Stachniewski said it best when he came to analyse the residual Calvinism of Milton's *Paradise Lost*:

Whatever Milton may have deliberately believed, and believed himself to be exhibiting in the poem, the full weight of imaginings in which his compatriots had acquiesced bears down on the experience the poem portrays. Had this pressure not registered, an imaginative poverty would have made itself felt. Attractive as a serenely consistent, morally superior, alternative system of values might be, it would feel like an evasion of, not an advance on, the theological and social ambience out of which the epic emerged.[8]

Indeed, when considering the abstract presence of ineffability in Milton's early religious sensibility, the sort of residual, orthodox pressures Stachniewski detects in *Paradise Lost* appear more acutely and are harder to ignore, especially given that Milton is always consistently orthodox on the fundamental Protestant belief in the authority of the Bible. Like Calvin, Perkins, Ames, and many other Protestant theologians and thinkers before him, Milton always upheld the supreme integrity, sufficiency, and ultimate literality of the Bible and clung to the belief that the Holy Spirit allows every elect reader to rightly read and understand the biblical text. In *The Reason of Church-Government* a young, relatively anonymous Milton earnestly spoke for an entire generation of godly Protestants when he

---

[7] *YCP* ii. 548.

[8] Stachniewski, *The Persecutory Imagination*, 332. Compare, however, with Fallon's analysis of Milton's notion of 'peculiar grace' and the anxieties it betrays which proceeds precisely from the unavoidable fact that in *Paradise Lost* at least there is an anomalous Calvinist irruption in the Father's phrase: 'Some I have chosen of peculiar grace | Elect above the rest' (III. 183–2). As Fallon convincingly argues, this irruption is not a concession to Calvinism as such, but a mark of Milton's irreconcilable desire to be 'elect by both birthright and merit' (*Milton's Peculiar Grace*, 188).

snubbed the Laudian bishops: 'Believe it, wondrous Doctors, all corporeal resemblances of inward holinesse & beauty are now past; he that will cloath the Gospel now, intimates plainly, that the Gospel is naked, uncomely, that I may not say reproachfull.'[9]

For Milton, however, the central Protestant belief in the individual authority of 'inward holinesse' quickly established itself as the cornerstone of his belief in radical and socially active Christian liberty and the absolute freedom of religious conscience, independent of stifling orthodoxy or any extra-biblical dictate. This core belief, given minor adjustments, remained a constant throughout his life and carried with it a deep suspicion of unwarranted probing of unknowable and ineffable divine mysteries. Such deep fear and suspicion of mystery was the product of a highly adaptable Protestantism which holds in tension— to use two of Milton's formative teachers as models—an intellectual indebtedness to the Calvinist–Perkinsian Puritanism of Milton's early tutor and *smectymnuus* author Thomas Young on the one hand, and the Platonic rationalism and tempered Protestant humanistic optimism of Alexander Gil, the elder, on the other.[10] Alexander Gil—Milton's headmaster at St Paul's—is especially instructive here. Gil was an ardent defender of the role of reason in biblical revelation, but like Perkins, who also privileges the role of logic in scriptural exegesis, Gil must have taught Milton to respect the *limits* of reason and to avoid dangerous speculation as well. In 'The preface to the reader' to his *The Sacred Philosophie of the Holy Scripture* (1635), Gil anxiously defends the importance of applying rational thinking in reading the Bible. As a true humanist, Gil celebrates man's God-given rational faculties, but then, true to his Protestant beliefs, he also holds out the Word of God and its scriptural record as the only yardstick against which to measure such faculties:

And seeing man alone of all the visible creatures is framed and formed of God unto this search, by the outward sense and reason to finde the wisdome and power of God in the creature, that so honouring him therefore as he ought he might be made happie thereby: if it bee no way possible by reason and discourse

---

[9] *YCP* i. 828.

[10] For the special influence of both men on Milton see Hill, *Milton and the English Revolution*, 22–32; Lewalski, *The Life of John Milton*, chs. 1 and 2, and 'How Radical Was the Young Milton?', 49–52.

to come to this end, then should God want of his honour by some of those meanes by which it might be given unto him; then should the creature bee failing to man in the speciall use, which he should make thereof to God, then should reason the chiefe facultie of our soule, and principall means of our knowledge, have beene given unto man in vaine; that is, as sence is to the beasts, onely for this life; if it were either no helpe at all, or an unfit, or an insufficient meane to know that which is most necessary and worthy to bee knowne; and yet obscure, to stirre up our industrie, that as faithful servants we may improve those gifts wherewith God that intrusted us . . .

. . . for to the knowledge of naturall things, we have our owne witlesse experience to helpe us, and the deceitfull authoritie of mistaking men: but all those truthes whereon our faith relies, are grounded on the infallible rules of Gods owne word revealed by himselfe unto us, for this end, that we should not bee deceived or mistaken. And although it was impossible for humane reason ever to finde out the conclusions and most fundamentall points of our faith, as the mysterie of the Trinite, the incarnation of God, the resurrection of the body, & c. yet being by the cleer light of Gods own word made known unto us, we approve the same truth by the judgement and voice of reason.[11]

Once again we encounter here the familiar fideist-rational refrain: reason can only be used to work out what faith instructs us is true, not to prove what then must be accepted as a point of faith. It is very likely, indeed, that Milton inherited from Gil the confidence in his own rational faculties, but also a deep apprehension about their limits in matters of inexplicable religious mysteries and matters of faith. As Milton matured, however, the ultimate result of this tension between faith and reason would be a personal theology that is neither wholly Calvinist nor wholly Arminian, but ultimately rational on its own terms, honest to the point of superciliousness and profoundly literary.

At the extreme, the impulse of such scriptural rationalism often led Milton to deny altogether the existence of mystery, especially in key areas of Christian theology. Milton's denial of the Trinity is a good example. In *Of True Religion*, published in 1673, an old, impenitent Milton openly defends tolerance towards Arians and Socinians not on the grounds that their heterodox theology is necessarily defensible (perhaps it isn't), but on the grounds that the Trinity is not the mystery

---

[11] *The Sacred Philosophie of the Holy Scripture*, 'The preface to the reader'.

scholastic theologians have made it out to be. For Milton, in denying a Triune God Arius was applying a sensible 'Protestant maxim' in reading the Scriptures plainly and without excessive subtlety—whether or not one agrees with his conclusions is irrelevant:

The Arian and Socinian are charg'd to dispute against the Trinity: they affirm to believe the Father, Son, and Holy Ghost, according to Scripture, and the Apostolic Creed; as for terms of Trinity, Triniunity, Coessentiality, Tripersonality, and the like, they reject them as Scholastic Notions, not to be found in Scripture, which by a general Protestant Maxim is plain and perspicuous abundantly to explain its own meaning in the properest words, belonging to so high a Matter and so necessary to be known; a mystery indeed in their Sophistic Subtilties, but in Scripture a plain Doctrin. Their other Opinions are of less Moment.[12]

This sentiment captures the well-known essence of Milton's fiercely (but not unconditionally) tolerant,[13] because radically subjective, religious impulse: a righteous Christian, justified and confirmed in his faith, with the aid of grace bringing his God-given reason to bear on his reading of the Bible, can never go wrong in his understanding of those divine 'mysteries' and religious truths which are *necessary* for his salvation.

As we have seen with Perkins and Ames, the distinction between passages in the Bible which are either indifferent or necessary for salvation had always offered a convenient get-out clause for Protestants forced to concede that some passages in the Bible make no sense literally, and are very hard to interpret without slipping into increasingly unstable realms of metaphor and allegory. This argument is commonly found in most Reformation literature and can be traced, as we have

---

[12] *YCP* viii. 424–5.

[13] The context for Milton's toleration of heretical sects in *Of True Religion* is the proto-Whig politics of the early 1670s, where some defenders of nonconformity wanted to stress the wide scope for religious toleration under the overthrown republic. For all his rhetorical fierceness, therefore, Milton's advocacy of religious and political toleration in some polemical contexts should not be taken *out* of these immediate contexts and is rarely, if ever, reflected in his major poetry in the simplistic sense which we tend to associate today with ideas of tolerance. On this subject, see Achinstein and Sauer, *Milton and Toleration.* Specifically on the subject of Milton's engagement with the Arian controversy see Martin Dzelzainis, 'Milton and Antitrinitarianism', in the same collection (pp. 171–85).

seen, partly and ironically to Erasmus. For his part, Milton unequivocally states this basic 'Protestant Maxim' in his *De Doctrina Christiana*
(which is in fact much less tolerant than the later *Of True Religion*):[14]

The Scriptures, then, are plain and sufficient in themselves... Through what
madness is it, then, that even members of the reformed church persist in
explaining and illustrating and interpreting the most holy of truths of religion,
as if they were conveyed obscurely in the Holy Scriptures? Why do they shroud
them in the darkness of metaphysics?... As if scripture did not contain the
clearest of all lights in itself: as if it were not in itself sufficient, especially in
matters of faith and holiness: as if the sense of the divine truth, itself absolutely
plain, needed to be brought out more clearly or more fully, or otherwise
explained, by means of terms imported from the most abstruse of human
sciences—which does not, in fact, deserve the name of science at all! The
Scriptures are difficult or obscure, at any rate in matters where salvation is
concerned, only to those who perish.[15]

Milton's concreteness of thought in this passage, with its open contempt
for (or is it fear of?) the 'darkness of metaphysics (*metaphysicorum...*
tenebris)', is a direct symptom of his guarded rationality. As Georgia
Christopher has argued long ago now, in her compelling analysis *Milton
and the Science of the Saints*, it would not be unreasonable to suppose
that if the later Milton consistently demystified the idea of a religious
mystery he did so because, for all his manifold heterodoxies and heresies, he remained throughout his life a creature of the Reformation for
whom the discourses of a literary theology collapsed the distinctions
between an active and a contemplative religion, and which substituted
things for words. While this is true in a very general sense, we ought to
admit, however, the fraught nature of this paradoxical idea. As I have

---

[14] Following the recent publication of Campbell, Corns, Hale, and Tweedie's
authoritative findings into the provenance of Milton's *De Doctrina* manuscript, *Milton
and the Manuscript of 'De Doctrina Christiana'* (Oxford, 2007), Professor Hunter's
misgivings about the attribution have been put to rest permanently. As Campbell *et al.*
conclude, there is no doubt that *De Doctrina Christiana*, a systematic theology most
likely compiled in the late 1650s and then abandoned as work-in-progress, rightly
belongs in the Milton canon. Since Hale's new and much anticipated translation of
the retranscribed Latin of the manuscript is yet to be published at the time of writing,
I have relied circumspectly on John Carey's still very reliable translation from the Yale
edition of the *Complete Prose Works*, despite his tendency (for reasons of clarity no doubt)
to break up the paratactic sentences of Milton's Latin and rearrange its syntax.
[15] *YCP* vi. 580.

intimated in my discussion of Reformation thought in the previous chapter, the most that such a shift can achieve is to dislocate the moment of ineffable surrender from its traditional place at the heart of the religious experience and locate it, indeterminately, outside the scriptural horizon of the Reformed Christian's religious life. However, that same ineffable presence still hovers on that horizon, insinuating itself into the gaps between the words of the Word, putting any conceivable Protestant 'speech-act' under the tremendous strain of having to contain within it ineffable presence even while precluding it. The more mature Milton found creative ways to accommodate or suppress this strain, but in his youth many of his early poetic experiments register a degree of spiritual and consequently poetic irresolution in the face of ineffable mystery.

Although the mature Milton's monist metaphysical views have been rightly characterized as something approximating 'animist materialism', the younger Milton of the Latin elegies and *A Masque Presented at Ludlow Castle* was still very much a straightforward Neoplatonic dualist who held that the divine rational soul forever yearns to escape the prison of the material body and ascend towards God.[16] Equally, his earlier rational distrust of metaphysics was a more uncomplicated symptom of his ardent Protestantism as filtered to him through the teachings of Gil and others. Fear, not impatience, is a much better word for the younger Milton's attitude to mystery who, having read, for example, Eusebius' *Life of Constantine*, notes in his commonplace book the following sentiment about presumptuous demystifiers: 'That the profound questions concerning God, which the human reason explains or comprehends with considerable difficulty, should either not be thought about or should be suppressed in silence lest they be proclaimed to the people and from this source a cause of schisms be given in the Church, Constantine very wisely admonishes in a letter to

---

[16] The phrase 'animist materialism' was first used in relation to Milton's mature poetry by Stephen Fallon, who argues that in *Paradise Lost* Milton, after a manner, echoes Spinoza by 'assimilating matter to current notions of mind and mov[ing] toward the position that all corporeal substance is animate, self-active and free' (*Milton Among the Philosophers*, 81). Fallon's analysis in the section between pp. 79–83 in particular offers a helpful, if brief, analysis of the early dualist-Neoplatonic stages of Milton's thought which nevertheless contain, as Fallon argues, some intimations of Milton's future monism.

Alexander and Arius.'[17] This reflection, probably recorded during the Horton period (1635–8),[18] hardly accords with the future poet for whom tactful silence, up until the late 1660s at least, was poetic and theological anathema. Neither does it accord with Milton's future anti-trinitarianism, monist materialism, or his ardent belief, set forth later in *Areopagitica*, in the need to put religious 'truth' through the dialectical 'wars' of contradictory public opinion precisely as an antidote to schism.[19]

Such fear of mystery does accord, however, with Milton's early religious sentiment, which comes across quite strongly, for example, in his earliest extant poem, the free paraphrase of Psalm 114. It is not unreasonable to speculate that when the teenage Milton decided to paraphrase Psalm 114, perhaps as a school exercise, he could not allow his raw imaginative instincts to interfere with the rational concreteness of the original Psalm's distilled religious meaning as he saw it. As a result, even though the idea of the paraphrase as such was no longer a source of overt transcendental anxiety as it had been for Erasmus almost a century earlier, a peculiar sense of discomfort about ineffable mystery and metaphoric circumlocution nevertheless creeps into Milton's paraphrase experiment. In Psalm 114 some of the more obvious embellishments of Milton's English version are political. When Milton expands the 'Israel' of the first verse into 'the blest seed of Terah's faithful Son', he is sharpening the paraphrase's political subtext by alluding to the English nation's near escape from the threat of Terah-like Roman Catholic idolatry when Charles and Buckingham's mission to woo the Spanish Infanta met with failure.[20] Other embellishments—such as the additions of adjectives in Jordan's 'froth becurled head' or the 'high, huge-bellied' mountains—are decorative lyrical expansions inserted for metrical and poetic effect. Taken together, however, the embellishments offer something more: an overriding sense of strangely opaque logic. In the original Psalm the elliptic Hebrew requires the reader

---

[17] *YCP* i. 380 (trans. from Latin).

[18] Ibid., n. 3.

[19] See the famous *Areopagitica* passage: 'And though all the windes of doctrin were let loose to play upon the earth, so Truth be in the field, we do injuriously by licencing and prohibiting to misdoubt her strength. Let her and Falsehood grapple; who ever knew Truth put to the wors, in a free and open encounter' (*YCP* ii. 561).

[20] Psalm 114 was sung in St Paul's in October 1623 when Charles and Buckingham returned from Spain empty-handed. See Hill, *Milton and the English Revolution*, 27.

to make metaphorical leaps over the logical gaps in the text. The AV and most other English versions before Milton's retain this sense of elliptic mystery, for example between the first and second verses. Here is the AV:

1. When Israel went out of Egypt, and the house of Jacob from a people of strange language;
2. Judah was his sanctuary, *and* Israel his dominion.

The AV translation is as literally faithful a translation from Hebrew into English as can be. The 'Israel' of the first verse denotes the people under bondage, but the 'Israel' in the second verse already connotes the same people's new habitation in the Promised Land, having been freed from bondage. The hand of God in this momentous act of deliverance, migration, conquest, and re-habitation is numinously present in the gaps between the words and the causal relationship between the two clauses making up the two verses. For the young Milton, on the other hand, such silent textual lacunae only suggest a space that urgently demands lyrical amplification. The result is a form of poetic *horror vacui*:

> When the blest seed of Terah's faithful son,
> After long toil their liberty had won,
> And passed from Pharian fields to Canaan land,
> Led by the strength of *the Almighty's hand*,
> *Jehovah's wonders* were in Israel shown,
> His praise and glory was in Israel known.
>
> (1–6, my emphases)

Not only does Milton tell us that it was the Almighty's hand that led the people of Israel out of captivity; he also names the Almighty as 'Jehovah', using the only biblical name for God, traditionally held to be itself unspeakable. Again, whereas the Hebrew Psalm mysteriously alludes to the sacred space of God's Tabernacle by referring to 'his sanctuary', using the possessive pronoun 'his' to collapse any distinction between the Israelites and their God, Milton talks more generally of a time when 'Jehovah's wonders were in Israel shown'. It is extremely revealing that Milton chooses to emphasize here the demonstrability of Yahweh's power. God's act of deliverance is a demonstrable one; it can be seen in the parting of the Red Sea, in the ultimate triumphs of the Israelites over their many enemies, and in the immanence of God's habitation in the Sanctuary. For the young Milton these demonstrable 'wonders' are only wondrous, therefore, in a speculative sense. One might indeed wonder why God chose his people, or speculate about the hidden workings of his providence, but such speculations are unnecessary since the only thing that matters is what these 'wonders' *show* the devout, and what is shown leads to certain knowledge, not of God as he is in himself but of his providential presence in the history of his chosen people: 'His praise and glory was in Israel known.' Where the original Psalm celebrates the overpowering numinous presence of God acting within creation in mysterious ways, Milton focuses only on the demonstrable historical outcome of God's actions.

Milton's next move in the paraphrase, moreover, clinches this sense of rational discomfort by completely eliding the original Psalm's use of impassioned apostrophe. Most English versions, as well as the Latin version of the Vulgate, render the original Hebrew apostrophe to the ocean in verse 5 (*ma-lekha*, מַה־לְּךָ) as 'what ailed thee' or 'what ayleth thee' (the Vulgate reads: 'Quid est tibi'). The figure of apostrophe is a self-referential, reflexive metaphor that usually heightens the speaker's sense of detached otherness and even loneliness, echoing the speaker's thoughts back across a great metaphorical chasm. Jonathan Culler famously argues that most readers of poetry find apostrophe, or rather the vocative mood inherent in the use of apostrophe, embarrassing. Many critics of poetry, argues Culler, 'reduce apostrophe to description' so that they can 'state the alternatives which confront the subject in [the] poem . . . but . . . eliminate the vocative, which is precisely the attempt to bring about the condition to which it alludes: the condition of the visionary poet who can engage in dialogue with the universe'.[21] The more mature Milton would grow into precisely such a visionary poet, but in his youth he seems to have been indeed deeply embarrassed by the vocative. In Psalm 114 the string of apostrophes to the 'sea', 'Jordan', 'mountains', and 'little hills' raises a series of powerful rhetorical questions which paint in contour the inscrutable power of God's irresistible presence in the created world. Culler's theoretical insight, again, is informative: multiple apostrophes, he argues, 'function as nodes or concretizations of stages in a drama of mind. This internalization is important because it works against narrative and its accompaniments: sequentiality, causality, time, teleological meaning.'[22] In other words, multiple apostrophes, especially to rocks, trees, and other

---

[21] Culler, *The Pursuit of Signs*, 143.   [22] Ibid. 148.

inanimate objects, animate these objects as participants in a universal drama which acknowledges and celebrates a profound sense of ineffable mystery in the imaginative workings of the mind as it responds, in this case, to the mystery of God's creation. In Psalm 114, where, as elsewhere in the Psalms, the divide between man and God is a condition of the Fall, the apostrophes moreover register deep elegiac loss even as they remove, as Culler says, 'the opposition between presence and absence from empirical time and locat[e] it in a discursive time'.[23] The speaker of the Psalm, for example, does not simply ask questions of creation, he identifies with it and its hidden Creator, projecting onto its myriad shapes and awe-inspiring natural forces his own sense of humble gratitude, and by impli-cation a sense of finitude as well. Here is the AV:

5. What *ailed* thee, O thou sea, that thou fleddest? thou Jordan, *that* thou wast driven back?
6. Ye mountains, *that* ye skipped like rams; *and* ye little hills, like lambs?
7. Tremble, thou earth, at the presence of the Lord, at the presence of the God of Jacob;
8. Which turned the rock *into* a standing water, the flint into a fountain of waters.

Milton, however, paraphrases as follows:

> Why fled the ocean? And why skipped the mountains?
> Why turned Jordan toward his crystal fountains?
> Shake earth, and at the presence be aghast
> Of him that ever was, and ay shall last,
> That glassy floods from rugged rocks can crush,
> And make soft rills from fiery flint-stones gush.

> (13–18)

Without the numinous perspective supplied by the apostrophe in the original Hebrew and faithfully retained in most translations, the subsequent imperative, 'Shake earth, and at the presence be aghast', points to a presence that is imagined and rationalized but never felt.[24] In

---

[23] Ibid. 150.
[24] In his later paraphrase of Psalm 114 into Homeric Greek verse, Milton retains the apostrophe in his 'Τίπτε σύ' (*CSP*, line 12, p. 235). However, this does not necessarily reverse Milton's attitude to mystery in the earlier English paraphrase. The apostrophe in the Greek version serves to reinforce the paraphrase's Homeric decorum, where direct addresses to anthropomorphic forces of nature enhance a sense of polytheistic sympathy

his own way, Milton too poses rhetorical questions which assert the inscrutable power of God's presence, but the point of view is one of rational bewilderment, not religious engagement. Instead of a reflexive metaphor which invites ultimate silence we have a voice wanting to know, almost objectively, 'why fled the ocean? And why skipped the mountains?' 'Aghast' is Milton's embellishment, and it speaks volumes: the terror implied here is akin to that of Otto's *mysterium tremendum*. One either stands aghast in speechless amazement, or one is not aghast and so can speak freely about the need to be so. The 'earth' stands 'aghast' at the presence of its Creator, while the poet recoils away from the ineffability of attenuated divine presence and seeks comfort in the alliterative music of his own verse. Milton's 'rocks can crush' and 'flint-stones gush' are beautiful and even majestic evocations of God's inscru-table power, but they are delivered with the clarity of observation, not the distraction of religious feeling. Even at this very early stage, it seems, Milton can be read as instinctively assuming a detached, pedagogic point of view—while the 'earth' and the rest of God's creation is rendered fearful and speechless at the presence of God, Milton will use his skills of poetic suggestion to say everything that *can* be said about this presence for the benefit of those who are rendered speechless.

The desire to impose rational or indeed ideate clarity on lyrical form governs many of Milton's early poetical experiments. In a letter of 1637 he confessed to Diodati:

For though I do not know what else God may have decreed for me, this certainly is true: He has instilled into me, if into anyone, a vehement love for the beautiful. Not so diligently is Ceres, according to the Fables, said to have sought her daughter Proserpina, as I seek for this idea of the beautiful, as if for some glorious image, throughout all the shapes and forms of things ('for many are the shapes of things divine'); day and night I search and follow its lead eagerly as if by certain clear traces.[25]

and energy. Whereas in the English paraphrase Milton's prime concern is to maintain an appropriately solemn atmosphere of Protestant religiosity, in the Greek paraphrase he is attempting to emulate Homer in the process of fusing ancient Greece with ancient Israel. See Hale, 'Milton as a Translator of Poetry', 250–4, and Einboden, 'The Homeric Psalm'. Einboden especially demonstrates the lengths Milton goes to in his effort to copy 'Homeric' idiom and diction.

[25] *YCP* i. 326–7.

Crucially, Milton voices here his desire to immerse himself not in the pursuit of superficial beauty but in the *idea* of the beautiful. The manner in which he then draws the analogy with the fable of Ceres only reinforces, moreover, the Picoesque Platonic intellectual undertow which views pagan myth as the hidden repository of potential ideate divine wisdom. When we recall that the broadly Catholic Pico was a fundamentally anti-poetic exponent of dignified religious 'poetry', the potential problems for Milton holding a similar position become even more acute, given that Milton is also a Protestant. For Milton, especially in the earlier years of his intellectual uncertainty, the 'glorious image' of Beauty was always going to be found in the rational sequiturs of coherent ideas, not the intricacy of form, but as a poet honing his craft he clearly delighted in the intricacy of form and sound as well. This brings us back to the well-documented argument between Stanley Fish and John Rumrich. In *Surprised by Sin*, Fish argues that Milton was indeed faithful to a long Platonic–Puritan tradition of rational didacticism in holding with Plato (and we can add Ficino and Pico) an absurdly anti-poetic stance which rejects 'fleshy (rhetorical) style'.[26] Rumrich, however, challenged this view by reminding us that, although there is no doubt that 'Milton prized reason and distrusted ungovernable passion,...his vocational commitment was to an Orphean art, which *Of Education* characterizes as "simple, sensuous, and passionate" [*YCP* ii. 403], and whose magical power to move audiences he repeatedly celebrated'.[27] In fact, both Fish and Rumrich point in the right direction, to a state of mind divided against itself. In the case of the more mature Milton of *Paradise Lost*, one can see how he would not have perceived an inherent contradiction between his Orphic pretensions and his rational didacticism: he wanted to move readers with the sensuous power of poetry and wanted to do so with passionate reason (or rational passion as the case may be). This is a paradox, to be sure, but one which is absolutely central to Milton's aesthetic sensibility and his emerging power as a movingly intellectual poet. In his youth, however, Milton lacked the intellectual maturity and the sheer experience of singular excellence and vocational certainty to embrace this paradox fully.

[26] Fish, *Surprised by Sin*, 89.
[27] Rumrich, 'Uninventing Milton', 255.

WANTING TO SOAR

Given Milton's imposing achievement in *Paradise Lost*, a critic might be forgiven for wanting to detect, and indeed finding, signs of Milton's epic pretensions in his earlier poetry, but as Stella Revard has pointed out, young Milton was 'sporting'. In the years leading up to the publication of his inaugural 1645 volume, *Poems of Mr. John Milton Both English and Latin Compos'd at several times*, Milton 'had yet to decide what kind of poet he was to be'.[28] The poems Milton wrote leading up to the 1645 publication—be they trivial school and college exercises, occasional diversions, or official commissions such as *A Masque*—are all, in a profound sense, experimental. They are experimental both in the obvious technical sense, but also on a deep intellectual level: they are experiments in poetic flight. Despite his spiritual commitment to the radical perspicuity of the revealed Word of God and its immutable scriptural record, the early Milton of the 1620s to 1640s could not—indeed, would not—divorce his own sense of self-worth from a poetic frame of reference dominated by the vatic, Neoplatonic–Hermetic desire to soar in the service of the ineffable and nameless God, with or without the aid of the living words of the Word. Stephen Fallon has recently analysed in great detail the dichotomy at the heart of Milton's desire to soar in rapt flight. 'The dialectic of flight as reward for virtue and flight as dangerous overreaching', argues Fallon, 'gives rise to a drama of self assertion and self-occlusion in many of Milton's major works.'[29] This drama has direct bearing on the problem of mystery, since it posed before the young Milton a potentially crippling poetic and religious conundrum: how does one soar numinously in verse without sacrificing prosaic scope and intelligibility?

Even in the early Cambridge poem 'At a Vacation Exercise', intended to display Milton's poetic wit and little else, the young poet could not help but muse that his true calling lies in 'some graver subject' (30):

---

[28] Revard, *Milton and the Tangles of Neaera's Hair*, 8. For a good discussion of the early volubility of Milton's Protestant identity see Swaim, 'Myself a True Poem'. For an equally good and complementary discussion of how this volubility comes across in *Poems 1645* see Evans, 'The Birth of the Author'.

[29] Fallon, *Milton's Peculiar Grace*, 52.

> Such where the deep transported mind may *soar*
> Above the wheeling poles, and at heaven's door
> Look in, and see each blissful deity...
>
>   (33–5, my emphasis)

Milton may be presuming to soar in these extravagant lines merely towards the pagan heaven of Mount Olympus, described earlier in 'On the Death of a Fair Infant' as being of 'ruined roof' (43). But he may by then have set his sights on another mountain altogether—Mount Oreb. Having mastered (so he claims) Hebrew as well as Greek, Latin, French, and Italian, in 'Ad Patrem' Milton hints of his desire not merely to become a *poeta-vates* in the classical, pagan sense of the term, nor even a Christian *vates* as Dante and Du Bartas were (as the reference to Italian and French may suggest this), but audaciously to outdo and pre-empt all these by becoming a 'Palaestinus...vates' uttering 'mysteries':

>   tuo pater optime sumptu
> Cum mihi Romuleae patuit facundia linguae,
> Et Latii veneres, et quae Iovis ora decebant
> Grandia magniloquis elata vocabula Graiis,
> Addere suasisti quos iactat Gallia flores,
> Et quam degeneri novus Italus ore loquelam
> Fundit, barbaricos testatus voce tumultus,
> Quaeque Palaestinus loquitur mysteria vates.
>
>   (78–85)

Best of fathers, when the eloquence of the Roman tongue had been made accessible to me, at your expense, the beauties of Latin and the high-sounding words of the sublime Greeks, words which graced the mighty lips of Jove himself, then you persuaded me to add to my stock those flowers which are the boast of France, and that language which the modern Italian pours from his degenerate mouth (his speech makes him a living proof of the barbarian invasions), and also those mysteries which the prophet of Palestine utters.[30]

Identifying a veiled reference to Moses in line 85 would have been mere conjecture were it not for the opening invocation of *Paradise Lost*, many years later, that appears to confirm which kind of muse, or poetic/prophetic

---

[30] *CSP* 160.

agency Milton sought to claim for his poetry. In 'Ad Patrem' Milton may have merely thought it, but in *Paradise Lost* he commands it:

> Sing heavenly Muse, that on the secret top
> Of Oreb, or of Sinai, didst inspire
> That shepherd, who first taught the chosen seed . . .
>
> (I. 6–8)

From the moment Milton decided to pursue a poetic career he seems to have wanted to soar as a poet-prophet who utters mysteries in the tradition of the Hebrew-speaking prophets of the Old Testament. But Milton's desire to 'utter mysteries' does not proceed from a genuine religious need to revel in the silence of the ineffable, as much as from his thoroughly Protestant instinct to confront his fear of the ineffable through the performance of ever more assertive poetic 'speech-acts'. This might explain Milton's early confusion about the types of prophetic authority available to him, and his attempts to reconcile two diametrically opposed prophetic models. Fallon helpfully identifies these two as 'the Pauline and Augustinian models' of humble prophetic appointment popular among contemporary Puritans, and the 'Aristotelian and Ciceronian humanist model of ethical proof' of a prophet's virtuous worthiness of prophetic appointment.[31] Milton's instincts as a poet tended to lean towards the latter, but as Fallon rightly argues, the resulting model of prophetic worthiness is inherently unstable.[32] The two conflated models are already apparent in the term 'Palaestinus vates', which marries the biblical prophetic model of the speech-impeded Moses with the classical model of the inspired vatic poet.

The conceptual problem with this difficult marriage is that genuine biblical prophets (at least genuine by reputation) all tend to suffer from a kind of Cassandra complex in that they are bound never to be rightly understood, let alone heeded. Such was the plight of Moses, of Samuel, of Elijah, of Isaiah, and of many other biblical prophets who followed in their footsteps. Indeed, the stuttering Moses, the archetypally humble prophet,

---

[31] See Fallon, *Milton's Peculiar Grace*, 39–44. See also Kerrigan, *The Prophetic Milton*, 17–82, and Lawry, *The Shadow of Heaven*. For Lawry, Milton often strikes a monist stance in a perpendicular line which unites man and God, fallen earth with heaven, but then also assumes pedagogic stances within the lateral line of fallen matter, death, and historical becoming.

[32] Fallon, *Milton's Peculiar* Grace, 41.

ultimately discovered that to hold unmediated discourse with Yahweh renders one speechless. Conversely, the inspired *poeta-vates* of the Virgilian classical tradition is more of an inspired *sacerdos* or votive priest than a prophet.[33] The vatic poet of classical antiquity offers his poetic creations to the gods as tribute for his god-given *ingenium*, which is divine at the source, but whose metaphoric and mimetic operation will always be intelligible because its application is human in scope—or as Calvin would say, intelligibly corrupt because fallen. In the balance between these two models lies an unstable theory of poetic inspiration which moves indeterminately from a view of the poet as the imaginatively free manipulator of unformed subject-matter, to one of the poet as the passive mouthpiece of preformed, transcendental subject-matter. This indeterminacy is registered, for example, in the dialectical movement between the pastoral frivolity of 'L'Allegro', with its 'unreproved pleasures free' (40), to the austere meditations of 'Il Penseroso', and then again within the meditative oscillations of 'Il Penseroso' itself. As 'Il Penseroso' accelerates to its ecstatic crescendo, Milton appears to lean towards the passive model when he pleads with Melancholy, 'Whose saintly visage is too bright, | To hit the sense of human sight' (13–14), to impress his mind with

> anthems clear,
> As may with sweetness, through mine ear,
> Dissolve me into ecstasies,
> And bring all heaven before mine eyes.
> And may at last my weary age
> Find out the peaceful hermitage,
> The hairy gown and mossy cell,
> Where I may sit and rightly spell
> Of every star that heaven doth shew,
> And every herb that sips the dew;
> Till old experience do attain
> To something like prophetic strain.
>
> (163–74)

---

[33] For a discussion of the sacral or 'cultic point of view' in Milton's poetry see Lieb, *Poetics of the Holy*, ch. 3, 'Sacral Poetics'. Lieb provides an eminently learned account of Milton's various sacral gestures as a complement to other studies of Milton's prophetic stance, but does not highlight sufficiently the inherent tension between the two models, resting too easily in the claim that, 'For Milton, as for the traditions that he inherited, the roles of sacerdos and vates were largely interchangeable' (p. 46).

The desire to be immersed in divine or 'solemn' music, generated in this case by the earthly notes of a 'pealing organ blow' accompanying a 'full-voiced' church choir (161–2), is anchored in the desire to be dissolved 'into ecstasies'. As the music penetrates the poet's ears from the outside, it dissolves him into ex-stasis, and so by stepping out of himself in a radically literal sense the passive poet-prophet relinquishes individual authority as he moves towards the ultimate source of divine illumination which such earthly music points to. However, never at ease with such modes of self-cancellation, Milton also qualifies the desire to immerse himself passively in external forces of divine inspiration by alluding to that desire's speculative, hypothetical tenor: after all, the music which the poet hears and which inspires him to rapture is not divine at its source, but merely that of a church choir. The 'gifts' of Melancholy, however they are defined, and the attendant moment of self-cancellation, are indefinitely deferred, 'Till old experience do attain | To *something* like prophetic strain' (173–4, my emphasis). What this rather vague 'something' might actually sound like, and what scope for poetic initiative it actually might allow, were not questions the young Milton was either willing or able to answer for himself, but he was prepared to frame such questions speculatively for the benefit of his future English readers. In the meantime, the poet must remain in the confines of an earthly church and be content to embody that church spiritually, where there is no direct access to the light of the *visio Dei* but only 'a dim religious light' (159–60) pouring through the embodied church's stained-glass windows.

By seeking, then, to realize his vatic ambitions in scriptural, prophetic terms the younger Milton faced a very hard sell as far as his intended Reformed audience was concerned. It is true that the type of unimpeded and crucially unmediated prophetic voice Milton lays claim to in his early poetry and prose was not uncommon among the more radical sectarians at the lunatic fringe of the Reformed English consensus, and was, as Nigel Smith has shown, a particular staple of the type of solipsistic spirituality advocated by those more idiosyncratic radicals branded by the High Calvinist orthodoxy as 'Levellers' and 'Ranters'.[34]

---

[34] Smith, *Perfection Proclaimed*, chs. 6–8. See also, more recently, McDowell, *The English Radical Imagination*.

However, the last thing Milton would have wanted as an aspiring, nationally inclusive, poet-prophet was to be written-off as another antinomian, 'ranting' solipsist. Milton appears to have been alert to this problem and to have acted appropriately. The early prose, particularly the anti-prelatical tracts, provided him with the perfect opportunity to place his future poetic designs into a thoroughly orthodox and— one should add—widely acceptable English Reformed context. The many autobiographical digressions in *Reason of Church-Government* and *An Apology against a Pamphlet* are explicitly designed to present Milton as a widely legitimate heir to what David Norbrook has discussed as the 'harmony of the King's Peace'.[35] Read in such a way, what Thomas Corns has also described as Milton's quest for a kind of learned, bourgeoisie 'respectability' in the early poetry and prose equally becomes, I believe, a quest for orthodox theological *acceptability*.[36]

Nevertheless, the type of dim Calvinist sensibility Milton bows to in his early poetry and prose, whether or not he actually subscribed to all of its theological ideas, conceptually at least impedes the sort of prophetic soaring he ultimately aimed for in his more solemn verse. To appreciate the extent of this problem for Milton's early thinking about his prophetic calling, we must look closely at one of the most famous of the early prosaic introductions to the future poet. Alluding to Isaiah's vision of the burning coal, Milton directly addresses in *Reason of Church-Government* his fellow Reformed Englishmen and proclaims his future plans to excel in sacred poetry. Having defended his desire to become a poet and extolled the edifying and salvific preaching qualities of solemn poetry (whether epic, tragic, or lyrical), he then makes his readers an equally solemn, and telling promise:

Neither doe I think it shame to covnant with any knowing reader, that for some few years yet I may go on trust with him toward the payment of what I am now indebted, as being a work not to be rays'd from the heat of youth, or the vapours of wine, like that which flows at wast from the pen of some vulgar Amorist, or the trencher fury of a riming parasite, nor to be obtain'd by the invocation of Dame Memory and her Siren daughters, but by devout prayer to that eternall Spirit who can enrich with all utterance and knowledge, and sends out his Seraphim with the hallow'd fire of his Altar to touch and purify the lips

---

[35] Norbrook, *Writing the English Republic*, 162.
[36] Corns, 'Milton's Quest for Respectability'.

of whom he pleases: to this must be added industrious and select reading, steddy observation, insight into all seemly and generous arts and affairs, till which in some measure be compast, at mine own peril and cost I refuse not to sustain this expectation from as many as are not loath to hazard so much credulity upon the best pledges that I can give them.[37]

What immediately stands out in this passage is Milton's rejection of secular over sacred poetry in terms that call for the intercession of an external, divine agency. He dismisses poetic endeavours that come out of strictly secular, or temporal, exigencies, whether through the wine-induced heat of lust, the economic pressures of patronage, or even— which is especially curious in Milton's case—the unqualified lapsarian source of inspiration that comes with the appeal to 'Dame Memory and her Siren daughters' (presumably pagan classical literature and history). As the Yale editor of *Church-Government* notes, this last image is a mixed metaphor that marries the power of the muses, traditionally the daughters of Memory, with the Music of the Spheres where the Platonic Sirens may be found. Milton thus intimates that any Platonic appeal to the muses and the powers of *harmonia mundi* outside the sacred context of 'devout prayer' is a waste of one's divinely inspired poetic or vatic gifts. It is likely, moreover, that this is how Milton himself indeed felt with regard to his belated poetic achievements. He registers this sentiment not only in 'At a Vacation Exercise', but also in the much-discussed letter to an anonymous friend drafted in the Trinity Manuscript, where he confesses his life to be 'as yet obscure, & unserviceable to mankind'.[38]

However, is Milton's 'devout prayer' in the *Church-Government* passage truly humble? A. D. Nuttall, for example, concludes his brief but penetrating analysis of Milton in *Overheard by God* by wondering aloud how, and even if, the 'ageing Milton' prayed.[39] Although the focus here is on the older, presumably more defiant Milton, this question might well apply to Milton of the 1640s. The question is of course rhetorical—Nuttall's analysis, side by side, of Herbert and Milton leads him to conclude that, unlike Herbert, Milton could never abase himself in self-effacing prayer. However, in the opening of Book XI of *Paradise Lost*, as we overhear the fallen Adam and Eve at

[37] *YCP* i. 820–1.   [38] Ibid. 319.
[39] Nuttall, *Overheard by God*, 111.

their penitent prayers, Milton delivers a powerful encomium of Herbertian prayer in all of its 'unutterable' power:

> Thus they in lowliest plight repentant stood
> Praying, for from the mercy-seat above
> Prevenient grace descending had removed
> The stony from their hearts, and made new flesh
> Regenerate grow instead, that sighs now breathed
> Unutterable, which the spirit of prayer
> Inspired, and winged for heaven with speedier flight
> Than loudest oratory...

> (XI. 1–8)

As with many of the narrator's didactic asides in *Paradise Lost*, this description of regeneration through prayer is inserted to make a theological point, in this case about the nature of 'prevenient grace', which although preceding human action is not, as Calvin would argue, irresistible: Milton of *Paradise Lost* believed that grace may be either rejected or accepted by the stony heart in need of regeneration. The same culpably human Milton—a fallen child of Adam and Eve even at the best of times—breaks through the didacticism of this reflection as he extols Adam and Eve's humble prayer with genuine emotion and regret. Moreover, the 'unutterable' dimension of such prayer captures the unique intimacy between God, the praying subject, and the agency of the 'mercy-seat' (revealed in the next lines as a metaphor for the Son, 'their great intercessor', XI. 19) mediating between them. The Son, for Milton, indeed embodies this ethos of silent, ineffable communication. After the Son concludes his important speech in Book III of *Paradise Lost*, in which he offers himself to atone for man's sin, the narrator reflects how even though he had finished speaking, 'his meek aspect | Silent yet spake, and breathed immortal love | To mortal men' (III. 266–7). This is also echoed in the earlier *De Doctrina* passage in which Milton reflects on the efficacy of silent prayer, where Moses stands in as a type for Christ's mediatory office, followed by the example of Hannah:

It is not necessary that our prayers should be always audible; the silent supplication of the mind, whispers, even groans and inarticulate exclamations in private prayer, are available. *Exod* xiv. 15. *Jehovah said unto Moses, Whereto criest unto me?* though he was saying nothing with his lips, and only praying inwardly. I Sam. i 13: *Hannah spoke with her mind; though her lips moved, her voice was not heard.* If we pray like this our prayers will be more private, and so we shall obey the injunction of Matt. vi. 6.[40]

In such intimate, private spaces of silent prayer and grace 'loudest oratory' has no place, but as a poet Milton must use his best oratorical skills to allude to the existence of such unutterable spaces. For all his emotional investment in the idea of Adam and Eve's penitent prayers, the didactic tone of the observation suggests that the epic poet at least, looking down (or is it up?) at Adam and Eve in ruefulness, is somehow uninvolved in their unutterable devotion. If the epic poet ever prays, the only prayer we have of him is the poem itself—a votive offering which is anything but 'unutterable' and consists of the loudest oratory conceivable.

This basic contradiction also inheres in Milton's 'devout prayer' in the *Church-Government* passage which mysteriously invokes the 'eternall Spirit' to enrich him with 'all utterance and knowledge'—for the ability to speak, and in a sense to know, all that is, whether from within or without creation. Milton's prayer to have *all* utterance which in turn leads to *all* knowledge is not a Calvinist–Perkinsian prayer for proof of his elect ability to speak at one with the revealed Word of God, or even a qualified Arminian prayer for 'prevenient' grace—it is an unabashed prayer for direct prophetic, not to say apostolic, inspiration. Milton reinforces the extraordinary claims of his 'devout prayer' with reference to Isaiah, explicitly pointing out that his is a prayer for biblical prophetic appointment: for the 'eternall Spirit' to send 'out his Seraphim with the hallow'd fire of his Altar to touch and purify the lips of whom he pleases'—in this case Milton. Just as in the Midrashic fable about Moses's moment of prophetic election as a baby, the object pressed by angels to Isaiah's lips (Isaiah 6: 6–7) is a powerful metaphor for the double processes of purification and maiming which attend the gift of prophetic speech. Isaiah's coal, indeed, figures widely in Christian homiletic and theological literature as a symbol for the unmediated encounter between fallen man and divine presence. For Roman

---

[40] *YCP* vi. 671. It is important to note that Milton's Latin here ('vox non prolata semper, sed vel nulla, vel submissa, vel etiam gemitus in privatis precibus valent') mirrors in its elliptic economy the idea of unutterable prayer. Carey's 'inarticulate exclamations', meant to intensify his translation of 'gemitus', is unnecessary since he already has 'whispers' (also a very free, though apt, translation of 'vox . . . nulla').

Catholics, the link between muteness and purity was salutary,[41] and the ability of Isaiah's coal to purge the flesh from its lapsarian sins—and especially the impurities of fallen, post-Babel languages—traditionally lent itself to profound mediations on the administration of the Eucharistic sacrament. In Milton's England, apologists for the Catholic integrity of the English Church and its ceremonies similarly exploited the metaphor of the coal to insist on the salvific expediency of taking Holy Communion in an elevated manner which celebrated and sought to regulate the numinous character of the religious occasion. Here, for example, is Richard Field's *Of the Church* (1628): 'Let us come and receive the body of him that was crucified, let us partake of that divine burning coale that the fire of desire being kindled in us by that coale, may burne up our sinnes, and lighten our hearts, and that being changed into that devine fire, wee may become fire, and be in a sort deified, and made partakers of the divine nature.' And also Lancelot Andrewes in his 1598 St Giles sermon on Isaiah 6: 6–7: 'for the Angell tells the prophet, that his sinnes are not only taken away, but that it is done sacramentally, by the touching of a Cole, even as Christ assureth us, that we obtain remission of sinnes by the receiving of the Cup.'[42]

For most Puritans, on the other hand, Isaiah's burning coal is a metaphor for the purifying effect of grace on the contrite sinner. The inner, spiritual space of intimate and silent communication between fallen man and God, mediated through the agency of the Incarnated Christ, finds its typological resonance in the concrete mediation of a burning, searing object: Moses—the type—is literally unable to speak;

---

[41] See e.g. the 1605 English translation of the Dominican Counter Reformation theologian Giacomo Affinati's *The dumbe divine speaker, or: Dumbe speaker of Divinite A learned and excellent treatise, in praise of silence*: 'I purpose to deliuer the excellencie of Silence, and how it is much better to keepe silence, then to talke, in regard of the numberlesse offences, that men do fall into by their tongues only' ('To the Reader'). The offences Affinati has in mind here include not only blasphemy and lying, but more importantly the sort of doctrinal heresies associated with Protestant teachings. Perkins's superficially comparable discussion of 'holy silence' is therefore strikingly different from Affinati's, since it seeks to define the rational limits of 'godly speech', not to suppress speech altogether.

[42] Field, *Of the Church*, Book III, p. 56; McCullough, *Lancelot Andrewes: Selected Sermons and Lectures*, 143. For a discussion of this sermon in relation to Andrewes's literary sacramentalism see my 'Textual Sacraments: Capturing the Numinous in the Sermons of Lancelot Andrewes', *RS* 21: 5 (2007), 662–78. See also Julian Davies, *The Caroline Captivity of the Church*, 206.

Christ—the antitype—reduces the praying man to humble silence through the workings of grace. Whereas ceremonialists like Andrewes seek to emphasize the concreteness of the coal as a sacramental object, the English divines who continue in the Reformed traditions of Geneva and Zurich tend to insist, in the spirit of either Zwinglian 'memorialism' or Perkinsian 'parallelism', that the coal is merely a metaphor for the cleansing power of the Holy Ghost as it operates in the heart of believers who receive the Word clothed in the flesh of lapsarian languages.[43] The moderate Puritan divine Edward Leigh, for example, glosses in his *Annotations upon all the New Testament... vindicated from the false glosses of papists and hereticks* (1650) the word 'baptize' in Matthew 3: 11 in the following terms:

It must be expounded metaphorically, or rather prophetically with reference (say some) to the History of the fiery cloven tongues, the visible representation of the Holy Ghost on the day of Pentecost. *Acts* 2.2.3, or to *Esay* 6.6, 7 (saith *Capellus*) where one of the Seraphims is said to have taken a burning coal from the Altar, and with it to have touched the lips of the prophet, by which coal the Holy Ghost was signified, or his most efficacious force of purging, and by those words *thy iniquity is taken away*, inward baptisme (which wholly consists in the purgation and expiation of sinnes) is noted.[44]

Milton's interest in the image of the burning coal, however, both in the 'Nativity Ode' and in *Reason of Church-Government*, is not in his own state of sinfulness and regeneration in the conventional Protestant sense, but in his privileged moment, as it were, by the burning bush of prophetic appointment, where lapsarian words purged from their equivocal maladies are transformed into an inspired voice speaking unadulterated truth.

---

[43] English Reformers following Calvin in seeking a compromise between Lutheran consubstantiation and Zwinglian memorialism in their explication of reformed sacramental theology began to advocate either a process of 'symbolic parallelism' or 'symbolic instrumentalism' in the sacramental ritual. Parallelists such as William Perkins, for example, refined Zwingli and taught that there was a parallel, rather than strictly memorial, relationship between the sacramental symbols and their transcendental referents. Such parallelism, or as Perkins calls it, 'the sacramental relation' (*The Golden Chaine*, in *Works*, i. 72), was seen to be exclusively predicated on faith and to be efficacious only in assuring, or 'sealing' the elect in their Justification. See Gerrish, *Grace and Gratitude*, 167, and Spinks, *Sacraments, Ceremonies and the Stuart Divines*, p. xiii.

[44] Leigh, *Annotations upon all the New Testament*, 7–8.

Granted, most Perkinsian English Calvinists were taught to think of the office of preaching as prophetic in character. In *The Arte of Prophecying*, for example, Perkins influentially argued that 'Preaching the word is Prophecying in the name and roome of Christ, whereby men are called to the state of Grace, and conserved in it'.[45] Jameela Lares, for example, indeed goes out of her way to show that Milton is not attempting in the *Church-Government* digression to offer sacred poetry as an alternative to preaching, but rather to 'turn' poetry 'to account for the ministry'.[46] According to Lares, Milton criticizes Cavalier court poets and Laudian preachers for debasing and corrupting both the office of poetry and the office of preaching, and declares his intention to pursue both vocations as a united divine office of sacred, hortatory poetry. However, what is striking about Milton's claim of prophetic authority in the *Church-Government* passage is its unabashed literalness. In seeking to assert himself as divinely inspired poet-prophet destined for great things, Milton embraces the literalness of the type rather than its spiritual-symbolical meaning (for most Christians, indeed the only true *literal* meaning) of the antitype. Milton's poetic imagination already implicates him in a trope which sees him emerge as a prophet not in a metaphorical, evangelical sense, but in a literal biblical sense. This is also echoed in the third draft for the dramatic poem, or play, 'Adam Unparadised', recorded in Milton's Trinity Manuscript, where Moses is introduced as the speaker of the dramatic prologue (the manuscript has 'Moses προλογίζει'), who steps onto the imaginary stage and recounts 'how he assumed his (*a*) true bodie, that it corrupts not because of his with god in the mount declares the like of Enoch and Eliah, besides the purity of y(e) pl that certained pure winds, dues, and clouds præserve it from corruption'.[47] This sketch of Moses's opening speech is

---

[45] Perkins, *Works*, ii. 646.

[46] Lares, *Milton and the Preaching Arts*, 47. Lares's attempt (pp. 44–5) to also weaken the link between the type of secular soaring poet we find in Sidney's *Defence of Poesie* and the type of poetic soaring Milton envisions in the *Church-Government* passage is too circumstantial. While it is certainly true that the context for each writer's defence of poetry is different, and that Milton puts greater emphasis on sacred poetry as opposed to Sidney's emphasis on the virtuous character of individual poets, Milton was patently inspired by Sidney's discussion of the poetic imagination as creatively free and of having limitless potential in creating a 'second nature'. Milton would have also been alert to the sensitive way in which Sidney frames this discussion within a Protestant meditation on Original Sin.

[47] *Facsimile from the Manuscript in Trinity College*, 33.

significant because it highlights Milton's desire to impose Mosaic biblical authority on the original scheme of the tragic poem. Moses, the author of Genesis, would have stepped forward and alluded to his unique election as a prophet who saw the ineffable face of God on Mount Sinai. He would then have proceeded by explaining how it is that he 'assumed his true bodie' and came to stand before the audience, as it were, in the flesh: the 'purity' of the place has preserved his otherwise mortal body in a state of animated stasis. Significantly, Milton originally wrote in the manuscript 'assum'd *a* true bodie' and then scratched out the 'a' and inserted the word 'his' above it. Clearly, it was significant to him that his readers, or audience, imagined here nothing less than the great prophet himself standing before them. It is literally Moses who comes forward and speaks plain truth, not a type or an allegorical shadow of the archetypal prophet; not, indeed, an actor. The literalness of the meta-poetic trope here and its implications for Milton's poetic claims is crude but effective: Moses is preserved in a state of perpetual immortality not just by virtue of being rooted ontologically in the 'purity' of a sacred place, but also by virtue of being both the product and typological source for Milton's sacred inspired art.

Conceptually, however, the 'divine' gift of speech implied by such literal prophetic appointment, whether in the Trinity Manuscript draft or the *Church-Government* passage, can never be fully intelligible because the ultimate tenor of its transcendental metaphors is absolutely ineffable; to wish to have one's lips burned by a coal, to wish oneself free from the curse of Babel, is paradoxically to wish the loss of one's intelligible lapsarian speech, and Milton never willingly sacrifices intelligibility. While I think, then, that Lares is probably correct in pointing out Milton's desire to yoke the office of preaching onto his vatic calling as a poet, we ought to appreciate that the sort of inspired poetic preaching Milton is fantasizing about in this passage is one which in its aspiration for 'all utterance and knowledge' marries the Neoplatonic vatic tradition with a model of biblical prophecy which far exceeds the narrow salvific remit of the Word described by Perkins, for example, as 'the field which in the Preacher must containe himselfe'.[48] Indeed, Milton seems to have been aware that the type of overreaching activism implied in his 'devout prayer' would have been registered by many

---

[48] Perkins, *Works*, ii, 646.

contemporary readers as dangerously hubristic. When he claims in the *Church-Government* passage, therefore, to think it is no 'shame' to enter into a 'covnant with any knowing reader', he is deeply aware he *ought* to be feeling shame for what he is about to promise. To mitigate this, he couches his offer of a covenant in distinctly elect Genevan jargon. It is a solemn, holy covenant that Milton, an elect reader of Scripture, seals with fellow 'knowing *readers*', who 'know' presumably not only how to read and interpret the Bible, but also how to 'read' their own personal state of election. The sort of election Milton prays for, however, is not simply one which would entail recognizing his place among a fallen community of elect saints, but one which calls for his unique elevation above the common Puritan herd as an Isaiah- or Moses-like prophet feeding his flock of readers poetic manna from heaven.

PRETENDING TO SOAR

Having promised his elect readers in *Reason of Church-Government* a solemn 'work' wrought from 'devout prayer . . . to the eternall Spirit who can enrich with all utterance and knowledge, and sends out his Seraphim with the hallow'd fire of his Altar to touch and purify the lips of whom he pleases', Milton appears to make good his promise by opening the 1645 volume of his collected poems with his most solemn poem to date—'On the Morning of Christ's Nativity', written many years earlier in 1629, not long after his twenty-first birthday. This seems to be the confident, exuberant expression of a young poet assured of his divine calling. Stirred into what appears to be a conventional mode of religious devotion occasioned by the liturgical calendar ('This is the month, and this the happy morn', 1), the poet invokes the aid of the 'heavenly Muse' of Christian poetry to sing a 'humble ode' (24) to the infant Christ. There is a pause between the proem's third and fourth stanzas as the muse presumably discharges her service, and the resulting choral 'Hymn' follows. It is only natural to assume—as this is what the poem encourages us to do—that since in the proem the poet requests that his inspired Hymn may join its 'voice unto the angel quire' (27), the Hymn that follows necessarily does just that, at least in our imagination. This is supported, as Tuve and Broadbent have noted, by the poem's underlying celebration of the Incarnation.[49] As God descends into flesh, forsaking 'the courts of everlasting day' to choose 'with us a darksome house of mortal clay' (13–14), the merely mortal poet seeks to sing a hymn uttered by Isaiah-like prophetic lips, purged from semantic sin with hallowed fire from out of God's 'secret altar' (28). However, as I have argued so far, wanting to soar towards God in one's speech is one thing, succeeding is quite another. If Milton's hymning lips in the 'Nativity Ode' were truly touched with God's 'hallowed fire', 'unsufferable' as the light of the Son's glory, his resulting 'Hymn' would have been rendered radically unintelligible to those who dwell in 'a darksome house of mortal clay'. The conundrum would appear to be insoluble, but Milton nonetheless succeeds in altogether suppressing its implications in the 'Nativity Ode' by only ever *pretending* to soar.

The hymning poet certainly seems to project himself into the Ode as an all-knowing, all-uttering seer, effortlessly describing the universal impact of the Incarnation on Nature's lapsarian 'deformities', on the ocean and stars, on the rustic shepherds, on the pagan gods. He successfully avoids the crippling implications of his prophetic conundrum by *sounding* assertive, by beguiling the reader with the rhyming, alliterative music of his verse. Had he really wanted to, of course, Milton could have chosen the sacramental road of negative capability and paradox in an effort to re-create the numinous feeling of ineffable mystery at the heart of the Nativity narrative. Whereas Tuve indeed reads the poem as a celebration of a 'mystery' rather than a description and comment 'upon an event',[50] Broadbent rightly argues against Tuve that 'the direction Milton takes in his poem—and, traditionally, need not have taken—is away from the incarnate towards the ideate'.[51] In other words, Milton celebrates the 'mystery' of the Incarnation by demystifying its more personal and uncanny implications and Platonically drawing out its abstracted, universal essence. This was not the traditional road taken, for example, by the Catholic convert Richard Crashaw, whose near-contemporary Nativity poem, as its title declares, is 'An Hymn of the Nativity, sung as by the Shepherds'. After a rather

---

[49] Tuve, *Images and Themes in Five Poems by Milton*, 37–72; Broadbent, 'The Nativity Ode', in Kermode, *The Living Milton*, 12–31.

[50] Tuve, *Images and Themes*, 37.

[51] Broadbent, 'The Nativity Ode', 23.

lengthy antiphon between the shepherd Thyrsis and the chorus, the two voices are joined in Crashaw's Hymn into a 'full chorus' which proceeds to celebrate, and antithetically re-enact, the emotive power of the Incarnational paradox:

> Welcome, all wonders in one sight!
>   Eternitie shut in a span.
> Summer in winter. Day in night.
>   Heaven in Earth, and God in man.
> Great little one! whose all-embracing birth
> Lifts earth to heav'n, stoops heav'n to earth.
>
> (79–84)[52]

However, whereas Crashaw sings as one with the lowly, awestruck shepherds, Milton pretends in his Hymn to fly high above such mystified voices, observing rather from a great distance of effable clarity the 'shepherds on the lawn...simply chatting in a rustic row' (85–7). Unlike the soaring poet, these merely pastoral shepherds are limited in their intellectual capacity, their 'silly thoughts' unable to grasp the full universal magnitude of the Incarnation:

> Full little thought they then,
> That the mighty Pan
>   Was kindly come to live with them below;
> Perhaps their loves, or else their sheep,
> Was all that did their silly thoughts so busy keep.
>
> (88–93)

The hymning poet's remote point of view, observing the shepherds from a great distance, strongly implies that unlike such (sacramental) rustics our poet has ascended, angel-like, to the full measure of the Incarnational miracle, which in turn sustains the power of his poetic soaring. Milton does not deliberately trip, therefore, over his own words as Crashaw does in perplexed ecstasy, but assertively sings of the divine-human vistas his elect soaring has enabled him to observe, aloofly, outside space and time.

---

[52] Crashaw, 'A Hymn of the Nativity, Sung as by the Shepherds', in Colin Burrow (ed.), *Metaphysical Poetry*, 140.

Granted, the distinction in this context between pretending to soar and actually soaring might sound overly speculative and forced with reference to a poem whose very existence *as* a poem points to an act of imaginative, as opposed to real, flight. But what is uniquely interesting in the 'Nativity Ode' is that Milton allows the poetry itself to evoke the wide gap between potential and mediated poetic power and actual, unmediated prophetic power. Readings of the poem which ignore this gap consequently tell only half of its story. As J. Martin Evans notes in his argument with Lieb, Christopher, and others, the 'Nativity Ode' is a poem of absence—the poet's persona finally dissolves into the 'our' of the 'angel quire' as he recoils from his own sin and, at one with fallen Nature's 'naked shame, | Pollute with sinful blame' (40–1), seeks to hide his 'foul deformities' (44) under a show of a purified, heavenly choral song.[53] Evans goes on to conclude that Milton's Ode is a 'quintessentially Puritan' poem,[54] not on the grounds Christopher proposes, but because by stripping away all personal authority from its voice, Milton invites the reader to gaze directly at the babe in the manger without the use of any mediating agency. Such claims are problematic, however, because doctrinal Puritans tended to conflate the denial of mediation (other than the agency of the incarnated Word of Christ itself, of course) with an interiorized holiness which often insists on its elect singularity in the wider context of the community of saints, and Milton the poet never felt comfortable with the self-effacing implications of such communal singularity. Nevertheless, Evans's claim is convincing to the extent that here at least, more than anywhere else in Milton's early poems (with the exception of 'The Passion', of which more below), we find the youthful Milton meditating in a fairly conventional Protestant sense on his own state of sinfulness, but in a very unconventional, roundabout way. The result is a poem

[53] Evans, *The Miltonic Moment*, ch.1. Evans's reading rightly challenges that of critics who detect an uncomplicated Protestant Miltonic persona in the Ode's proem and hymn. Evans has in mind here especially Georgia Christopher's reading in *Milton and the Science of the Saints*, 23 ff. See also Lieb, 'Milton and the Kenotic Christology'. I think, however, that Evans insists too strongly on Milton's self-erasure in the poem. While his persona—especially an early prophetic persona—suffers in the poem from diminishing presence and power, it still insinuates itself into the poem, as my reading below will suggest, until its ultimate surrender to silence in the final stanza.
[54] Evans, *The Miltonic Moment*, 16 ff.

which both pretends to soar above sin, but also denies ever attempting such audacious feats; a poem which, as Richard Halpern argues persuasively, both assertively celebrates the miracle of the Incarnation, but also points to its babe-like, speechless infancy, where the *kenosis*, or the emptying of God, becomes also the emptying of the poet's as-yet infant (and hence relatively speechless) poetic powers.[55] Indeed, once we break from the spellbinding effect of Milton's fluid cadence and pay attention to what the voice in the poem actually *says*, we soon discover that the vocal power of the poet's flight is elusive and illusory.

To begin with, the opening invocation to the heavenly muse is *not*, as far as we can tell, ever answered. The invocation does not open with an imperative petition as in *Paradise Lost*'s 'Sing heavenly Muse', but with a hesitant enquiry:

> *Say* heavenly Muse, shall not thy sacred vein
> Afford a present to the infant God?
> Hast thou no verse, no hymn, or solemn strain,
> To welcome him to this new abode...
>
> (15–18, my emphasis)

Uncertain of his ability to sing at one with the muse, the poet desires of it first to 'say' in a language he can understand whether or not their joint song is at all possible, given his lowly lapsarian condition. The implicit answer to this question, at least in the poem before us, is no, not at the present time, not in your lifetime. The heavenly muse cannot afford any verse, or hymn, or solemn strain that fallen humans, elect though they may be, may ever hope to utter or understand so long as they dwell in a 'darksome house of mortal clay'. The muse's silence is indeed as loud as the poet's eager impatience in the proem's next and final stanza:

---

[55] R. Halpern, 'The Great Instauration: Imaginary Narratives in Milton's "Nativity Ode"', in Nyquist and Ferguson, *Re-Membering Milton*, 3–24. Halpern discusses Milton's fractured presence in the Ode in the Lacanian terminology of the 'mirror stage' and concludes that, 'in effect, the "Nativity Ode" reproduces the Lacanian practice of constructing an evolutionary narrative and then breaking it. It announces the birth of the subject into history by insisting that something *happens* there; and its own iconoclastic presence is the sign of that traumatic, poetic nativity' (p. 21). For a similar reading see Quint, 'Expectation and Prematurity in Milton's *Nativity Ode*', who also reads the poem as an admission that young Milton 'expected too much of himself, too much of poetry itself', even as he offers in the poem a 'pledge of greater things to come' (p. 216).

See how from far upon the eastern road
The star-led wizards haste with odours sweet:
O run, prevent them with thy humble ode,
And lay it lowly at his blessed feet;
Have thou the honour first, thy Lord to greet,
    And join thy voice unto the angel quire,
From out his secret altar touched with hallowed fire.

(22–8)

Milton exhorts the muse to lay her gift of a 'humble ode' at Christ's 'blessed feet', and thus to have the 'honour first, *thy* Lord to greet, | And join *thy* voice unto the angel quire' (my emphasis). But surely these lines should have read, '*my* Lord to greet, | And join *my* voice unto the angel quire'.[56] There is an ambiguity here that is as deliberate as it is destabilizing. Clearly, the interpretation of these lines depends on whom we understand to be the addressee of the impatient exhortations to 'see', 'run', 'prevent', and 'lay'. To allow for the standard reading of the poem in which it is assumed the muse assents to the poet's request, the exhortations must be read as referring to the ode about to be written: at one with the muse, the poet stirs *himself* into poetic action. Such a reading, however, supplies a positive answer to the third stanza's query which is never guaranteed in the poem. However, if we read the proem's third and fourth stanzas as one fluid utterance, then the exhortations to 'see', 'run', and 'prevent' continue the petition to the heavenly muse who is yet to supply her contribution to the poet's verse. Read in this way, stanza 4 shows the poet surrendering to the silence of the muse in deference to her divine authority, or as Gregory Goekjian aptly puts it, 'in his use of the muse, Milton asserts his authority even while denying it'.[57] Lurking beneath the assured presumption of the poet's voice is the tacit concession that it would be better for the muse, at least for the present, to sing with the angel choir what the poet actually knows himself to be incapable of. For his part, the poet of the opening stanzas desires instead to lay his limited, *written* poetic gift not at the feet of the infant Christ, but at the feet of an imagined lapsarian readership. And it is for the sake of this readership, as it were, that the

---

[56] Christopher, *Milton and the Science of the Saints*, 23, indeed, rewrites these lines to suit her argument and substitutes in square brackets 'his' for 'thy'.

[57] Goekjian, 'Deference, and Silence', 122. See also Belsey, *John Milton*, 20.

poet must remain in regenerate darkness. This darkness may be shot with some measure of elect light, but it is a rather pale light compared to 'that light unsufferable' of the Son's glory.

However, while the hymning voice in the poem insists on exhibiting the limited powers of its essentially lapsarian utterance, the actual drama of the Hymn celebrates the transformation of such lapsarian utterances into inexpressible heavenly music. The Hymn's opening sequence portrays the created universe as semantically in need of repair. Gripped in the lapsarian vice of post-Babel utterance, the humble poet portrays a world animated by speech that on a sudden becomes 'fair' and 'mild' at the immanent presence of the infant Incarnated *logos*. Thus we read how Nature 'woos the gentle air' with '*speeches* fair' (37–8), how the trumpet of war '*spake* not to the armed throng' (58), or how the winds '*whisper*' so that the '*mild* ocean' may now forget how to '*rave*' (64–7, my emphases throughout). This mellowing of cosmic utterances is then followed at the centre of the Hymn by a verse description of the song the angel choir is suddenly heard singing to the infant Christ. Crucially, in describing what the angels' song sounds like, the poet effectively positions himself outside the angel choir to which he had hoped to be joined in the proem.[58] And yet, by describing the impact of this song on the shepherds' hearts and ears, which, as the previous stanza establishes, are far more lowly than the poet's, Milton ingeniously sustains a semblance of detached prophetic authority while still conceding that he too cannot in actuality sing *with* the angel choir.

The otherwise absent Miltonic persona, therefore, suddenly positions itself in these stanzas, if only for a brief moment, as a prophet-like mediator standing within earshot of both heaven and earth, somewhere between the rustic shepherds' 'chatter' and the angels' song:

> When such music sweet
> *Their* heart and ears did greet,
>   As never was by mortal finger strook,
> Divinely-warbled voice
> Answering the stringed noise,
>   As all *their* souls in blissful rapture took:
> The air such pleasure loth to lose,
> With thousand echoes still prolongs each heavenly close.
>
>   (93–100, my emphases)

[58] Kerrigan, *The Prophetic Milton*, 200.

Milton's interest in music and musical figures is well documented.[59]
Song marries words with music in a way that rationally circumscribes the
affective powers of music within effable meaning. To impose words on
music is to transform the fundamentally ineffable power of music into an
articulated, syntactically linear utterance, memorably Platonized by
Milton in the later 'At a Solemn Music', in the invocation to the 'Blest
pair of sirens, pledges of heaven's joy, | Sphere-borne harmonious sisters,
Voice, and Verse' (1–2). John Carey has cogently argued that 'Voice' and
'Verse' do not represent the conjoined powers of 'music' and 'poetry',
as is often assumed, but rather the marriage of specifically unaccompa-
nied song with the measured rhythms of versification. As Carey points
out, 'the idea of song, and of song as opposed to songless music, was vital
to [Milton's] creative impulse and can be traced in the choices his
imagination made'.[60] This idea is clearly noticeable in the imaginative
choice Milton makes in the 'Nativity Ode', where the 'music sweet'
heard by the shepherds is immediately qualified as 'divinely-warbled
voice' singing either with or without words. Milton thus briefly insinuates his persona's belated hope for prophetic power into the stanza's
ambiguity by effectively allowing the possible interpretation of the
'divinely-warbled voice' as that of his own Hymn, pretending, if only
for a moment, to be at one with the angel choir. For the brief space of
two stanzas (IX–X) the poet thus toys with the possibility that it is in fact
his inspired Hymn which the shepherds are actually listening to, and
which potentially at least 'Could hold all heaven and earth in happier
union' (108).

Two stanzas later, however, we learn that the 'divinely-warbled voice'
the shepherds hear is in fact not the poet's but that of 'The helmèd
cherubim | And swordèd seraphim' who appear amid 'a globe of circular
light', 'Harping in loud and solemn quire, | With *unexpressive* notes to
heaven's new-born heir' (109–16, my emphasis). The adjective 'unexpressive', first coined by Shakespeare in *As You Like It*, III. ii. 10 to
capture (for all the comedy involved) the ineffability of intense desire,

---

[59] Spaeth's *Milton's Knowledge of Music* remains the definitive study on this subject.
See also Hollander, *The Untuning of the Sky*, 315–31; Spitzer, *Classical and Christian
Ideas of World Harmony*, 103–7; and the essays by L. Stapleton and J. Hollander in
Barker, *Milton: Modern Essays in Criticism*, 31–57.
[60] Carey, 'Milton's Harmonious Sisters', 247.

normally denotes that which is inexpressible. It can also mean, however, that which is itself incapable of expressing anything semantically meaningful. While Shakespeare's Orlando only has the former meaning in mind, in Milton's use of the adjective both meanings uneasily coexist. The seraphim's song is ultimately 'unexpressive' in a prelapsarian, pre-Babel sense, in that it does not express itself at all in normal language. The brief marriage of the hymning voice and the angel choir in stanzas IX and X thus disintegrates on the turning of this one ambiguous adjective, as stanzas XI through XVI gradually deflate the poet's claims of prophetic power. The poet's voice—the one we are actually reading and listening to in our head—is clearly expressive, while the angels' song, as the poet now concedes, is not.

Milton's timid prophetic persona thus begins to lower, imperceptibly, the height of its ambition, and moves from asserting the illusory union between its voice and that of the singing angels, to conceding the actual gulf between them. Having drawn attention to this gulf between the two voices, vying against each other within the Hymn, the hesitant lapsarian voice of the mere man lurking behind the inspired confidence of the prophetic poet begins at this point to intrude into the Hymn by parenthetically qualifying its vocal illusion of power: 'Such music (as 'tis said) | Before was never made' (117), or 'Once bless our human ears, | (If ye have power to touch our sense so)' (127). Parenthesis then fluidly gives way to open statement, as actual power recedes into deferred millenarian promise: 'For if such holy song | Enwrap our fancy long, | Time will run back, and fetch the age of gold' (133–5). Retreating back again into his 'darksome house of mortal clay', the poet plummets rather than soars, looking ahead with the rest of lapsarian humanity towards Judgement Day, when 'to those ychained in sleep, | The wakeful trump of doom must thunder through the deep' (155–6).

The Hymn, however, does not end here. As if unwilling to finish on a note of conceded weakness, the poet's voice gathers strength again as it asserts its power over that which lies in pagan ignorance beyond the salvific pale of the Word. The positioning of the traditional Nativity component of the 'cessation of the oracles' at this juncture in the Hymn allows Milton's prophetic persona to once again reassert its qualified control and to begin soaring again by picking on its pagan inferiors. Once again the imagery reverts from that of music and song to that of mere speaking voices. In contrast to the favourable mellowing of speech in the opening sequence of the Hymn, however, the impact of the Incarnation and its attendant 'unexpressive' angelic song on the pagan gods is stark. The descent of the divine *logos* into the world renders the pagan oracles 'dumb', stripping their voices of any coherent expression. Since the poet, however, clearly does have words with which to describe the vocal violation of the pagan gods, he once again positions himself outside his subject, describing in triumphant succession a host of Graeco-Roman and Semitic idols in various postures of incoherent vocal defeat—shrieking, weeping, lamenting, sighing, and mourning.

Empowered by his parading of humiliated and defeated gods, tightly imprisoned within the power of his rhyming metre, itself immensely free and liberated, the poet finally ends his Hymn with yet another deliberately ambiguous address, perhaps to the reader, perhaps to himself, perhaps to the muse:

> But see the virgin blest,
> Hath laid her babe to rest.
>   Time is our tedious song should here have ending,
> Heaven's youngest teemed star,
> Hath fixed her polished car.
>   Her sleeping Lord with handmaid lamp attending.
> And all about the courtly stable,
> Bright-harnessed angels sit in order serviceable.
>
> (237–44)[61]

Perhaps 'our' song, as Evans suggests, is inclusive of reader, poet, muse, and angels, its 'tediousness' pointing to its overall spent choral power. 'Tedious' is a form of *occupatio*, but for all of Milton's improvisatory flair and the impetuous overflow of his alternating rhyme-scheme, there is an undercurrent of strain as the poet struggles to sustain his prophetic voice alongside the 'unexpressive' song of the angel choir. Beneath the Ode's vibrant playfulness, there is an inescapable sense that both reader and poet are left feeling hoarse with the effort. Even so, the illusory

---

[61] In the 1673 edition of his collected poems Milton revised the punctuation of this stanza, amending the full stop after 'car' into a comma, and the full stop after 'attending' into a colon.

power of the poet's utterance has had its desired effect, and we the fallen readers are at least left feeling elated in the comforting image of sympathetic stars and serviceable angels attending to 'our' well-earned rest as well as to that of the God-man 'babe' in the manger. Even though the poet has actually conceded that what he had in mind all along was beyond his poetic reach, he nonetheless leaves us with an unqualified sense of power at the occasion of a traditional Nativity scene made universally glorious through the sheer audacity of his poetic will.

The implicit straining of the prophetic voice in 'Nativity Ode' turns into outright crisis in the poetic *aporia* which is 'The Passion'. Even stranger is the fact that Milton chose to publish it at all. Contemporary readers of *Poems 1645* would have read through the 'Nativity Ode' and the two subsequent paraphrased Psalms, which, as Milton's headnote declares, were 'done by the Author at fifteen years old', noting the tender age in which the poet accomplished such admirable poetic feats. After such clear signs of early poetic promise Milton may have intended his readers to forgive the ensuing poetic oddity of 'The Passion', which, as the 1645 postscript declares, was abortive: 'This subject the author finding to be above the years he had when he wrote it, and nothing satisfied with what was begun, left it unfinished.' But the positioning of the poem in the volume soon after the 'Nativity Ode', and the addition of the explanatory postscript, only account for what Milton expected his readers to do with the unfinished poem once they read it in its published context. It does not explain why Milton wanted to publish it in the first place.

If my argument about Milton's early fear of ineffable mystery so far holds, one or two probable answers suggest themselves. First, Milton's early failure to grapple with the subject of the Passion was in itself clearly significant to him. It was especially significant in the context of his projected poetic ambition to tackle with complete verbal perspicuity subject-matter which traditionally falls under the conceptual categories of the ineffable and the numinous. I suspect Milton's failure to grapple with the subject of the Passion had little to do with the immaturity at the time of his poetic talent. The Passion of the Christ is far more mysterious than the Incarnation which precedes it. It fulfils the grim promise of the Incarnational intimacy. It reminds Christians what sinful creatures they are, and how great is the love of their Creator who would suffer unspeakable torture and death to atone for their sinfulness. The

Passion is meant to render the lapsarian voice dumb, to humble it in reflective silence, to overwhelm it with paradox, and Milton, ever anxious to assert his voice, was simply not equipped, temperamentally, to sing of God's suffering on the cross. The experience likely humbled him, however, and it is for the sake of communicating this redemptive sense of humility that he may have desired to share this experience with his readers. There is, however, another, strictly conceptual, poetic reason for the inclusion of 'The Passion' in *Poems 1645*. The failure of 'The Passion' poignantly qualifies the limited success of the 'Nativity Ode' which precedes it, not, as Louis Martz argues, by pointing to the earlier Ode's poetic 'immaturity',[62] but to the illusory character of its vocal power. 'The Passion' is important, therefore, not only for being a failure, but also in the way it shows itself failing.

The received wisdom on 'The Passion' is that the deeply irrational nature of its mystery and Milton's refusal to take the road of paradox results in the highly self-referential, tortured tone of the poem: 'my song', 'my flattered fancy', 'my woe', 'my sorrows', 'my plaining verse', and so on. As Lewalski surmises, Milton's 'Protestant imagination was not stirred by the Passion, and he found no way in elegy, as he had in the Nativity Ode, to move from the personal and local to the universal. So his conceits become ever more extravagant and the text becomes painfully self-referential.'[63] To say that the Passion did not stir Milton's imagination because he was a Protestant oversimplifies the problem, to put it mildly. The subject of the Passion certainly did not fail to stir the devotional imaginations of such Protestant sacramentalists as Donne in his '*La Corona*', 'The Cross', 'Upon the Annunciation and the Passion falling upon one day', or 'Good Friday Riding Westward' (to name only four obvious examples), and Herbert's 'The Sacrifice', 'The Agony', 'Redemption', 'The Thanksgiving', and of course 'The Reprisal', with its similar admission of failure: 'I have considered it, and find | There is no dealing with thy mighty passion' (1–2). What I suspect Lewalski probably means is that Milton's Reformed sensibility and his fear of ineffable mystery meant he was more comfortable writing about the Incarnation and the Nativity than about the Passion. However, the Passion clearly did stir Milton's Protestant imagination, otherwise

---

[62] Martz, *Poet of Exile*, 51.
[63] Lewalski, *The Life of John Milton*, 38. For a similar view see Parker, *Milton*, i. 71–2.

he would not have attempted this poem to begin with. What is more, Lewalski assumes that the self-referential pain of the poem results from Milton's difficulty with the subject, when in fact, as I would argue, it is the other way round: it is Milton's insistence on a peculiarly conceited self-reference which causes him pain and ultimately fails the poem.

The opening stanza of 'The Passion' explicitly points to the earlier 'Nativity Ode' and invites comparisons with it:

> Erewhile of music, and ethereal mirth,
> Wherewith the stage of air and earth did ring,
> And joyous news of heavenly infant's birth,
> My muse with angels did divide to sing;
> But headlong joy is ever on the wing,
>   In wintry solstice like the shortened light
> Soon swallowed up in dark and long out-living night.
>
> (1–7)

This one stanza tells the entire story of the poem's failure. The voice unequivocally identifies itself with that of the allegedly soaring poet of the 'Nativity Ode'. There is a sense of false confidence, however, as the poet seeks to carry over the apparent success of the earlier poem's beguiling utterance into a contemplation of the deeply ineffable mystery of the Passion. The voice alludes to the universal scope of vision in the earlier poem, where the 'stage of air and earth did ring' with the power of his song. The next line, perhaps the most significant in the poem, then seeks to suppress the illusory character of the earlier ode's power by asserting the unity and harmony of the human voice sharing his song with that of the angels—voices which in the earlier poem were effectively presented as distinct and remote from one another. The gulf between the divine and the human lurking as a suppressed presence beneath the earlier poem's assertive diction is almost casually dismissed as the poet claims that it was in fact '*My* muse' who 'with angels did *divide* to sing' (my emphasis). 'Divide to sing' is a remarkable coinage in this context. As Carey points out in his notes to the poem, 'divide' 'can mean execute "divisions" or rapid melodic passages, and "share" (with the angels)'.[64] This ambiguity is indicative, moreover, of the inherent

---

[64] *CSP* 123.

dichotomy between the two voices. Although the two voices may appear to share in one song, they are nonetheless divided. 'My muse' did sing and 'I' did sing are not, after all, the same thing, just as the 'song' the poet does end up writing down in the 'Nativity Ode' is divided into quantifiable metrical verses whereas the angels' 'unexpressive' song clearly is not.[65]

This expression of doubt has, however, a peculiar effect. Rather than deflating the poet's hope of coherent song and stimulating an outpouring of paradox, the poet becomes obsessed with the sound of his own voice. Milton does not attempt to replicate his strategy from the 'Nativity Ode' and merely move from the personal to the universal. Instead, he impossibly attempts to subsume the universal into the personal as if to swallow up altogether Isaiah's burning coal of prophetic utterance. The poet in 'The Passion' desperately snatches the 'harp' from the hands of the 'harping' cherubim and seraphim of the earlier ode, as he declares: 'For now to sorrow must I tune *my* song, | And set *my harp* to notes of saddest woe' (8–9, my emphases). Egged on by his anxious desire to sound sublime and prophetic, the poet attempts to graft the mystery of the Passion onto his own lapsarian voice, so that once again he may assert vocal control in the face of a deeply ineffable religious mystery. However, without a minimum degree of humble distance between the authority of his poetic voice and its subject, Milton is unable to create the numinous space necessary for the idea of the Passion to expand its ineffable presence in the poem. His anxious ego intrudes with such force that the reverberating sounds of its utterance divest the Passion of its essential numinous character entirely.

---

[65] On the symbolic significance in Milton's poetry of sacred images of division and disjunction see Budick, *The Dividing Muse*, esp. ch. 2, pp. 13–31. My own analysis of the 'Nativity Ode' and 'The Passion' is in many ways complementary to Budick's analysis of images of separation in these poems that promote an idea of mystical silence that somehow becomes a vital differentiated component of the divine harmonies produced by the 'angel quire'. Budick traces these ideas of 'sacred disjunction' to Clement's and Philo's discussion of the dividing *logos* and their allegorical interpretation of the Mosaic blueprint for the 'mercy seat' above the Ark of the Covenant in Exod. 25: 17–22. Milton apparently alludes to the mercy seat of the Ark in ll. 143–4 of the 1645 version of the 'Nativity Ode: 'Th'enamelled arras of the rainbow wearing, | And mercy set'. It should be noted, however, that in his revision of these lines for the 1673 edition Milton weakened this allusion by cutting out the explicit reference to 'Th'enamelled arras' of the Ark. Budick explains this away by implying that Milton hated being obvious.

Unable, therefore, to create an illusion of power as he had done in the 'Nativity Ode', the poet turns to nervous petition for alternative agencies of poetic inspiration. He reflects how he will need 'softer airs' and 'softer strings' (27), and the guiding powers of a different muse (since the heavenly muse from the earlier ode has once again deserted him). He appeals to personified 'night best patroness of grief' (29), and when that fails, invokes Ezekiel's chariot, 'That whirled the prophet up at Cedar flood' (37). This last invocation is particularly interesting since it alludes to a rich mystical-kabbalistic tradition which is centrally concerned with the idea of soaring, or ascending towards the ineffable Godhead. Moreover, as Michael Lieb has shown, there is a direct link between early kabbalistic readings of the first chapter of Ezekiel and what is known as *merkabah* ('chariot') mysticism, with the later syncretic Neoplatonism of Pico, Reuchlin's Christian kabbalistic treatises, Francesco Giorgio's *De Harmonia Mundi Totius Cantica Tria* (1525), through Bruno, Henry More, and even—which is most significant to Milton—Alexander Gil's *The Sacred Philosophie of the Holy Scripture* (1635).[66] More and Gil's contribution to the ubiquitous presence of *merkabah* symbolism in the English religious psyche is probably too late to be of direct relevance to 'The Passion', which is putatively dated to 1630, but we would do well to remember, as Lieb points out, that 'although Milton never uses the term *merkabah* as such, its pervasiveness throughout Renaissance Neoplatonic thought renders its influence inescapable'.[67] That influence is best characterized not as indebtedness to a well-defined philosophical and mystical idea, but as a biblical humanist *topos* which becomes in the period, like Jacob's ladder, a symbol for Neoplatonic ascent.

The strange and elaborate imagery making up Ezekiel's chariot vision—the four-faced, four-winged *chayyoth* ('animals' or 'living beings', translated by the AV as 'creatures' and usually interpreted as cherubim), the wheel within a wheel, the ring full of eyes, the spectrum of dazzling colours—become loaded kabbalistic-Neoplatonic metaphors in the hands of Pico and his disciples, who then deploy these metaphors in various numerical speculations and formulae about creation and deity and the possible mystical movement between them. In 'The Passion' Milton presumably invokes the Ezekiel image in an effort to yoke Ezekiel's prophetic voice to

[66] See Lieb, 'Encoding the Occult'.
[67] Ibid. 65–6.

his own lament for the crucified Christ. Like the previous appeal to apostrophized 'night', the aim is to be consumed by a 'holy vision' wherein the poet-prophet's 'soul' might fruitfully reflect on the Passion 'In pensive trance, and anguish, and ecstatic fit' (41–2). The entire Ezekiel sequence, however, is itself consumed by implicit frustration as the two prophetic models of soaring cancel out one another: the solipsistic Hermetic poet vies with the passive biblical agent of transcendental prophecy for space and authority. As a result, an indeterminate Miltonic persona eagerly anticipates ineffable rapture at the prospect of being swept away by 'some transporting cherub' (37) who might bear the poet, Ezekiel-like, to 'where the towers of Salem stood, | Once glorious towers, now sunk in guiltless blood' (39–40), but simultaneously resists this rapture. After all, his carefully constructed tears, 'fitly fall[ing] in ordered characters', are far too rehearsed and orderly in their regular metrical cadence to render the inarticulate loss of emotional and verbal control that comes with genuine 'ecstasy' and 'anguish' the poet so mechanically hopes for.

The result is defeat. All that remains is for the poet to toy with the conceit that perhaps he ought to sing in solitude on some 'mountain wild', where

> The gentle neighbourhood of grove and spring
> Would soon unbosom all their echoes mild,
> And I (for grief is easily beguiled)
>   Might think the infection of my sorrows loud,
> Had got a race of mourners on some pregnant cloud.
>
>   (50–5)

Surrendering to his solipsistic impulse, the poet is left alone with the echoes of his own voice and muses that maybe if he shouted loud enough heaven would at least reward him with the conceit of its response, a welcome fancy. This too, however, is denied as the poem recedes into an uneasy silence and abruptly ends, a proem without a hymn. For what is supposedly an unfinished poem, this is a rather powerful ending. As it stands, 'The Passion' is a remarkable expression of forced un-expression, the last stanza of its orphaned proem in many ways encapsulating the essence of young Milton's prophetic conundrum. Of course, the nature of this conundrum dictates that, given Milton's sense of poetic destiny, such a failure could not have been allowed to speak for itself, and so Milton added in 1645 the postscript which declares it to be an unfinished poem, a temporary setback.

'The Passion' is followed by the two experimentally 'metaphysical', so-called English odes, 'On Time' and 'Upon the Circumcision'. Of the two, 'Upon the Circumcision' is of some interest if only for the relationship it bears to the two previous liturgical poems, the 'Nativity Ode' and 'The Passion'. It is significant that Milton places 'Upon the Circumcision' after and not before 'The Passion', as the liturgical calendar would have dictated otherwise. It shows him returning to the more manageable devotional terrain of the Nativity, taking a step back from the failure of 'The Passion' to reassert the potential and hoped-for power of his prophetic voice. In many ways 'Upon the Circumcision' is a compromise. Its opening lines echo those of 'The Passion', looking back to the 'Nativity Ode' and the poet's 'triumphant song | First heard by happy watchful shepherds' ear' (3–4). The shorter, compact poem that follows, however, is decidedly un-Miltonic in character and the most 'metaphysical' of Milton's early collection. Inverted antithetical lines such as 'O mere exceeding love or law more just? | Just law indeed, but more exceeding love!' (15–16) expose the prophet-to-be as mere 'frail dust' (19), a humble mortal far removed from the 'flaming powers and winged warriors bright' (1) invoked at the outset of the poem in a weak moment of lapsarian prayer. Viewed in isolation, 'Upon the Circumcision' is neither more nor less experimental than the 'Nativity Ode'—it is simply another poetic attempt to strike an appropriate religious tone when dealing with deeply spiritual, even numinous subject-matter. However, when we read 'Upon the Circumcision' in the sequence of *Poems 1645*, we come to it with the highs and lows of the 'Nativity Ode' and 'The Passion' fresh in our mind, so that suddenly it seems that in *this* poem there is neither a sense of prophecy nor a sense of verbal power. What begins with the 'Nativity Ode' as a promising— and one might add, daring—attempt to produce solemn verse with 'all utterance and all knowledge', recedes several religious poems later into diverting 'metaphysical' prayer.

STANDING STILL

If the first important step towards resolving a problem is to admit to oneself there *is* a problem, then 'At a Solemn Music', following in the 1645 volume immediately after such problematic poems as the

'Nativity Ode', 'The Passion', and 'Upon the Circumcision', emerges in the overall context of *Poems 1645* as precisely such an admission. Positioned as it is in the volume, 'At a Solemn Music' can be likened to a deep intake of breath, a pause for poetic and intellectual reflection. Unlike the previous poems, 'At a Solemn Music' celebrates nothing. The single imperative sentence making up (at least in its published form)[68] the first twenty-four lines of the poem creates what critic Russell Fraser has aptly described as 'a stirring panorama, resonant but static' where 'nothing happens'.[69] 'At a Solemn Music' does not reach out after an unattainable mode of poetic utterance, but seeks rather to explain why such modes of poetic expression are, at present, unavailable to the poet who has sung with such difficulty on the Nativity and the Circumcision, and with outright failure on the Passion.

'At a Solemn Music' is perhaps the most self-explanatory of Milton's early poems about the potential powers of inspired poetic song. It portrays solemn poetry as song or 'solemn music', imperfectly mirroring but nonetheless resonating with the harmony of God's prelapsarian vocal creation. Its reference to the harmonious and continuous song of the 'thousand choirs' of the 'cherubic host' (12) in the presence of an enthroned God mirrors the 'music sweet' described in the 'Nativity Ode'. It paints, moreover, an eschatological picture of God's elect as the 'just spirits that wear victorious palms, | Hymns devout and holy psalms | Singing everlastingly' (4–6), accompanied by the angels in heaven on 'immortal harps of golden wires' (13). The nuanced title, '*At* a Solemn Music', as opposed to, say, 'Of Solemn Music', captures the poem's occasional mood. The adverbial preposition 'at' denotes the lapsarian occasion of the poem's creation as opposed to the 'Solemn Music' it describes. The poet hears a melody—perhaps someone singing, perhaps a concert—and in a fleeting moment of transient rapture is transported to heaven with visions of a decreed future, temporarily deferred. This brief moment is in turn frozen in time within the mimetic grip of the poet's verse, which thus analogically creates an imperfect written simulacrum of

---

[68] What was to become in *Poems 1645* a single uninterrupted sentence is divided in the final third draft of the poem in the Trinity MS into two sentences with a full stop at l. 16. On the possible millenarian significance of this revision see Moschovakis, 'Great Period'.

[69] Fraser, 'On Milton's Poetry', 189.

the 'Solemn Music' it lovingly describes. Unlike Aquinas's theory of analogical predication, this poetic analogy is radically imperfect in the pseudo-Dionysian sense outlined by Cusanus, similar in principle to Cusanus' theory of a polygon trapped within a circle. Milton's poem can only describe the idea of 'Solemn Music' by using the analogy of created human music, but such music can never fully represent the transcendental *idea* of 'Solemn Music' to which it aspires. Moreover, the poem drives home the impact of Original Sin on our ability to participate in non-lapsarian heavenly harmonies: because Adam and Eve brought discord to God's harmonious creation by transgressing, 'we on earth' consequently sing or talk with lapsarian voices that are discordant. The first-person pronouns of 'The Passion' dissolve in 'At a Solemn Music' into the humbly fraternal 'we' of the Genevan community of saints, so 'That *we* on earth with undiscording voice | May rightly answer that melodious noise' (17–18, my emphasis). In short, 'At a Solemn Music' may be read as a clear poetic expression of Milton's early anxiety about his prophetic calling. Its static contemplation appears to explain why 'The Passion' was a failure, and exposes the vocal activism of the 'Nativity Ode' as divided against itself.

However, as usual with Milton, things are not as simple as they originally seem. Does Milton truly erase his own poetic persona from the inclusive 'we' of the closing lines? Is Milton's identification with fallen humanity sincere, or is it reluctant? Once we attend to the poem's uneven structure, the latter rather than the former emerges as the more likely interpretation. The poem's underlying message about the gulf between the divine and the human capacity to produce expressive song is reiterated twice in the poem in very similar terms. Both instances are identical in content but crucially differ in their syntactical, and hence conceptual, function in the poem. The central uninterrupted sentence of the first twenty-four lines is sealed with an earnest prayer:

> O may *we* soon again renew that song,
> And keep in tune with heaven, till God ere long
> To his celestial consort us unite,
> To live with him, and sing in endless morn of light.
>
> (25–8, my emphasis)

This prayer is addressed to God. The 'we' of line 25 is inclusive of both poet and fallen humanity. This is the humble praying Milton, at one with his fellow man, praying for the millenarian honour of being among those elect who 'ere long' shall be united to the 'celestial consort' through the ability to sing as the angels in the unmediated presence of God. As Fish points out, this last 'till' may imply 'not in this lifetime', for if the poet were to be joined *now* to the celestial consort his own individual poetic voice would be drowned forever by the heavenly harmony: 'Properly understood, then, the wish that we be united with God's celestial "consort"... is a wish that we not be heard, that we utter sounds in such a way as to remain silent. The man who wants to sing alone is like a man who wants to stand alone, raised by his own merit to some bad eminence.'[70] Fish's analysis here would seem to support the type of theological crisis I have argued Milton exposed himself to by seeking to clothe his vatic persona in biblical prophetic robes. Fish appears to argue almost the exact same thing when he places his reading of 'At a Solemn Music' within the wider context of what he terms Milton's 'impulse to action', which, as Fish assumes, is always 'sinful because it has its source in a desire to be separate, to break away from the corporate existence of those who live and move in God'.[71] However, this is not as simple as Fish allows. To begin with, the type of separation implied in Milton's activism, as I have argued in relation to the *Church-Government* passage about 'devout prayer', would have been perceived as sinful only by those who live and move not 'in God', but in God's Word. This is precisely, moreover, why Milton must insist on his personal predestined appointment as a prophet—so that he alone among the elect *would* be made separate in his ability to sing as one with the fully unmediated Word.

For example, the first time Milton appears to communicate the same idea in the poem, he embeds it into the poem's main prolonged sentence:

> That *we* on earth with undiscording voice
> May rightly answer that melodious noise;
> As once *we* did, till disproportioned sin
> Jarred against nature's chime, and with harsh din

[70] Fish, *How Milton Works*, 312.   [71] Ibid.

Broke the fair music that all creatures made
To their great Lord, whose love their motion swayed
In perfect diapason, whilst they stood
In first obedience, and their state of good.

(17–24, my emphases)

This clause qualifies the opening invocation to the 'Blest pair of sirens',
'Voice, and Verse'. However, unlike the prayer with which Milton
concludes the poem, the Miltonic persona here is implicitly and cleverly
separate from the 'we on earth' of line 17. By shrewdly invoking at the
outset of the poem Voice and Verse as remote, transcendental ideas, the
poet effectively demystifies his own poetic ability to marry the human
singing voice with metrical verses. When the poet then goes on to enlist
the power of such Platonized 'Sphere-borne harmonious sisters', he
pretends to be doing so for the collective benefit of mankind, so that
Voice and Verse may 'to *our* high-raised phantasy present, | That
undisturbèd song of pure concent' (5–6, my emphasis).[72] But surely
the one who in this case presents to his readers' 'high-raised phantasy'
the potential powers of heaven's 'undisturbèd song' is the poet, who, in
writing a poem about music, marries the 'sounds' of voice and verse in
the poem to begin with.[73] By thus implicitly presenting himself as able
to produce quasi-divine harmonies, the poet marks himself as separate
from ordinary mankind—indeed, as a prophet. In theory at least, 'At a
Solemn Music' succeeds where the 'Nativity Ode' falters because it
merely suggests the poet's potential to achieve an 'undiscording voice'
without the burden of having to perform something that he at least
knows to be impossible. Young Milton may have been unable to prove
his ability to reproduce heaven's ineffable music in practice, but he
could certainly assert his desire and theoretical ability to do so. Although
it may not have been much of a solution to his underlying prophetic

---

[72] The 1645 version of the poem should read 'undisturbèd song of pure *content*'. As
Carey notes, however, all drafts of the poem in the Trinity MS read 'concent', the variant
which also appears in the final edition of 1673. This and other evidence suggests that the
word 'content' in all 1645 editions of the text was probably a printer's error that Milton
corrected in 1673. See *CSP* 168.

[73] That verse can produce 'sound' on its own is, of course, extremely odd, but as
Carey speculates, its sound may have been one which 'Milton heard only in his head—a
Platonic idea of sound, pre-sonic, intellectual' (Carey, 'Milton's Harmonious Sisters',
251).

conundrum, allowing his prophetic persona space in which to make such an assertion made it possible for him to proceed and demonstrate in the remainder of the volume his considerable prophetic as well as poetic potential.

It is significant that there are no other overtly religious poems in the 1645 volume after 'At a Solemn Music', whether in English or in Latin. Having subtly suppressed the vexed problems of his vatic authority and reasserted his prophetic potential, Milton quietly drops the subject. The rest of the volume is arranged in this context as a pleasant diversion from the troubled religious sequence of the opening. When Milton does return here and there to the themes of heavenly music and the human singing voice, he does so in the manageably lapsarian realms of pastoral. Such is the Genius of the Wood's digression in *Arcades* on the power of music and the 'heavenly tune, which none can hear | Of human mould with gross unpurgèd ear' (72–3). In the context of the 1645 volume, these words expose the Arcadian Genius of the Wood as a thinly disguised pastoral manifestation of the defeated Miltonic persona from the earlier religious poems. Masquerading as the local deity of an imaginary landscape peopled by woodland nymphs and shepherds, the Miltonic Genius of *Arcades*, though powerful within the pastoral realm of his fabulous wood, is significantly weakened at the thought of heaven. In *A Masque Presented at Ludlow Castle*, published as the concluding English poem of the volume, Milton can be seen to develop this theme into a complex dramatic *agon* between two fleshed-out characters: the chaste Christian Lady whose inner, distinctly Protestant spiritual power manifests itself ultimately in song and the *refusal* to speak, and the lascivious pagan enchanter Comus, who is a master of rhetorical manip- ulation and who assaults the Lady's virginal ears with 'well-placed words of glozing courtesy | Baited with reasons not unplausible' (161–2).[74]

Particularly poignant in the context of these ideas is the Lady's song to Echo midway through the masque, which alludes to the possible power of divinely inspired song, gathering strength amid the many dangers of the dark and tangled fallen world, to tame, redeem, and spiritually overwhelm even a pagan enchanter descended from Homer's witch Circe (the genealogy of Comus is Milton's invention), who is

---

[74] On the importance of gendered silence and its relation to early modern notions of female chastity see Graham, 'Virgin Ears'.

clearly associated with the bestializing and dehumanizing powers of licentious musical rapture. The Lady's song *sounds* to Comus distinctly otherworldly and ineffable. Upon hearing its 'raptures', the pagan enchanter notes how the Lady's voice does not break the silence as normal speech would, but 'sweetly' floats, extraordinarily, 'upon the wings | Of silence, through the empty-vaulted night | At every fall smoothing the raven down | Of darkness till it smiled' (248–51). As the experience of hearing the Lady sing overwhelms him, Comus wonders aloud, 'Can any mortal mixture of earth's mould | Breath such divine enchanting ravishment?' (243–4). Initially, this statement sounds like a straightforward rhetorical question: the apparent heavenly power of the Lady's song suggests to Comus that she is in fact no mere 'mortal mixture of earth's mould'. This reading is supported within the masque both by the abstracted Platonic terms in which the Elder Brother describes his sister's potential power to resist temptation, and within the brief space of the song's immediate effect on Comus. In the grip of a momentary epiphany, the pagan enchanter is moved to concede that 'such a sacred and home-felt delight | Such sober certainty of waking bliss | I never heard till now' (261–3).

As Carey points out in his notes to *A Masque*, the use of an Echo scene was a common plot-device in Elizabethan and Jacobean drama, where an Echo persona repeats the ends of a character's sentences (Carey cites as a typical example the graveyard scene in Webster's *The Duchess of Malfi*, V. iii). The use of an Echo figure, however, is also a common pastoral trope used to intensify a speaker's sense of grief and loss, for example in the exchange between Philisides and Echo in Sidney's 'The Second Eclogues' to the *Old Arcadia*. Milton, however, characteristically moulds and reshapes both traditions to make an intellectual statement that is uniquely his own. The song to Echo was probably inserted into the masque to allow Alice Egerton to display her singing, and as William Shullenberger shows in his compelling analysis of the Lady's spiritual rite of passage in the masque, for all its 'sweetness' the song to Echo is 'a lyric of strenuous redemptive imagination'.[75] Indeed, the song is the most distinctly Miltonic feature of the masque, where it is clear that Milton allowed himself to explore a theme very close to his

---

[75] Shullenberger, 'Into the Woods'.

own heart, namely the relationship between sacred song, youthful chastity and promise, and the threats of fallen discourse that can overwhelm the fragile hope of realizing such promise. John Hollander rightly points out that the song to Echo is crucially 'self referential in two senses', in that it addresses 'itself to its own resonating effects' as well as 'covertly refer[ring] to the Lady herself and her own predicament'.[76] This double self-reference is important; it allows the Lady's song to assume a complex body of ideas that is only indirectly related to the theme of female chastity on which Milton had been presumably commissioned to write the masque in the first place. Dramatically speaking, the Lady is singing a perfectly straightforward request to the familiar figure of Echo to tell her where her brothers are ('Canst thou not tell me of a gentle pair | That likest thy Narcissus are?', 235–6) and, if Echo has hidden them in a cave, to 'Tell me but where' (239). Crucially, however, the Lady's song is an appeal to Echo without an echo. It is, as Hollander rightly says, not the typically 'malicious' Echo of, say, Webster's graveyard, but a personified body of ideas relating to heavenly music and eloquence.[77] Rather than doubling back on her, the Lady's words presumably penetrate the dark forest canopy in an effort not only to find her brothers, but to reach heaven as well (or at least the Attendant Spirit sent from heaven). The Lady's song thus subverts contemporary conventions by omitting the traditional 'response' of the echo and transforming the song, through layered mythological allusions to Ovid's Narcissus, Echo, and Philomela ('the love-lorn nightingale', 234), into a moving meditation on the fear of speechlessness and self-annihilation that attends the worldly temptations of self-love, self-indulgence, and self-worship embodied in the Narcissistic myths and in the figure of Comus himself, who constantly threatens the Lady with implicit Philomela-like spiritual, if not physical, rape.

What the Lady says as she sings is equally significant, therefore. Rather than singing about how lonely and fearful she is, as perhaps would be expected from her dramatic predicament, she concludes her song with a heaven-bound prayer on behalf of personified Echo, 'the sweet queen of parley', that she may be purged of her lapsarian

---

[76] Hollander, 'Milton's Renewed Song', in Barker, *Milton: Modern Essays in Criticism,* 43–57, at 46. See also Hollander, *The Figure of Echo,* 55–60.

[77] 'Milton's Renewed Song', 48.

deformities and rise to heaven: 'So mayst thou be translated to the skies, I And give resounding grace to all heaven's harmonies' (241–2). Although it makes little dramatic sense, the Lady's song ends with a distinctly Miltonic prayer for the redemption of fallen language, and it is extremely revealing that such a prayer has little to no long-term effect within the unfolding dramatic action of the masque itself. Although he is so thoroughly moved by the Lady's song, Comus hastens to reassert his power of lapsarian eloquence over the Lady's melody: 'I'll *speak* to her I And she shall be my queen' (264–5, my emphasis). He then proceeds to seduce the Lady into his palace, and by the time the action resumes between the two protagonists, the song to Echo, with its ineffable resonance and internal mythological echoes, is quite forgotten as Comus waves his phallic wand and binds the Lady's body to the enchanted chair at the heart of his corrupting domain. In the final analysis, then, the overall dramatic action of the masque ultimately provides a sobering response to Comus's now not-so-rhetorical question, which is altogether different from the initial one: yes, the Lady is in fact only mortal, and no, she cannot in effect sing to save herself. The Lady's song to Echo, therefore, gains all the more poignancy in Milton's masque for its inability to exert any real power over the lascivious enchanter and save the chaste Lady from rhetorical rape.

The final ineffectiveness of the song to Echo in actually redeeming the Lady exposes the precarious nature of the Lady's power as a remote Platonic abstraction. The Lady—a complex allegorical distillation of solemn music, virginal chastity, and Platonic Christian idealism *in potentia*—is dramatically and poignantly rendered powerless in Comus's suggestively Spenserian woodland domain of error and temptation, not for allowing her 'corporal rind' to be 'immanacled' (663–4), but for having a 'corporal rind' in the first place. For all his lascivious paganism, Comus is no fool. He can intellectually grasp the ineffable Platonic idea which the Lady represents, and it this intimated transcendental presence which ultimately fills him with dread: 'Sure something holy lodges in that breast, I And with these raptures moves the vocal air I To testify his *hidden* presence' (245–7, my emphasis). But this 'holy' and numinous presence cannot protect the Lady's 'corporal rind', suggesting a deep dichotomy between them. It is only through the strangely allegorical powers of Sabrina, the Christian-British-maternal nymph, that the Lady is finally freed from the enchanted chair and

Comus is (temporarily) put to flight. The song to Echo, then, is an elaborate trope for the Lady's irredeemable loneliness as a religious and poetic ideal; a loneliness which in turn renders the Elder Brother's rather academic encomium of 'the arms of chastity' (439) distinctly hollow in the masque's dramatic context. From Milton's personal perspective, the commission to write the masque must have provided his imagination with an irresistible opportunity to explore the drama of his own personal poetic vocation and the worldly threats arrayed against its vatic claims. The Lady's predicament was one that Milton believed he himself faced as a would-be poet-prophet desperately seeking to remain chaste and pure in a fallen world. In *Elegia Prima*, for example (a verse letter Milton addressed to his friend Charles Diodati from London, probably in the spring of 1626), he tellingly describes his immanent return to the studious halls of Cambridge from the unruly town life of London as escaping the 'infamous halls of faithless Circe' ('malefidae infamia Circes | Atria', 87–8), recalling the imaginative pedigree of Comus, the son of Circe, in the later masque.[78] Like his creation, the chaste Lady, the young Milton, known to his Cambridge chums as the 'Lady of Christ', was also an unwilling prisoner in a 'corporal rind' who often thought of himself as a victim of Comus's enchantment—a mere mortal trapped within the ineffectual voice of his own lapsarian poetic creations, with no real hope of ever soaring 'with no middle flight' towards the dizzying heights of heaven.

Only 'Lycidas' and 'Epitaphium Damonis', Milton's most accomplished early poems, twined in the English–Latin sections of the 1645 volume, begin to envision a way forward for the future poet-prophet. If we accept that 'Lycidas' is an intensely autobiographical poem—not in the straightforward sense suggested by Tillyard, but in J. Martin Evans's qualified, meta-poetic sense—then we can indeed see that 'beneath the marmoreal formality of the [pastoral] surface . . . Milton can be observed in the process of discovering some of his deepest anxieties'.[79] Depending on the context in which we read the poem, however, the sort of 'personal' Miltonic anxieties 'Lycidas' discovers change in tone and

---

[78] *CSP* 23–4.
[79] Evans, *The Miltonic Moment*, 72. See also Creaser, '"Lycidas": The Power of Art', 125. For the traditional autobiographical reading refined by Creaser and Evans see Tillyard, *Milton*, 70 ff.

perspective. These deep anxieties are of one nature if we read the poem in its original incarnation as J.M.'s nearly anonymous concluding English contribution to *Justa Eduardo King naufrago* (1638), and of quite another nature if we read 'Lycidas' in its subsequent incarnation as the penultimate English poem in Milton's inaugural 1645 volume. In the context of *Poems 1645* (and *only* in this context), the remembered and reflected anxieties are less about the need to liberate pastoral artifice and poetic vocation from numbing grief, and more about the need to reassert and proclaim prophetic authority. The 'uncouth' pastoral poet who sings the elegy becomes, in *Poems 1645*, the defeated prophet of 'The Passion' and 'Upon the Circumcision', who bemoans his 'fingers rude' that 'Yet once more' must prematurely struggle to pluck the 'berries harsh and crude' of poetic inspiration, 'before the mellowing year' (1–5). There are no guarantees for the reconfigured grief-stricken Miltonic persona who ponders aloud, in a moment of acute despair, whether or not the pursuit of a belated prophetic-epic voice is even appropriate:

> Alas! What boots it with uncessant care
> To tend the homely slighted shepherd's trade,
> And strictly meditate the thankless muse,
> Were it not better done as others use,
> To sport with Amaryllis in the shade,
> Or with the tangles of Neaera's hair?
>
> (64–9)

The speculative road from 'L'Allegro' to 'Il Penseroso' is overwhelmed in 'Lycidas' by grief, but also plotted anew through the grim realties of life's 'canker...Or taint-worm...Or frost' (45–8). 'Lycidas', positioned just before *A Masque* near the end of the English section of the 1645 volume, invites some comparison with the 'Nativity Ode' which opens the section. The reference to the melancholic 'thankless muse' of sacred poetry exposes Milton's 'heavenly Muse' (not *any* old pastoral muse) as an unforgiving taskmistress. Reduced to the level of the chatting 'rustic shepherds' from the earlier ode, the elegizing pastoral swain hears on a sudden the voice of Phoebus, an oddly baptized agency of poetic prophecy, who reminds him that as 'all-judging Jove...pronounces lastly on each deed, | Of so much fame in heaven expect thy meed' (82–4)—no more, no less. The image is ambivalent; by touching

the speaker's 'trembling ears' (77) Phoebus reminds the Virgilian pastoral poet of his true calling in a 'higher mood' (87), and so implicitly
calls him to premature action. At the same time, however, by reminding
the merely pastoral poet that 'Fame is not the plant that grows on
mortal soil' (78), he also points out that such sacred vocation can only
be pursued in complete submission to the will of 'all-judging Jove', who
will reward the poet only *after* he ceases to be merely mortal and ascends
to heaven.

Throughout 'Lycidas' (whether we read the poem in its 1637 or 1645
contexts), a shattered Miltonic persona—shattered, like the 'leaves of
the mellowing year' (5), by grief and by vocational frustration—goes
through successive cycles of pastoral introspection which seek to liberate
the swain from the fear that he might share in Lycidas's premature
death, and like Orpheus be abandoned by the lesser muse Calliope to
the Bacchanal 'rout that made the hideous roar' (61). The fear of
Orphic dismemberment when confronted by the hideousness of ecstatic, animalistic roars once again betrays Milton's deep Protestant anxiety
about the loss of personal voice when the merely human is overwhelmed by ecstasy and ineffable mystery. This theme informs not just the
subject of 'Lycidas' but also its structure. In the headnote to the poem,
Milton describes 'Lycidas' as a 'monody'—an ode in a single voice—but
the very notion of a pastoral 'monody' is in some sense oxymoronic.
The uncouth swain vies in the poem against pastoral and finally Bacchic
polyphony in an effort to assert a unified, singular voice. The parade of
mourners give added force to the sense of implied post-Babel vocal
discord that dominates the swain's seemingly uncouth, but in fact
highly elaborate and carefully structured, monody. The poem's symme-
try, carefully balanced repetitions, and emerging paradox of cyclical
progress[80] offer a unified and increasingly transcendental vision of
poetic and salvific aspiration. In 1637 such moving through grief
redeems and validates the pastoral voice and the art Milton associates
with it; in 1645 the poem seems to redeem more specifically the
prophetic vocation of a reconstituted, public Miltonic persona.

Especially poignant in the 1645 context of prophetic rediscovery is
the angry diatribe of St Peter, 'The pilot of the Galilean lake' (109), on

---

[80] For the best analyses of these important features of the poem see Rajan, *The Lofty
Rhyme*, 44–55, and the Evans and Creaser studies cited above.

whose scriptural and conventionally pastoral attack on the corrupt
clergy in 1637 the 1645 Milton pins his vaunted claims for prophecy
in the amended headnote to the poem: 'And by occasion foretells the
ruin of our corrupted clergy then in their height.' In 1637, however,
when Milton wrote the poem, the point of the attack on the clergy is not
so much a specific topical allusion to the rampant High Churchmanship
of the Carolinian episcopacy (Milton's St Peter, after all, shakes his
'mitred locks', 112), but an attempt to address a scriptural *topos* which
links ministerial calling and pastoral care with the calling of sacred
poetry.[81] Granted, in *Reason of Church-Government* this *topos* is overtly
politicized, but in 'Lycidas' the pilot's diatribe assumes a parabolic,
typically pastoral quality reminiscent, among many other possible examples, of Spenser's 'Maye Eclogue' from *The Shepheardes Calendar*.[82]
The dim and disarmingly pleasant pastoral mode once again reveals
itself as the playground of meta-poetic self-recrimination; the Miltonic
persona shadowed in the swain seeks to lay the blame for his poetic-
prophetic belatedness on the false poet-prophets and unnatural 'blind
mouths' who 'scarce themselves know how to hold | A sheep-hook, or
have learnt aught else the least | That to the faithful herdman's art
belongs!' (119–21). Milton significantly conflates in these lines the
image of pastor and pastoral poet, describing corrupt pastors as false
poet-prophets who bring musical discord to the Reformation project:

---

[81] See Alpers, *What is Pastoral?*, 100–1 and Revard, 'Lycidas', in *CM* 254–5. The
biblical *topos* of the bad shepherds is taken from Ezek. 34: 2–10. Revard dismisses overly
specific political readings of the 'pilot' sequence on the grounds that Milton 'was
concerned in this passage less with the sufferings of the faithful than with the outrages
of the guilty' clergy in a more abstract Reformed sense (p. 254). Accordingly, Revard
challenges John Leonard's reading of 'trembling ears' in l. 77 as a topical allusion to the
fate of the Puritan pamphleteers William Prynne, John Bastwick, and Henry Burton,
whose ears were chopped off in June 1637, following their conviction by the Star
Chamber for seditious libel. Leonard's and Revard's readings, however, need not be
mutually exclusive. While the poem clearly appeals to pastoral conventions and *topoi*, it
also introduces contemporary political themes without straining these conventions
(though I tend to agree with Revard that these themes do not form the poem's overall
subject). For other political readings see Hill, *Milton and the English Revolution*, 49–52;
Norbrook, *Poetry and Politics in the English Renaissance*, 270–84; Dietz, ' "Thus sung the
Uncouth Swain" '.

[82] Compare Spenser's 'Tho gan shepheards swaines to looke a loft, | And leave to live
hard, and learne to ligge soft: | Tho under colour of Shepherds, somewhile | There crept
in Wolves, ful of fraude and guile, | That often devoured their owne sheepe, | And often
the shepheards, that did hem keepe' ('Maye', 124–9).

> What recks it them? What need they? They are sped;
> And when they list, their lean and flashy songs
> Grate on their scrannel pipes of wretched straw,
> The hungry sheep look up, and are not fed . . .

(123–5)

Milton himself, after a manner, had hoped to feed the sheep of the elect with solemn poetic manna, or was at least toying with such dreams in 1637 when the death of Edward King, a fellow scholar and poet as well as a recently ordained pastor, must have filled the nearly 29-year-old Milton with a morbid sense of urgency. If corrupt pastors—from the 'privy paw' (128) of overbearing crypto-Catholic bishops to English Jesuits lurking in the shadows—were responsible in Milton's eyes for so much that was wrong in the Reformed English Church, was it not at least possible that in some insidious way they were also indirectly responsible for contaminating his powers of divine inspiration? Far-fetched as these ideas might sound, there is, however, an important sense in which the transition from the 'dread voice' (132) of St Peter to the commingled soothing waters of Alpheus and Arethusa in the subsequent pastoral tableau encourages us to dismiss such wild fears as irrational: the swain's grief can only be negotiated in the imaginary realms of pastoral conceit, not in the distractingly real world of politics and apocalypse to which the mitred pilot belongs. Perversely, it is the busy world of politics—not the remoteness of transcendental realms—which proves here to be threatening, supernatural (as well as unnatural), and finally ineffable.

Rather than silencing the poet, therefore, the remote echoes of the pilot's dread voice stir him into busy pastoral action, but it is action which must contend with the menacing threat of the supernatural and super-pastoral manifesting itself as ineffable fissures in the swain's pastoral craft. The poet's weakness after the thundering voice of St Peter, with his enigmatically apocalyptic 'two-handed engine at the door', ready to 'smite once, and smite no more' (130–1), is palpable.[83] The swain dallies in 'false surmise' (153) as he turns to deck the hearse of Lycidas and crafts an

---

[83] Speculations abound, of course, as to what Milton's 'two-handed engine' signifies, and it is one of the few instances in Milton criticism where competing interpretations enjoy equal and even cumulative plausibility. Whether it signifies Michael's two-handed sword, God's Word, decrees of election and damnation, the Old and New Testaments, St Peter's twin keys, or the axe that beheaded Laud, it is plainly apocalyptic and offers a menacing and appropriately obscure image of Judgement Day. See Carey's headnote to the poem, *CSP* 242.

elegiac monument in his honour with pretty but merely decorative flowers. What is often missed, however, is with what painstaking care the Miltonic swain clings to his 'false surmise' as he dallies with the flowers in minute and loving detail. Alpers, for example, has rightly pointed out that the flower sequence is brimming with confident action, as the swain commands the pastoral surroundings to throw 'all your quaint enamelled eyes' (139) on the imaginary and, in a sense, absent hearse.[84] And yet, at the same time, it is also a fleeting afterthought, a self-referentially artificial *faux* painting where the poet, not nature, enamels the flowers' 'sad embroidery' (148). When we consider this in relation to the Renaissance Neoplatonic tradition of the poet as divine maker, the Miltonic swain emerges as an idolatrous Protestant, clinging to the insubstantial trappings of his ineffectual, because as yet uninspired, poetic craft.

In this broader contextual sense, 'Lycidas' emerges as an extended meditation on the crisis of a poet who must find ways to liberate his aspiring prophetic voice from the inherited dichotomy at the heart of the Protestant-humanist confrontation with ineffable presence. Initially it seems that all that remains of the swain's dreams of prophecy is to look ahead to life after death, when, like Lycidas, he too shall join at last the inclusive heavenly choirs and become one of many anonymous 'saints above' who entertain the Lamb with 'unexpressive' music. This 'unexpressive', radically ineffable music, however, is 'nuptial', its marriage suggesting not only the union of fallen man with God but also the elusive unity of the pastoral and elegiac mood with the sacral and the prophetic:

> So Lycidas sunk low, but mounted high,
> Through the dear might of him that walked the waves;
> Where other groves, and other streams along,
> With nectar pure his oozy locks he laves,
> And hears the *unexpressive* nuptial song,
> In the blest kingdoms meek of joy and love.
> There entertain him all the saints above,
> In solemn troops, and sweet societies
> That sing, and singing in their glory move,
> And wipe the tears for ever from his eyes.
>
> (172–81, my emphasis)

---

[84] Alpers, *What is Pastoral?*, 101–2.

Initially, this beatific description of heaven with its 'unexpressive' vocal song appears to echo the type of passive resignation Milton had expressed on this subject in 'At a Solemn Music'. By inserting the 'unexpressive nuptial song' into the distinct eschatological imagery of Revelation 7: 17 ('For the Lamb which is in the midst of the throne shall feed them, and shall lead them unto living fountains of waters: and God shall wipe away all tears from their eyes'), Milton relegates it to the remote future of a widely familiar apocalyptic prophecy. This remote prophecy, moreover, sealed in its scriptural idiom, is recited by the Miltonic alter ego of the 'uncouth swain', whose oxymoronic multivocal monody confusedly loiters in the past tense of its disharmonious lapsarian expression. The promise of Apocalypse and the gentle caress of 'ooze', 'laves', and 'wipe' is at once comforting and stifling. On one hand, it gives hope to the grief-stricken poet, who must take some comfort in the belief that those whose 'thin-spun life' is 'slit' by the 'blind Fury with th' abhorred shears' (75–6) will one day sing with the Lamb of God an 'unexpressive nuptial song'. On the other hand, this is small comfort to the poet still trapped in the present tense of his ineffectual and poetically frustrating grief.

Strangely, however, there *is* a sense in which this last scriptural beatific vision of heaven restores repressed prophetic powers to the Miltonic persona. By poetically paraphrasing the words of Revelation, the poet appropriates the prophetic words of Scripture only to expand them with the power of his hybrid Hermetic-Protestant ego. This expansion gives biblical weight to the poem's monodic authorial voice, as it uses the thunder of prophecy to smooth out the pastoral 'uncouthness' of a poet on a sudden grown in biblical sophistication. The poet remains the same 'country swain', but line 186 introduces a new sense of sober clarity to the swain's song which relegates his previous oscillations to the dead past ('Thus sang the uncouth swain to the oaks and rills'). However, it is also possible to register a change in the swain's song earlier in line 182, immediately following the beatific image of heaven:

> *Now* Lycidas the shepherds weep no more;
> Henceforth thou art the genius of the shore,
> In thy large recompense, and shalt be good
> To all that wander in that perilous flood.
>
> (182–5, my emphasis)

The word 'Now' abruptly breaks with the past tense of the pastoral, and consequently the words which follow see the Miltonic swain slowly emerging from his pastoral stupor and receding into the past. The time for pastoral elegy is now over; the discordant, chatting shepherds 'weep no more' and are silent. Once again uplifted by the promise of heaven's 'unexpressive nuptial song', of a musical vocal marriage between heaven and earth, the poet crowns Lycidas—the pastoral object of his elegy—as the 'genius of the shore'. Revard's reading of this passage is important:

> While the Christian pastor-poet is entertained in heaven, he retains a numinous aspect on earth in the form of a pagan 'genius'. But he is not a genius of the wood or meadows, haunting those places where he lived, having left a part of himself behind to console his fellow shepherds. No; he becomes a genius of the very element that destroyed him—the perilous flood, almost as though the poet were having a last word with those water deities who did not protect Lycidas.[85]

Indeed, the suitable epithet of 'genius' invites comparison with the Genius of the Wood we encountered earlier in *Arcades*, who inhabits an unruly, discordant pastoral realm of untamed natural beauty. As the example of *A Masque* demonstrates, such pastoral woods may seem beautiful and alluring but are nonetheless places of great lapsarian danger, their tangled shrubs and dense trees admitting very little of the light of heaven. The 'shore', on the other hand, is a liminal boundary between the concreteness of earth and the vast, unfathomable and ineffable depths of the ocean. As the presiding power of this metaphysical boundary, Lycidas can now exert his new-found mediating powers and, Christ-like, bridge heaven with the fallen earth for the sake of all mortals who must still struggle for salvation, wandering 'in that perilous flood'. The biblically loaded image of the 'perilous flood' metaphorically expands in this way from the Irish Sea in which Edward King had drowned to signify the 'perilous' fallen world awaiting Judgement Day more generally. The apotheosis of the drowned Lycidas offers the swain a vehicle for the apotheosis of his pastoral songs; from now on the poet will look to Lycidas, the 'genius of the shore', for poetic inspiration of a different kind. With renewed powers of poetic inspiration close at hand, the rejuvenated Miltonic swain, now turned *vates*, once more warbles with 'eager thought' his 'Doric lay' (189), even as he

---

[85] Revard, 'Lycidas', *CM* 259–60.

looks ahead to the 'fresh woods, and pastures new' (194) of future, distinctly unpastoral poetic achievements.

The same process of rapture and apotheosis is mirrored in the much more personal Latin elegy on the death of Diodati, 'Epitaphium Damonis', which seals the Latin section of *Poems 1645* and where, again, Milton exhibits his own considerable poetic mastery of the pastoral to make a negative statement about the extremely limited solemn range of such a voice. The early, experimental Milton, however, does not view this limitation as any reason for abandoning the pastoral voice, whose inability to accommodate the 'dread' voice of the supernatural and the ineffable is both consoling and liberating to a poet still content to craft his poems from fallen matter. Grief, however, strains the pastoral voice to breaking point (or rather to epic point), but in 'Epitaphium Damonis' consolation is found in the ceremonial meditation on the strain itself rather than its ultimate poetic implications. Take, for example, Milton's use of the conventional pastoral trope of the shepherd's pipes breaking up when having to produce solemn music:

> Ipse etiam, nam nescio quid mihi grande sonabat
> Fistula, ab undecima iam lux est altera nocte,
> Et tum forte novis admoram labra cicutis,
> Dissiluere tamen rupta compage, nec ultra
> Ferre graves potuere sonos, dubito quoque ne sim
> Turgidulus, tamen et referam, vos cedite silvae.

(155–60)

And I—for my pipe was sounding some lofty strain, I know not what, eleven nights and a day ago, and I had by chance set my lips to a new set of pipes, when their fastening broke and they fell apart: they could bear the grave notes no longer—I am afraid that I am being high-flown, but still, I will tell of that strain. Give place, woods.[86]

Typically of the egocentric, meta-poetic Milton, the point of ultimate grief over the death of his beloved Diodati turns into a personal statement of poetic grief over the loss of a metaphorical musical instrument. He not only laments the dissolution of his inspirational friendship with Diodati, but also the consequent dissolution of his metaphoric *cicutae* (shepherd's pipes) at the mere attempted utterance of some 'grave sound'—be it the

---

[86] *CSP* 285.

strained attempt to put unspeakable grief into words, or the effort to describe in verse the solemnity of heaven and its inexpressible harmonies. The breaking of the pipes is a common pastoral metaphor for the breaking of poetic inspiration, associated, for example, with Spenser's alter ego, Colin Clout.[87] Milton, however, typically universalizes the metaphor through the oddly circumlocutory manner of specifying a time ('ab undecima... altera') which echoes 'alter ab undecimo' in Virgil's eighth Eclogue.[88] The Latin poem clearly at the back of Milton's mind is about loss of childhood innocence, apple-picking and the beginning of sexuality as a kind of fall—*ut vidi, ut perii*—whereas the lost years of childhood become in Milton's poem the dwindling days and nights of pastoral poetic powers. The singing voice associated with the shepherd's pipe breaks and dies away to make room for the sober, austere reflections outlined speculatively in the earlier 'Il Penseroso'. Echoing this time Virgil's tenth Eclogue, Milton commands the pastoral woods to give way ('vos cedite silvae'),[89] as inarticulate grief hardens into prophetic urgency.

As in 'Lycidas', however, Milton does not discard the pastoral and its conventions in 'Epitaphium Damonis', but seeks to sublimate its pagan machinery through the agency of the apotheosized Damon, so that Amor (Cupid) is found in heaven, shooting his arrows of rapture and desire not at the 'base hearts of the rabble' but among the 'heavenly spheres', so that his shafts 'kindle holy minds and the forms of the gods themselves'.[90] The imagery in the final lines of the elegy gathers tremendous ineffable force as the sedate but highly eroticized realms of pastoral song give way to a paradoxically virginal Bacchic frenzy amid the 'hosts of heaven'. This is the closest Milton comes in his early poetry to confronting the devotional but also erotic core of ineffable mystery, and he locates it, ingeniously, not in the apocalyptic scripturalism of

---

[87] See *Shepheardes Calender*, 'Januarye', 72; *The Faerie Queene*, VI. x. 18.

[88] 'alter ab undecimo tum me iam acceperat annus, I iam fragilis poteram ab terra contingere ramos. I ut vidi, ut perii! ut me malus abstulit error!' (39–41); 'My eleventh year finished, the next had just greeted me; from the ground I could now reach the frail boughs. As I saw, how I was lost! How a fatal frenzy swept me away'. *Virgil*, trans. Fairclough (Loeb edn.), i. 59.

[89] Echoes Virgil's 'concedite silvae', *Ecl.* 10.63.

[90] 'Nec tenues animas, pectusque ignobile vulgi I Hinc ferit, at circum flammantia lumina torquens I Semper in erectum spargit sua tela per orbes I Impiger, et pronos nunquam collimat ad ictus, I Hinc mentes ardere sacrae, formaeque deorum' ('Epitaphium Damonis', 193–7). Trans. *CSP* 285.

'Lycidas' but in pastoral's cultic roots of the Bacchic. Milton's rousing image at the end of the poem is violently iconoclastic, as he turns the iconic Bacchic impulse to lose oneself in a religious frenzy—which, again, also carries the Orphean threat of dismemberment—into the ecstasy and rapture of inexpressible heavenly songs under the auspices of Zion's 'thyrsus':

> Ipse caput nitidum cinctus rutilante corona,
> Letaque frondentis gestans umbracula palmae
> Aeternum perages immortales hymenaeos;
> Cantus ubi, choreisque furit lyra mista beatis,
> Festa Sionaeo bacchantur et orgia thyrso.

> (215–19)

Your radiant head circled with a gleaming crown, the joyful, shady branches of leafy palm in your hands, you will take part for ever in the immortal marriage-rite, where singing is heard and the lyre rages in the midst of the ecstatic dances, and where the festal orgies rave in Bacchic frenzy under the thyrsus of Zion.[91]

The chaste, virginal Damon, with his 'radiant head circled with a gleaming crown', is not just a type of Christ but also a baptized Bacchus, presiding over an 'orgia festa' (festive orgy) of angelic hymns. The oxymoronic image of a festive heavenly, and therefore (one assumes) chaste, orgy offers one of many strong indications in Milton's early poetry that fear of ineffable mystery—of speechless spiritual rapture—was intimately bound up in his imagination with fear of potentially contaminating sexual intercourse and physical ecstasy. Physical and spiritual purity are inseparable for Milton, as are the consequences of allowing himself to be overwhelmed either by grief, desire, or holy ambition to the point where he must step outside of himself and either fall silent or be overwhelmed by 'unexpressive' singing voices. The physical–spiritual dialectic implied here defines Milton's early poetic ambitions: Milton's desire to lose himself in the heavenly 'frenzy' must be deferred until he can prove his worth as a holy poet, and in order to prove his worth he must *not* lose himself in any form of earthly 'frenzy' or physical ex-stasis. Bacchus, the god of wine and intoxication, is also the patron god of the alien, the foreign, and all that is radically other or

---

[91] *CSP* 286.

ex-trinsic. To confront the ineffable at the heart of any religious mystery is to confront the radical otherness of the supernatural, and to wish to lose oneself in it is to wish not to be human anymore. For the Greeks, being 'human' meant being Greek-speaking and civilized; for Christians in the Pauline-Augustinian tradition, however, being human is to be subject to sin, and to wish to rise above sin is therefore to wish to rise above the human. In invoking Damon's divine powers of inspiration in their Christ-like mediatory capacity, however, Thyrsis nevertheless holds onto the promise of an 'undiscording voice' ('At a Solemn Music', 17) that will be heard amid rapture and silence even though it is deeply embroiled, figuratively and substantially, in the fallen world's 'harsh din' of 'disproportioned sin' (At a Solemn Music', 19–20).

The pastoral conclusion of *Poems 1645* allows the collection to end on a rather hopeful note, but without offering any real resolution to the underlying Protestant dread that the ineffable might overwhelm the poet's desire to speak more than his allotted share and consign him to oblivion. What begins with a bold declaration of prophetic intent in the 'Nativity Ode' ends with the hopeful resignation that the time has not yet come for the poet-prophet to fulfil his destiny. In 1645 Milton had not yet reached the intellectual clarity needed to resolve the underlying prophetic conundrum of his poetic ambition effectively. Although he tended to suppress the overarching theological implications of the type of poetic voice he wanted to achieve, he nonetheless manages in the early poems to sustain a measure of illusory prophetic power. In all of the poems I have analysed so far I have pointed out how Milton repeatedly finds a way to suggest a space where the poet-prophet may be found in his element, somewhere between the overwhelmingly verbal world of Calvin's elect on the one hand, and the divine Godhead shrouded in its ineffable mystery on the other. In these, often brief, imaginary moments of prophetic power, somewhere above the sinful world but still far below God, the prosaic Protestant in Milton relents so that the young poet may finally begin to soar in 'the high region of his fancies with his garland and singing robes about him'.[92] Though brief, these moments must have sustained the younger Milton in

---

[92] *Reason of Church-Government*, *YCP* i. 808.

prophetic hope and encouraged him in his plans for greater poetic projects. The next time we encounter Bacchic frenzy in Milton's poetry we find that Milton no longer wishes to assimilate its raptures into his sacred song. In the invocation to Book VII of *Paradise Lost*, Milton pleads of Urania, the heavenly muse:

> But drive far off the barbarous dissonance
> Of Bacchus and his revellers, the race
> Of that wild rout that tore the Thracian bard
> In Rhodopè, where woods and rocks had ears
> To rapture, till the savage clamour drowned
> Both harp and voice; nor could the Muse defend
> Her son. So fail not thou, who thee implores:
> For thou art heav'nly, she an empty dream.
>
> (VII. 32–9)

The more mature Milton, grown in sophistication and vocational confidence, will no longer require the gentle prop of baptized pastoral origins to soar effectively in poetic flight. In *Paradise Lost*, Zion's thyrsus is discarded for Zion itself, Parnassus for 'Sion's hill' (I. 10), while the Doric lays of Milton's youthful experimentations, overwhelmed by the 'barbarous dissonance' and 'savage clamour' of sin and chaos, are consigned to the pastoral past. In *Paradise Lost*, Calliope's ineffectual patronage proves nothing but an 'empty dream', and the fear of Orphic dismemberment, of sacrificing monist coherence and individual distinctness amid a cacophony of sounds and dissenting voices, crystallizes into the poetics of singularity and exclusion, where the ineffable itself becomes both the subject and the lack which will allow Milton to sing about man's greatest loss of all.

4

Paradise Lost: pretending
to say the unsayable

Paradise Lost is an epic poem about epic loss. The loss is spiritual, occasionally political, always universal, but also a deeply personal loss of innocence, of obedient and truly harmonious filial as well as conjugal love, and of access to total divine meaning and truth as well. Composed in large part after the Restoration by a defiant, politically disillusioned, still desperately idealistic, and very isolated Milton, now 'fallen on evil days...and evil tongues; | In darkness, and with dangers compassed round, | And solitude' (*Paradise Lost*, VII. 25–8), it aligns the defeat and futility of temporal ideology with Satanic betrayal and the evil forces of idolatry and self-worship which led to man's first, original, and most fatal disobedience. Ineffability permeates *Paradise Lost*; it is to be found, of course, in the ineffable divine light to which the blind poet stretches his hand in his attempt to 'see and tell | Of things invisible to mortal sight' (III. 54–5), but it is also a symptom of the unspeakable condition of darkness and blindness in which the inspired poet-prophet takes dictation from the 'heavenly Muse' and shapes his poetic vision. From the speculative history of ineffability, through the emerging Renaissance dichotomy between Neoplatonic humanism and Reformation theology, to Milton's attempts to grapple with this dichotomy in some of his most accomplished early poems—all of the material I have covered and analysed in the previous chapters coalesces in *Paradise Lost* into a singular renegotiation of traditional apophatic theology and imagery. As in his early poetry, Milton's deep spiritual commitment to the Reformed ideals of scriptural rationality and literal perspicuity drive him to situate the traditional tropes of apophatic mystical theology in a discursive and explicitly didactic framework which objectifies the concept of ineffability as a discrete metaphysical and semantic category, without once submitting to its imperatives of silence. As I will argue, however, the resulting poetry achieves its enormous affective and imaginative power precisely by setting itself *against* the deeply ineffable background that permeates the silent gaps which lurk between metaphor and matter, or spoken words and the otherworldly sounds (or even smells, in God's case) that may be attached to such words. Throughout this sustained preoccupation with the limits of fallen speech and the implications of ineffability, the idea of loss itself—of absence and exclusion—becomes the poem's central metaphor about the unbridgeable gulf between what the poem actually says on the level of words and what the poetry shows on the level of poetic affect 'about' that which is unknowable, ineffable, and finally lost.

UNBLAMED EXPRESSION

> Thee Father first they sung omnipotent,
> Immutable, immortal, infinite,
> Eternal King; thee author of all being,
> Fountain of light, thyself invisible
> Amidst the glorious brightness where thou sitst
> Throned inaccessible, but when thou shad'st
> The full blaze of thy beams, and through a cloud
> Drawn round about thee like a radiant shrine,
> Dark with excessive bright thy skirts appear,
> Yet dazzle heaven, the brightest seraphim
> Approach not, but with both wings veil their eyes.
>
> (*Paradise Lost*, III. 372–82)

In this rapturous hymn Milton's angels celebrate the gloriously dark and inaccessible *Deus absconditus* of traditional Christian mysticism and Reformation theology as Milton interpreted them. Although the angels are non-lapsarian beings who dwell in relative proximity to God's ineffable glory, and although their song is a 'charming symphony' where 'no voice but well could join | Melodious part, such concord is in heaven' (III. 368–71), the terminology they use is recognizably 'fallen' in its reliance on common tropes of negative theology and apophasis.[1] God's hidden presence is

---

[1] See Lieb, *Poetics of the Holy*, 205–7.

figured in the familiar terms of negative theology's bright cloud of darkness, also reminiscent of the Mosaic theophany on Mount Sinai. True to the Mosaic subtext, this ineffable brightness, moreover, assumes ontological cultic immanence in the shape of a shrine: the angels worship the hidden God at one remove by worshipping the dark cloud which veils God's full glory, where he nevertheless sits anthropomorphically 'Throned inaccessible'. The hymn offers an important reminder that our inability to comprehend, let alone talk about, the radical otherness of God as he in himself is not a condition of the Fall, but an ontological barrier that marks the transcendental *difference* between Creator and creature, *numen* and sign. It also brings us very close to Milton's dazzlingly corporeal angels, where the difference between their melodious concord—equally ineffable in its elusive otherworldly remoteness—and our putative ability to sing a similar hymn has *everything* to do with the Fall, which has divorced man from such rapturous, heavenly concord.

Milton's mediating bard, however, is sufficiently inspired to render what he describes in 'At a Solemn Music' as the 'melodious noise' (17) of angelic hymns with content and form. Read in isolation, the content and form of the angelic hymn is much like Spenser's humbly apophatic 'An Hymne of Heavenly Beautie', with its similar celebration of 'the great glory of that wondrous light' which hides the enthroned God's 'brightnesse from the sight | Of all that look thereon with eyes vnsound' (176–9).[2] It points to the dark, numinous core of Milton's poem and gently reminds us that the poet of *Paradise Lost*, inspired though he may be, cannot presume to see God and talk about him any more than the angels can (which in itself is a significant Orphic presumption). It also places Milton's startling desire to 'assert the eternal providence, | And justify the ways of God to men' (I. 25–6) in its proper context: the most that Milton can hope to do is to render the ways of fallen men to God inexcusable in the process of educating 'a fit audience…though few' (VII. 31) of fellow lapsarian readers in the tragic enormity of our loss of Paradise.[3] For Sharon Achinstein, moreover, such a pedagogic process involves implicating the 'fit'

---

[2] *Edmund Spenser: The Shorter Poems*, ed. Richard A. McCabe.

[3] As Jason Rosenblatt has shown, the term 'justify' cannot be extricated from its Hebraic ramifications and distilled into a simplistic Pauline paradigm of justification by faith: 'God's justice might best be understood as legal rather than evangelical, inherent rather than imputed' (*Torah and Law in 'Paradise Lost'*, 70).

revolutionary reader in 'perplexing' acts of reading.[4] The paradoxes of hell's 'darkness visible', of seeing with blind eyes, of unstable and unpredictable allegorical figures, of mirroring the divine creation of the universe by creating an epic poem out of dark, chaotic matter—these are all deliberate paradoxes designed to encode the poem's relentless groping in the dark, where 'darkness' becomes 'a figure for [the] condition of hermeneutic struggle, inverting the common sense in which darkness connotes a spiritual condition of abjection from God'.[5]

At the same time, however, there is also a problem with Milton's irradiated darkness which many of the epic's un-'fit' readers (that is, readers who have long ago now lost any immediate political sympathy for Milton's engagement with revolutionary discourse) have often registered, and which, not inconceivably, even contemporary 'fit' readers may have noticed. The angelic hymn does not stand alone, but follows hard after the epic presentation of a dialogue between the Father and the Son in which the central theology behind the drama of the Fall is set out and clearly explained in moving tones of rebuke and regret to the penitent reader. Achinstein is right, of course, that Milton 'scatters hard-to-read passages all over his text as a means to test his readers' strenuousness',[6] but surely not when God delivers his sermon on obedience, accountability, and free will. This clash between clarity and obscurity in the didactic apparatus of the poem indeed dramatizes a hermeneutical struggle, but in doing so, somewhere between the clarity of divine speech and the apophasis of the angelic hymn, something other than Paradise gets lost. The affective power of ineffable mystery, so central for any traditional meditation on God's hidden ways, loses its numinous character so that, in Milton's heaven at least, the paradox of bright darkness becomes a paradox of bright brightness.

For a very long time, a common response to the apparent lack of mystery in the poem was to attack Milton's representation of heaven and God: Milton violated a cardinal rule of metaphysics and, in a way, of literature too—you can talk 'about' God (that is, about the experience of *failing* to talk about him), but you can never actually talk about him as he is in himself, let alone assume God's point of view and presume to talk *for* him. On these terms, Marvell's initial 'severe' misgivings about the poem, that

---

[4] Achinstein, *Milton and the Revolutionary Reader*, 210–23.
[5] Ibid. 219.   [6] Ibid. 210.

Milton would ruin the sacred truths of the Bible by turning them into mere fables, still seem to some justified: 'the argument | Held me a while misdoubting his intent, | That he would ruin (for I saw him strong) | The Sacred truths to fable and old song' ('On Mr Milton's *Paradise Lost*, 5–7).[7] A. J. A. Waldock, a famous anti-Miltonist whose critique of the poem has been roundly dismissed,[8] nevertheless pinpoints the problem with perfect clarity: 'perfection, quite strictly, is unportrayable, for as soon as the process of portrayal begins we, the readers, begin a corresponding, and quite involuntary and irresistible, process of translation; we translate into the terms of limitation and imperfection. Indeed, the translation in a sense is already effected for us, for the portrayal itself is translation.'[9] Waldock's argument is simple: when Milton portrayed God as a protagonist in an epic poem, the breach of literary decorum was the least of his problems. As we have seen in Chapter 1, St Augustine memorably captured the essence of the paradox Milton would face when he pointed out that, 'if what cannot be spoken is unspeakable, then it is not unspeakable, because it can actually be said to be unspeakable'. We can modify Augustine's statement to apply to Milton's problem as Waldock sees it: 'if God who is unportrayable in lapsarian language can be portrayed, then he is no God, because he can actually be portrayed.' Augustine goes on to suggest that Christians should altogether avoid thinking about such entanglements and devote themselves instead to prayer and participation in the sacraments. Does Milton, then, resort at all to what may be termed 'sacramental language'? The poet and critic Paul Mariani defines 'sacramental language' as 'language that pays homage to the splendid grittiness of the physical as well as the splendor and consolation of the spiritual'.[10] And if we accept, as I think we can, Mariani's speculative definition, we can see why such sacramental expression was simply not an option for Milton, who revels everywhere in *Paradise Lost* in the 'grittiness of the physical' and the splendour of the spiritual, but rarely if ever allows this splendour to be in any meaningful sense consoling. I suppose this last assertion must remain in the realm of subjective religious feeling (or the lack of it), but I think we can safely say that, generally speaking, Milton is not a poet of religious consolation in any obvious

---

[7] *The Poems of Andrew Marvell*, ed. Nigel Smith.
[8] The most eloquent answer to Waldock's criticism can be found in Frank Kermode's 'Adam Unparadised', in Kermode, *The Living Milton*, 85–123.
[9] Waldock, *'Paradise Lost' and Its Critics*, 97.
[10] Mariani, *God and the Imagination*, 234.

sense.[11] His poetry lifts up, instructs, beguiles, and humbles, but is never itself humble, and it is because of his refusal to avoid the paradox of ineffability in mere humble prayer that Milton ran into innumerable difficulties in his portrayal of heaven.

This common assessment of the poem, however, has not gone un-challenged. One critic who for decades now has insisted that Milton's God is in fact much more mysterious than most allow, and indeed is sacramentally so, is Michael Lieb. As Lieb points out, 'Milton is as "dark" as any other poet (or theologian) that the early modern period produced. His God is the consummate embodiment not only of the light with which he is so often associated but of a darkness in which he is said to reside.'[12] The darkness Lieb has in mind here is not the hermeneutical darkness Achinstein detects in the poem's dialogue with its intended readership. Lieb's darkness is the absolute, hyper-essential darkness of divine alterity and difference, where difference is under-stood not in Derridean terms but as the *ens* of Christian-Platonic, but chiefly Hebraic theology. It is the other which lies beyond creation and yet is deeply implicated in it fabric and its signs, or as Milton's Michael says to the fallen Adam, 'of his presence many a sign | Still following thee, still compassing thee round | With goodness and paternal love, his face | Express, and of his steps the track divine' (XI. 351–4). The materialist, gloriously vivid universe Milton creates in *Paradise Lost*, though very dark in places, seems to admit very little of this *other* kind of darkness. It is true that the angels in their hymn in Book III sing about this darkness and point to it, but at no stage in the poem is there an obvious mimetic effort to actually evoke such darkness in the traditional apophatic sense of absence and aphaeresis, either in heaven or as it is filtered through prelapsarian creation. Discussions about the

---

[11] Note for example Stephen Fallon's provocative assertion that Milton, 'though very much a theological writer, is hardly a religious writer at all' (*Milton's Peculiar Grace*, 38). Fallon arrives at this assertion by noting the glaring absence of conviction of sin in Milton's self-representations and autobiographical digressions in the poetry and prose. While Milton shared with contemporary Puritans much by way of theology, he did not share in the religious feeling such Puritans, especially Quakers, attached to such theology. But this assertion can be misleading: it is not that Milton is not a religious poet, but only that he is not a religious poet in the conventional sense. Milton's poetic exploration of blameless singularity is after all religiously expressed and presented with the force of something like religious conviction.

[12] Lieb, *Theological Milton*, 5.

poem's metaphysical theology of the kind produced by Lieb, Fallon, and others, therefore, can help readers assess the relativity of literalness and mimesis in the poem with little fear of paradox, but they also tend to divert attention from the natural and even visceral discomfort many readers (even readers with no apparent religious sensibility) feel when confronted by the violent dislocation of mystery in the poem.

In this respect, Gordon Teskey's recent attempt to shed light on the nature of mystery in *Paradise Lost* points in the right direction. If Milton's God does not inspire us with reverential awe in the same way as Dante's truly hidden deity in the final canto of the *Paradiso*, it is because Milton's God is self-referentially Milton's creation. As Teskey says, 'the more artistically brilliant is the poet's justification of the ways of God to men—in particular, the account of Creation—the more the God he justifies, the Creator with a capital C, disappears behind the brilliance of that justification'.[13] For Teskey, this is the result of a poetry governed by principles of shamanistic 'delirium', where the poet's creative energy 'flows as a consequence of his having to alternate rapidly between opposite terms' of reality and hallucination.[14] The opposite terms Teskey has in mind here, however, are also the familiar ones I have already discussed of the Hermetic poet, self-propelling himself towards God in ever-more ambitious poetic flights, and the passive prophet, lying in his bed as the 'heavenly Muse' dictates accommodated divine truths to him in verse. These opposite terms allow Milton to vacillate between radically human and transcendental points of view, and both have their source in the text of the Bible, which is the repository of God's accommodated Word, as well as the palette for Milton's unique poetic creation. If Milton's God the Father comes across as too emotionally involved or cynical in his mockery of the rebel angels, therefore, we need only glance at the Bible to appreciate that such an accommodated picture is entirely biblical in character.

However, *Paradise Lost* is not a biblical poem as Du Bartas's *La Sepmaine* is. It is a poem made up of dismembered biblical parts rearranged around a vast quantity of extra-biblical material—a dynamic Frankensteinian creation, 'unattempted yet in prose or rhyme' (I. 16),

---

[13] Teskey, *Delirious Milton*, 27. See also Ferry, *Milton's Epic Voice*, 46; Quint, *Origin and Originality in Renaissance Literature*, 207–19.

[14] Teskey, *Delirious Milton*, 27.

which rises out of its biblical bedrock to the music of Milton's poetic imagination. Problematically, however, Milton continually plays an authorial game in *Paradise Lost* where he simultaneously asserts and eschews the demiurgic powers of his poetic creativity. In Book I he alerts us to this ambivalence towards the Hermetic paradigm of the poet as divine creator by conjuring the hellish counter-image of such creativity when the devils use 'wondrous art' (I. 703) to erect their phantasmagorical creation of Pandaemonium. Echoing the myth of Amphion, who used the magical lyre given to him by Hermes to create the lower city of Thebes, the devils' architectonic wonder rises fully formed 'like an exhalation, with the sound | Of dulcet symphonies' (I. 711–12) from the material stuff of hell. 'Exhalation' suggests the foul, insubstantial, and even illusory nature of this structure, which holds up a distorted mirror to the idea of *in*-spiration which governs Milton's ability to create through poetic utterance what he allegedly receives fully formed from the muse on her nightly visitations. The counter-image of Pandaemonium serves both to warn against and empower Milton's unique creative authority. Despite its physical splendour, Pandaemonium's huge 'fabric' remains the creation of 'spirits reprobate' (I. 697), and its insubstantial halls and Grecian splendour house only fallen angels; Milton's elect poetic utterance, on the other hand, produces a substantially coherent universe from which Milton as the passive-active amanuensis of God carves out a fully imagined hell in which to confine the rebel angels. William Kerrigan calls this the paradox of 'artless art',[15] where Milton forces us to accept an impossible truth: 'He reminds us of those mystics who hit the target by not aiming, of those biblical prophets who wrote the words of God in books that bear their own names. Milton is both author and amanuensis. He has both everything to do and nothing to do with *Paradise Lost*.'[16] There is no denying Milton's prophetic pretensions, but, again, it is doubtful whether we can seriously entertain the notion of Milton ever pretending to be mystical. There is something askew about the comparison between Milton's method in *Paradise Lost* and 'those mystics who hit the target by not aiming', because Milton never gives the impression of 'not

---

[15] Kerrigan, *The Prophetic Milton*, 137. See also Entzminger, *Divine Word*, 119–21.
[16] Kerrigan, *The Prophetic Milton*, 138.

aiming'.[17] Like Luther and Calvin before him, Milton does not cancel out the ineffable, but violently dislocates its presence away from its natural place with God to rest finally with himself, or rather with the mysterious sources of his divine inspiration which allow him to speak *for* God. Milton's created God, then, is not mysterious and ineffable, but the powers of poetic inspiration which allow Milton to speak on behalf of the truly hidden God are ineffably mysterious in the extreme.

The four proems sung by the Miltonic poet-prophet are primarily designed to effect this dislocation. As Lewalski argues, the imagery of the proems 'resist full explication as does the topic they treat, the springs of Milton's poetic creativity'.[18] Lewalski goes on to explore the generic structure of the four proems, but rightly avoids speculating about the precise nature of Milton's 'divine' poetic powers, since these are deliberately shrouded in mystery. Taken together, the four invocations to Books I, III, VII, and IX continually insist on the mysterious ambiguity of the divine agent/s inspiring the poet. Throughout, the equivocating structure of 'and/or' dominates. In Book I, for example, Milton invokes the aid of the 'heavenly Muse' (I. 6) that gave Moses the Torah on the top of Mount Sinai (or Oreb), *and* also the mysterious Spirit— presumably the *logos* or utterance of God which created the world and 'satst brooding on the vast abyss | And mad'st it pregnant' (I. 21–2). In Book III it is the 'holy light' (III. 1) of God, which *is* God, as well as that of the *logos, or* the equally ineffable and mysterious 'pure ethereal stream, | Whose fountain who shall tell?' (III. 7–8). In Book VII it is the ancient muse of Astronomy, 'Urania, by that name | If rightly thou art called' (VII. 1–2), but whose 'meaning, not the name I call' (VII. 5). And finally, in Book IX it is yet again the unnamed, mysterious 'celestial patroness' (IX. 21) who makes nightly visitations to the sleeping prophet

---

[17] That is not to say, of course, that *Paradise Lost* may not have a 'mystical' design written into its poetical scheme, where 'mystical' is understood as an implied anagogical structure. See Crump, *The Mystical Design of 'Paradise Lost'*, echoing Anne Ferry on Milton's 'creative patterns': 'Milton fashioned as perfect a poem as he could, a poem that bore witness in as many ways and as fully as possible . . . to the continuing presence of the creative imagination in the divine scheme' (p. 27). However, detecting numerological patterns and anagogical schemes of cyclical perfection in the poem is one thing; to conclude that Milton was therefore writing mystical poetry is quite another.

[18] Lewalski, *'Paradise Lost' and the Rhetoric of Literary Forms*, 38.

and dictates to him 'slumbering, *or* inspires | Easy my unpremeditat-
ed verse' (IX. 23–4, my emphases).

Of the four proems, the invocation to light in Book III is the most
relevant to the traditions of ineffability and apophasis I have charted in
this study. It introduces us to the blind Mosaic poet-prophet who turns
his inward eye away from the paradox of hell's 'darkness visible' (I. 63)
to the inverse paradox of heaven's 'unapproachèd light' (III. 4):

> Hail[,] holy light, offspring of heaven first-born,
> Of the eternal co-eternal beam
> May I express thee unblamed? since God is light,
> And never but in unapproachèd light
> Dwelt from eternity, dwelt then in thee,
> Bright effluence of bright essence increate.
> Or hearst thou rather pure ethereal stream,
> Whose fountain who shall tell? Before the sun,
> Before the heavens thou wert, and at the voice
> Of God, as with a mantle didst invest
> The rising world of waters dark and deep,
> Won from the void the formless infinite.
>
> (III. 1–12)

For Louis Martz, this passage points to the poet's 'modesty and humility',[19] while Bauman argues that Milton strikes here an 'uncertain
chord' and covers 'all the possibilities'.[20] Jason Rosenblatt, in a useful
analysis of the Moses type informing this sequence, links its imagery to
the Sinai theophany where Moses 'apprehended divinity in darkness'.[21]
As usual, however, it is Lieb's similar assessment which offers the most
detailed contextual analysis. Lieb places the invocation to light in its
proper intellectual context by tracing the history of light worship in
pagan and Christian thought, from Plato's parable of the cave in *The
Republic*, through Neoplatonic and Hermetic reflection on light as the
supreme radiance of the One, to early and medieval Christian mysticism
and liturgical preoccupation with the Johannine theological concept
of light.[22] Indeed, Lieb's survey of Western mystical and liturgical

---

[19] Martz, *Poet of Exile*, 97.
[20] Bauman, *Milton's Arianism*, 222–3.
[21] Rosenblatt, *Torah and Law in 'Paradise Lost'*, 139.
[22] See Lieb, *Poetics of the Holy*, ch. 9, esp. pp. 195–210.

traditions preoccupied with the light-stream motif runs a parallel course to the history of ineffability I have charted in Chapters 1 and 2, and in particular to the metaphor of the bright cloud which recurs in Denys' *Mystical Theology*, Nicholas Cusanus's *De Docta Ignorantia*, and Pico's *De Ente et Uno*. The scriptural cornerstone of this apparently traditional invocation is 1 Timothy 6: 16 ('dwelling in the light which no man can approach unto'), a patristic and Protestant *locus classicus* for any discussion of the utter transcendence of the hidden God. Milton then constructs around this scriptural cornerstone a sequence of images deriving from Patristic, Platonic, and Neoplatonic apophatic traditions. The light expressed here is both spiritual and physical; it is both the symbolical manifestation of God as well as the direct radiance of God's 'bright essence increate'.[23] It is also, however, the divine, uncreated light which joins with the *logos*, 'offspring of heaven-first born', in the act of creating the world with its lesser, created lights, and which the suppliant blind bard prays may 'invest' him 'as with a mantle', just as it had done 'The rising world of waters dark and deep' well before physical light was created.

Crucially, the invocation marries and then juxtaposes the limits of sight with the limits of speech, as the poet moves from contemplating the ineffable 'holy light' of heaven to delineating the limits of his expression and inward vision wherein the 'celestial light' (III. 51) irradiates the mind and plants there eyes so that the poet may '*see* and *tell* | Of things invisible to mortal sight' (III. 54–5, my emphasis). But in seeing *and* telling Milton is already making an anti-mystical gesture. The word 'mystery' derives from the Greek verb μύειν (*müein*), which means to close or shut one's eyes or lips. Initiates into mysteries were expected never to reveal the secrets of their mystical experience. When initiates into hidden mysteries (be they pagan celebrants at the mysteries of Eleusis or Christian monks contemplating the hidden God) broke this prohibition and spoke of their experiences to non-initiates, they had to do so without actually opening their lips. Negative theology is the metaphorical consequence of this prohibition: its practitioners will never tell you what God is, but only what he is not. So is Milton's prayer to be able to 'see and tell | Of things invisible to mortal sight' similarly

---

[23] See Haan, '"Heaven's purest Light"', 117; Nuttall, *Overhead by God*, 91–3.

obedient and tight-lipped? Indeed, can it be said to be *apophatic* at all?
Lieb argues that it is:

> The poet can only question the basic assumptions upon which the invocation is
> built: the results are those of perplexity before the incomprehensible and
> unapproachable... But it is an enlightened perplexity, a perplexity in which
> the poet himself delights, as *sacerdos ludens*... Milton's song to 'holy Light,'
> as a 'playful' act of expressing the inexpressibility of the ineffable, is his way
> of declaring his devotion to the mysterium. It is nothing less than an act of
> worship.[24]

Lieb's notion of the *sacerdos ludens* (playing priest) echoes Cusanus'
experiments in a metaphysical *serio ludere*, where the mystic evokes an
overpowering sense of ineffable mystery in his writings by playing a
serious literary game with semi-efficacious metaphors and negative
expressions. However, once we read Milton's invocation to 'holy light'
in the context of the ensuing narrative of Book III and the dialogue
between the Father and the Son, it emerges as much more than an act of
worship. Lieb himself senses that the invocation may be pulling in other
directions when he concedes the paradox of 'enlightened perplexity'.
'Enlightened perplexity' is an apt oxymoron, insofar as it captures the
sense of play which underlies the invocation, but this playfulness is
heuristic and vatic, not merely sacral. Just as he had done in 'At a
Solemn Music', Milton lifts up the merely praying voice of the suppliant poet by continually proclaiming his wish to do much more than
worship in perplexed ecstasy. The invocation to 'holy light' is extraordinary in the larger context of the poem, because Milton is not about to
celebrate the ineffable, but potentially to do extreme violence to it.

When the blind bard speculates, 'May I express thee unblamed?', this
is not the refrain of a negative theologian content in the failure of
representation, but the genuine worry of a poet who must defend his
ensuing expression, which is anything but mystical. The word 'express'
has a variety of possible meanings here which enrich the overall tenor of
Milton's invocation. First there is the common usage of the word
'express' to mean the act of putting into words a thought, an idea, or
an emotion (*OED* II 8*a*). But there is also the more specific meaning of
expressing a concept symbolically—whether analogically or allegorically

[24] Lieb, *Poetics of the Holy*, 186–7.

(*OED* II 6)—as well as the complementary painterly meaning of expressing something real figuratively, that is, engaging in an act of mimesis (*OED* II 5*a*). We can thus paraphrase 'May I express thee unblamed?' in a number of ways. One paraphrase can be: 'Do I even have the mental capacity to express unblamed the *idea* of holy light at all?' Another paraphrase can be: 'May I express the holy light unblamed using a variety of metaphorical representations?' And yet another paraphrase can be: 'May I portray the holy light unblamed as if it were a tangible object and not an abstract concept?' These three possible meanings of 'express' overlap and undercut one another, even as a final possible pun on 'express' in the sense of 'squeeze out' (*OED* I, esp. 3: to 'press or squeeze out the contents of') suggests that the poet will attempt to express the holy light out from its natural place in ineffable abstractness into realms of mimetic metaphor, resulting not in humble silence but in poetry.

By framing these layered meanings with images of created and uncreated light which refer to a diverse apophatic tradition, Milton effectively queries his own place within that tradition. 'May I express thee unblamed?', then, is a rhetorical question which appears to state that it is impossible to say or portray the ineffable either as idea, concept, or object without some blame. But blame of what exactly, and blamed by whom? Blamed for attempting the impossible and forbidden, or for failing the attempt? Blamed by his fallen peers, by himself, or by God? Whatever the answer, it is clear that the poet intends to do precisely what he thinks might be impossible. The entire movement of the invocation is one which attempts to force, indeed to squeeze-express, the inexpressible light of heaven into the realms of mimesis and move from the apophatic to the symbolic. However, whereas the pseudo-Dionysius stands on the symbolic or kataphatic to reach into the hidden truth which is apophatic, the Miltonic bard inverts the process of mystical theology so that he may hold onto the promise of hidden truth even as he asserts the redemptive power of the deficient symbol.[25]

The mystical inversion underlying the invocation to Book III is directly related to the theme of blindness. We may recall that in *De Ente et Uno*

---

[25] See Budick, *The Dividing Muse*. For Budick, Milton is engaged in *Paradise Lost* in a process of imagistic divestiture which is finally liberating and redemptive, where the aim is to achieve 'a kind of poetic vision that would set loss or exclusion at its very heart' (p. 92).

Pico describes the moment of mystical rapture as being 'blinded by the darkness of divine splendour'. As I argued in Chapter 2, Pico invests this traditional apophatic formula with his belief in the microcosmic dignity of man; to be blinded by darkness in this way is the greatest reward that awaits the man who actively explores his innate divinity and becomes one with the angels. Significantly, however, the only darkness in Milton's invocation is finally the darkness of *physical* blindness, where the abject reality of eyes rolling vacantly 'in dim suffusion veiled' (III. 26) reinforces the poet's sense of alienation from shared human delight in God's created world, or book of nature ('book of knowledge' in line 47), and its ultimate celebration in fallen human companionship:

> Thus with the year
> Seasons return, but not to me returns
> Day, or the sweet approach of even or morn,
> Or sight of vernal bloom, or summer's rose.
> Or flocks, or herds, or human face divine;
> But cloud instead, and ever-during dark
> Surrounds me, from the cheerful ways of men
> Cut off, and for the book of knowledge fair
> Presented with a universal blank
> Of nature's works to me expunged and razed,
> And wisdom at one entrance quite shut out.
>
> (III. 40–50)

For the blind poet-prophet, however, the 'universal blank' of his physical blindness is also the blank canvass of his universal, divinely inspired poetic art which allows him to 'see and tell' of invisible divine vistas.

Throughout the invocation, therefore, the blind poet's sense of loneliness translates into claims of inspired singularity. Between line 26, which alludes to Milton's physical blindness, and the lines quoted above, which carve out for the poet a space of prophetic authority, the Miltonic bard meditates on the nature of virtuous poetic-prophetic ambition itself and offers one of the most striking metaphors for the epic's poetics of ineffability as a whole. The poet pleads with the divine light to make him equal in 'renown, | Blind Thamyris and blind Maeonides, | And Tiresias and Phineus prophets old' (III. 35–6). With the exception of the blind poet Homer (Maeonides), the prophetic types of blind Thamyris, Tiresias, and Phineus are ambivalent, in that they all represent pagan prophets whose blindness was a form of punishment for presuming to peer into divine mysteries. Tiresias was either blinded by Athena as punishment for peering at her naked body, or by Hera for agreeing with Zeus that women derive more pleasure than men from sexual intercourse. The poet Thamyris, whose story is briefly told in Homer's *Iliad* (II. 594–600), was robbed by the Muses of his eyesight and lyre when he boasted he could outdo them in song, and, as Fowler adds, '"*Thamyras insanit*" was proverbial of those who ventured beyond their talents'.[26] Phineus is the blind Thracian king who gives Jason advice on how to capture the Golden Fleece. According to the myth recorded in Apollodorus' *Argonautika*, he was blinded by the gods for prophesying the future too accurately. It is unclear in Milton's invocation if the Miltonic bard believes he shares in the punishment of these 'prophets old', or if he thinks his blindness may in fact be a gift. He hopes to equal these pagan prophets 'in renown' (III. 34), but 'renown' tells us nothing about whether or not he views his blindness as a reward or punishment for his unique 'prophetic' sight. There is certainly ample autobiographical evidence to suggest that Milton was anxious to silence royalists who pointed to his blindness as a divine punishment for his defence of regicide. In the *Second Defence* Milton dismisses these suggestions by pointing out that a prophet's blindness is a gift, not a curse: 'Or shall I recall those ancient bards and wise men of the most distant past, whose misfortune the gods, it is said, recompensed with far more potent gifts, and whom men treated with such respect that they preferred to blame the very gods than to impute their blindness to them as a crime?'[27] As in the invocation to light, Milton goes on in the *Second Defence* to cite the examples of Tiresias and Phineus and adds to these the further examples of famous blind philosophers and statesmen. For Milton, the prophetic sight that comes with physical blindness is a gift, but not in the traditional apophatic sense. Like a mystic, the Miltonic bard also retreats inwardly and then begins to ascend, but at the point where his inner eye meets the unmediated radiance of God's 'unapproachèd light' we do not encounter the paradox of dark splendour, but the peculiarly Miltonic paradox of the nightingale's inarticulate song, singing *in* the dark, 'darkling':

[26] Fowler, *Paradise Lost*, 168, n. 35.
[27] *YCP* iv. 584 (trans. from Latin).

> Then feed on thoughts, that voluntary move
> Harmonious numbers; as the wakeful bird
> Sings darkling, and in the shadiest covert hid
> Tunes her nocturnal note...

>   (III. 37–40)

Like many of his Elizabethan predecessors, Milton often returns in his poetry to the image of the nightingale and its inescapable association with the myth of Procne and Philomela immortalized by Ovid. In much Elizabethan poetry before Milton the image of the forlorn nightingale tends to be used almost proverbially to denote the power of song to express a sense of loss that would be otherwise unspeakable; but in Milton's poetry, as we briefly saw in *A Masque*, for example, the nightingale usually denotes a meta-poetic reflection on the loss of poetic ability and creative belatedness.[28] In the invocation to light, however, the sense of belatedness Milton associates with the nightingale is transformed into a powerful symbol for the type of song the Miltonic bard will sing in his unmediated encounter with the *visio Dei*. This song is at once full of melody and expression and yet somehow impaired and inarticulate, in the 'shadiest covert hid'.

In this context, the gruesome myth of Philomela's rape, loss of speech through mutilation, and final metamorphosis into a nightingale becomes doubly significant; after all, as Fowler points out, can it be coincidence that in Plato's *Republic* 'the soul of Thamyris passed into a nightingale?'[29] When the blind poet imagines that the union between himself and holy light will produce a song similar to that of the melancholy nightingale,

---

[28] See e.g. Milton's Sonnet I. For a good discussion of the nightingale image in Milton's poetry in relation to poetic belatedness see J. Kerrigan, 'Milton and the Nightingale'.

[29] *Paradise Lost*, 169, n. 38. There is some confusion in the ancient mythological tradition as to whether it was Philomela or her sister Procne who was raped and brutally silenced, and also disagreement about which sister gets turned into a nightingale and which into a swallow. In most Greek versions of the myth it is the violated sister Philomela who turns into a swallow (a bird that never sings) and Procne, the grieving mother, who turns into a nightingale. Renaissance authors, however, were mostly familiar with Ovid's version of the myth, where Philomela is the victim of rape who then presumably turns into a nightingale (Ovid, *Metamorphoses*, 6.668–9, however, only states that the two sisters were turned into birds, 'quarum petit altera silvas, | altera tecta subit' ('One flies to the wood, the other rises to the roof'), and the construction does not unequivocally clarify which sister is which). For a good discussion of the nightingale motif in Western literature and the Procne/Philomela confusion see Williams, *Interpreting Nightingales*.

he is lamenting the painful loss of identity that comes with such collabora-
tions. Perversely, however, this loss of identity is also empowering.[30]
Milton harnesses the violent energy of the Philomela myth and redirects
it at the object of the ineffable *mysterium*. Like Philomela, the Miltonic
poet plans to violate the silence of divine presence by finding a voice to
utter the unutterable, but it is a violation the darkness and silence find
pleasing as they willingly give way to it. When the nightingale next sings
her 'amorous descant' in the prelapsarian night of Milton's Eden, we are
told that 'silence was pleased' (IV. 603–4). Like the Lady's song in *A
Masque*, the nightingale-poet's song does not merely break the silence, but
testifies to its 'hidden residence' by 'sweetly' floating 'upon the wings | Of
silence, through the empty-vaulted night | At every fall smoothing the
raven down | Of darkness till it smiled' (*A Masque*, 247–51). Similarly,
Milton never actually breaks the silence of divine presence, but only ever
gently floats on its 'wings' and, ultimately, this gentle musical encroach-
ment into the realms of apophasis produces mimesis. In the classical myth
loss of articulation is replaced with artistic representation when Philomela
communicates her suffering to her sister by weaving images representing
the events onto a piece of fabric which she then secretly sends to her. But in
order to produce mimesis, the holy light must be forced into a concrete
concept, readily grasped by the poet's imagination. Like the myth of
Philomela, the entire invocation to 'holy light' is thus dominated by
similar flux of verbal metamorphosis and a brooding anxiety over the
loss and recovery of the powers of representation. We move from the loss
of speech in the presence of God's uncreated light, or 'effluence', to the
blind poet's loss of created light which leaves him cut off 'from the cheerful
ways of men' (III. 46) and their implied lapsarian chatter, to the transformation of lost speech into inspired song, as the self-created poet-
prophet feeds on thoughts that 'voluntary move | Harmonious numbers'.
Throughout this process light itself undergoes metamorphosis, from the
ineffable 'unapproached light' of God to the created light/sound of
mimetic poetry.

Underscoring the image of the poet-nightingale's darkling song is a
subversive preoccupation with Christian-Neoplatonic ideas about the Orphic mystery of blind love which finds its biblical correlation in the Pauline

---

[30] See Maxwell, *The Female Sublime from Milton to Swinburne*, 21–4.

idea of love in Ephesians 3: 19: 'And to know the love of Christ, which passeth knowledge, that ye might be filled with all the fullness of God.' As Edgar Wind has shown, Pico's use of the Orphic mystery of blind love in *De Ente et Uno* and elsewhere derives from Proclus' *Commentary on the Timaeus*. In the *Timaeus* (33C) Plato put forward the idea that the demiurge created the cosmos as a perfect, all-encompassing spherical body that requires no eyes to see and no ears to hear since it is all things in itself, a self-sufficient entity outside of which nothing else exists. In his commentary Proclus inferred from this that 'the highest mysteries must be seen without eyes and heard without ears, and he claimed that Orpheus meant to refer to that secret when he "said Love to be eyeless"'.[31] Milton's comparable vision of ineffable rapture, however, is filled not with the darkness of God's divine presence, but with the sound of Orphic music that mysteriously creates out of the wound, or cut, of Milton's physical blindness perfectly harmonious verse. The song itself is not dark, but it is *sung* 'darkling', shrouded by the darkness of divine presence. In other words, the poet's inspired song, hatched in the chaotic, boundless deep of Milton's imagination, assumes concrete mimetic substance while retaining the apophatic markers of the *Deus absconditus* who authorizes such creation in the first place: it is a song that is simultaneously present and hidden, immanent and yet perpetually mysterious. Milton prays of holy light to be able to sing in the darkness of apophasis, not that he may be content in failing, but that he may 'irradiate' the darkness of ineffability with his blazing song.

Paradoxically, therefore, there is a sense in which 'May I express thee unblamed?' actually *asserts* the poet's putative or wished power to express the ineffable. Just as he had done in his prayer to the Spirit in *Reason of Church-Government*, Milton pleads here for a totality of vision which is at once solipsistic and inspired. Milton's blindness, however, allows him not just to see hidden visions of the *mysterium*, but also to rise to the fullness of his implied Hermetic and Christian divinity so that—like Cusanus' contracted *maximum*, or Platonic microcosm—he may pretend to be all in all and so need no ears to hear and no eyes to see *all* things. But since for Cusanus only Christ is the perfectly maximal man, Milton's comparable ambition is astonishingly hubristic *if* it

[31] Wind, *Pagan Mysteries*, 57.

is confined to Cusanus' and Pico's Catholic mystical perspective. It is precisely the Protestant perspective of biblical prophecy, therefore, propped up in the invocation by the lesser types of 'Blind Thamyris and blind Maeonides, | And Tiresias and Phineus prophets old', which ironically liberates Milton from the constraints of mysticism and allows him to invest the apophatic imperatives of negative theology with his urgent desire to express unblamed 'something like a prophetic strain'. John S. Lawry long ago said that for Milton 'epic *doing* can be the revelation of meditative *saying*. The human word spoken within the moving shadow of history will be inspired from the fixed dynamism of eternity, which it will in turn express.'[32] However, it is doubtful whether or not such eternity is ever actually *expressed* in the poem, and how 'fixed' is the supposed dynamism which underlines its conceptual contours. Contrary to what Lawry avers, *doing* and *saying* in *Paradise Lost* are fundamentally opposed to one another: epic doing shows precisely what meditative saying *fails* to say even as it *pretends* vociferously to say it. Thus, the invocation to the eternal and immutable holy light is not finally humble or uncertain, though it begins that way, but is deliberately vague. It begins by showing us a humble, blind bard timidly reaching for the 'unapproachèd light' of God, conceding his mortal weakness and limitations, when in fact it seeks to remind us that on the level of poetry we ought to distinguish between what the poet *wishes* to express, what he in fact *will* express, and what he wants his readers to *believe* he has expressed. In other words, we need to attune ourselves to Milton's complex theory of poetic accommodation which, as I will next argue, is deliberately paradoxical and holds an important key to understanding Milton's use of metaphor in the poem against the backdrop of ineffability, not only as presence, but also as absence.

THE PARADOX OF MONIST ACCOMMODATION

One of *Paradise Lost*'s most paradoxical ideas is its implied theory of accommodation. Milton was heir to a tradition which viewed the problems of ineffability as a consequence of epistemology. The hidden

---

[32] Lawry, *Shadow of Heaven*, 4.

God cannot be expressed in words because he cannot be known as he is in himself. In a semiotic system where words are believed to relate to things, knowledge of things is prerequisite before anything can be said about them. In such a world-view, any effort to say the unsayable necessarily involves a process of accommodation, where those who have access to ineffable knowledge must accommodate such knowledge in order to communicate it. Such a process of accommodation invariably involves the translation of abstract, ineffable concepts into analogical metaphors and allegories. A large number of notable scholars have given thought to this important idea in *Paradise Lost*. R. M. Frye and C. A. Patrides have briefly traced its rather unremarkable intellectual history, and many critics since then have attempted to explain the ways in which the theory, as employed by Milton, should shape our reading of the poem's most difficult passages, where the poet claims to see and then tells 'Of things invisible to mortal sight'.[33]

The key biblical passage usually associated with the theory of accommodation is Exodus 33: 20–3, when God once again talks directly to Moses on the mount following the fiasco of the golden calf:

And he said, Thou canst not see my face: for there shall no man see me, and live. And the Lord said, Behold, *there is* a place by me, and thou shalt stand upon a rock: And it shall come to pass, while my glory passeth by, that I will put thee in a clift of the rock, and will cover thee with my hand while I pass by: And I will take away mine hand, and thou shalt see my back parts: but my face shall not be seen.

Here indeed the AV translation of the Hebrew is as accurate as can be, especially of the enigmatic and comically bizarre phrase 'my back parts'. The crude anthropomorphism of the passage perfectly captures, however, its implied theological idea: God's 'face', his actual countenance and essence of being, cannot be seen or known, but only his 'back parts'. It is

---

[33] See Frye, *God, Man and Satan*, 7–13; Patrides, '*Paradise Lost* and the Theory of Accommodation', in Patrides, Hunter, and Adamson, *Bright Essence*, 159–64; MacCallum, 'Milton and Figurative Interpretation of the Bible'; Madsen, *From Shadowy Types to Truth*, 54–74; Shullenberger, 'Linguistic and Poetic Theory in Milton's *De Doctrina Christiana*'; Nuttall, *Overheard by God*, 98–100; Grossman, 'Milton's Dialectical Visions'; Swaim, *Before and After the Fall*, 163–74; Ronald Bond, 'God's "Back Parts": Silence and the Accommodating Word', in Blodgett and Coward, *Silence, the Word and the Sacred*, 169–81; Lieb, 'Reading God'; Treip, *Allegorical Poetics and the Epic*, 194–6; Gimelli Martin, *The Ruins of Allegory*, 7–24, 329–39; Graves, 'Milton and the Theory of Accommodation'.

impossible to determine what these 'back parts' actually stand for, but the metaphor does suggests that what man can see and tell of God in a lowly, limited capacity is inferior, even degrading, when compared to the true, hidden majesty of God.[34] The idea of accommodation is captured in the motion of God's hand which covers Moses's eyes as he passes by him. According to the traditional formulations of the theory of accommodation in the writings of Augustine, Aquinas, Luther, or Calvin, based on this and other scriptural passages, because God as he is in himself is radically ineffable, he chooses to accommodate his nature in the revelatory process to the limited intellectual capacity of his creatures using anthropomorphic-pathetic metaphors from the created world, that is, by covering our eyes and showing us only his 'back parts'. The many anthropomorphic-pathetic images of God in the Bible thus represent God not as he is, but in an accommodated manner which, though imperfect, is nonetheless satisfying since God himself is seen to guide and sanction the accommodation process by placing a metaphorical hand on the eyes of believers as he 'passes' by them in Scripture.

Biblical accommodation operates, therefore, along the lines of the analogical model, but there is one crucial difference between any theory of accommodation and theories of analogical predication: analogy is a figurative tool a mystic or a philosopher might use to say or intimate something 'about' God; accommodation (from a position of faith) is what happens when God tries to tell us something about himself. Right at the outset, therefore, we can see there is a problem. If Milton does indeed employ a 'biblical' theory of accommodation in *Paradise Lost*, we might well ask, what is it exactly that he 'accommodates'? One reasonable answer would be to suggest that Milton uses in *Paradise Lost* images of God that are all biblical in origin and hence already 'accommodated'. Another, equally reasonable, proposition is that Milton in fact employs a Platonic or Neoplatonic form of *creative* accommodation where the allegedly inspired Orphic poet communicates the ineffable truths conveyed to him through the agency of the 'heavenly Muse' by shrouding

---

[34] For the significance of this passage in Milton's *De Doctrina Christiana* see Lieb, *Theological Milton*, 80–2. Lieb's suggestion that there is something sexually voyeuristic about this passage and indeed in the very concept of theophany explored here is tantalizing and, despite Lieb's reservations, entirely appropriate to the theological idea being expressed.

them in elaborate allegories. Kathleen Swaim has proposed the idea that the biblical theory of accommodation belongs to the poem's postlapsarian discourse of Michael, while the Orphic theory of creative accommodation belongs to the prelapsarian discourse of Raphael. As Swaim argues, Michael is the dogmatic, Protestant angel with the clenched fist of logic and words of prophecy, while Raphael is the poet angel with the open hand of metaphor and transcending analogies.[35] Swaim's paradigm is convincing and genuinely helpful, but it neglects the role of the epic narrator whose meta-poetic intrusions destabilize either angel's rhetorical and didactic position in the baroque enactment of what Catherine Gimelli Martin has conversely analysed as Milton's theory of 'meta-allegory'.[36]

Take, for example, the poem's underlying monist-materialist philosophy. When Raphael delivers his monist-materialist speech in Book V ('one first matter all, | Indued with various forms, various degrees | Of substance', V. 472–4), he does so within the prelapsarian narrative frame of the poem. Clearly, however, Raphael does not intend this lecture to be understood as an analogy or metaphor for something else, but as literal fact. This literal fact serves an important didactic purpose within the poem's prelapsarian context; Raphael instructs Adam how to appreciate 'the scale of nature . . . From centre to circumference', so that Adam may 'In contemplation of created things | By steps . . . ascend to God' (V. 509–12). The allusion to the Hermetic metaphor which views God as a circle whose centre is everywhere and circumference nowhere is significant in this context. In the prelapsarian world which Adam shares with the angels, and where man and Paradise are at the centre of the created world, Adam can ascend and become what Cusanus calls the contracted *maximum* through degrees of distinctly unfallen empirical observation. Whereas in the fallen world man can never become the contracted *maximum* except through some ineffable mystical contemplation of Christ, in the prelapsarian world all that separates Man from God, the 'all' from which all matter extends, are *degrees* of animated matter. However, the problem with this philosophical-theological idea begins when we try and apply it to Raphael's poetic narration of the angelic war and the poem more generally. Stephen Fallon argues, for

---

[35] Swaim, *Before and After the Fall*, ch. 4.
[36] See Gimelli Martin, *The Ruins of Allegory*, ch. 5.

example, that those who seek to separate in their reading of the poem the spiritual from the corporeal, the metaphorical from the literal, are of the 'devil's party without knowing it'.[37] Are we then to believe that critics like Swaim and Gimelli Martin, who argue that Raphael instructs Adam through the use of transcending analogies and metaphors (Swaim), or multilevelled meta-allegory (Martin), are unwitting members of the devil's party? Hardly, since the philosophical construct which props up the poem's vital materiality is itself, at the end of the day, just that—an artificial construct constantly self-referencing its own artificiality. Milton may have believed in the underlying metaphysics of Raphael's lecture and may have invested his poem with the necessary props to support it, but it remains a *literary* feature of the poem. In other words, what Fallon terms the poem's 'animist materialism' provides the terms of reference which allow us to think of the poem as mimetic, but this metaphysical world-view is itself a product of these terms. The poem's sinewy physicality both authorizes and produces the mimetic fantasy of coherence and permanence which encourages us to imagine that the various layers of the poem's complex theological argument and mimetic representations deal with literal absolutes.

This fantasy is so brilliantly conceived, however, that it is very hard to break away from its spell even when its occasional logical incongruity becomes too difficult to process, let alone visualize in poetic terms. Milton's allegorical representation of Sin, Death, and Chaos is a case in point. Many readers have found the anomalous presence of what seems like straightforward Spenserian allegory in *Paradise Lost* inexplicable and distasteful. As ever, it was Samuel Johnson who sparked off the debate when he remarked that 'Milton's allegory of Sin and Death is undoubtedly faulty',[38] and numerous critics since then have attempted to defend Milton and argue that the allegorical figures are either not faulty at all or are at the very least *deliberately* faulty. However, what possible role does allegory have in a monist, animist materialist universe where spirit (tenor) and matter (vehicle) are one? Teskey and Fallon provide plausible answers to both questions. It is certainly significant that allegory is confined in *Paradise Lost* to hell and the abyss of Chaos. According to Fallon, the allegorical vehicles of Sin and Death amount to

[37] Fallon, *Milton Among the Philosophers*, 224.
[38] Johnson, 'Milton', *The Major Works*, 712.

'deficient ontology as well a deficient epistemology', where they represent the 'privation of being itself'.[39] In other words, Sin and Death only
exist in Milton's monist materialist universe as negative non-entities
that are nevertheless literally 'real' in the poem's imaginary landscape
because they take up negative ontological space: 'they function as
negative numbers in a universe created with positives only.'[40] Teskey's
similar assessment is slightly less paradoxical and more literary: the
grotesque Spenserian physicality of Sin and Death, who later build
together with 'wondrous art | Pontifical, a ridge of pendent rock |
Over the vexed abyss' (X. 312–13) of Chaos, serves to free 'Sin and
Death to become daemonic beings', not allegories.[41] Fallon and Teskey
are untroubled and even vindicated in their analysis by the strange
metaphorical vacuity of these allegorical beings, by their slippery indeterminacy, and by their incestuous relationship with the ideal, the
physical, and very real evil of Satan.

However, might it not be possible to suggest, as Nuttall has done,
that the good Doctor Johnson was actually right?[42] Surely it is valid to
argue that the 'faulty' allegorical presence in *Paradise Lost* contaminates
Milton's stable, materialist universe with symbolism. Curiously, none of
the critics I have cited so far, including Nuttall, actually stop to consider
what such dysfunctional allegories might actually refer to. Sharon
Achinstein, for example, makes a convincing case for reading these
allegories as subversive royalist tropes. Milton's allegories are 'faulty'
or 'unstable', she argues, because rather than yielding the typical royalist

---

[39] Fallon, *Milton Among the Philosophers*, 182–3.
[40] Ibid. 185.
[41] Teskey, *Delirious Milton*, 31. Teskey echoes Gimelli Martin, *The Ruins of Allegory*, 179.
[42] See Nuttall, *Overheard by God*, 85–93. Long before Fallon, Nuttall explored the strange materialism of Milton's epic, where the 'physicalism of the universe is, so to speak, a transfigured and exalted physicalism' (p. 91). However, Nuttall concludes that when it comes to the distinction between spiritual and 'corporal forms' in the poem Milton is not as consistent as Fallon would later argue he is, but the willing victim of a deliberate Platonic confusion which views all spirits as a form of matter. And on this account at least, according to Nuttall, Johnson was right to question both the physical integrity of Milton's allegories and his corporeal angels. But as Poole rightly argues, Johnson's criticisms may be founded but they are not fair, 'because it is impossible for Milton to meet them: Johnson assumes the ontological barrier of the Fall to be absolute, and then blames Milton for not being able to do anything about it' (*Milton and the Idea of the Fall*, 179).

tenor contemporaries would have associated with the allegorical imagery Milton deploys in his portrayal of Sin, for example, such allegories only confront the reader with the perplexing realities of tyranny, incestuous cannibalism, and hell's self-consuming nihilism.[43] However, too much insistence on what these allegories might signify, even negatively, ironically undermines their quite deliberate 'faulty' status. After all, if the allegories are deliberately faulty, might it not be also deliberate that hell's vacuity and semiotic indeterminacy spills over into the fallen world across the gulf of Chaos using the concreteness of rock as a bridge? One critic at least, Sarah Morrison, has bravely suggested as much, arguing that Milton actively seeks to bring the poem's 'naturalistic narrative' in conflict with its allegorical elements.[44] She then explains why: '[Milton's] highly fictionalized interpretation of sacred history must necessarily contain within itself subtle indications of its nature as an accommodated version of accommodated scriptural truth.'[45] Morrison represents here a long line of sceptical Miltonists who are suspicious of critics who suggest that *Paradise Lost* is anything other than a modestly biblical poem. The weapon of such critics is Milton's theory of distinctly biblical, not Orphic, accommodation as outlined in *De Doctrina Christiana* and apparently implemented throughout the poem. According to such critics, Milton's epic poem in its entirety (not just the postlapsarian books) is confined to accommodated biblical models of allegorical, typological, and symbolical representations as it moves from 'shadowy types' to scriptural 'truth', and makes no extravagant claims to *literal* truth beyond what the analogy of faith allows Milton and his 'fit audience' to glean from Scripture. I too agree that the allegorical and the literal are in conflict in *Paradise Lost*, but not because Milton wants to privilege one over the other. Milton's monist materialist world (or should we say prelapsarian world?) bleeds from a number of deliberate allegorical wounds, and these apertures allow us as readers to experience an oddly displaced sense of ineffable mystery in a fictional universe whose every corner is otherwise illuminated with bright light.

---

[43] Achinstein, *Milton and the Revolutionary Reader*, 193–9. See also Sauer's analysis of the gendered allegorical implications of Milton's Sin in *Barbarous Dissonance*, ch. 4.

[44] S. R. Morrison, 'When Worlds Collide: The Central Naturalistic Narrative and the Allegorical Dimension to *Paradise Lost*', in Pruitt and Durham, *Living Texts*, 178–97.

[45] Ibid. 179–80.

Here it is instructive to glance over at the *De Doctrina Christiana* manuscript.[46] If we view what Milton actually says about the biblical theory of accommodation in *De Doctrina*, it soon emerges that there are problems with the theory as Milton understands it even before we speculate about its possible relevance to *Paradise Lost*, whether or not we confine it to Michael's postlapsarian discourse. Having cited 1 Timothy 6: 16 (a quotation which is central, of course, to the invocation to holy light in Book III of *Paradise Lost* as well), Milton opens his discussion of accommodation in *De Doctrina* with the following orthodox statement: 'When we talk about knowing God, it must be understood in terms of man's limited powers of comprehension. God, as he really is, is far beyond man's imagination, let alone his understanding.'[47] In a strong Augustinian and Protestant mode, Milton then emphasizes that what God has revealed of himself in Scripture is accommodated 'as our minds can conceive and the weakness of our nature can bear'.[48] This leads to Milton's subsequent much-debated statement that 'we ought to form [in Latin, *capere*—capture] just such a mental image of [God] as he, in bringing himself within the limits of our understanding, wished us to form':

It is safest for us to form an image of God in our minds which corresponds to his representation and description of himself in the sacred writings. Admittedly, God is always described or outlined not as he really is but in such a way as will make him conceivable to us. Nevertheless, we ought to form just such a mental image of him as he, in bringing himself within the limits of our understanding, wished us to form. Indeed he has brought himself down to our level expressly to prevent our being carried beyond the reach of human comprehension, and outside the written authority of scripture, into vague subtleties and speculation.[49]

---

[46] Despite reaffirming the compositional date of *De Doctrina* to be in the mid- to late 1650s, which would put it very close to when, according to Aubrey, Milton began work on *Paradise Lost* in 1658, Campbell *et al.* warn that the two works have little in common and should not be compared without careful qualification and circumspection. While obviously written with very different aims in mind and in very different genres, and while it is also probably true, as Campbell *et al.* argue, that *De Doctrina* 'points . . . to a different lost paradise, that of a republican England . . . where no orthodoxy would go untested' (*Milton and the Manuscript of 'De Doctrina Christiana'*, 161), to suggest that none of the theological ideas contained in *De Doctrina*, *qua* ideas, would still be fresh in Milton's mind when composing *Paradise Lost*, or that he inexplicably abandoned them all during the following decade, is urging too much caution.
[47] I.ii. *YCP* vi. 133.   [48] Ibid.   [49] *YCP* vi. 133–4.

At the heart of Milton's discussion of biblical accommodation in *De Doctrina* is an implied theory of creative readership which is highly relevant for any discussion of Milton's use of the Bible in the creation of *Paradise Lost*. As H. R. MacCallum has shown, Milton's theory of accommodation as outlined in *De Doctrina* significantly differs from comparable formulations of the theory in either Luther or Calvin. Luther's and Calvin's conception of the theory is 'social' (perhaps 'pedagogic' is a better term), since 'they take up the position that the Bible was written for a popular audience consisting largely of simple, uneducated people'.[50] Milton's theory, on the other hand is purely 'epistemological, in the sense that it defines the limits of man's comprehension':[51]

The whole drift of his argument is calculated to encourage the reader to rest in the words and images of Scripture, not to penetrate behind them. Thus while the tendency of theories of social accommodation is to explain away the anthropomorphic descriptions of God, Milton's doctrine requires the acceptance of them at face value, without any distinction between the 'tenor' and the 'vehicle.[52]

However, as Nuttall explains, to accept the anthropomorphic descriptions of God in the Bible at face value without distinction between the 'tenor' and the 'vehicle' problematically requires a sort of 'pious bad faith':

If God is exactly as he represents himself the 'theory of accommodation' falls to the ground; no accommodation has occurred; if on the other hand he is not such as he represents himself to be then, once we understand this, it is only through (of all things) a sort of pious bad faith that we can continue to believe what is evidently untrue. A solution might have been to suggest that the 'accommodated picture' is a part but not the whole of the truth, but Milton does not clearly adopt it.[53]

---

[50] MacCallum, 'Milton and Figurative Interpretation of the Bible', 402.

[51] Ibid. 403.

[52] Ibid. For a similar analysis, see also Lieb, *Theological Milton*, 114–23, 143–8.

[53] Nuttall, *Overheard by God*, 100. Graves, 'Milton and the Theory of Accommodation', disagrees with Nuttall and argues that Milton does in fact adopt the idea that the accommodated picture is a part but not the whole of truth and is therefore synechdochal in nature. However, the fact that Milton uses neither the word 'analogy' nor the word 'synecdoche' to explain his theory of accommodation when such words were already current in theological debates about biblical hermeneutics should discourage us from imposing such terms on his theology. If this was Milton's idea here he would have stated it clearly.

Either way, then, there is a problem. If the theory of accommodation critics also detect in *Paradise Lost* is merely a 'social' pedagogic tool which explains things away, then it will only succeed in grinding this richly textured poem into fine scriptural dust. However, if MacCallum, Lieb, and others are right and the biblical theory as Milton understands and then presumably deploys it in *Paradise Lost* is merely epistemological, then, as Nuttall intimates, it requires a proper distinction between truth and falsehood which Milton never clearly supplies either in *De Doctrina* or in *Paradise Lost*. Milton, quite deliberately it seems, does not even explain, for example, in what semantic or metaphysical sense readers of the Bible might actually 'capture' an image of God. The process of epistemological accommodation—like that of poetic inspiration in *Paradise Lost*—is one of competitive collaboration. God determines the limits of representation, but it is the reader who forms the image of God in his mind, potentially at the expense of God's intentionality.

A possible compromise between MacCallum's and Nuttall's analysis might point out that Milton's theory appears only to discuss how elect and righteous readers of Scripture may form an image of God in their mind which *accords* with, rather than derives from, similar images in the Bible. This is, after all, how most Protestants viewed the act of inspired biblical readership in the context of what many of them term, and I briefly discuss in Chapter 2, as the 'language of Canaan'. A Reformed Christian must be alive to the Word in a way which makes the words of the Bible alive to him, and like most living things, such a literary organism, so to speak, would be subject to continual growth and change. For Milton, the Bible, with its distinct vocabulary, turns of phrase, and historical-prophetic narrative, was never mere grist for the mill of his poetic imagination (as his classical learning was), but the very life-blood of his creative impulse. However, Milton's theory of biblical accommodation seems to be contaminated at its source with the Orphic impulse of the creative poet who enjoys *unaccommodated* access to divine truths. It is not so much that Milton demands his readers' acceptance of biblical metaphors at face value, as that he implies that the 'logic' of biblical accommodation can be used to defend most anthropomorphic-pathetic representations of God that are 'biblical' in *character*. It does not matter if such representations are formed while actually reading the Bible or thinking about God more generally in

extra-biblical circumstances, because every thought Milton has about
God and every action he takes to express such thoughts creatively
proceeds from his eloquence in the 'language of Canaan' and his
profound spiritual relationship with the Word of God and its textual
record.

The next paragraph in the *De Doctrina* manuscript further reinforces
this difficult idea when Milton proceeds to caution against the use of
anthropopathy when interpreting God's self-representations in the
Bible:

In my opinion, then, theologians do not need to employ anthropopathy, or the
ascription of human feelings to God. This is a rhetorical device thought up by
grammarians to explain the nonsense poets write about Jove. Sufficient care
has been taken, without any doubt, to ensure that the holy scriptures contain
nothing unfitting to God or unworthy of him. This applies equally to those
passages in scripture where God speaks about his own nature. So it is better not
to think about God or form an image of him in anthropopathetic terms, for to
do so would be to follow the example of men, who are always inventing more
and more subtle theories about him. Rather we should form our ideas with
scripture as a model, for that is the way in which he has offered himself to our
contemplation. We ought not to imagine that God would have said anything or
caused anything to be written about himself unless he intended that is should
be a part of our conception of him. On the question of what is or what is not
suitable for God, let us ask for no more dependable authority than God
himself.[54]

Milton appears to repeat here the same Protestant 'logic' from the
previous paragraph. Anthropopathetic descriptions of God in the
Bible are *not* in fact anthropopathetic in a strict metaphorical sense
simply because God would not 'have said anything or caused anything
to be written about himself unless he intended that it should be a part of
our conception of him'. To the modern reader who finds it hard to
reconcile the odd logic of this statement Milton has his answer ready:
God is not human and therefore cannot be circumscribed by the
intricacies of human reasoning. Citing, for example, Genesis 6: 6,
where God repents the creation, Milton is not worried at all that if
taken literally such anthropopathetic descriptions might deny God's

foreknowledge: 'If *Jehovah repented that he had created man,* Gen. vi. 6, *and repented because of their groanings,* Judges ii. 18, let us believe that he did repent. But let us not imagine that God's repentance arises from lack of foresight, as man's does, for he has warned us not to think about him in this way: Num. xxiii. 19: *God is not a man that he should lie, nor the son of man the he should repent.*'[55] Anthropopathy is only anthropopathy when it is used to speculate about God in human rhetorical terms outside the textual remit of the Bible. Human rules of reasoning and human understanding of language clearly do not apply to God and his accommodated portrayal in the Bible, simply because 'Deus non est homo'. But surely the whole point of accommodation is precisely that God lowers himself so that the rules of human reasoning might negotiate his textual presence.

Even before we get to *Paradise Lost,* therefore, we encounter here a monist paradox. Milton assimilates into his imagination the accommodated text of the Bible so completely that they become one, but having fully assimilated the scriptural text he has no need for the accommodated text any longer. As an elect reader who never errs in his understanding of the biblical text, he assumes total authorship over the text so that its accommodated truths become his own *unaccommodated* truths. This simple and powerful religious idea of interpretative authority then allows Milton to claim as literally 'true' any extra-biblical discourse about God which adheres to an obscure model of scripture (*more scripturae*). Georgia Christopher rightly points out that the underlying Protestant principle behind such a 'model of scripture' is to be found with Calvin's *fides facet personam*—the idea that faith, in creating the regenerate man, also creates the regenerate man's corresponding perception of God. God himself is immutable, but man's perception of God as grounded in faith and Holy Scripture is not.[56] However, the problem for literary critics with this principle is that what Milton alludes to as the 'model' or 'custom' of Scripture is hardly a linguistic or literary criterion. It is not even an unstable hermeneutical criterion as is Calvin's *fides facet personam.* And it is precisely at this murky point that the theory of accommodation as outlined in *De Doctrina* finally links up with *Paradise Lost:* when Milton speaks for God in his poem he

---

[55] *YCP* vi. 134–5.
[56] See Christopher, *Milton and the Science of the Saints,* 115.

is not really 'rapt above the pole' (VII. 23), but wrapped up in the 'native element' (VII. 16) of his scriptural imagination.

Therefore, at the heart of the ongoing argument among critics about how to square Milton's theory of accommodation with his claim in the poem to portray ineffable vistas as they really were, or are, is a basic disagreement about the precise nature of metaphor and literalness in *Paradise Lost*; or rather, about the metaphor *of* literalness in the poem. Fallon's engrossing exposition of the animist materialism of Milton's poetic universe has placed such extraordinary emphasis on the poem's claims to literal (one assumes scriptural) truth, that few now question the poem's strangely physical literalness. 'From the time of *Eikonoklastes*', argues Fallon, 'Milton was done with fiction; his later poems are records of truth delivered directly, not through the mediation of allegories.'[57] Fallon is not alone, of course. Maureen Quilligan, for example, uses a comparison with Spenser's mediated vision in *The Faerie Queene* of the eternal city which 'earthly tong | Cannot describe, nor wit of man can tell' (I. x. 55) to point out that what Spenser's Redcross Knight sees can only be read on the mimetic-allegorical level of inadequate or incomplete earthly signs.[58] The movement in Spenser's epic, as Quilligan rightly says, is of the lapsarian creature looking up at heaven and the patterns of its ineffable light through an allegorical glass. Milton, on the other hand, assuming the prophetic mantle of Moses, reverses Spenser's allegorical process so that we the readers see ourselves, fallen though we are, 'as God sees us'.[59] The full implications of Quilligan's and Fallon's arguments are set out in William Franke's interesting analysis of Milton's 'figurative mode'. Franke asserts: 'Milton as a prophetic poet could surrender neither the image nor the truth. Using a third option, he retained both but disconnected them, so that the image no longer functioned as an outward manifestation and representation of how things really are, but rather fed the reader's personal experience of the poem, where truth could be encountered in spiritual immediacy.'[60] Since, however, according to Franke, such

---

[57] Fallon, *Milton Among the Philosophers*, 163.
[58] M. Quilligan, 'Milton's Spenser: The Inheritance of Ineffability', in Hawkins and Schotter, *Ineffability*, 65–79.
[59] Ibid. 72.
[60] Franke, 'Blind Prophecy', 88.

spiritual immediacy is only located in the emotional and didactic register of images which 'do not (nor are they meant to) adequately represent [the poem's] deeper meaning', Franke is forced to conclude that Milton's imagery 'is in this relative sense irrelevant'.[61] I accept Franke's theorization of Milton's 'third option' when it comes to his figuring of ineffable truths, but I think such an option renders Milton's imagery *deeply* relevant to the poem's ultimate meanings, as it is this very dissonance which forces the reader again and again to face up to the consequence of the Fall.

If, indeed, as Fallon, Quilligan, and Franke argue, Milton's *Paradise Lost* eschews the sacramental immanence of the sign that has been miraculously transformed into a sacred object, and if the poem's central epistemological claim is to the internal processes of interpretatively spiritual (that is, subjective) truth, then the poem's uniformity of vision and tactile materiality lend these processes real, indeed tangible, substance. After all, the Reformation movement did not do away with sacramental immanence; it merely sought to interiorize its miraculous operation so that scriptural words, rightly understood, become *spiritually* efficacious things through a process of 'sealing'.[62] In *Paradise Lost*, however, many of Milton's densely physical metaphors are unsealed, as it were, from any fixed relationship with 'sealed' scriptural or spiritual meaning through the poem's lack of sacramental effusion and the need to place the experience of loss at the heart of the reader's encounter with the poem. The resulting poetic vision is one of sinewy, often luxuriantly tactile, concreteness, which is nevertheless strangely unreal and ephemeral, where images evoking raw materials such as gold, silver, pearl, and other precious minerals are shaped into the 'sparkling orient gems' (III. 506) and 'liquid pearl' (III. 518) of heaven's ineffable fabric, as well as into the enamelled opulence of Paradise's equally ineffable and quite un-natural 'nature's boon' (IV. 242), where rivers run on 'orient pearl and sands of gold' (IV. 239) and 'fruit burnished with golden rind' hung 'amiable' (IV. 249–50). Milton goes on to say of the golden fruit of Paradise that they are 'Hesperian fables true, | If true, here only, and of delicious taste' (IV. 250–1). Such imagery suggests a wondrous mythology, a Hesperian fable wrought by the poet's artful fancy that

---

[61] Franke, 'Blind Prophecy', 92.   [62] See Ch. 3, n. 43 above.

'if true', so the poet muses, it can only be so 'here', in Paradise. But of course Paradise is *not* to be found 'here', in the mimetic grip of the verse, since it is in fact already lost. In this way, Milton's epic consistently opens onto ineffable worlds that are nevertheless bound together within the poet's all-encompassing vision in relative physical distance from our fallen, empirical earth.[63] Milton's power as a poet is such, however, that it is all too easy to lose ourselves in the depths and heights of his monist-materialist universe, where the conceit that we are admitted into the presence of prelapsarian and forbidden ineffable sights constantly evokes a sense of acute loss as we are reminded again and again that in fact the limits of art and scriptural decorum have *not* been transgressed, but merely temporarily obscured. Indeed, the day we accept Fallon's statement that *Paradise Lost* only deals in 'truth' and never in an 'eviscerated poetic truth',[64] we have no business as literary critics to interrogate the poem as a literary artefact. Fortunately for the critic, the concept of the 'literal' for Milton is itself always figurative—not in the sense that Milton's metaphors enfold spiritual truths in some mysterious Neoplatonic sense, but in the sense that the promise of spiritual-scriptural truth is ineffably contained in the workings of fallen language and Milton's richly affective imagery. Raphael's lecture on the monist principle which binds all creation within one, continuous animated matter is not allegorical or even figurative, but its position in the narrative within the prelapsarian encounter with Adam renders it as distinctly *lost* literal fiction, the truth of which we as readers must reconstruct amid the iconoclastic ruins of allegory and transcendence.[65]

It is in this context that our willingness to embrace the paradoxical nature of Milton's theory of accommodation becomes indispensable if we are ever to relate to Milton's drama of the Fall. Fallon mines, for

---

[63] For an excellent discussion of Milton's 'relative universe' see Gimelli Martin, *The Ruins of Allegory*, ch. 2.

[64] Fallon, *Milton Among the Philosophers*, 165.

[65] This accords, I think, with what Lana Cable discusses as Milton's iconoclastic 'carnal rhetoric'. Although Cable never applies her theory to *Paradise Lost*, her theoretical insight could be used to clarify the problem of inspiration and authority in Milton's use of metaphor in *Paradise Lost*: 'purely in logical terms, there can be no perceptible distinction between rhetoric that serves an unknowable divine will and that which serves the demands of mortal flesh. If it is apprehensible to human sense, rhetoric is by definition all carnal—representational, temporal, mortally flawed' (Cable, *Carnal Rhetoric*, 49).

example, Raphael's materialism speech for all the philosophical nuggets it is worth, but seems less sure of his ground when Raphael next employs what amounts to a theory of accommodation as he responds to Adam's request to hear more about what 'Hath passed in heaven' (V. 554) prior to the angels' fall:

> High matter thou enjoinst me, O prime of men,
> Sad task and hard, for how shall I relate
> To human sense the *invisible exploits*
> Of warring spirits; how without remorse
> The ruin of so many glorious once
> And perfect while they stood; how last unfold
> The secrets of another world, perhaps
> Not lawful to reveal? Yet for thy good
> This is dispensed, and what surmounts the reach
> Of human sense, *I shall delineate so,*
> *By likening spiritual to corporal forms,*
> *As may express them best, though what if earth*
> *Be but the shadow of heav'n, and things therein*
> *Each to other like, more than on earth is thought?*
>
>   (V. 563–77, my emphases)

For all of Milton's monism, the intellectual context of Raphael's words resonates with Augustinian and Platonic logocentric orthodoxy. Raphael is promising to apply in his description of the angelic war in heaven a form of literary accommodation very similar to what Augustine and Calvin argue God himself applies in communicating elements of his ineffable nature to Moses. We may recall that Augustine, for example, having contemplated the name 'I Am that I Am', states in *De Genesi ad Litteram* that 'the Divine Being is beyond words and cannot be spoken of in any way without recourse to expressions of time and place'.[66] 'Time' and 'place' are ontological parameters which proceed from the axiomatic belief in the existence of the hidden God, but which can never confine God to a specific ontology. In the spirit of this tradition, Raphael appears to concede that what Adam asks to hear about would be impossible to describe in a language a lesser creature such as he could understand without rooting an otherwise ineffable subject in an ontology which

---

[66] *The Literal Meaning of Genesis*, 6.16; Taylor, i. 166–7.

Adam can relate to. Raphael thus excuses in advance the imagery of his forthcoming narration of the war in heaven as some form of Platonic, if not Philonian, allegory where that which is ineffable would be described 'by likening spiritual to corporal forms'.[67] But there is a paradox here, because the monist materialist universe Raphael and Adam co-inhabit, we are told, cannot admit an implicitly dualistic allegorical or even meta-phorical dimension.

It is true that in *De Doctrina* Milton takes the words 'I Am that I Am' to mean that God is a spirit, that is, a single, mathematically 'simple' monist entity: 'From this it may be understood that the essence of God, since it is utterly simple, allows nothing to be compounded with it, and that the word hypostasis, Heb.i.3, which is variously translated sub-stance, or person, is nothing but the most perfect essence by which God exists from himself, in himself, and through himself.'[68] Given this theology, Fallon is perhaps right to say that Raphael's 'spiritual' and 'corporal' are merely 'relative terms';[69] angels for Milton are corporeally made up of the same created substance as man, but are simply more rarefied, because the closer any being is to God who is a 'Spirit', the more rarefied and simple—in the mathematical sense—it becomes. If 'spiritual' and 'corporal' forms are substantially of the same matter, however, accommodation can never take place, and the whole point of Raphael's apologetic speech about his ensuing narration of the angelic war evaporates. The war in heaven is not some stilted lecture on spiritual bodies, but a wildly imaginative, at times even comical, epic sequence, drawing on numerous literary models of heroic warfare to instil in the reader a sense of exaltation and awe at the poet's ambitious vision and its underlying moral lesson about angelic heroism, rebellion, and divine justice. Only the most imaginative poetry can achieve such feats, and by insisting too strongly on the materialist argument we petrify the energy of this poetry. Whether or not Milton actually believed in corporeal angels is beside the point. What matters is that we, as readers responding

[67] Milton's use of the adjective 'corporal' seems to mean 'having a body' (corporeal), not 'relating to the body' more generally. However, as Fowler notes, Milton 'did not observe this distinction regularly, if at all' (*Paradise Lost*, 317, n. 573). See *OED* 'corporal', *a.*, 1c but also 2: 'Of the nature of body or matter; corporeal, material, physical. *Obs.*'

[68] *YCP* vi. 140–1.

[69] Fallon, *Milton Among the Philosophers*, 143.

to Milton's art, want to believe in Milton's corporeal angels because they are so brilliantly conceived *metaphorically* using the terms of a monist materialist philosophy.

Granted, the literalist who has no patience for the paradox of a material metaphor might still counter by pointing to Raphael's next, desperately speculative affirmation of radical monism: 'though what if earth | Be but the shadow of heav'n, and things therein | Each to other like, more than on earth is thought?' We can take these words to mean that since earth and heaven are indeed 'one matter all', what appears to us as accommodation is simply a question of relativity. But the speculative, wishful tone of these lines, not to mention the inescapable Platonic resonance implied in the very words 'shadow of heav'n', suggests that we are dealing here not with degrees of materialist substance but with epistemological problems of language and representation, where abstract concepts and ideas are, ultimately, shadowed in earthly metaphors and typology.[70] If the angels' 'invisible exploits' in heaven are indeed invisible in a physical, material sense then that would make the need for metaphorical representation all the more acute—how else will Raphael describe what Adam is simply unable to conceptualize? As William Poole points out, what begins with the promise of simile (comparing like with like) devolves during the narration of the war into explicit metaphor (like with unlike) and finally into aporia: 'They ended parle, and both addressed for fight | Unspeakable' (VI. 296–7).[71] Given this process of gradual rhetorical *aphaeresis*, what possible bearing do seventeenth-century philosophical speculations about materialism have on Adam's ability to appreciate the truly adverse implications of rebellion and the underlying moral dimension of this cautionary tale? I am not suggesting that the poem's presentation of a monist-materialist universe is either inconsistent or negligible. On the contrary, its implications for the poem's metaphorical concreteness are irrefutable, but the very physicalism of the poetry displaces a sense of ineffable mystery which the narrator then reintroduces into the poem through the back door of lapsarian sensibilities.

---

[70] See Madsen, *From Shadowy Types to Truth*, 54–74; Swaim, *Before and After the Fall*, 159–64.
[71] Poole, *Milton and the Idea of the Fall*, 177.

Later in the poem, for example, when the Miltonic poet is about to compete with the Bible in his retelling of the Genesis account of creation (the *Hexamera*) through the foil of Raphael's lecture, he immediately inserts the following disclaimer:

> Immediate are the acts of God, more swift
> Than time or motion, but to human ears
> Cannot without process of speech be told,
> So told as earthly notion can receive.

(VII. 176–9)

This second, more straightforward announcement of accommodation complicates Raphael's previous speech from Book V even further, because the two conceptually overlap and cause a meta-poetic split in the narrative presentation of Raphael's prelapsarian lecture. Now it seems that we must interpret the movement from 'spiritual' to 'corporal' forms as a reduction of ineffable concepts into 'earthly notions'. It forces us to stop and ask ourselves: who is the angel really addressing when he says 'Yet for thy good | This is dispensed'? It is very difficult to read through the stirring events of the angelic war without wondering whether or not unfallen Adam would have been able at all to comprehend Raphael's edifying story. Would he have known what to make of shields, chariots, swords, or the firepower of 'engines and their balls | Of missive ruin' (VI. 518–19)? God may have endued Adam with the necessary knowledge needed to name the animals according to their 'nature', but surely it would be too much to assume that Adam in his prelapsarian state could have even grasped the abstract horror implicit in the sin of disobedience, let alone the concept of war. But whereas prelapsarian Adam could not possibly have had any 'earthly notion' relevant to the understanding of 'engines' of war and gunpowder cannons, most seventeenth-century readers certainly did have such notions.[72] Raphael's accommodation speeches invite us to imagine the narrator, not Raphael, addressing us the fallen readers in a brilliant flash of meta-poetry, where the relationship between Raphael and Adam effectively becomes the Platonic 'shadow' of the narrator's complex relationship with his intended lapsarian audience. Raphael could have

---

[72] Ibid. 179.

said to Adam: 'what surmounts the reach of *your* (prelapsarian) sense', but instead he says 'what surmounts the reach of *human* (lapsarian) sense', thus implicitly addressing Adam as the archetypal human whose 'sense' is not merely far removed, epistemologically, from all things divine, but is in some manner already corrupt. Since, however, there is no indication that Raphael has access to God's foreknowledge beyond what he has been told, it is hard not to detect an authorial intrusion at this moment in the dialogue, where Milton the didactic poet tugs at our sleeve and tells us, 'this is as much addressed to you as it is to Adam'.

Nevertheless, whether or not they are intentional, the meta-poetic anomalies in Raphael's theory of accommodation complicate the underlying presentation of the theory because it breaks with the illusion of one continuous matter. As soon as we sense what Milton is whispering to us below the surface of the words we are hard pressed not to consider the relevance of the theory not only to the 'pavilions', and 'brazen chariots' of the warring angelic armies, but also to Milton's portrayal of heaven in general, and God in particular. Suddenly we must wonder whether or not the entire poem is itself an exercise in accommodation, where the only criterion for literal truth is the mysterious narrator's subjectivity. This is not helped, moreover, by the tone of Raphael's accommodation speech, which betrays a peculiarly Miltonic anxiety about the *permissibility* of such accommodation. Raphael is not asserting the materialist imperative with confidence, but wondering speculatively whether the fact that he and Adam are one matter is any excuse for disclosing 'the secrets of another world, perhaps | Not lawful to reveal'. Later on in the poem, when an over-curious Adam wants to know more about the hidden mysteries of planetary motions, the same Raphael who earlier muses 'though what if earth | Be but the shadow of heav'n, and things therein | Each to other like, more than on earth is thought?', now suddenly asserts:

> God to remove his ways from human sense,
> Placed heaven from earth so far, that earthly sight,
> If it presume, might err in things too high,
> And no advantage gain.
>
> (VIII. 119–22)

This discrepancy is usually explained away by pointing out that Raphael's lecture distinguishes between necessary or permissible knowledge and unnecessary, non-permissible knowledge. In this pre-lapsarian context, the criterion for the necessity of certain knowledge is not salvific but precautionary: God sends Raphael to 'render man inexcusable' ('The Argument', Book V) and to ensure that he is 'suffi-cient' to stand. The edifying story about the fall of the rebel angels is necessary to instruct Adam about the moral of obedience; speculations about astronomy are of no value whatsoever. The silent Eve's reaction to Adam's improper questions about planetary motions speaks volumes. In a wonderful moment of suburban ennui, when Eve notices the counte-nance of her husband 'Entering on studious thoughts abstruse' (VIII. 40), she prudently gets up with 'lowliness majestic' (VIII. 42) and leaves the bower to potter in the garden—she has better things to do then to sit there and listen to speculative nonsense. But Eve's sudden onset of prudent boredom obfuscates another meta-poetic anomaly here. As Regina Schwartz has pointed out, we must never forget that Urania, Milton's heavenly muse invoked in the opening of Book VII, is the ancient muse of astronomy, indicating therefore that the Miltonic poet gains his inspiration from the wrong side of permissible knowledge. However, as Schwartz then qualifies this, Milton associates Urania (whose meaning, not the name, he invokes) with the allegorical Wisdom of the Book of Proverbs, which was present at the moment of creation and is 'qualified to offer knowledge, not rumor or quaint opinions of it... Milton thereby converts star-gazing, the emblem of presumptive curiosity, into a divinely sanctioned quest'.[73]

All paradoxes, it seems, lead then to the poem's ambivalent active-passive narrator, but where does this leave the equally paradoxical theory of active-passive monist accommodation which the narrator supposedly performs on our behalf? Significantly, one of the central metaphors in the poem for the underlying difficulty of this paradox is the very instrument of star-gazing—the telescope. As an instrument devised by man to see into the far reaches of heaven, the telescope is a suspect device for Milton, and he usually associates the sort of insights one might gain from a telescope with diabolic delusion and deception. And yet, the relatively frequent reference to this image in the poem suggests

[73] Schwartz, *Remembering and Repeating*, 59. See also E. Cook, 'Melos versus Logos, or Why Doesn't God Sing: Some Thoughts on Milton's Wisdom', in Nyquist and Ferguson, *Re-Membering Milton*, 197–210.

that Milton was fascinated with the astronomical analogy it offered him. Early on in the epic, for example, when the reader is still trapped in hell with the devils, the narrator likens Satan's shield to the moon,

> whose orb
> Through optic glass the Tuscan artist views
> At evening from the top of Fesole,
> Or in Valdarno, to descry new lands,
> Rivers and mountains in her spotty globe.
>
> (I. 287–91)

Given that Milton admired Galileo (the 'Tuscan artist') and visited him in 1638, a number of critics have worried about the association of Galileo with Milton's Satan.[74] Unfortunately, the simile does seem to suggest that if you look through a telescope at the moon long enough in an effort to 'descry new lands' you will only find Satan looking back at you. This idea is reinforced when later, in Book III, Satan lands on the 'orb of the Sun': 'There lands the fiend, a spot like which perhaps | Astronomer in the sun's lucent orb | Through his glazed optic tube yet never saw' (III. 588–90). Renaissance astronomers, including Galileo, considered spots on the sun to be a worrying sign of its translunary (as opposed to sublunary) mutability and corruption,[75] and Milton uses this idea to suggest that Satan's presence genuinely corrupts the sun like no spot any astronomer can actually claim to see with his telescope. The word 'perhaps', however, softens the negative force of the simile so that the spots on the sun astronomers *can* see using a telescope may have something Satanic about them after all. The point is not that astronomers are overreaching fools, but that Satan, for all his otherworldly ponderousness, is much too close to us for comfort in his 'spotty' physicality. The Satanic spot on the sun links up with 'spotty' in the moon simile from earlier in Book I. As

---

[74] See Fowler, *Paradise Lost*, 78, nn. 286–91; Lewalski, *The Life of John Milton*, 93–4. However, if the autobiographical passage in *Areopagitica* alluding to Galileo is anything to go by ('There it was that I found and visited the famous *Galileo* grown old, a prisoner to the Inquisition, for thinking in Astronomy otherwise then the Franciscan and Dominican licencers thought', *YCP* ii. 537–8), it is likely that Milton admired Galileo more for the fact that he had defied the Catholic Church and was under house-arrest than for his astronomy as such; though Milton had probably read Galileo's *Dialogo…sopra i due massimi sistemi del mondo, tolemaico, e copernicano*, published in 1632 and banned by the Church in 1633.

[75] See Fowler, *Time's Purpled Masquers*, 68–70.

A. D. Nuttall puts it, in his brilliant analysis of this extended simile, the word 'spotty' is 'low, almost brutal' and points to the moon's degraded fallen nature[76]—like Lucifer, the morning star, it has been implicated in sin, for how else can the New Science detect its blemishes and then speculate about their possible meanings? But, of course, the sun which Satan next corrupts with his speculative presence is also a Neoplatonic metaphor for divine effluence, and when Satan discovers it to be 'beyond expression bright, | Compared with aught on earth, metal or stone' (III. 590–1), the echo of 'may I express thee unblamed?' from the invocation to holy light earlier in the book is deliberate. It contrasts the limits of fallen, empirical knowledge, which cannot even supply the scientist with terms to express the created light of the sun, with the limits of spiritual knowledge which has to contend with the uncreated light of God. When standing against an inexpressible background, therefore, Satan becomes all too visible to us because everything about him for Milton is *fallen* matter, 'earth, metal or stone'. It is in this lapsarian, epistemological sense that telescopic vision is ultimately implicated with Satanic vision.

The image of Satan blighting the sun with his fallen presence is a powerful metaphor, therefore, for the way in which all fallen accommodated matter is corrupted by the symbolism which material things lend themselves to and into which they need to be reworked for them to transcend the limits of matter or the *merely* literal. But what if the accommodating telescope was held, not by a fallen being looking up at heaven, but as Quilligan intimates, by an angel or an inspired poet looking at earth from the ineffable remoteness of heaven? When Raphael descends from heaven to Paradise, he views all of God's creation in one swoop of his telescopic sight, as things far away from him quickly come into view as he flies down towards them. Milton cannot resist the analogy, and adds that Raphael sees the earthly Paradise 'As when by night the glass | Of Galileo, less assured, observes | Imagined lands and regions in the moon' (V. 261–3). Raphael's downward flight embodies in the most literal analogy the principle that accommodation can only move in one direction—from the heavenly down to the earthly. Peer at heaven with Galileo's 'less assured' telescope and you see only 'imaginary lands'; peer at Heaven (with a capital 'H') using Milton's inverted angelic or inspired telescope and you see God's prelapsarian creation in its fully imaginable splendour. However, even if we allow the poem's materialist philosophy to become in this way a tool of literary analysis and argue that the narrator/Raphael merely intends to adjust the earthly lens of his inverted telescope through which we can perceive more rarefied subject-matter, the hidden God remains quite literally out of the picture. The underlying monist-materialist philosophy which grounds the project of mimesis in *Paradise Lost* explains everything but solves nothing. Once we apply the narrator/Raphael's theory of monist accommodation to Milton's portrayal of God and the heaven he inhabits, none of what Raphael or the narrator says about accommodation makes any kind of sense whatsoever. When it comes to Milton's God, we are forced to retreat into traditional realms of biblical accommodation which the monist structure of the poem otherwise repudiates, and the paradox of Raphael's theory of accommodation as outlined above still stands. There is, however, a degree of deliberate inadvertency about this paradox. It allows Milton to reintroduce into the poem ineffable mystery even as he asserts the poem's oddly obfuscated sense of revealed literal clarity.

INEFFABLE SPEECH EFFECTS

When Milton's God speaks, the overall didactic integrity of the poem comes under threat. Notwithstanding Campbell's (*et al.*) recent warning against following Maurice Kelley in using *De Doctrina* as a gloss on *Paradise Lost*, it is very difficult to read the *De Doctrina* statement dismissing anthropopathy, especially the parenthetical remark describing it as 'a rhetorical device thought up by grammarians to explain the nonsense poets write about Jove', without thinking with an ironic smile of Milton's God. Although there are very few isolated figurative descriptions of God in *Paradise Lost* that may qualify as strictly anthropopathetic, Milton does appear to invest the speech of God throughout the epic with what can be read (and indeed often has been read) as extremely potent and at times visceral anthropopathy. To give the most famous example, the content of the Father's speech to the Son during the council in heaven in Book III is straightforward and clear: it is a perfectly thought-out and executed logical sermon on Milton's theology, summarizing Milton's (not God's) key positions on grace, election, and free will. That the theology is recognizable as idiosyncratically Miltonic need not worry us, since it was Milton, after all, who famously asserted that 'it is the custom of poets to place their own opinions in the mouth of their great characters',[77] and I think it is safe to assume that in *Paradise Lost* Milton's greatest character in a very literal sense is God. But then Milton's God the *dramatis persona* also problematically says the following about man's future fall caused by the perversion of Satan's 'false guile' (III. 93):

> For man will hearken to his glozing lies,
> And easily transgress the sole command,
> Sole pledge of his obedience: so will fall,
> He and his faithless progeny: whose fault?
> Whose but his own? Ingrate, he had of me
> All he could have; I made him just and right,
> Sufficient to have stood, though free to fall.
>
> (III. 94–9)

The injured tone of 'whose fault? | Whose but his own?', and in particular the word 'ingrate', strikes such a petulant chord in our ears that the tightly condensed theological dogma so crucial to the poem's project of 'justification' contained in 'I made him just and right, | Sufficient to have stood, though free to fall' is hard, if not impossible, for some readers to digest.

As many critics have argued, it is possible for the modern reader to over-complicate the problem by placing too much emphasis on his or her own unsolicited emotional response to the speech. Enter the theory of biblical accommodation: the tone of righteous indignation Milton attributes to his speaking God is entirely commensurate with similar biblical passages where the biblical God expresses dismay or frustration with his creatures.[78] Such is the tone, as Milton himself points out, in Genesis 6: 6, or indeed in Numbers 14: 11: 'And the Lord said unto Moses, How long will this people provoke me? and how long will it be

---

[77] *First Defence, YCP* iv/i. 446. 'sensum fere suum poetae personis optimis affingere solent', *Defensio Prima, CCW* vii. 326. The context for this quotation is Milton's argument against tyrants where, after quoting to that effect Seneca's *Hercules Furens*, Milton makes the point that when Seneca placed a comment against tyrants in the mouth of Hercules he was effectively voicing what many upright men secretly believed about Nero during the emperor's reign: 'significabat et quid ipse, et quid omnes viri boni, aetate etiam Neronis, faciendum tyranno consuerint', ibid.

[78] See Hughes, *Ten Perspectives*, 122, or Lieb, *The Sinews of Ulysses*, 76–97.

ere they believe me, for all the signs which I have shewed them?' But is it really possible to excuse Milton's use of occasional anthropopathy in God's speeches in *Paradise Lost* on literary-poetic grounds simply because it accords with an ill-defined principle of biblical hermeneutics? Michael Lieb thinks it is. Lieb argues that, since Milton fully divinizes the emotional life of God and seeks to reclaim passibility as a distinct category of deity, we should introduce into Milton's hermeneutical and related poetic theory the idea of *theopatheia* as opposed to *anthropopatheia*. According to Lieb, the term *theopatheia* (God-like emotion) captures the idea that 'for Milton, the emotional life of God is real and indeed holy. It originates in God, inheres in him, and is bestowed upon his offspring as manifestations of the *imago Dei*.'[79] So far so good; but when Lieb turns to consider how this profoundly abstract principle might operate poetically in *Paradise Lost* he loses his reader in a maze of apophatic speculation and circumlocution, continually saying and not saying what he and by extension Milton mean to say when they try and say the unsayable. Lieb focuses, rather problematically, for example, on the terms of description Milton's angels use to talk about God in their apophatic hymn in Book III. He alludes to the way in which the angels use negative expressions to affirm something about God—the traditional practice of negative theology—and offers such theologically accurate but literarily opaque statements as: 'At the very point that the language denies accessibility, however, it invites conceptualization.'[80] He finally concludes that 'the poet places himself in the profoundly unique position of offering his poem as the vehicle through which the voice of God is able to speak',[81] but, again, this statement cannot be taken literally, unless we are willing to admit that Milton actually did have direct access to God's mind and was attempting therefore to say the unsayable. However, if it is not to be taken literally, Lieb is entirely unclear how his argument should be understood *poetically*. All that remains in the admission that '*Paradise Lost* is not the Bible, and Milton's God does not possess the same authorized presence as he does in the Bible', followed by the rather desperate assertion that nevertheless 'As far as Milton is

---

[79] Lieb, 'Milton and the Anthropopathetic Tradition', 231. See also *Theological Milton*, ch. 4.
[80] Lieb, 'Milton and the Anthropopathetic Tradition', 233.
[81] Ibid. 237.

concerned, however, [or is it as far as Lieb is concerned] his poem is the most authoritative re-enactment of what happens in the Bible as one can possibly imagine' (p. 162). What is missing from Lieb's theory of *theopatheia* is a meditation on the literary process which allows Milton to pretend to say the unsayable, as opposed to *actually* saying it; after all, when Milton's God shouts out his 'ingrate', it is Milton the poet, not God, who is ultimately registering his disgust with fallen humanity. I am not suggesting that Lieb's analysis is untenable. His fundamental claim that Milton read the biblical God as 'a fully passible being' is probably true and important for what it can teach us about *Paradise Lost*, but Lieb's application of this idea as a tool of literary analysis is too blunt and its conclusions too difficult to follow once it assents to the circular logic of Milton's paradoxical theory of accommodation.

Another, equally unsatisfying, solution to the problem is to propose that Milton may not have considered the speech he had placed in God's mouth in Book III as anthropopathetic at all (or *theopathetic*, for that matter). In fact, some have argued that since the speech is a product of a theology grounded on the 'right' interpretation of Scripture based on 'human reason', *emotion* never plays into it. According to such a reading, God is not being defensive or petulant but merely logical, and a word such as 'ingrate', as Fish, for example, argues, thus becomes 'a term not of reproach, but of definition'.[82] Gary Hamilton in his own way concurs with Fish when, altogether ignoring the 'ingrate' outburst, he describes the speech (or at least a sanitized version of it) as a 'well-organized and carefully planned lesson in theology'.[83] Such readings place important and justified emphasis on what Dennis Burden has analysed as the epic's strong logical impulse to 'establish the reasonableness of God's anger'[84]—a rationalism which in Milton's heaven at least, as Richard Strier has shown in a splendid essay, indirectly undermines the theology of free will which is so central to Milton's theodicy.[85] But readings of this type are surely lacking when they seek to deny the equally didactic tonal register of God's speech, which is neither anthropopathetic nor really theopathetic, but profoundly dramatic. Paul

[82] Fish, *Surprised by Sin*, 64.
[83] Hamilton, 'Milton's Defensive God: A Reappraisal', 92–3.
[84] Burden, *The Logical Epic*, 13.
[85] Strier, 'Milton's Fetters, or, Why Eden is Better than Heaven'.

Stevens, for example, retains both readings and more convincingly argues that the emotional thrust of God's speech is ultimately justified by the 'literary context' of both Homer and the Bible within which Milton conceived it. Stevens is, moreover, right to criticize Irene Samuel's claim that God's speech merely states 'what is',[86] and to point out that it is rather 'an expression of anger that is meant to elicit a response—both in the reader and the Son'.[87] No matter how forcefully Fish insists that God's speech in Book III is 'non-affective',[88] the speech undeniably delivers a powerful affective punch; it is designed to arouse powerful emotions of shame and guilt in the reader which place the cold meditation on the doctrinal pronouncements of the speech in their proper salvific context.

The problem with divine speech in *Paradise Lost* is not, therefore, what God says, but *how* he says it. Some critics, unnecessarily attempting to salvage the numinous integrity of divine speech in the poem, argue that Milton designs God's speeches to sound otherworldly in their non-lapsarian integrity. Entzminger and Fish, for example, argue that the syntax and grammar of God's several speeches in the poem are eminently clear and carefully attuned to the theological content being expressed.[89] So, for example, when 'God's decrees refer to eternal matters, his speech has a high incidence of abstract nouns that are likewise immutable in meaning and use'.[90] God's words in the poem are never ambiguous, according to Entzminger, because their vocabulary and syntax promote the idea of a Platonically perfect language, that is, a language which is both 'prior to and inclusive of the reality [it] indicates'.[91] According to such a reading, the words Milton puts into the mouth of God amount to nothing less than a Lutheran consubstantive sacrament, where words do not refer to objects but *become* those objects: 'The Father's word "Grace," for instance, is itself "gracious" (III. 142, 144).'[92] However, as I have argued in relation to Luther's theology in Chapter 2, such a consubstantive approach to sacred language would dislocate the ineffable with considerable force, so that

[86] Samuel, 'The Dialogue in Heaven', 603.
[87] Stevens, *Imagination and the Presence of Shakespeare in 'Paradise Lost'*, 152.
[88] Fish, *Surprised By Sin*, 62–8.
[89] Entzminger, *Divine Word*, 127–35. See also Fish, *Surprised by Sin*, 74–80.
[90] Entzminger, *Divine Word*, 132.
[91] Ibid. 130.   [92] Ibid.

meaning, at least non-literal meaning, gets lost. The literal meaning that *would* remain under such conditions, however, must exist at the expense of subjectivity, because if we are to sustain the absolutist illusion of literalness we can never allow either the subjectivity of the reader, or even the subjectivity of the poet for that matter, to interfere with the interpretation of what God says literally. So if we are to accept the readings of Entzminger and Fish, we must also accept that when we interpret what Milton's God says in his allegedly Stoic, artless scriptural manner, it is never therefore *our* interpretation because we are asked to accept literally what is already interpreted, accommodated, and digested at the moment of utterance. This experience in many ways defines the typical hostile reaction to divine speech in *Paradise Lost*, where its clarity is seen to be much too bright, and the Lutheran paradox of consubstantive literalness which generates such clarity at the expense of ineffable mystery makes for bad theology, and for some, even worse poetry.

However, Milton removes any sense of ineffable mystery from the actual words his God utters precisely because he is aiming for the immediacy of direct parental rebuke which depends on eliciting from the reader a very specific emotional as well as rational response. *Paradise Lost* is not a laconic monody, but a dramatic-epic poem, where characters deliver speeches within a wide range of affective registers and where ineffable mystery is not suppressed but carefully displaced and diffused to give numinous support to the didactic clarity of words. Divine speech in *Paradise Lost* is always reported within the didactic epic frame of the inspired poet's narrative, and its cumulative effect must be weighed against the imaginary backdrop of the poem as a whole. Therefore, given the sensitivity of these passages when God speaks, it is a rather alarming phenomenon that few modern critics seem to attach any significance to the apophatic conventionality in which Milton *introduces* his speaking God. At the extreme, such omissions produce a view of Milton's God that is as hostile as it is unbalanced. Critic Warwick Orr, for example, accuses Milton's God of irrecoverable self-diminution through the 'very otiose reasoning' employed in his rationalistic defence, which in turn renders the total presence of the deity in the poem as 'perpetually other than himself, a "meaning" virtually without "form" '.[93] But this is to ignore the important

---

[93] Orr, 'Milton and the Defeat of Sacredness', 106.

way in which the epic narrator prefaces in Book III and elsewhere the
actual divine speech with a description of God the Father on his throne:

> Now had the almighty Father from above,
> From the pure empyrean where he sits
> High throned *above all height*, bent down his eye,
> His own works and their works at once to view:
> About him all the sanctities of heaven
> Stood thick as stars, and from his sight received
> Beatitude *past utterance*...
>
> (III. 56–62, my emphases)

The significance of this description, which insists on the apophatic
character of God's unmediated presence, *is* that it is conventional.
Thomas Corns, one of those who do find the conventionality of the
imagery itself significant, thinks that 'Milton would like us to respect
this vision as a difficult metaphor of the edge of human understanding'.[94] Similarly, in an earlier essay Marshall Grossman helpfully describes Milton's use of such traditional apophatic imagery within the
dynamics of what he calls Milton's twin 'dialectical visions'—one
temporal, the other revelatory. As Grossman contends, Milton 'uses
continuing metaphors in varied contexts to imitate, in the reader's
experience, the inadequacies of empirical judgement. The vehicles of
these metaphors form the discursive surface of the text while the tenors
provide the literary illusion of grace.'[95] The traditional anthropomorphic references to God 'sitting' and 'bending his eye' are thus balanced
by the idea that God sits, transcendentally, 'above all height' and
that the beatitude he bestows on the angels is 'past utterance'. As Lieb
has shown, moreover, this imagery is closely bound up with Judaeo-
Christian traditions which talk of God's divine 'dwelling' (*Shekinah*) in
the world as light and presence.[96] The reference to God 'sitting',
moreover, specifically alludes to God's throne, echoing traditional
Jewish 'Throne Mysticism', which informs Paul's famous account of
his rapture to the third heaven where he had heard 'unutterable words',
and which also informs Milton's 'impetus for transforming cultic

---

[94] Corns, *Regaining 'Paradise Lost'*, 18–19.
[95] Grossman, 'Milton's Dialectical Visions', 29.
[96] See Lieb, *Poetics of the Holy*, 212–45.

precedence (worship of the *Shekinah* in the sanctuary) into visionary form (the *visio Dei*)'.[97]

Once God's speech is concluded, moreover, the narrator hastens to add:

> Thus while God spake, ambrosial fragrance filled
> All heaven, and in the blessèd spirits elect
> Sense of new joy ineffable diffused...
>
> (III. 135–7)

This extraordinary olfactory image, suggesting that God's words fill heaven with 'ambrosial fragrance', colours the speech which we have just read with a profound sense of otherworldly mystery that ingeniously proceeds from the inherent anthropomorphism of the imagery. The anthropomorphic God who sits and talks also produces sweet breath *as* he talks. But this anthropomorphic breath does not behave as normal breath does—God, we are reminded, is not a man—for as the breath spreads throughout all heaven its 'ambrosial fragrance' causes a new sense of *ineffable* 'joy' to spread among the angels who smell it. By the force of the same trope, God's otherwise literal words are not merely heard in heaven, but are in fact felt as a total sensory and emotional experience. By framing God's literal speech with a sense of profound apophatic mystery, Milton effectively inverts the traditional apophatic formula. He points out in this way not that what we are about to hear is in fact ineffable and therefore not to be taken literally, but that what we read when God speaks, and must understand literally, is in fact radically ineffable at its source. This kind of apophatic inversion instantly creates, as Grossman indicates, a split in the representation of God in the poem, since it points out that were God the Father to speak directly to the reader the experience would overwhelm us. It obliquely points to the truly transcendental and aweful God whose numinous presence lords it over the 'circuit inexpressible' of the poem's extended metaphysical scope, while highlighting the important function in the poem of the inspired poet-prophet mediating on our behalf with his telescope of paradoxically monist accommodation. This process of inversion, moreover, attaches the ineffability of deep emotion and fear usually associated with the mystery of God's unmediated presence

---

[97] Ibid. 228.

to the literalness of his words, so that what God says carries with it throughout the epic a deep, resounding authority.

This is the strategy again in Book V, when Raphael introduces God's speech in the following terms:

> Thus when in orbs
> Of *circuit inexpressible* they stood,
> Orb within orb, the Father *infinite*,
> By whom in bliss embosomed sat the Son,
> Amidst as from a flaming mount, whose top
> Brightness had made *invisible*, thus *spake*.
>
> (V. 594–9, my emphases)

Once again, it is within this traditionally evoked frame of invisible power that God is then described, with yet another unsettling dose of anthropopathy, 'smiling' to the Son as he sardonically mocks the rebel angels by feigning panic:

> Let us advise, and to this hazard draw
> With speed what force is left, and all employ
> In our defence, lest unawares we lose
> This our high place, our sanctuary, our hill.
>
> (V. 729–32)

Without the benefit of the previous description of the utterly transcendental 'I Am', God speaking 'as from a flaming mount', one might have been forgiven for blanching with astonishment at Milton's cynical God. The paradox of Milton's monist accommodation, however, encourages us to accept the literalness of God's mockery without losing sight of the infinite power which produces such oddly accommodated anthropopathy. The same accomodation process is then repeated when the Son speaks next, but here the effect is slightly different. When the Son replies to the Father, 'thy foes | Justly hast in derision' (V. 735–6), reinforcing our sense of the rebel angels' absurdity in attempting to overpower in military combat an omnipotent, omniscient deity, the narrator also introduces his answer in the following terms: 'To whom the Son with calm aspect and clear | Lightning divine, ineffable, serene, | Made answer' (V. 733–5). The syntax here retains both meanings of the homonym 'aspect'. When we look at the Son's countenance, or 'aspect', through Milton's accommodating monist lens we see a scriptural vision

similar to that of the angelic power revealed to the prophet Daniel
(10: 6): 'his face as the appearance of lightning.' But unlike Daniel's
vision, the Son's aspect of divine, clear lightning is paradoxically 'calm'.
This hard image is necessarily apophatic and it serves to counterbalance
the equally paradoxical yet very real anger of God's mocking infinitude.
'Aspect', however, is also the act of looking at something (*OED* 1*a*, but
also *b* in the sense of a 'glance', citing Milton), so when the Son answers
the Father with 'calm aspect' he is also looking directly at the hidden
God who embosoms him. In this sense, the Son's ineffability is not a
product of apophatic metaphors but a literal divine attribute imparted
to him from the Father. This literalism hardens the metaphor of 'clear
lightning' into a physical trait, so that it reinforces not only the literal
sense of what the Father and the Son say, but also the ineffable parameters of the subordinate relationship between the Father, who is
appropriately biblical in his anger, and the Son, who sits 'in bliss
embosomed' *within* the infinitude of the Father. In the course of the
poem both are referred to as God and both are ineffable in equal
measure, but the presence of ineffability itself, as an attribute, is imparted from the Father to the Son in a form of inexpressible effluence.

The Son for Milton is subordinate to the Father because he is the
efficient expression of the Father's will, and so in essence external to
him. God the Father begets the Son, or *logos*, by uttering him and then
creates the universe by uttering *with* him. The relationship between the
Father and the Son is in principle a reflection of an idealized Aristotelian
semiotic theory where God's mental content finds literal expression in
the words he utters. But whereas for Aristotle the process is more or less
empirical, in that things in the world make impressions on the mind by
forming likenesses of the perceived objects which can then be expressed
in words corresponding to these likenesses, God's Word reverses this
process—it populates reality with objects which are direct physical
expressions of his free and un-necessitated thought or will. It is precisely
at this point that Aquinas, for example, for whom the epistemological
realms of rational enquiry and revelation are distinct from one another,
recommends the analogical model: when we speak of the first two
persons of the Trinity as Father and Son, we do so adjectively and
analogically, since in reality the two are one essence. For Milton,
however, what can be gleaned from Scripture with the aid of reason is
fully revelatory and, consequently, scriptural terms such as 'Father' and

'Son' must be understood *literally*. This is the logic behind one of *De Doctrina*'s most quoted anti-trinitarian passages:

It does not follow, however, that the Son is of the same essence as the Father. Indeed, if he were, it would be quite incorrect to call him Son. For a real son is not of the same age as his father, still less of the same numerical essence: otherwise father and son would be one person. This particular Father begot his Son not from any natural necessity but of his own free will: a method more excellent and more in keeping with paternal dignity, especially as this Father is God.[98]

God's ineffability reflects on the Son or is imparted to him in the semiotic sense that the Son expresses the Father's ineffable nature in all that he does.[99] When the Father commands the Son as the kingly Messiah to arm himself in readiness for battle with 'my mighty arms | Gird on, and sword upon thy puissant thigh', the angel/narrator immediately qualifies the literal iconicity of the imagery which conjures the scriptural image of Israel's warlike anointed king David by adding that when the Father thus speaks to the Son, and to us in an accommodated manner, 'on his son with rays direct | Shone full, he all his Father full expressed | *Ineffably* into his face received' (VI. 719–21, my emphasis). This dynamic of ineffable effluence underscoring biblical images and typological metaphors points to Milton's attempt throughout *Paradise Lost* to literalize the very concept of ineffability.

As a quality or attribute of God, ineffability ceases to behave in the poem adjectivally or analogically, but rather substantively. It is not a condition of absence around which the poetry must trace an apophatic path, but, as we have seen with divine speech more generally, an attribute attached to what is said, perhaps in an accommodated manner, lending scriptural and non-scriptural metaphors literal and quite ineffable substance. When the Son-Messiah, armed for battle, next begins his speech in which he expresses his 'filial Godhead' (VI. 722) in language resonating with scriptural images of kingly power enfolded in the Father's eternity, the monistic 'all' that is God and all who obey him accrues tremendous ineffable weight that is felt throughout the

---

[98]   *YCP* vi. 209.
[99]   For a good discussion of the many different ways in which Milton reflects on the Son's subordination to the Father in the poem, and especially on the Son's mutability as opposed to the Father's fixity, see MacCullum, *Milton and the Sons of God*, 71–8.

speech in a very physical sense as a binding principle, not just of the theology but of the poetry as well:

> Sceptre and power, thy giving, I assume,
> And gladlier shall resign, when in the end
> Thou shalt be all in all, and I in thee
> For ever, and in me all whom thou lov'st...
>
> (VI. 730–3)

Milton objectifies in this way the presence of the ineffable so that it becomes a central piece of furniture in his metaphysical setting. This is not a process of demystification as such, but one of literary concreteness, where the attribute of ineffability is imparted not just to the Son but ultimately to the inspired epic narrator as well, who, like God the Father, ineffably irradiates the darkness of apophasis with his 'literal' utterance.

This strategy is not confined in the poem to divine speech. The objectifying of the ineffable as an attribute which characterizes the inspired or divine speaker allows Milton to suggest throughout the poem that what characters say in our presence is often at odds with how they say it. As we move away from God, whose literal words derive their ineffable authority from the apophatic imagery framing them, the dissonance between the content of speeches and how we are then asked to imagine the *effect* of these speeches on those who hear them grows more extreme; true to the principles of Milton's monism, the farther we are from Milton's God, the greater the divide between the didactic import of speeches we read and their affective register as things we might hear. Take, for example, the three opening lines of Book VIII which Milton added for the 1674 edition of the poem:

> The angel ended, and in Adam's ear
> So charming left his voice, that he awhile
> Thought him still speaking, still stood fixed to hear...
>
> (VIII. 1–3)

Everything Raphael says to Adam in his lectures is clear and unambiguous in terms of its didactic import. The imperatives of accommodation require Raphael to use highly metaphorical language, but such metaphors function under the aegis of the wider epic metaphor of animate matter, conceived within the poem's meta-poetic monist theory of accommodation, which in turn encourages us to understand what

Raphael says literally. But, again, Milton seems to appreciate that too much emphasis on literalness might obscure the fundamental fact that Raphael is an angel who is superior to prelapsarian Adam, at least in terms of his proximity to God, and so while what Raphael says is perfectly clear to us, his voice as he talks *sounds* divine. Milton exploits the epic convention of the pregnant pause after a long speech to make a profound semantic and epistemological statement. Having to digest the didactic import of the angel's lecture, Adam stands still in deep thought, but Milton crucially invests this familiar situation with the power of otherworldly sound. When Raphael finally stops speaking, Adam thinks he can hear his angelic voice lingering on in the silence. The 'charming' musical notes of Raphael's voice have a mesmerizing, hypnotic effect on Adam, who believes the angel is still speaking to him long after he has fallen silent. Given the poem's materialist physicality, however, this extraordinary image raises many insoluble questions. When Adam thinks the angel is still speaking, what is it that he thinks the angel is saying to him in this brief moment of rapture? Can he hear specific words, or is it perhaps just noise? Is he hearing the mere echo of, say, the angel's last sentence, or is it something else? This brief image suggests that the process of angelic speech has a distinctly ineffable character to it which is overridden by didactic exigencies, but which still persists as ineffable presence behind the literal surface of the words. 'Still stood fixed to hear' suggests that Adam simply sits there in a trance waiting for the angel's literal meaning, as it were, to catch up with his unspoken words, and this points, again meta-poetically, to the lapsarian gaps in our understanding as readers confronted with a narrative containing the faint echoes of another, unspeakable world.

However, not just angelic speech is represented as something other than what it sounds in our mind when read in isolation. As we move down Milton's materialist chain of being from non-lapsarian angels to prelapsarian man, we come much closer to the realities of human speech but are still at one lapsarian remove. When prelapsarian Adam and Eve sing their morning hymn, for example, the narrator introduces their song in the following terms:

> Lowly they bowed adoring, and began
> Their orisons, each morning duly paid
> In various style, for neither various style

> Nor holy rapture wanted they to praise
> Their maker, in fit strains pronounced or sung
> Unmeditated, such prompt eloquence
> Flowed from their lips, in prose or numerous verse,
> More tuneable than needed lute or harp
> To add more sweetness, and they thus began.
>
> (V. 144–52)

The impression here is that prelapsarian prayer is somehow freer and more genuine than lapsarian prayer. As Fowler notes: 'Before the fall there is no antagonism between formal elaboration (various style) and inspired spontaneity (rapture).'[100] The actual hymn Adam and Eve sing, however, is closely patterned on Psalm 148, with a possible echo of Psalm 19 as well.[101] As usual, the narrator's framing imagery offers a meta-poetic critique of the lapsarian world, where 'various style' in Church liturgy comes at the expense of personal, unmeditated 'rapture'. The implications of prelapsarian rapture, however, extend beyond prayer to the idea of 'prompt eloquence' more generally. As John Leonard argues, the patterning of the hymn on familiar Psalms does not contrast prelapsarian eloquence with lapsarian liturgy, but rather points to an existing tension between unmeditated inspired songs (the Psalms) and the loss of rapture that may come when such rapturous songs are forced into a set form of organized prayer.[102] Unlike fallen man, for whom it is impossible to speak coherently (where coherence means an imposed order such as one gets with set prayers) while being gripped by musical or ecstatic 'rapture', Adam and Eve manage a distinctly liturgical coherence even as they are overtaken by 'holy rapture' when addressing God as 'Unspeakable, who sits above these heavens | To us invisible or dimly seen' (V. 156–7). As readers, however, we have to take the narrator's word for it that Adam and Eve's hymn is rapturous and that it is, in fact, an unmeditated prayer unburdened by contrivance. As Edward Said long ago noted, there are many moments in *Paradise Lost* when we are asked as readers to take the angel's or the

[100] Fowler, *Paradise Lost*, 289–90, nn. 145–52.
[101] See Radzinowicz, *Milton's Epics and the Book of Psalms*, 148–56; See also D. McColley, 'Eve and the Arts of Eden', in Walker, *Milton and the Idea of Woman*, 100–19.
[102] Leonard, *Naming in Paradise*, 246.

narrator's word for it, and *it* is the *only* thing we have, 'not a thing, certainly, and not more than an assertion that depends on other words and an accepted sense-giving code for support'.[103] Indeed, we are asked to see through the poet's contrivance at something purer, intimated, and finally ineffable not in epistemological terms, but on the level of poetic feeling. Strangely, when Milton employs this strategy with God's divine speech the effect is somehow less startling, because we expect God to be ineffable but not literal, and the conceit that the speech prepared by the poet for God is both ineffable *and* literal remains in the realm of paradox. But in Adam and Eve's case the dissonance between what they sing and *how* they sing causes us as readers to feel the smart of the Fall all the more strongly. I take this to be part of what Balachandra Rajan describes as the poem's 'destitutive energy',[104] whereby we are asked to accept that what we recognize as liturgically mundane in Adam and Eve's prelapsarian prayer is in fact somehow ineffable and therefore obliterated by the Fall.

This growing dissonance effectively introduces a moral or ethical dimension into Milton's poetics of ineffability. Despite his quarrel with Calvin on predestination, Milton firmly believed, like Luther and Calvin before him, that the presence of the ineffable in religious discourse poses not just a semantic-epistemological problem, but a salvific one. The Reformed Christian, fighting against silence in the struggle for justification and salvation, constantly has to renegotiate the moment of ineffable surrender in the devotional experience. Milton's poetics of ineffability in *Paradise Lost* allows him to objectify and diffuse ineffable presence through what I have discussed so far as ineffable 'speech effects'. But as we descend into hell (or rather, begin with hell in Books I and II), similar speech effects when Satan and the devils speak point to the dark side of ineffability, where silence is not just a threat for salvation but also a punishment, and where the illusion of eviscerated rhetorical meaning devolves into the 'dismal universal hiss' (X. 508) of condemned snakes. Long before this final degradation, however, when the mock-heroic Satan is about to open his mouth to speak for the first time, still cutting a remarkable figure of power and injured merit, the narrator says this: 'To whom the archenemy, | And

---

[103] Said, *Beginnings*, 280.
[104] Rajan, '*Paradise Lost*: The Uncertain Epic', 117.

thence in heaven called Satan, with bold words | Breaking the *horrid silence* thus began' (I. 81–3, my emphasis). What is striking about these lines is the idea of 'horrid silence' which Satan's bold words break. The proverbial idea of speech as broken silence gains a peculiar paradoxical significance in Milton's hell. T. S. Eliot, for example, famously objected to the paradoxical image of hellish flames that give off no light but only 'darkness visible' (I. 63), on the grounds that it is too difficult to imagine, but the idea of *silence* in hell is even harder to imagine since it seems to suggest that hell's inferno not only does not give off any light, but also produces no sound. *Pace* Fowler's impressive marshalling of patristic evidence to suggest that 'darkness visible' is 'obviously not meant as physical description',[105] it is very hard to ignore the physical context of these metaphors, where Satan and the fallen angels suffer very real physical as well as mental torments. Despite a vividly evoked landscape that includes a burning lake with 'tossing...fiery waves' (I. 184) and vast desolations where the fallen angels are 'o'erwhelmed | With floods and whirlwinds of tempestuous fire' (I. 76–7), Milton's hell is as silent as the grave, because it is a semiotic grave, and it is this aspect of hell which makes it particularly 'horrid' in the context of Milton's universe. It is a grave where the mind and its ability to express things in words meet only oblivion in the very physical *absence* of spiritually 'literal' truths.[106]

When Satan defiantly says: 'The mind is its own place, and in itself | Can make a heaven of hell, a hell of heaven' (I. 254–5), this is, of course, terribly ironic, because Satan's false sense of Stoic *apatheia* depends here on an interiority that has just been emptied of any meaningful substance by his ejection from heaven. The lie to Satan's *apatheia* is given later in Book IV, when the soliloquizing devil implodes and admits: 'Which way I fly is hell; myself am hell' (IV. 75). This corresponds to the idea expressed moments earlier, when the narrator reports how Satan's 'conscience wakes despair | That slumbered, wakes the bitter memory | Of what he was, what is, and must be | Worse' (IV. 23–6). The unremitting Calvinistic terror attached to the word despair, pulling down the weight of the line into the slumber of bitter memory in the next line, is inescapable. Satan's predicament is that of utter reprobation, which is

[105] Fowler, *Paradise Lost*, 63, nn. 62–4.
[106] See Sharon-Zisser, 'Silence and Darkness in *Paradise Lost*'.

all the more horrific in the Arminian context of the poem for being self-inflicted: by abdicating his free will Satan effectively falls into acute, Bunyan-like, Calvinistic despair. Moreover, the resulting despair and the loss implied in the idea of memory itself results in a poignant parody of the Tetragrammaton, where memory of what he 'was, is and shall be' becomes 'Worse' in Satan. This corruption of God's unsayable name indicates that God has utterly withdrawn his monist essence from Satan, effectively leaving him an empty mechanical shell, which, 'like a devilish engine back recoils | Upon himself' (IV. 17–18), fit for the incestuous relationship with the allegorical Sin and Death.

As Sanford Budick observes in relation to Milton's Satan, 'what interests Milton is not, as has sometimes been suggested, Satan's strategies of the big lie, but rather the inevitable failure of the imagination that has become oblivious to the transcendent structure of creation'.[107] A radically fallen being like Satan cannot speak in any meaningful sense without great difficulty and without causing himself pain in the process. Like the darkness around him, therefore, the silence of hell is finally a reflection of its 'new possessor' (I. 252), whose vacuous, idolatrous, self-loving interiority contains only roving, disembodied words that, 'interwove with sighs', must find 'out their way' (I. 621) whenever he wishes to express something. In the specific context of what ensues once words do find out their way, that 'something' is a rousing speech meant to plant desperate hope in the minds of the gathered hosts of fallen angels, but it has the ironic effect of someone attempting to fill a void with insubstantial nothings:

> O myriads of immortal spirits, O powers
> Matchless, but with the almighty, and that strife
> Was not inglorious, though the event was dire,
> As this place testifies, and this dire change
> Hateful to utter: but what power of mind
> Foreseeing or presaging, from the depth
> Of knowledge past or present, could have feared,
> How such united force of gods, how such
> As stood like these, could ever know repulse?
> . . . .
>   But he who reigns
> Monarch in heaven, till then as one secure

---

[107] Budick, *The Dividing Muse*, 87.

Sat on his throne, upheld by old repute,
Consent or custom, and his regal state
Put forth at full, but still his strength concealed,
Which tempted our attempt, and wrought our fall.

(I. 622–30; 637–42)

The bravado underlying the appeal to 'immortal spirits' and 'powers
matchless' is framed in the opening line by the forlorn and hollow echoes
of the two 'O's—two graphic-phonetic holes reverberating across the
silence of hell's semantic void.[108] 'O' is a phonetically empty and curiously
mournful interjection, suggesting here lamentation as well as desperate
pleading. Milton's God too, of course, uses similar language later in Book
III. After the Son offers himself as sacrifice to redeem man, God addresses
the Son in a language that registers deep emotion: 'O thou in heaven and
earth the only peace | Found out for mankind under wrath, O thou | My
sole complacence!' (III. 274–6). A less charitable reader might point out
that God is feigning joy and surprise in these lines, but the use of
anthropopathy in the apostrophe to the Son serves a dramatic-didactic
purpose. God's 'O's also register implicit lament, in this case for having to
redeem man in the first place 'under wrath', but also joy for the Son's self-
sacrifice and unflinching demonstration of 'filial obedience' (III. 269).
Such joy, however, is not God's as much as the reader's, who is invited
across the lapsarian divide symbolized by apostrophe's copula 'O' to share
with God this moment of thanksgiving. When 'O's resound in heaven the
sense of lack attached to such semantic voids points to our remoteness
from heaven but also the hope of one day returning to it, while in hell such
sounds embody an absolute, irrevocable distance.

Unlike God's speech, then, Satan's rousing words evoke only acute grief
and loss. The enjambed adjective 'Matchless' at the start of line 623,
divorced from its noun 'powers' ending line 622, stands alone and is unequal
to the devastating logical clause, 'but with the almighty', which not only

---

[108] Some Lacanian literary theorists, for example, discuss the textual use of 'O' as a
mark of the ineffable 'real', especially in relation to Shakespearean formulations of desire.
See Joel Fineman's analysis of 'abject Os' in *Othello*, where he develops psychoanalytical-
ly Frank Kermode's observation that 'Othello's "hollowness" is materialized in the sound
of O' (Fineman, 'The Sound of O in *Othello*', in *The Subjectivity Effect in Western
Literary Tradition*, 143–64, at 151). See also Shirley Sharon-Zisser, 'True to Bondage:
the Rhetorical Forms of Female Masochism in "A lover's complaint"', in Sharon-Zisser,
Critical Essays on Shakespeare's 'A lover's complaint', 179–90.

concedes God's omnipotence but also forces out of Satan the next shifty, double negative: 'that strife | Was not inglorious'. Satan's sense of 'glory' is ephemeral and painfully subjective, as opposed to the ontological reality of a 'dire' 'place' which is 'hateful to utter' in a very objective sense. The rhetorical trope of words interwoven with feigned sighs thus gains in the context of hell's materiality and ontological negativity the added dimension of inverted, cursed ineffability. Like divine speech, satanic speech also has an ineffable quality to it, but it is one of unspeakable despair, not inexpressible plenitude. Whenever Satan speaks he instantly sighs with implicit grief because his words express only loss and degradation. The result in this particular speech is an outpouring of condescension and political diminution of God: the tormented liar attempts to convince himself and his fallen peers that none could have foreseen their demise against a tyrant 'upheld' omnipotent 'by old repute, | Consent or custom' (I. 639–40), and that in hiding his true powers God therefore 'tempted our attempt, and wrought our fall' (I. 642). William Empson is the one critic who famously thought Satan was actually onto something in this speech,[109] but the rhetorical position here is one of negative confidence, not the airing of genuine grievances.

An impaired negative theology, it seems, bereft of a positive correlative, thrives in hell as a form of perverse Machiavellianism. Each instance of Satan's use of negative language or false positives points to that which is entirely absent in hell, and hence in a profound christological sense positively extrinsic to it. It is a state of semiotic privation bordering on nihilism, where the fallen creature, as the nihilist Belial wishfully reflects, can only hope to be 'swallowed up and lost | In the wide womb of uncreated night, | Devoid of sense and motion' (II. 149–51), rather than face a state of eternal despair and privation where the immortal 'intellectual being' (II. 147) with its 'thoughts that wander through eternity' (II. 148) must ultimately wander nowhere, beyond Being itself. I am not suggesting that Milton perversely anticipated Nietzsche or modern semiotic theories, but I am suggesting that in exploring the moral emptiness of Satan Milton could present the predicament of satanic atheism as an imposed state of divine privation which entails a complete withdrawal from a logocentric world and the semiotic theories underpinning it. On these terms, Milton's Satan does indeed

---

[109] Empson, *Milton's God*, 47.

emerge as an early modern reluctant champion of something like the Nietzschian 'will to power', except that what Nietzsche would call the metaphysical lie of inert divine anti-nature is in Milton's hell the ultimate truth and source of life which casts a dark, paradoxical light on Satan's radically fallen and therefore *vacuous* anti-nature.

The devils' roving, inexpressible thoughts—inexpressible because meaningless in the poem's logocentric materialist sense—fizzle out into nothing in the 'womb of uncreated night', but this is the same dark 'womb' of chaotic matter where the inspired narrator's song is first conceived metaphorically and from which it rises as an equally dark and magnificent creation, but which, unlike Pandemonium, has poetic and moral substance. For all the verbal power of his epic diction, Milton wants the *effect* of the poem as a whole to be itself deeply ineffable, and to elicit from us an appreciation similar to that of his Adam when he asks of Raphael to hear of things that may not be 'lawful to reveal':

> though what thou tellst
> Hath passed in heaven, some doubt within me move,
> But more desire to hear, if thou consent,
> The full relation, which must needs be strange,
> *Worthy of sacred silence* to be heard . . .
>
> (V. 553–7, my emphasis)

Fowler draws our attention here to the echo of Horace in the words 'worthy of sacred silence'. The reference is to Horace's Ode II. xiii, where, after having suffered a narrow escape from a falling tree, the poet contemplates how near he was to making the final journey to Hades. Once there, the poet imagines seeing Sappho and Alcaeus singing songs to the shades, who 'marvel at both as they utter words worthy of reverent silence' about 'the woes of seaman's life, the cruel woes of exile, and the woes of war'.[110] The point of Sappho's and Alcaeus' chthonic recital is that the subject of war and suffering, not to mention the otherworldly setting in which they sing, is quite literally

---

[110] *Horace: Odes and Epodes*, trans. Bennett (Loeb edn.), p. 141. The original Latin runs: 'Sappho puellis de popularibus | et te sonantem plenius aureo, | Alcaee, plectro dura navis, | dura fugae mala, dura belli. | utrumque sacro digna silentio | mirantur umbrae dicere' (25–30).

nefarious.[111] So is the core story in *Paradise Lost* of Satan's monstrous, and hence 'strange', rebellion against God, and the 'cause' that 'Moved our grand parents in that happy state, | Favoured of heaven so highly, to fall off | From their creator' (I. 29–31). However, once the demiurgic poet pretends to speak the unspeakable it is, as Augustine put it, no longer unspeakable and hence very hard to greet with an equal measure of 'sacred silence'. Indeed, how many readers of *Paradise Lost* who have recorded their experience have ever greeted the poem with silence? If there is one thing the poem does it is to elicit from its readers a powerful response, be it a cry of approval or a studied counter-defence. Silence is finally inimical to the underlying didactic, and ultimately dialogic, 'speech-act' which governs the poem's relationship with its intended 'fit' audience of elect readers trained at reading sacred texts 'rightly'. Silence, we are reminded, remains the final and irrevocable punishment God ordains for the rebel angels: 'Therefore eternal silence be their doom' (VI. 385). The great paradox of *Paradise Lost* as a poem—for some, its most fundamental interior inconsistency—is in its irreconcilable desire to be at once a gloriously vivid epic and an object for solemn, if not speechless, contemplation. But Milton deserves our abiding admiration for trying the impossible, not our censure for failing to succeed where no poet can.

To summarize then, *Paradise Lost* is a deceptively apophatic poem, but quite unlike anything produced in that tradition. It plots its own unique *via negativa* amid the ontological positives of luminous matter and literal truths, as its poet-narrator assertively fills the void of silence with images and sounds that point to their own created self-sufficiency as the inspired truths of a merely fallen poet, dreaming of lost or hidden worlds. True to its roots in Protestant theories of inspiration and interiority (where heaven, Paradise, and hell are as much interiorized states of mind as they are real, ontological places), the radically ineffable core of the poem is not to be found in its depiction of forbidden heavenly sights and sounds, nor in the baroque, manufactured opulence of a lost Paradise, but in the mysterious powers of inspiration which allow the poet-prophet to conjure mimetically such forbidden or

---

[111] From the Latin *nefas*, 'abominable', related to *fari*—'to speak', and hence 'unspeakable'—*nefandum*.

impossible images to begin with. Milton lights up the darkness of apophasis, paradoxically, with dazzling sound so that he may speak from within the darkness of ineffability and give a true, poetic account of his privileged, spiritual vision. He manages this by pretending to say the unsayable and to have access to literal, absolute truths that he then accommodates for his fallen readers; but also by simultaneously denying that such accommodation can ever take place, and allowing his poetic imagery to reveal itself as intrinsically fallen, mimetic matter. Milton evokes the majesty of God's ineffable presence, or the otherworldly voice of angels, or the unspeakable evil of Satan, through a form of ineffable dissonance, where traditional apophatic imagery lends literal words their numinous or nefarious quality. Throughout this process, spoken words are often set at odds with their putative affective impact on those who read or hear them. The concept of ineffability—objectively deployed in the poem's metaphysical setting as a defining attribute of the hidden God, imparted to the Son, and finally inflicted as punishment on the devils—in turn accrues ethical significance; it becomes both the object of the poem's loss as well as a final mark of the Fall itself, where the devils' denial of God results in nihilistic silence. This will be important to bear in mind as we turn to the final piece in this puzzle: the 1671 volume of *Paradise Regained* and *Samson Agonistes*, where the ethics of ineffability inform a prolonged and profoundly spiritual meditation on the potential rewards and punishments implied in the idea of an individual's complete submission to sacred silence when confronting the ineffable presence of God, not as he is in himself, but in his revealed ways with his chosen creatures.

5

Paradise Regained and *Samson Agonistes*: the ineffable self

The 1671 volume of *Paradise Regain'd a Poem. In IV Books. To which is added Samson Agonistes* was licensed for publication in the summer of 1670, three years after the first publication of *Paradise Lost*. Milton, long since completely blind and now subject to the 'detested thraldom of kingship'[1], was 61. A decade had passed since the king's triumphal restoration to the throne. During this time, unlike many of his revolutionary friends, Milton escaped the scaffold and was only briefly imprisoned. His public and literary personae, on the other hand, were less fortunate. On 27 August 1660 Milton had to endure the public burning of his books at the hands of a hangman in London. I only mention these well-known facts because both *Paradise Regained* and *Samson Agonistes* are said to reflect the dark and troubled times of Milton's Restoration years in which he most likely wrote or finished them. Although we will never know for certain when exactly he wrote either one of these poems, it is generally agreed that they are 'late'. *Paradise Regained*, perhaps (though this is unlikely) drafted in part before the Restoration, was almost certainly written in its entirety or finished *c.*1667–70; and *Samson Agonistes*—despite continuing controversy on this issue—in all probability also belongs to the Restoration era (though in this case earlier stages of writing during the 1640s and 1650s are far more plausible).[2] Regardless of

---

[1] *Readie & Easie Way, YCP* vii. 357.

[2] I follow the general consensus today, contrary to Parker's insistence on an earlier date for the poem, that *Samson Agonistes* was largely composed after the Restoration, and so avoid entering into the dispute surrounding the date of its composition. For my purpose, what is significant is that Milton chose to publish it together with *Paradise Regained* in 1670. For a brief summary of the problems surrounding the dating of *Samson Agonistes* see Carey's headnote in his edition of the poem, *CSP* 349–50, and Lewalski, *The Life of John Milton*, 492–4.

the date in which either poem was first conceived, it is widely agreed that both poems, as we have them, reflect in different ways Milton's political and ideological bitterness after the failure of the revolution, and offer a subversive political commentary on Restoration culture.[3]

The vast majority of studies published on Milton's late poetry since the mid-1980s have focused almost exclusively on its political subtext, as social historians and cultural-materialist scholars seek to rescue the seventeenth-century, revolutionary Milton from the clutches of 'late twentieth-century, liberally oriented university don[s]'.[4] While discussions about Milton's religious politics (or political religion, as the case may be) can shed interesting, broadly contextual light on the late poetry, they generally seek to resolve unnecessarily much in these poems which is insoluble and mysterious, and make conjectural claims about Milton's agreement and/or disagreement with contemporary dissenters that is largely unknowable. Moreover, if, as Peggy Samuels for instance says, historians have succeeded in undoing the 'false dichotomy between the poetical and the political Milton', then such undoing should work both ways.[5] After all, if Milton brooded over his personal failure as a revolutionary and contemplated the means to overcome this failure, than in all probability he also questioned, or at the very least reassessed, his success as a uniquely elected, 'divinely inspired' English poet and the ability of his poetry to teach and instruct. It is this aspect of Milton's later poetry that most concerns me here. The subject of personal and national redemption to which Milton turned in *Paradise Regained* forced him

---

[3] Rushdy's *The Empty Garden* is one of the most intricate, and arguably one of the better, studies of Milton's late poetry as a political-philosophical commentary. Rushdy presents a compelling case for reading Milton's late poetry in terms of an implicit dialogue with Hobbes. For the overall 'Restoration ambiance' of the later poems see also, more generally, Hill, *Milton and the English Revolution*, 413–48; Worden, 'Milton, *Samson Agonistes*, and the Restoration'.

[4] The words are those of Robert Fallon, *Captain or Colonel*, 14. Fallon argues that the image of a pacifist 'late' Milton is a twentieth-century liberal anachronism. Other historicists who have developed this approach include Wilding, *Dragons Teeth*; Loewenstein, *Milton and the Drama of History*, and 'The Revenge of the Saint'; Achinstein, '*Samson Agonistes* and the Drama of Dissent'; Samuels, 'Labor in the Chambers'; Norbrook, 'Republican Occasions in *Paradise Regained* and *Samson Agonistes*'; Coffey, 'Pacifist, Quietist, or Patient Militant?' Though not strictly speaking a historicist study, Michael Lieb's *Milton and the Culture of Violence* has also played a major role in further questioning modern assumptions about Milton's late poetry.

[5] Samuels, 'Labor in the Chambers', 153.

not just to point to the ineffable mystery at the heart of the Protestant election-and-regeneration narrative, but to confront that very silence and finally surrender to it. That he should then also write (or rework an older draft of) the tragedy of *Samson Agonistes* and append it to *Paradise Regained* suggests just how vexing this final confrontation of silence and ineffable *aporia* at the heart of Protestant ideas of interior holiness and contemporary political ideologies really was for the ageing poet. We will never know if the joint publication of the two poems was a calculated literary gesture on Milton's part or merely serendipitous, but there is no denying that the two poems, as the volume now stands, are starkly juxtaposed in a way which invites comparison between them. I will seek to add to those who have explored the close intellectual relationship between *Paradise Regained* and *Samson Agonistes* along the lines of the two poems' comparable conceptual concern with silence, language, and interpretation. Both poems deal with similar themes and similar ideas about the precise nature of Christian heroism and what it takes to do right in the eyes of God, and although the climactic outcome in each poem is very different, they end by delivering complementary didactic messages about the dangers and rewards of remaining true to the Protestant spiritual ideal of the 'language of Canaan' and its attendant narrative of ineffable individual holiness and election.

THE END OF SILENCE

As we have seen throughout the previous chapters, thinking about the ineffable involves conflict. It involves conflict not only with intellectual paradox, but also with opposed ideas about how to negotiate ineffable presence in one's religious experience. As we move from *Paradise Lost* to *Paradise Regained*, it is not Milton's attitude to the ineffable as such which changes, but the subject of the poetry which forces him to renegotiate the language of apophasis in the process of confronting not the ineffability of a transcendental deity, but the ineffability at the core of the Protestant religious encounter with God's words and pro-mises as recorded in Scripture and mobilized in the service of temporal history and politics. Milton could have chosen any episode from the gospel accounts of the life, death, and resurrection of Jesus as an appropriate theme for a brief epic about the regaining of Paradise. His choice to focus on the synoptic temptation narratives not only allowed him to align *Paradise Regained* with *Paradise Lost* through the reintroduction of the character of Satan, but also to rewrite the quintessential Christian narrative of a single individual's conflict with the satanic forces of the temporal world arrayed against his efforts to secure salvation. The choice of subject arguably reflects Milton's intellectual state of mind at the time of writing the poem, when he contemplated the ways in which he might regain the spiritual 'paradise within . . . happier far' alluded to at the end of *Paradise Lost* (XII. 587). The ensuing conflict is not physical but verbal, waged in a typological desert wasteland that is as much an interior psychological battleground as it is a historical-biblical one. Jesus and Satan contend by exchanging scriptural quotations and rhetorical positions rather than physical blows. The presence of silence and the ineffable in this ongoing conflict looms over the contestants as the inescapable end of discourse. For Satan it will be the end in a very literal and final sense; for Jesus it is the end of action, which finds fulfilment in the underlying ineffable presence of God the Father to whose will the passive Jesus submits by clinging both to the spirit and the letter of the Word whose flesh he is.

A large number of critics have analysed the redemptive function of language, silence, and hermeneutics in Milton's brief epic.[6] Two critics in particular, Ken Simpson and Regina Schwartz, have tied all of these themes to what I have discussed throughout this study as Milton's engagement with a poetics of ineffability.[7] Simpson's reading of 'lingering voices' and 'telling silences' in *Paradise Regained* fits very nicely into my argument so far. He differentiates between the silence of Jesus which points to the 'creative presence' of God's Word, and the 'shameful silence' of Satan (IV. 23) which 'reveals the silent void of faithlessness'.[8] According to Simpson, the triumph of *Paradise Regained* as a poem lies in its ability to capture the presence of the ineffable through speech,

---

[6] See Martz, *Poet of Exile*, ch. 15; Laskowsky, 'A Pinnacle of the Sublime'; Mustazza, 'Language as Weapon in Milton's *Paradise Regained*'; Entzminger, *Divine Word*, 102–19; Goldsmith, 'The Muting of Satan'; Blythe, 'The Cloistered Virtue'; Davies, *Milton*, ch. 4; Radzinowicz, 'How Milton Read the Bible', in *CCM* 202–18; Rushdy, *The Empty Garden*, ch. 3.

[7] Simpson, 'Lingering Voices, Telling Silences'; Schwartz, 'Redemption and *Paradise Regained*'.

[8] Simpson., 'Lingering Voices', 191.

whereby Milton 'demonstrates that silence and the Word are not mutually exclusive, but mutually dependent aspects of representation'.[9] Schwartz has produced a complementary argument and has shown, moreover, that the poem's working of redemption includes a process of verbal denial, or *aphaeresis*, where everything that Satan falsely says about redemption must be discarded on the basis of Scripture and submission to the will of God, until we end in the presence of silence that is redemptive in what it shows, ineffably, without saying.[10]

Both analyses are borne out by what other critics have said about the language of the Son in the poem.[11] Milton's Jesus responds to Satanic temptation, as he does throughout the gospels, in elliptic, deeply mysterious language which simultaneously inhabits the literal and the figurative, the outer and inner man, the flesh and the Word. When, for example, Satan tempts Jesus with the wisdom of classical learning, Jesus replies 'sagely':

> Think not but that I know these things, or think
> I know them not; not therefore am I short
> Of knowing what I ought: he who receives
> Light from above, from the fountain of light,
> No other doctrine needs, though granted true;
> But these are false, or little else but dreams,
> Conjectures, fancies, built on *nothing firm*.
>
> (IV. 286–92, my emphasis)

This is the language of paradox at its most extreme. Jesus' opening sentence twists and turns around the words 'knowing' and 'not' with such apparent evasiveness that by the time he actually concedes that he *does* already know what Satan hopes to tempt him with, the reader cannot escape feeling that there is something nevertheless mysterious about the extent of Jesus' knowledge. This sense of mystery is entirely appropriate, for as soon as Jesus next refers to the divine 'Light from above', his syntax suddenly becomes clear and precise. As in many comparable moments where Jesus speaks in this poem, the movement from the obscurity of perplexing, circumlocutory

---

[9] Ibid. 184.

[10] Schwartz, 'Redemption and *Paradise Regained*', 41–6.

[11] See in particular the analyses of Martz, Entzminger, Davies, and Rushdy cited above.

aphorisms to the precision of a scripturally informed light that needs 'no other doctrine' re-enacts the poem's symbolic movement from an external space of literal equivocation to the inner space of luminous spiritual clarity, where the 'light' of Jesus' scriptural wisdom disentangles the rhetorical snares of his adversary. Moreover, whether or not Jesus has actually read the Greek philosophers, or, as he says earlier, 'what concerns my knowledge God reveals' (I. 293), he seems to know enough to expose the philosophers' 'smooth conceits' as 'Conjectures, fancies, built on nothing firm'. The phrase 'nothing firm' is particularly poignant in this context. The entice-ments of extra-biblical wisdom, and in particular of Platonism, which Milton always admired, are by far the most dangerous because, unlike wealth or glory, they are of some value to the Christian mind, providing of course that they are subordinated to Christian teachings. As we have seen in Chapter 1, Philo is the first recorded monotheistic exegete to insist that the wisdom of Moses, cryptically encoded in the Hebrew Bible, prefigures and anticipates that of Plato—a point which most Church Fathers subsequently adopted and which Milton's Satan directly chal-lenges: 'All knowledge is not couched in Moses' law' (IV. 225). In his response, therefore, Jesus does not reject pagan wisdom categorically; his dismissal of Plato as one who 'to fabling fell and smooth conceits' (IV. 295) only criticizes Plato's literary delivery, not his actual philosophy. But in a striking prolepsis, Jesus prophetically anticipates Colossians 2: 8 and Augustine's celebrated attack on the Neoplatonists in Book X of *De Civitate Dei* by condemning pagan philosophy's spiritual infirmity. The word 'firm', as Jesus uses it, refers of course not to the solid foundation on which one builds any kind of earthly structure, be it a temple, or a philosophy grounded in the phenomenal world, but to the firmness of faith in things not of this earth. The language of Milton's Jesus is unique in that, much like the idealized Protestant 'language of Canaan', its true 'literal' meaning is often the figurative, spiritual one.

Throughout the temptations, therefore, Satan is thwarted by his inability to grasp the ineffable complexity of the Son-of-God paradigm and his compulsion to read biblical and historical narratives pragmati-cally and literally. Discussing at length the 'doubt motif' in the poem, for example, Rushdy shows how, 'having constituted a world where doubt—to the degree of doubting the Spirit—is an epistemological norm, Satan is in turn constituted as a being incapable of employing the spirit and judgement necessary to understand Jesus' construction of

his world—the world of the spiritual kingdom within'.[12] Satan cannot
make any sense, for example, of the dove descending on Jesus' head at the
moment of baptism ('whate'er it meant', I. 83), thinks the Son's prophe-
sied kingdom is perhaps an earthly one ('A kingdom they portend thee,
but what kingdom, | Real or allegoric I discern not', IV. 389–90), and is
infuriated by the ambiguity of the words 'Son of God':

> The Son of God, which bears no single sense;
> The Son of God I also am, or was,
> And if I was, I am; relation stands;
> All men are Sons of God . . .
>
> (IV. 517–20)

It is not the case, however, that Satan is incapable of conversing in
highly figurative language. Satan is a master of rhetorical manipulation,
and as Jesus points outs, was known to disseminate through the pagan
oracles false prophecies that were deliberately and maliciously ambiguous:

> But what have been thy answers, what but dark
> Ambiguous and with double sense deluding,
> Which they who asked have seldom understood,
> And not well understood as good not known?
>
> (I. 434–7)

The difference is not between figurative and non-figurative speech, but
between speaking at one with God or against God. Satan, in other
words, is unskilled in the 'language of Canaan' underpinning Jesus'
incarnated, and therefore 'inward', oracular divinity:

> God hath now sent his living oracle
> Into the world, to teach his final will,
> And sends his *spirit of truth* henceforth to dwell
> In pious hearts, an *inward oracle*
> To all truth requisite for men to know.
>
> (I. 460–4, my emphases)

In the Augustinian tradition which Luther and Calvin revived and which
Milton adopted, there are two types of literal readings: that of the Law, or the

---

[12] Rushdy, *The Empty Garden*, 218.

letter which 'killeth'; and that of the Gospel and the spirit which gives life.[13]
We can never really tell what Satan knows or does not know in the poem, or
what he can or cannot comprehend, but if we accept that he must be in some
way spiritually impaired, then it follows that his ultimate downfall results
from his difficulty in glimpsing, or even sensing, the ineffable presence of the
numinous glowing mysteriously behind Jesus' cryptic spiritual responses. As
in *Paradise Lost*, Satan's unspeakable moral emptiness manifests itself as a
semiotic impairment where that which is truly divine can only be experi-
enced in modes of expression which are 'without sign of boast, or sign of
joy, | Solicitous and blank' (II. 119–20), and which result in something like
Calvinist despair and acute pain. When an unmoved Jesus reminds Satan
about his inevitable destruction at his hands ('my promotion will be thy
destruction', III. 202), Satan, 'inly racked' (III. 203), delivers his most
candid (and most manipulative) speech in the poem as an irredeemable
reprobate. Having resigned himself to the inexorability of his doom, Satan
echoes Belial's nihilistic speech from Book II of *Paradise Lost* in a bid to
move Jesus to pity, and concedes that where there is no hope of redemption
ceasing to be is a wished-for blessing: 'I would be at the worst; worst is my
port, | My harbour and my ultimate repose, | The end I would attain, my
final good' (III. 209–11).

The hermeneutical theme of the figurative versus the literal, the
pragmatic versus the spiritual, indeed manifests itself in the poem in
the continued reference to Jesus' mysteriously divine interiority and
Satan's vacuous, damaged interiority. Both Louis Martz and Stevie
Davies discuss at length the poetics of interiority in *Paradise Regained*,
which they believe is the main driving force behind the poem's inward-
looking, categorical critique of language. Martz, for example, detects
a 'mode of renunciation' in the poem's retracting, frugal style, while
Davies calls the poem 'a soliloquist's narrative, exilic from the corporate
body of language'.[14] Both critics in essence echo Stanley Fish, who in
a much-cited essay on the theme of inaction and silence in *Paradise
Regained* asserts that Milton seeks in the poem to deliver himself and his
readers from 'the frame of reference from which poetry (and all language) issues'.[15] But as Entzminger and Goldsmith rightly argue, the

---

[13] See MacCallum, 'Milton and Figurative Interpretation of the Bible', 397–9.
[14] Martz, *Poet of Exile*, 247; Davies, *Milton*, 155.
[15] Fish, 'Inaction and Silence', in Wittreich, *Calm of Mind*, 25–47, at 26.

poem seeks to redeem human language, not to suppress it.[16] Granted, Martz and Davies significantly highlight the way in which the language of the poem points towards an inward space where human speech ultimately cannot penetrate, but they fail to observe that it is strictly the language of Satan which is denied access to this inviolable inner space, or holy of holies, where Jesus' divine nature resides.

However, while the mysterious language of Jesus continually points to his more than human, twofold nature, it is never entirely clear in the poem in what capacity he actually resists temptation. Indeed, a large body of criticism has been devoted to the question whether or not Milton's Jesus ever exercises in the poem divine power. One school of thought argues that since Milton's God declares Jesus to be a 'perfect man, by merit called my Son' (I. 166), Jesus necessarily responds to Satan's temptations only as a 'perfect man', through a humanly achievable blend of insight, common sense, and vast erudition.[17] But the term 'perfect man' is hardly unambiguous. Just as a 'perfect man' is not God, neither is he a mere man, and he may be reasonably expected to have greater insight than lapsarian humans, and an altogether superior intelligence. It is true that Milton focuses unambiguously on Jesus' humanity in the poem, particularly in Jesus' opening soliloquy, and that many of Jesus' powers—for example, his ability to see through Satan's disguise in Book I—may be put down to astute human intelligence. In *De Doctrina* at least, as has often been noted (if we can assume that Milton's position on this theological point had not changed by the late 1660s), Milton shies away from making any pronouncements on the mystery of Christ's twofold nature:

So since we must believe that Christ, after his incarnation, remained one Christ it is not for us to ask whether he retained a two-fold intellect or a two-fold will, for the Bible says nothing of these things. For he could, with the same intellect both increase in wisdom, Luke ii. 52, after he had emptied himself, and know everything, John xxi. 17, that is, after the Father had instructed him, as he himself acknowledges.[18]

---

[16] Entzminger, *Divine Word*, 102–19; Goldsmith, 'The Muting of Satan'.

[17] See Pope, '*Paradise Regained*', 13–26; Carey, *Milton*, 124–30; Weber, *Wedges and Wings*, 86; Webber, *Milton and his Epic Tradition*, 173–4.

[18] *YCP* vi. 425.

If the Bible 'says nothing of these things' neither will Milton, and his subsequent choice to focus in the poem on Jesus' humanity not only accords with the theme of the 'second Adam', but also with the general biblical portrayal of Jesus: 'It is more useful for the Bible to distinguish the things which are peculiar to his human nature'.[19] The point of all these qualifications, however, is not that Jesus necessarily operates exclusively in his human capacity, but that we as human readers, like the poet, cannot know where his humanity ends and his divinity begins. It is unnecessary, then, to read too much into the term 'perfect man', which may be little more than theological shorthand for the traditional belief, endorsed by Milton, that Jesus was born a second Adam, free from Original Sin and hence perfect.[20] In any case, the term 'perfect man' should not be taken as somehow indicative of how Jesus actually operates in the poem, or to suggest that Jesus' sinless goodness necessarily imputes to him divine powers. To insist that Milton's Jesus operates either exclusively as a man or exclusively in his divine capacity is to impose a false dichotomy on the mysterious God-man paradigm which no Christian, including Milton, could ever countenance. What the term does suggest is that, as the Incarnated Word of God, Jesus is a man who need never fear the presence of the ineffable in his speech, because the divinity which authorizes his speech and gives it its spiritual shape and meaning is itself fundamentally ineffable.

The question we ought to ask, therefore, is not whether Milton's Jesus exhibits supernatural powers, but how he exhibits in this most verbal and dialectical of poems his sinless and ineffable perfection. The answer appears to be in Jesus' use of scriptural language. Jesus' actions in the poem are at once louder than ordinary words, and yet *are* words, and, as Schwartz suggests, it is how we read these words and the silence that they point to that determines our ability to participate in the poem's implicit work of redemption. Indeed, there is a sense in *Paradise Regained* that there is a 'right' and a 'wrong' way of going about reading its meaning. After all, like most devout Protestants of his day, Milton

---

[19] Ibid. 427.

[20] In *De Doctrina*, I.xi (*YCP* vi. 383–9) Milton endorses the Pauline view that all men sin in Adam, but objects to Augustine's term 'Original Sin' on the grounds that it is too narrow. Sin also 'took possession of Adam after his fall' (p. 389), and therefore cannot be merely original. As Kelly points out, however, Milton nevertheless employs the term 'Original Sin' in *Paradise Lost*, IX. 1003–4: 'Wept at completing of the mortal sin | Original.'

firmly believed that through the workings of grace a righteous Christian may 'rightly' read the Bible and arrive at its spiritually literal meaning. And since he proclaims in the opening invocation of *Paradise Regained* that his poem narrates actual biblical events, 'unrecorded left through many an age, | Worthy t'have not remained so long unsung' (I. 16–17), it is not unreasonable to suppose that he believed his own poetic creation would reveal its full meaning only to a 'fit' audience of righteous and elect readers conditioned to read, as it were, in the 'language of Canaan'. I am not suggesting that only a righteous Christian can rightly read the poem (I, for one, would be excluded from its 'meaning'), but that it is important to bear in mind that there are certain hermeneutical criteria in operation in the poem that may, once taken into account, shape our reading of its underlying didactic message. The blurring of the semiotic boundaries between the literal and the figurative in *Paradise Regained* is a symptom of a literary mind poetically engaged in a hermeneutical aesthetic where figurative expression must be deciphered in its proper scriptural light using that mysterious Protestant exegetical method known as the 'analogy of faith'. Consequently, anyone who attempts to decipher the poem's didactic meaning by looking for its use of self-evident metaphors either finds very few and so concludes that the poem is aesthetically unrewarding, or decides that the whole poem is one complex, insoluble metaphor and so enters the realms of wild allegory. It is in this context that the strictly literal readings of the poem, as the example of Satan demonstrates, are the 'wrong' ones, and the figurative, 'spiritual' readings, following the example of Jesus' use of language, are the 'right' ones.

To demonstrate what I mean by this line of reasoning we must turn to the controversial pinnacle scene at the end of the poem. Milton follows Matthew and Luke in presenting the temptation on the pinnacle of the Temple as a last-ditch effort on Satan's part to force an obedient, humble Jesus to break in some way—any way—with God. Traditionally, the exegetical crux of this episode has always rested on the interpretation of the Evangelists' use of the Greek word, *to pterugion*, which the AV translates (following the Vulgate) as 'a pinnacle'.[21] The word *pterugion* can either mean a flat roof or parapet on which it is reasonably possible to stand, or a tall point or spire on which it is presumably

---

[21] See McClung, 'The Pinnacle of the Temple'. For the typological significance of the temple structure in this scene and throughout the poem, see my 'Spiritual Architectonics: Destroying and Rebuilding the Temple in *Paradise Regained*', *MQ* 43:3 (2009), 166–82.

impossible to stand. Either way, the temptation remains one of presumption, but if Jesus *can* physically stand on the pinnacle then the temptation is only symbolic, and if he cannot feasibly stand, then the temptation is altogether more literal—Jesus must perform an ostentatious miracle and prematurely display his divine powers. Reactions to this scene among Miltonists have been just as varied as those of scriptural exegetes contending with the original gospel narratives, with some favoring a more abstract, almost allegorical reading and others confining themselves to a more literal reflection on the act of standing and its feasibility. But as Margaret Kean points out, the standing on the pinnacle is 'at one and the same time a literal and metaphoric victory' which renders the question as to whether or not the pinnacle is precarious rather redundant.[22] In his essay on 'lingering voices' and 'telling silences' in the poem, Ken Simpson argues that Jesus' ability to stand on the pinnacle consists of, or is underwritten by, the combined power of speech and silence, which in turn 'reveals the incarnate Word as a union of divinity and humanity, of unsayable presence and the words of the Word'.[23] Simpson's reading makes perfect theological and conceptual sense, but is hard to reconcile with what is, after all, a physical act of standing. How can the act of standing on the pinnacle literally consist of speech and silence? Simpson is already making an assumption about the non-literal dimension of the poem, which, while accurate, needs to be stated more clearly.

Milton's Jesus resists temptation and ultimately stands on the pinnacle not by making a claim to Godhead, nor merely by performing a humanly possible balancing feat, but by citing the written Word whose flesh he is and submitting himself obediently to the will of the Father: '*Also it is written,* | Tempt not the Lord thy God, he said and stood' (IV.560–1, my emphasis).[24] These words are as simple and straightforward as they are mysterious: whether Jesus says 'don't temp God', or indeed 'don't temp me who am God', the point is simply that Jesus *does* stand on the pinnacle, and that this act of standing is paradoxical and mysterious—at once a physical, literal act of standing but also

---

[22] M. Kean, '*Paradise Regained*', in *CM* 429–43, at 432.

[23] Simpson, 'Silence and the Word', 181.

[24] This was the standard Reformed understanding of Christ's active obedience to the will of God in the gospels. See Hunter, 'The Obedience of Christ in *Paradise Regained*', in Wittreich, *Calm of Mind*, 67–76.

something else, more mysterious and transcendentally powerful. I am not suggesting that our reading of the pinnacle scene should be allegorical, but that we should be willing to admit the possibility that the act of speaking the Word and then standing is itself figurative in terms of its *meaning*, and that its spiritually literal meaning is to be found not in the act itself but in what it signifies in the accumulated scriptural valence of the scene. It is not the case, therefore, as Fish surmises, that 'a successful reading of the poem...will be marked by a *re*valuing of the Son's passivity, which implies of course a *de*valuing of assertive action and self-expression'.[25] Fish's forensic acumen misses its mark in this instance. He goes on to apply his dictum to the pinnacle scene and concludes that 'the man who wraps himself in the Scriptures, as Christ does here, becomes an adjunct of them and ceases to have an independent existence'.[26] But this is a rather curious way to discuss an act of obedience which, for pious Christians at least, far from ceasing or cancelling existence, gives an otherwise pointless existence profound religious meaning.

The type of either/or 'act' Satan tries to force Jesus into is that which in fact 'devalues assertive action'. The point of Satan's final and most audacious temptation, as Milton presents it, is to rob Jesus of the possibility of meaningful, obedient action by trapping him in his own insoluble ambiguity as the Word made flesh, and in a sense to subject him to the physical laws of gravity suggested by the 'glorious Temple' rearing its 'pile' (IV. 547) high above the towers of Jerusalem:

> There stand, if thou wilt stand; to stand upright
> Will *ask thee skill*; I to thy Father's house
> Have brought thee, and highest placed, highest is best,
> Now show thy progeny; if not to stand,
> Cast thyself down; safely if the Son of God:
> For it is written, he will give command
> Concerning thee to his angels, in their hands
> They shall uplift thee, lest at any time
> Thou chance to dash thy foot against a stone.
>
> (IV. 551–9, my emphasis)

---

[25] Fish, 'Inaction and Silence', 38 (emphasis original to the text).
[26] Ibid. 43.

Satan places Jesus within a paradox which he believes should force him either to expose his full divinity if the Son of God, or fall and die if only human. Satan's error lies once again in his literal, uninspired misunderstanding of the concept of 'action'. Satan believes that standing up on the pinnacle will require a demonstrable, exterior act of 'skill'. 'Skill' is an interesting word in this context. Earlier in the poem Satan flatters Jesus as one who is 'so apt, in regal arts, | And regal mysteries' (III. 248–9). As Carey points out in his notes to the poem, in the seventeenth century the words 'skill' and 'mystery' were interchangeable in some contexts. The phrase 'regal mysteries' could mean either 'state secrets' or 'the skills of government' and is ironically contrasted with Matthew 13: 11: 'It is given unto you to know the mysteries of heaven.'[27] In Satan's earthbound vocabulary, 'skill', even if it is magical or supernatural skill, is directly at odds with the type of 'skills' Jesus will require in his redemptive mission on earth. The kind of skill Satan has in mind is that which allows him to conjure up a magical banquet in the desert, or to show Jesus a view of Italy from the top of Mount Niphates. In the latter instance, Milton revisits his astronomical telescope analogy from *Paradise Lost* as the narrator indeed speculates that Satan could only achieve such a feat by either subjecting Jesus to some sort of astronomical displacement ('parallax'), some other optical illusion, or literally handing him a skilfully designed telescopic contraption: 'By what strange parallax or optic *skill* | Of vision multiplied through air, or glass | Of telescope, were curious to inquire' (IV. 40–2, my emphasis). There is, admittedly, a degree of mystery about the method of Satan's supernatural powers, but by speculating about their method the poet trivializes their supernatural scope. Asides of this sort do more than preserve a sense of reality in the poem. They demystify the diabolic to make room for the divine, so that the merely logical finally gives way to genuine divine mystery in Jesus' unfolding victory over Satan.

Watching Milton's Satan exercising supernatural powers, therefore, is like watching a magician pull a rabbit out of a hat. There is a sense of mystery involved, but one which is evoked by the exhibition of superior skill, or sleight of hand, not the miraculous. When Satan thus says to Jesus on the pinnacle, 'to stand upright | Will ask thee *skill*', he once again falls into his own trap since he and Jesus do not conceive of

[27] Carey, *CSP*, p. 473, iii. n. 249.

supernatural skill at all in the same way. As Jesus cites Deuteronomy 6: 16, 'Ye shall not tempt the Lord your God', and stands, he performs a perfect, 'non-skilful' act of obedience which reinforces, rather than resolves, the insoluble mystery of his twofold nature as the Word made flesh. The didactic import of this 'act' seems clear: only by obediently submitting to the spirit of the Word can regenerate humans find the strength to stand where all other men must fall. However, since in the poem this ultimate act of redemption is performed by the living incarnation of the Word itself, it is neither passive nor active, but finally reflexive. That which is ineffable opens its mouth and speaks, and it is this final glimpse of the truly miraculous which smites Satan in 'amazement' and causes him to fall, not the act of standing itself. The meaningful silence that follows in the brief moment when Satan falls and the angels lift Jesus from his 'uneasy station' (IV. 584) on the pinnacle is not merely the silence of a language that has been cancelled or consumed, but that of the ineffable making its presence known at the expense of fallen speech.

'PROMPTED SONG ELSE MUTE'

So far I have outlined how the hidden presence of the ineffable manifests itself in *Paradise Regained*. This presence is implicit in the language of Jesus and the method by which he thwarts satanic temptation. However, there are other forces at work in the poem which introduce a sense of conflict into these themes, for as soon as Jesus makes present that which is ineffable, the poem's narrator strives to cancel out the ineffable character of this presence. In *Paradise Lost* Milton's strategy was one of sustained poetic expression in the face of loss. There, the objective was to mystify the inspirational and creative powers of the narrator so that the epic voice could sing, Philomela-like, from *within* the darkness of apophasis. This imposition of sound on silence allowed Milton to objectify the ineffable and deploy it as a demonstrable attribute extrinsic to the poet's ability to speak for God and those beings whose speech is otherwise transcendental, otherworldly, and ineffable in quality. In *Paradise Regained*, however, the emphasis on discursive introspection reverses this process as the previously mysterious 'interior' of the poet's inspired ability to create gives way redemptively to the

Word through a process of self-retraction and occlusion. The narrator's epic voice deliberately falls silent and allows the scriptural words of Christ to speak through him and *for* him. Paradoxically, however, the final result of this introspective process of silencing is a radical gesture of self-assertion, not as inspired poet, but as redeemed man.

E. M. W. Tillyard long ago made the provocative observation that the character of Christ in *Paradise Regained* is partly an 'allegorical figure, partly Milton himself imagined perfect'.[28] In her own study of the poem Barbara Lewalski applies the significance of Tillyard's observation to the role of the narrator's voice. She claims that there is an 'inevitability and even an appropriateness' in Tillyard's observation, since the heightened objectivity and restraint exhibited by the narrator in *Paradise Regained*, as opposed to the far more involved narrator of *Paradise Lost*, derives 'from the almost complete fusion of the narrator's point of view (as redeemed man) with that of his Redeemer'.[29] The closing of the gap between the narrator and his subject cancels out the space that was so vital to allow the idea of prophecy to assume its imaginative power in *Paradise Lost*, and especially in the early 'Nativity Ode'. The Miltonic bard does not pretend to soar in *Paradise Regained*. There is either inspired song, fully at one with the Word, or complete silence: 'prompted song else mute' (I. 12). At one with the Word, the narrator of *Paradise Regained* inhabits a diminished space between heaven and earth and has no need, therefore, to accommodate hidden sights to 'mortal sense'. The poet who 'erewhile the happy garden sung, | By one man's disobedience lost', now sings 'Recovered Paradise to all mankind' (I. 1–3), and the song is perfect, like a hawk's 'prosperous wing full summed'. Emulating Jesus, the poem's main 'above heroic' hero, the narrator's voice also promotes itself as the 'perfect' vehicle to 'tell of deeds | Above heroic, though in secret done, | And unrecorded left through many an age, | Worthy t' have not remained so long unsung' (I. 14–17). The words 'secret', 'unrecorded', and 'unsung' all point to the forbidden, hidden space of ineffable mystery—a sheltered interior under the Law, since then made accessible to all mankind through Christ, now an inner space of redeemed personal sanctity. The Miltonic audacity of these lines outdoes that of the presumption to

---

[28] Tillyard, *Milton*, 259.
[29] Lewalski, *Milton's Brief Epic*, 327–8.

undertake theodicy in *Paradise Lost*. The narrator implies that the 'true' events which he is about to narrate in song were worthy to remain 'so long unsung' until his final maturity as a sacred poet. The 'worthiness' implied in 'Worthy t' have not remained so long unsung' is finally metonymic. It is the poet, not just the poem, who is worthy at long last to sing this particular kind of song. Looking back at a long poetic career, the Miltonic persona contained within the 'I' of the opening line concedes that his arrival at this poetic threshold took time to evolve. There would have been no *Paradise Regained* without *Paradise Lost*, no *Paradise Lost* without *A Masque*, the 'Nativity Ode', and 'Lycidas'. It is a re-formed Miltonic persona who finally declares his worthiness to successfully sing, as he had hoped early on in the failure of 'The Passion', of 'His godlike acts; and his temptations fierce' (24). The humble, mature poet of *Paradise Regained* declares his ability to finally triumph where his younger, discarded poetic persona so long ago failed.

The diminishing presence of the narrator in *Paradise Regained* insists in this way on the parity between his and Jesus' voices. However, this should not imply that the narrator of *Paradise Regained* is somehow passive. It is true that his intrusions into the poem are far more subtle and infrequent than those of the narrator in *Paradise Lost*, but they are not any less significant—with diminished capacity comes far greater control. The storm scene in Book IV is an interesting example of this. After Jesus rejects Satan's offer of pagan learning, Satan brings him back to the wilderness. While Jesus sleeps Satan accosts him with 'ugly dreams' (IV. 408), which are then mirrored by a violent, highly tropological storm raging across the night sky. The narrator's description of the storm soon makes way to direct apostrophe:

> and either tropic now
> 'Gan thunder, and both ends of heaven, the clouds
> From many a horrid rift abortive poured
> Fierce rain with lightning mixed, water with fire
> In ruin reconciled: nor slept the winds
> Within their stony caves, but rushed abroad
> From the four hinges of the world, and fell
> On the vexed wilderness, whose tallest pines,
> Though rooted deep as high, and sturdiest oaks
> Bowed their stiff necks, loaden with stormy blasts,
> Or torn up sheer: ill wast thou shrouded then,

> *O patient Son of God, yet only stood'st*
> *Unshaken,* nor yet stayed the terror there,
> Infernal ghosts, and hellish furies, round
> Environed thee, some howled, some yelled, some shrieked,
> Some bent at thee their fiery darts, while thou
> Sat'st unappalled in calm and sinless peace.

                                        (IV. 409–25, my emphasis)

Lewalski has highlighted the apocalyptic, prophetic nature of the storm which 'points to the violent upheavals of nature at Christ's death' recorded in Matthew 27: 51–2, and has identified the subsequent apostrophe as a familiar epic device which allows the narrator to express his deep emotion at Jesus' foreshadowed suffering in the Passion.[30] However, as Lewalski herself points out, the narrator of *Paradise Regained* is decidedly anti-epic. The triumphant apostrophe celebrates Jesus' ability to withstand a storm that is both physical and external, but also meta-poetically internal—a diabolic assault on the reader's imagination made up of distinctly pagan imagery which evokes the sublime images of Milton's hell and Chaos from Books I and II of *Paradise Lost.* The four winds of classical mythology join forces with 'infernal ghosts' and 'hellish furies' to unleash a storm of 'Fierce rain with lightning mixed, water with fire | In ruin reconciled', which is contrasted with Jesus', and by association the present narrator's, inner state of 'calm and sinless peace'. The apostrophe seems to do two things. On the one hand, it allows the narrator to identify with the Jesus' triumph while still acknowledging that he is far weaker than Jesus and must rely on his example. On the other hand, it exhibits the narrator's credentials as a poet whose voice is itself 'above-heroic' and no longer reliant on the pagan trappings of classical mythology and the fallen epic mode associated with them. After all, the storm scene itself is a worn cliché of classical literature,[31] and it is not incidental that this episode follows immediately after Jesus' renunciation of classical, pagan learning associated with such mythological machinery. By re-creating such a conventional scene and then setting his voice against its imagery, the poet declares his ability to redeem his art from 'infernal ghosts' and

---

[30] Ibid. 311, 329.
[31] See e.g. Lucan, *Civil War,* 5.430–55, 540-653; Virgil, *Aeneid,* 1.81–123; Ovid, *Metamorphoses,* 11.474–572; and Seneca, *Agamemnon,* 465–578.

'hellish furies' and to release the idea of literalness from the allegorical vacuity of Sin and Death which in *Paradise Lost* haunts its spiritual integrity.

A similar meta-poetic act of textual redemption also occurs at the end of the poem after the pinnacle scene, when Satan falls for a second time and is finally vanquished. First, the narrator deploys two epic similes from pagan Greek mythology to describe the magnitude of Satan's final demise. He likens Satan's fall to the death of Antaeus the giant at the hands of Hercules (IV. 563–8), and more poignantly, with the suicide of the Sphinx who hurls itself from the acropolis at Thebes when Oedipus solves its riddle with the answer, man (IV. 572–5). As Satan falls with 'dread and anguish' (IV. 576), he drags down with him the pagan imagery used to describe this fall and confines the pagan imagination, not unlike the pagan gods in Book I of *Paradise Lost*, to the implied pit of hell in 'Ruin, and desperation, and dismay' (IV. 579). Then, as the narrator continues with this triumphant description of the vanquished devil, his syntax purges the fiend from the text altogether:

> So Satan fell and straight a fiery globe
> Of angels on full sail of wing flew high,
> Who on their plumy vans received him soft
> From his uneasy station, and upbore
> As on a floating couch through the blithe air . . .
>
> (IV. 581–5)

Without any punctuation after 'Satan fell', the subject of the entire sentence ought to be Satan, but the 'him' of line 583 clearly refers to Jesus. In one deft syntactical move the narrator effectively deletes Satan as if he never existed, and allows Jesus to assume his rightful place in the sentence as the subject of the narrator's adoration. Satan, it seems, literally falls out of the poem. This display of meta-poetic force captures the narrator's active involvement in the poem's work of redemption. Following the example of Jesus, the narrator also asserts his own ability to overcome satanic temptation and stand firm through the act of redeemed speech by expelling Satan from the grammar of his spiritual landscape.

In emulating the Redeemer, therefore, the narrator of *Paradise Regained* retracts to make room for the speaking ineffable, but then blurs the distinction between his and Jesus' voice so that he too might in a sense speak while remaining silent. When, for example, Jesus responds to the temptation of pagan learning and literature, his ensuing encomium of biblical poetry reaches out of the poem to pat the narrator on the back:

> Or if I would delight my private hours
> With music or with poem, where so soon
> As in *our native language* can I find
> That solace? All our Law and story strewed
> With hymns, our psalms with artful terms inscribed,
> Our Hebrew songs and harps in Babylon,
> That pleased so well our victor's ear, declare
> That rather Greece from us these arts derived;
> Ill imitated, while they loudest sing
> The vices of their deities, and their own
> In fable, hymn, or song, so personating
> Their gods ridiculous, and themselves past shame.
> Remove their swelling epithets thick-laid
> As varnish on a harlot's cheek, the rest,
> Thin-sown with aught of profit or delight,
> Will far be found unworthy to compare
> With Sion's songs, to all true tastes excelling,
> *Where God is praised aright, and godlike men,*
> *The Holiest of Holies, and his saints,*
> *Such are from God inspired,* not such from thee;
> Unless where moral virtue is expressed
> By light of nature not in all quite lost.

(IV. 331–52, my emphases)

The disparaging view of classical literature when compared to the Bible is a commonplace in Milton's thought. There is no need to apologize for these lines, or to read them as Milton's way of performing a post-humanist act of 'self-mutilation'.[32] Even as a young man, Milton was noticeably ambivalent about the merit of pagan literature and had set his sights on emulating in his English poetry the themes, style, and genres of the Bible, with its models for prophetic song in the Psalms issuing from 'Sion hill' (*Paradise Lost*, I. 10).[33] It is not unreasonable to assume that Milton indeed thought of *Paradise Regained* very much as a poem 'where God is praised aright, and godlike men, | The Holiest of Holies, and his saints'. Even though the

---

[32] Davies, *Milton*, 165.
[33] See Radzinowicz, 'How Milton Read the Bible', in *CCM* 202–5.

narrator here is silent, his Miltonic presence shines through Jesus' words. Jesus is not only condemning Satan, he is also implicitly congratulating Milton the poet on perfecting the art of sacred songs 'such are from God inspired'. The harmonious coexistence of Jesus and the Miltonic narrator indeed finds its most eloquent expression in the words 'our native language'. 'Our' is inclusive of both Hebrew-speaking Jesus and the English-speaking poet who has now fulfilled his pledge made long ago in 'At a Vacation Exercise' to his 'native language' (1) that 'The daintiest dishes shall be served up last' (14).[34] Theirs, then, is a prelapsarian 'native language' of Paradise, an unmeditated (not unpremeditated), prompt (not prompted) eloquence, perfect in its univocal harmony and power to work redemption in the lapsarian world.[35] In this qualified conceptual and religious sense, Milton's English is indeed the new Hebrew, a new and poetical 'language of Canaan'. When Jesus asks the rhetorical question, 'where so soon | As in *our native language* can I find | That solace?' the hidden English-speaking narrator has an answer ready for us: in the Bible, as well as in the inspired poetry of a certain John Milton, Englishman.

Milton's intellectual triumph over his peculiarly Reformed anxieties regarding ineffable presence in *Paradise Regained* is almost complete, but it comes at a price. After a lifelong struggle to reconcile his vaulting literary ambition with his deepest commitment as an elect and righteous Protestant, he finds in *Paradise Regained* both the subject and the voice with which to religiously express his 'inner oracle'. Here at last his theology and poetry meet in perfect harmony, and the result is a poem 'in tune with heaven' ('At a Solemn Music', 26), and so, much like its hero, made 'perfect'. However, *Paradise Regained* is a lesser *poem* than *Paradise Lost* precisely because it is completely consistent with its own ideas. Once Milton drives away ineffable presence from its last guarded stronghold in the inspired poet's imagination, his poetic language loses its power to move and astonish. The light of its clarity is much too bright, and as many readers have noted, it leaves us cold.[36] The coldness of the poem serves a clear didactic purpose, but there is simply not enough inexpressible

---

[34] We now know, of course, that Jesus' 'native tongue' was Aramaic, but Milton's Jesus is clearly talking about the Hebrew poetry of the Psalms, 'Our Hebrew songs and harps in Babylon'.

[35] Leonard, *Naming in Paradise*, 244.

[36] See for e.g. Hyman, 'The Reader's Attitude in *Paradise Regained*'; Fisher 'Why is *Paradise Regained* So Cold?'

darkness in the *poetry* of *Paradise Regained* against which to appreciate the brilliance of Milton's art.

At the end of the poem, the narrator retreats into private obscurity together with his subject: 'he unobserved | Home to his mother's house private returned' (IV. 638–9). Dayton Haskin has convincingly argued that Mary's function throughout the poem, and especially in this closing line, is one of primary hermeneutical significance. After presenting compelling evidence to support this unusual claim, Haskin argues: 'Milton presents Mary as one who mediates the Word—first to Jesus himself, then to the New Testament writers, and ultimately to Christians in every age . . . She exercises the authority roles of preserving, interpreting, and combining diverse texts into a unique personal synthesis.'[37] By showing Jesus returning to his mother's house at the end of the poem, Milton holds before his readers both the instrument and measure of personal salvation, encouraging individual Reformed Christians to be assiduous and inspired collators of sacred biblical truths in their personal salvific interests. *Paradise Regained* does not conclude on a quiet note of introspective, maternal solitude, but tensely looks ahead to the unfolding of a collated gospel narrative which will see Jesus finally leaving his mother's house to begin his redemptive public ministry, culminating in his ultimate sacrifice on the cross. This suspended, untold narrative, however, can only unfold at the end of *Paradise Regained* in the silence of the 'fit' reader's mind, waiting on Christ's redemption not just to gather the elect into the glory of God, but also to sit in judgement on the damned. Politically speaking, the poem teaches reserved and even angry apocalyptic patience rather than quietist pacifism: the Second Coming and millennium is always around the corner, and the blind poet can only cling to the hope—or violent fantasy, rather—that the many satanic enemies of the Reformation, from papists to decadent Church of England royalists, will one day soon be trodden under Christ's foot.[38] In the meantime, however, a veil of silent interpretation falls between Milton and his community of readers: each to his own redemptive narrative, each to his own hopes and dreams, each to his own 'mother's house'. In the final analysis there is an elusive sense in *Paradise Regained* that the poet has indeed found his way to a truly ineffable 'fairer Paradise' (IV. 613), but few

[37] Haskin, *Milton's Burden of Interpretation*, 138.
[38] See Knoppers, *Historicizing Milton*, 137; Coffey, 'Pacifist, Quietist, or Patient Militant?'

of his readers—then and now—can rightly follow in his footsteps. Milton, it seems, regains Paradise only for himself.

UNDER THE SEAL OF *SAMSON*'S SILENCE

> Yet I pity
> His wretchedness, though he is my enemy,
> For the terrible yoke of blindness that is on him.
> I think of him, yet also of myself;
> For I see the true state of all us that live—
> We are dim shapes, no more, and weightless shadow.
>
> (Sophocles, *Ajax*, 121–6)[39]

These words of Sophocles' Odysseus, uttered upon the dejected sight of the once-heroic Ajax wallowing in the blood of slaughtered animal carcasses which the great hero has killed in a fit of distracted madness, aptly describes how many readers feel when they first lay imaginary eyes on Milton's Samson, and how some readers still feel, even more acutely, when they finally put down the text. Milton's Samson is not the reader's enemy, but he hardly arouses obvious sympathy either. Among ancient Greek tragic heroes, Sophocles' Oedipus and the Heracles of both Sophocles and Euripides are usually offered as models for Milton's Samson,[40] but Sophocles' Ajax was probably at the back of his mind as well. Ajax's curse of 'blindness' and subsequent suicide are instructive here. What Odysseus recognizes in Ajax is the terrible curse of *atē*—not physical, but rational blindness:[41] Ajax

---

[39] The translation is John Moore's, from the Chicago edition of *The Complete Greek Tragedies: Sophocles II*, ed. Grene and Lattimore, 13.

[40] The most obvious Sophoclean model for *Samson Agonistes* is *Oedipus Coloneus*, but parallels with *Oedipus Rex* and the Heracles of the *Trachiniae* have also been suggested. From Euripides, whom Milton admired (and quoted from) more than Sophocles, the Heracles plays (*Alcestis, Heracleidae*, and the *Heracles*) have also been plundered for echoes, and from Aeschylus, *Prometheus Unbound* as well. See Brewer, 'Two Athenian Models for *Samson Agonistes*'; Maxwell, 'Milton's Samson and Sophocles' Heracles'; Kessner, 'Milton's Hebraic Herculean Hero'; Wilson, *Mocked with Death*, ch. 7.

[41] Moore's 'terrible yoke of blindness' is an apt translation of the difficult phrase 'ἄτῃ συγκατέζευκται κακῇ'. 'ἄτη' (*atē*), often the name of the personified goddess of mischief and discord is a difficult word to translate, but it usually means 'reckless impulse, caused by judicial blindness sent by the gods' (Liddell and Scott). In any case, Moore's translation is much better than the Loeb's vague 'cruel affliction' (trans. Lloyd-Jones, p. 45).

slaughters helpless dumb animals thinking them to be actual men on whom he wishes to avenge himself for cheating him out of the prize of Achilles' armour. Moreover, it is the angry, partisan goddess Athena who inflicts this curse on Ajax. A direct comparison between Sophocles' *Ajax* and Milton's *Samson Agonistes* would be difficult; the differences are far more striking than the similarities: Athena curses Ajax with temporary mental blindness to stop him committing slaughter on men she defends; God allegedly lifts Samson's mental blindness so he may precisely commit mass slaughter on pagan men deemed God's enemies. But the overall theme of heroic degradation followed by an act of redemptive suicide—redemptive at least in the eyes of those who remain and continue to suffer—offers a compelling analogy about heroism 'tangled in the fold, | Of dire necessity' (*Samson Agonistes*, 1665–6).

The violent poem of *Samson Agonistes* indeed follows after the elusive tranquillity of *Paradise Regained* in the 1671 volume like a troubling and enigmatic qualification. The tragic structure and transmuted biblical subject-matter of the poem scrutinize the complexities of human psychology and human drama, not divine mysteries. There is in this poem no soaring of any kind, no glimpse of the transcendental. God's justice, a central theme in the poem, is viewed through a glass darkly in Samson's wretched contemplation of his present shame and the Chorus's running interpretation of the action. *Samson Agonistes* is everything *Paradise Lost* (and *Paradise Regained*, for that matter) is not. It is episodic, elliptic, and very much of *this* world. This can be misleading, however. Although the categorically *other* world of the hidden God is not the direct subject of the poem, its ineffable presence in *Samson Agonistes* is one of the most menacing in Milton's poetry, if not in any poetry. *Samson Agonistes* resonates with a profound ambience of ineffability which is intimately related to the tradition of apophasis, but from a radically Protestant perspective where the individual champion of God must contend with *aphaeresis* and *apophasis* at the core of his election narrative. The nightmare of *Samson Agonistes* is a Sophoclean (or Euripidean) distillation of the nightmare lurking behind the Protestant assumption that salvation depends on acts of reading that can, as Haskin has shown, go terribly wrong;[42] and when acts of reading go

---

[42] See Haskin, *Milton's Burden of Interpretation*, esp. chs. 5 and 6. For Haskin, the interpretative models of *Paradise Regained* and *Samson Agonistes* encourage the reader 'to

wrong in a Protestant context, reprobation and hell always lurk around the corner. Whereas *Paradise Regained* links self-effacing silence with redemption as a form of poetic *mysterium, Samson Agonistes* examines the tragic consequences of self-annihilation when a divine, ineffable mystery is violated, and personal salvation is divorced from the greater narrative of national salvation through history.

The presence of the numinous in *Samson Agonistes* is felt negatively as oppressive despair, as something denied. It arises from Samson having profaned that which is sacred and ineffable in an objective, numinous sense. Samson has betrayed his vows as a Nazarite of God by speaking unlawfully and divulging to Dalila the 'capital secret' (394) about his strength. The pun in 'capital' reinforces the double, literal–figurative significance of this violation: Samson both profanes the actual hair where his strength 'Lay stored, in what part summed' (395), but also that which is summed in his hair—a divine covenant of capital importance for his nation's salvation. He 'divulged the secret gift of God | To a deceitful woman' (201–2), and so violated that which is sacred, forbidden to be revealed, and hence unspeakable. The recurring image in the poem that captures this sense of unholy betrayal is the notion of violated sacred 'silence'.[43] In his opening soliloquy, a tormented Samson berates himself:

> Whom have I to complain of but myself?
> Who this high gift of strength committed to me,

reflect upon the process by which the canonical Scriptures had been produced ... by setting in motion contests of interpretation in which an urge for closure [i.e. *Samson Agonistes*] is pitted against a disciplined, responsible patience that delights in continuing interpretative activity [i.e. *Paradise Regained*]' (p. 119).

[43] For previous discussions about the thematic importance of silence in the poem see Landy, 'Language and the Seal of Silence in *Samson Agonistes*' and Mustazza, 'The Verbal Plot of *Samson Agonistes*'. My reading significantly differs, however, from that of Landy and Mustazza, who align the theme of silence in the poem with Samson's spiritual growth and inward movement from vain words to silent deeds which finally culminate in the silent calm of catharsis. Such readings assume, of course, that the catharsis enjoyed by the Chorus at the end of the poem is also shared by the reader (which I doubt), but more importantly they fail to distinguish between the conflicting presence in the poem of two types of silence—the silence which signifies God's ineffable approval of an elect person's spiritual holiness, on the one hand (the sort of silence celebrated in *Paradise Regained*), and the nihilistic silence which results when God *excludes* from the light of the Word an elect person fallen from grace, on the other. As I argue, it is never sufficiently clear in the poem which silence finally consumes Milton's Samson.

In what part lodged, how easily bereft me,
Under the seal of silence could not keep,
But weakly to a woman must reveal it,
O'ercome with importunity and tears.
O impotence of mind, in body strong!

(46–52, my emphasis)

A broken 'seal of silence' then becomes an abandoned 'fort of silence', which Samson confesses to have deserted at a mere 'peal of words (O weakness!)' (235). The parenthetical exclamation '(O weakness!)', itself weakened by the parenthesis, points to the semiotic nature of this desertion and the irony that mere words can so easily penetrate and bring down the impregnable 'fort' of one's ineffable covenant with God. That such guarded secrets, or spaces of divine intimacy, function as a kind of ineffable *mysterium* is reinforced again later when, after Manoa bewails his and his son's misfortunes, Samson reminds everyone who cares to listen that he alone is to blame, 'who have profaned | The *mystery* of God given me under pledge | Of vow, and have betrayed it to a woman, | A Canaanite, my faithless enemy' (377–80, my emphasis). Soon Manoa himself alludes to Samson's violation of 'the sacred trust of silence' (428), and even Dalila, in her hollow suit for pardon, stings Samson by reminding him of the particular nature of his transgression: 'Was it not weakness also to make known | For importunity, that is for naught, | Wherein consisted all thy strength and safety?' (778–80).

Allusions to the violation of ineffable mystery in *Samson Agonistes* obliquely reflect on Milton's similar violation, or at least the potential for such violation, in *Paradise Lost*. The penalty Milton's Samson pays for opening his lips and breaking the 'seal of silence' is the loss of physical as well as inner sight. Having profaned the sacred 'mystery' of his covenant with God, Samson feels he is lost not just to the light of day, but chiefly to the life-affirming light of the Word itself. In a particularly poignant sequence in the opening soliloquy Samson hints at the paradox of his predicament. He has fallen from having free access to the unmediated light, or will, of God, previously given to him under a 'seal of silence', into physical as well as inner darkness where the light of God, or the Word, cannot penetrate and therefore *falls* silent. The ironic echoes of the epic narrator's invocation to holy light in Book III of *Paradise Lost* are inescapable:

> O dark, dark, amid the blaze of noon,
> Irrecoverably dark, total eclipse
> Without all hope of day!
> O first-created beam, and thou great word,
> Let there be light, and light was over all;
> Why am I thus bereaved thy prime decree?
> The sun to me is dark
> And *silent as the moon*,
> When she deserts the night
> Hid in her vacant interlunar cave.
>
> (80–9, my emphasis)

Like the invocation to light in *Paradise Lost*, the phrase 'silent as the moon' links Samson's blindness to speech, but here there is no inner sight that can 'see and tell' of invisible things but only the metaphor, partly based on Pliny, of the moon's 'vacant interlunar cave'. The cave is 'vacant' because it is a figment of the imagination, a conceit dreamed up by men wildly speculating about what happens to the moon when it sets. Note that we are back in the forbidden, speculative realms of astronomy, and the image of Satan's ponderous moon-like shield from the opening of *Paradise Lost* should never be far from our minds. Since Samson is blind and can never see the 'eclipsed' sun rise again, his mind is permanently trapped in vacant realms of fruitless and potentially sinful speculation and, yes, semantic indeterminacy as well. Georgia Christopher, one of many critics who see Milton's Samson undergoing a process of regeneration in the poem, argues that Samson emerges in the wake of the tragic catastrophe as a 'Hebrew hero who is an honorary puritan saint'.[44] But the poem seems to me to represent such typological sainthood, as far as Milton's Samson is concerned, as finally elusive and potentially flawed. Lost to the Word, Samson's state of spiritual, psychological, and physical darkness impairs his ability to participate in any kind of meaningful discourse or 'speech-act', unless, of course, we are willing to countenance the difficult idea that his final and fatal act in enacting the catastrophe, like Jesus' standing on the pinnacle, is in some way uttered and not performed.

---

[44] Christopher, *Science of the Saints*, 226.

Insofar as Milton's Samson is trapped, therefore, in a circular predicament of typological prolepsis where he must regain his ability to 'read'
his life's story and recuperate his former biblical persona encapsulated
in the Chorus's nostalgic memory of 'That heroic, that renowned, |
Irresistible Samson' (125–6), he has become to all intents and purposes
illiterate. In Milton's religious vocabulary the blind, dejected Samson is
a metaphor, superimposed on the traditional Christian typology, for the
loss of one's elect ability to read and rightly understand the silent gaps of
Scripture, or at the very least for the potential danger of misreading such
gaps. The whole action of the poem, such as it is, indeed unfolds *within*
such a gap, or vignette in the biblical text. This was a common approach
to biblical hermeneutics among Protestants. As Christopher notes,
Luther spoke of the Old Testament stories as 'lattices', urging 'the
exegete to weave himself into the sense by filling in the interstices
with details of situation and psyche from his own experience'.[45] All
that the Bible tells us is that enough time elapses in the prison house for
Samson's hair to grow long again, and presumably, therefore, for him to
make amends with God: 'Howbeit the hair of his head began to grow
again after he was shaven' (Judg. 16: 22). The marginal gloss in the
Geneva Bible on this verse makes explicit what the Judges narrative
obliquely implies: 'Yet had he not his strength again, til he had called
upon God.' Milton, however, exploits the silent gap suggested by this
verse to cast doubt on the process of exegesis itself. Wittreich, for
example, has argued that 'the poem can be seen, in terms of the
conceptual model provided for it by the Book of Judges, as engaged
in a variety of fiction-making operations'.[46] These include, in Wittreich's analysis, the processes of 'condensing', 'displacing', and 'encoding' various elements of the biblical narrative. He points out that the
three main events of Samson's life that are retold from the most varied
perspectives in the poem are Samson's birth, marriages, and the jawbone
episode. For Wittreich, however, when 'Milton uses repetition to create
an alignment between the beginning and end, the past and present, of
Samson's life, the effect is not of revealing a Samson realizing his
potentiality as a minister of his deity but of reinforcing the point
that, because of his persistence in error, Samson falls short of that

---

[45] Ibid. 68.
[46] Wittreich, *Interpreting ' Samson Agonistes',* 61.

potentiality'.[47] Samson's opening soliloquy indeed condenses two isolated narrative elements from the Judges story that are directly related to the mysterious power of his hair. The first fragment is embedded in his reflection on his moment of birth, when Samson was proclaimed a Nazarite unto God: 'why was my breeding ordered and prescribed | As of a person separate to God' (30–1). The second fragment echoes and directly relates to the first, alluding to the moment of Samson's betrayal by Dalila (48–51). By isolating these two narrative fragments from the elliptic flow of the Judges account, Milton highlights the poem's central preoccupation with the theme of covenant-making and covenant-breaking and the doubts and fears that beset the religious individual seeking to mend that which is broken. Wittreich, however, then goes on to claim that the aim of Milton's manipulation of the biblical text is to 'wring from scriptural history its highest truths'.[48] Far from distilling the 'highest truth' from Samson's biblical story, I believe that, given the subtext of ineffability in the poem, the tragedy of Samson is presented as a metaphor for the potential *failure* of such a process, when exegesis yields not a single truth but only the silence of ambiguity. This is surely the implication if we deny, as Wittreich does, that Milton's Samson is finally redeemed, and Wittreich himself seems to have come round to see this when, in his later work, he argues that Milton's aim was to use the traditional Samson story against itself, 'to frustrate, not foster, platitudinous Christianity'.[49] The tragedy of Milton's Samson is that of a biblical hero grasping at straws in his desperate attempt to define his role within a scriptural narrative shaped by dogmatic readings and incomplete Christian typologies. It is not a case of Samson either failing or succeeding in this process, but of the process of interpretation itself finally overwhelming the agonist, leaving the reader as well with unanswered, and finally unanswerable, questions.

---

[47] Wittreich, *Interpreting 'Samson Agonistes'*, 150.
[48] Ibid. 60.
[49] Wittreich, '*Samson Agonistes*: Thought Colliding with Thought', in Kelley and Wittreich, *Altering Eyes*, 98–131, at 99. Essay reprinted in *Shifting Contexts: Reinterpreting 'Samson Agonistes'*. Despite Anthony Low's and Philip Gallagher's disparaging reviews of Wittreich's *Interpreting 'Samson Agonistes'*, where they cast severe doubt on his use of sources in reconstructing a Protestant intellectual history which viewed Samson as a negative exemplum, Wittreich's actual *reading* of the poem remains as provocative and as valid as it was when he first published it.

Indeed, if the ineffable character of *Paradise Regained* can be defined as one of epic retraction ending in silence, then the ineffable character of *Samson Agonistes* is undoubtedly dramatic, where *generic* silence and formal tragic lacunae speak volumes, ineffably. In the preface, 'Of That Sort of Dramatic Poem Which is Called Tragedy', Milton calls our attention to the dramatic genre of *Samson Agonistes*. After a short encomium of the morally edifying format of Greek tragedy, he mentions, almost in passing, that the 'Division into act and scene referring chiefly to the stage (to which this work never was intended) is here omitted'.[50] All drama is necessarily elliptic, in that its confined onstage action often unfolds with reference to implicit action taking place offstage in the greater inferred world which the characters inhabit. By staging a drama, moreover, a director or producer supply their own interpretation to a dramatic text in a way which usually locks that text into a single consistent dramatic reality. By stressing that *Samson Agonistes* was never intended for stage production, Milton emphasizes his poem's call for intimacy with the individual reader and his or her subjective predilections. Dramatic speech evokes an immediacy and intimacy which, in tragedy at least—certainly most Greek tragedy— enhances the sense of illicit voyeurism that sets the process of catharsis in motion. Nicholas Jose takes the view that the destruction of the Philistine theatre at the end of the poem signifies Milton's rejection of false 'theatrical values' in anticipation of 'another mode, "legend" and lyric "song"'. In light of this, Jose then reads the claim that the work was

---

[50] *CSP* 357. I place myself among those critics who read Milton's parenthetical statement quite literally—'never intended for the stage' means 'never intended for the stage'—any stage. I therefore do not think that this statement specifically alludes in a qualified sense to the 'Restoration' stage, or that it implies, as Timothy Burbery most recently argues, that the blind Milton simply had no links with the theatre and therefore could not stage the drama even if he wanted to, therefore implying that if he could he would have staged it (*Milton the Dramatist*, 96–7). Burbery continues to argue that since the text appears to contain embedded stage directions (or what Burbery *reads* as stage directions and cues) which help us visualize its action, it clearly *was* intended for *a* stage—a hypothesis he seeks to reinforce by the irrelevant fact that the poem has been successfully staged throughout the twentieth century. While *Samson Agonistes* is clearly not a closet drama in the Elizabethan-Senecan sense, as Elizabeth Sauer, for example, argues ('The Politics of Performance in the Inner Theatre: *Samson Agonistes* as Closet Drama', in Dobranski and Rumrich, *Milton and Heresy*, 199–215), it does seem fairly clear that Milton wanted his readers to visualize the poem's dramatic action through a textual, aural encounter, not a staged, visual one.

never intended for the stage as 'a tactical move in the interests of higher truth'.[51] It seems to me, however, that far from promoting the interests of a 'higher truth', Milton's insistence that his poem was never intended for the stage effectively undermines any attempt to arrive at such absolutes. However we interpret *Samson Agonistes*, it is to remain a personal experience; each reader, the preface implies, must recognize and create his own catharsis, his own moment of 'truth'.

Given the controversy surrounding the poem, such an analysis might seem disingenuously equivocal, but once the generic structure of the poem is aligned with the themes of broken silence and the violation of ineffable mystery, it appears that there is an intentional, didactic pre-miss behind the poem's calculated dramatic ambiguity. The poem opens, for example, with the image of Samson addressing an invisible person:

> A little onward lend thy guiding hand
> To these dark steps, a little further on;
> For yonder bank hath choice of sun or shade.

(1–3)

These arresting opening lines immediately subject the reader to Samson's blindness. Who is Samson talking to? Is there an actual person on the imaginary stage lending him a hand? As is well known, these lines echo similar opening scenes in Sophocles' *Oedipus Coloneus* and Eur-ipides' *Phoenician Maidens*, but in these examples we know the identity of the addressee (Antigone in the former, Tiresias' daughter in the latter). However, with the absence of any stage directions or any real performance in mind, *Samson Agonistes* is enacted and performed in our mind's eye, and the vision stirred up by the opening scene is a deliber-ately ambiguous one, calling for our moral and intellectual readership. Could Samson be addressing himself in an effort to gather strength? If there is someone with him, who is that person? Perhaps a Philistine jailor, or maybe a random pedestrian who meets Samson outside the prison. Of course, as Stevie Davies suggests, Samson could be praying to God, the hold of whose hand 'the hero lost before he became blind'. For Davies, 'it is God's withdrawal and man's savage sense of rejection that

---

[51] Jose, *Ideas of the Restoration in English Literature*, 157–8.

Samson Agonistes mourns, and this larger guidance that the agonist solicits'.[52] However, it is also possible to argue that Samson is addressing, meta-poetically, the reader. It is ultimately up to us to guide his 'dark steps' and make our own choice on his behalf of 'sun or shade'.

From the outset, therefore, Milton presents his Samson as a moral and psychological riddle, pulling in two directions at once. Significantly, the biblical Judges account indeed revolves around a central riddle offered in the story as a metaphor for the mystery of Samson's gift withheld from the heathen mind, as well as for the prospect of hope and redemption that the Samson story entails within the wider context of the Book of Judges. The Bible tells us that Samson slays a lion with his God-given strength. He later returns and finds 'a swarm of bees and honey in the carcase of the lion' (Judg. 14: 8). Next, during the wedding-feast with the Timnite woman, for no apparent reason, Samson presents her thirty companions with a riddle which they have to solve within the seven days of the feast: 'And he said unto them, Out of the eater came forth meat, and out of the strong came forth sweetness. And they could not in three days expound the riddle' (14: 14). What happens next ominously foreshadows things to come. The wedding guests manipulate Samson's bride into coercing her husband to disclose the answer to his riddle before the seven days are up, and after many importunities Samson relents, reveals the answer to his bride, and is betrayed, leading to his famous saying, itself riddling and circumlocutory: 'If ye had not plowed with my heifer, ye had not found out my riddle' (14: 18). This bizarre episode was probably inserted by the biblical editors of the so-called 'Deuteronomistic History' (Deut.–2 Kgs.) to allow for the inclusion and allegorical interpretation of the Samson story—an ancient Semitic solar myth—within the wider context of the Book of Judges's redemptive narrative of sin, repentance, and national salvation.[53] The significance of the riddle seems clear enough: out of the

---

[52] Davies, *Milton*, 180.

[53] Contrary to the erroneous etymology, current in Milton's time, which glossed Samson's Hebrew name as meaning 'there the second time', Samson's Hebrew name, *Shimshon* (שִׁמְשׁוֹן), is almost certainly derived from the Hebrew for sun, *shemesh* (שֶׁמֶשׁ). This and other themes in the story—the strength residing in his long hair (sunbeams), the recurrent motif of fire and burning—all suggest the presence of an ancient solar myth. Krouse, *Milton's Samson*, 23–30, gives a concise summary of the early traditions associated with the Samson myth. See also Blenkinsopp, 'Structure and Style in Judges 13–16'.

death of the mighty eventual good will issue; out of the demise of the destroyer will issue new hope for spiritual sustenance. By putting forth this riddle, the biblical Samson unwittingly foresees his own destruction and eventual self-sacrifice for the greater good of Israel. The words previously spoken by the angel to Samson's mother thus come into sharp focus, as it is made clear that Samson will only trigger a process, not see it to fulfilment: 'for the child shall be a Nazarite unto God from the womb: and he shall *begin* to deliver Israel out of the hand of the Philistines' (Judg. 13: 5, my emphasis). 'Begin' does not imply that Samson's act of self-sacrifice will be abortive, but that it will retain its providential significance within a wider national narrative in which Samson only plays a part.[54]

The centrality of Samson's riddle to traditional Protestant, not to say Puritan, meditation on the Samson myth is important, especially the typological metaphor of the honey extracted from the lion's carcass. Here, for example, is Bunyan in the preface to his *Grace Abounding* (1666), addressing fellow godly readers who are about to 'taste' from the sweet 'honey' of his spiritual autobiography:

I have sent you here enclosed a drop of that honey, that I have taken out of the Carcase of a Lyon, *Judg. 14. 5, 6, 7, 8.* I have eaten thereof my self also, and am much refreshed thereby. (Temptations when we meet them at first, are as the Lyon that roared upon Sampson: but if we overcome them, the next time we see them, we shall finde a Nest of Honey within them.) The Philistines understand me not. It is a Relation of the work of God upon my Soul, even from the very first, till now; wherein you may perceive my castings down, and raisings up: for he woundeth, and his hands make whole.[55]

---

[54] See J. P. Rosenblatt, 'Samson's Sacrifice', in Boesky and Crane, *Form and Reform in Renaissance England*, 321–37, at 329. Rosenblatt's 'monistic' reading of *Samson Agonistes* might indeed demonstrate that Milton uses a 'positive typology' to 'emphasize God's continuous ways with all his creatures' (p. 340) but it does not follow that such a reading would 'acknowledge the humanity of the Chorus, its capacity for fellow-feeling, and its considerable spiritual and intellectual development' (p. 329).

[55] Bunyan, *Grace Abounding to the chief of Sinners*, in Stachniewski, *'Grace Abounding' with other Spiritual Biographies*, 3. See also Anthony Burgess's *Spiritual refining: or A treatise of grace and assurance Wherein are handled, the doctrine of assurance. The use of signs in self-examination. How true graces may be distinguished from counterfeit. Several true signs of grace, and many false ones* (1652): 'our happinesse, and the ground of all our peace, lyeth not in what we have done, but what we have received, and in what Christ hath done for us. This doctrine is like the hony *Sampson* found in the dead Lyon, in Christ crucified, which we are to instruct all burthened sinners in' (p. 324).

As John Stachniewski points out in his note on this passage, when Bunyan says defiantly, 'The Philistines understand me not', he is reflecting on the common Puritan belief 'that the language of their spiritual experience was foreign to the worldly'. Then, referencing the *Pilgrim's Progress*, Stachniewski adds: 'They sometimes called it "the Language of Canaan".'[56] Indeed, the ideal of interior spirituality contained in the typological metaphor of the 'language of Canaan' is implicit in the idea of 'honey' as well, since Canaan is, after all, 'a land flowing with milk and honey' (Exod. 3: 8). Samson can only be a type of the Puritan saint—as he is in Bunyan's preface—when his riddle yields 'honey', that is, when the riddle of his violent suicide in the context of Old Testament redemption yields its desired spiritual sustenance in the Christian antitypes of triumph over temptation and adversity for which Job, not Samson, is the ultimate Old Testament model.

It would seem, then, that if we want to sustain a reading of Milton's Samson as an unequivocal type of a Puritan saint complementing the model of Job-like patience and perseverance depicted in *Paradise Regained*, we must also look to his riddle and its implied honey; but Milton significantly omits from the poem any mention of the actual content of the biblical riddle and especially of the honey associated with its solution. The Chorus alludes to the slaying of the lion in its opening song, but it omits any reference either to the honey or the riddle: 'who tore the lion, as the lion tears the kid' (128). By omitting in this way the typological key with which to put Samson's feat of strength into a spiritual context, the Chorus presents Samson's power at this stage of the poem only in its heroic and destructive capacity. The Chorus alludes to the riddle again towards the end of the poem, and here too the reference is deliberately and significantly elliptic. Weighing Samson's diatribe on the inconstancy of women, the Chorus recalls the riddle because of the Timnite woman's previous treachery:

> It is not virtue, wisdom, valour, wit,
> Strength, comeliness of shape, or amplest merit
> That woman's love can win or long inherit;
> But what it is, hard is to say,
> Harder to hit,

[56] *Grace Abounding*, 229.

(which way soever men refer it)
Much like thy riddle, Samson, in one day
Or seven, though one should musing sit...

(1010–17)

The Chorus is mocking Samson. It suggests that Samson's riddle—so central to the meaning of the biblical text in which it originally appears—is as insoluble and difficult to discover, indeed 'Harder to hit', than the mysterious power a woman's love might have over a man. Moreover, it implies that, in allowing himself to be effeminized by the treacherous women in his life, Samson has now lost his ability to answer his own riddle. Samson himself reinforces this point of view when, several lines later, the Chorus observes the mock-heroic giant Harapha approaching. As if to test Samson's ability to communicate figuratively, the Chorus warns Samson of the imminent danger by describing it as an approaching storm:

> But had we best retire, I see a storm?
>   *Sam.* Fair days have oft contracted wind and rain.
>   *Chor.* But this another kind of tempest brings.
>   *Sam.* Be less abstruse, *my riddling days are past.*
>   *Chor.* Look now for no enchanting voice, nor fear
> The bait of *honeyed words*; a rougher tongue
> Draws hitherward, I know him by his stride,
> The giant Harapha of Gath, his look
> Haughty as is his pile high-built and proud.

(1061–9, my emphases)

This short stichomythia places Samson's blindness in a wider semantic, and distinctly Protestant, spiritual context. Because he is blind and literally cannot see the figure of Harapha approaching, Samson is unable to complete in his mind the Chorus's metaphor. Because of his physical blindness, unrecompensed by the gift of divine sight, he can only grasp at the literal meaning of the Chorus's figurative, riddling words and so naturally assumes it is about to rain. Samson's literal misinterpretation of the Chorus's words puts him in harm's way and exposes the extent to which he has fallen from his 'riddling days' as an elect deliverer of Israel, thereby also rendering the subsequent boasting-match with Harapha and the pledge to fight as God's champion distinctly hollow. Even if the exact allegorical content of the biblical riddle, or 'honey', withheld from us in the poem ever did bear any significance for Samson, it is now lost forever in the insoluble maze of his mind. Far from being eloquent in the 'language of Canaan' and its spiritual honey, this deeply flawed type of Protestant sainthood, a victim of what the Chorus describes in deep scriptural irony as Dalila's 'honeyed words', is thoroughly illiterate in any spiritual vocabulary and therefore quite ignorant of his place within the implied scriptural narrative he inhabits.

However, if my argument about the potential breakdown of the so-called 'language of Canaan' in the opening and middle sections of the poem so far holds, what are we to make of the equally enigmatic catastrophe at the end of the poem? Does Samson finally regain his 'skill' in the 'language of Canaan' and so fulfil his typological destiny? Many Christian thinkers throughout history have argued on the basis of the catalogue of saints in Hebrews 11 (all deeply flawed biblical heroes of the Old Testament who sinned in the eyes of God) that Samson's life and death typologically foreshadow the death and resurrection of Christ, and represent a virtuous model of strength in weakness through faith. Since the author of the epistle cites Samson among other Old Testament heroes who, despite their shortcomings, relied on faith to achieve extraordinary things, many argue that Milton uncontroversially follows Hebrews in portraying Samson as a type of Christian saint who undergoes spiritual growth. The fundamental problem with such readings, however, is that the idea of strength through faith promoted in the Epistle to the Hebrews deliberately subverts all notions of physical strength associated with Old Testament heroics. Hebrews's is a deeply *spiritualized* idea of strength. The heroes cited in the epistle are used to teach the Hebrews, who are still trapped under the Law and its legalistic Old Testament vocabulary, that 'faith is the substance of things hoped for, the evidence of things *not seen*' (Hebrews 11: 1, my emphasis). To use faith merely to 'subdue kingdoms' or 'stop the mouths of lions' (11: 33) is an example of how faith was used under the Law to which Milton's Samson (notwithstanding Joan Bennet's commanding analysis and argument to the contrary in *Reviving Liberty*) remains in bondage, not how it should be used to promote the Spirit. The epistle's point is that Gedeon, Barak, Samson, Jephthah, David, and Solomon are only made perfect in Christ, not in themselves: 'And these all, having obtained a good report through faith, received not the promise: God having provided some better things for us, that they without us should not be made perfect' (11: 39–40). All types are necessarily similar to their antitype in some way but also *dissimilar*, and when the dissimilarity outweighs the similarity the type can no longer function. The problem with Milton's Samson is that too much ambiguity and sinfulness at the source of the type disables its relationship with any conceivable antitype. Far from being a type of Christ who rises out of the ashes, as the Chorus implies, in mock resurrection 'Like that self-begotten bird' (1699), Milton's Samson is stripped by the ambiguous framework of the unstaged tragedy of his ability to function typologically in a redeemed Christian context precisely *because* of his inability to unequivocally re-enter the national narrative of salvation traced by the Chorus, itself trapped under the bondage of the Law, who sees in his death an act of phoenix-like redemption.

This leads us to the still-unresolved and controversial debate about the ultimate didactic moral of the poem, which usually boils down to Samson's 'rousing motions' (1382). Since it is impossible to say anything about *Samson Agonistes* these days without taking sides in this controversy, my answer, initially evasive like Stanley Fish's answer, is that we are never meant to know.[57] For Fish, however, the indeterminacy at the heart of the poem points finally to the antinomian certainty of its author and his biblical hero in the poem, 'who rests confidently in his knowledge of the truth and in his ability easily to discern the one obligation that it would be death to slight'.[58] The point for Fish is that Samson may know what he has to do, but we as readers cannot share in that knowledge. I, on the other hand, believe that it is not possible to hold such a view of the text without essentially refining the more categorically negative or sceptical interpretations of the poem. If we accept the traditional view proposed by Krouse, and comprehensively developed since then by Lewalski, Radzinowicz, Low, Christopher, and many others, that, as A. S. P. Woodhouse says, 'the latest experiences of Samson become a study in regeneration, and his act of fierce revenge the seal of his repentance and restoration',[59] then the poem can offer only hope of one kind or another.[60] But as I see it,

---

[57] See Fish, *How Milton Works*, chs. 12 and 13.
[58] Ibid. 477.
[59] Woodhouse, *The Heavenly Muse*, 296.
[60] See Krouse, *Milton's Samson and the Christian Tradition*; Stein, *Heroic Knowledge*; Steadman, '"Faithful Champion"'; Lewalski, '*Samson Agonistes* and the "Tragedy" of the Apocalypse'; Woodhouse, *The Heavenly Muse*, 292–319; Low, *The Blaze of Noon*; Hill,

Milton's Greek tragedy about the life and death of the biblical strong-man offers an awkward catharsis which is enjoyed, perversely, only by Manoa and the Chorus of Danites, while the reader is left with a stark cautionary tale about the danger of potentially misreading God's will in the process of 'making bad choices and succumbing to self-deceit'.[61] Samson's certainty, which Fish can be so certain of while remaining in doubt, is itself finally elusive.

I am far more inclined to adopt Derek Wood's finely tuned and well-argued reading which attempts to reconcile both approaches by acknowledging that the poem clearly *does* appeal to Christian typology and clearly *does* offer a reading which views Samson as a proto-Christian hero striking an apocalyptic blow for liberty, but which also recognizes that such readings are subjective to those who produce them and are dependent on the unverifiable, and potentially misleading, inner testimony of sinful men who call on God to account for their 'un-Christian savagery'.[62] Bunyan, like other authors of spiritual autobiographies in

---

Milton and the English Revolution, ch. 31; Radzinowicz, *Toward 'Samson Agonistes'*; Christopher, *Science of the Saints*, 225–54; Lieb, *The Sinews of Ulysses*, 98–138; Bennet, *Reviving Liberty*, ch. 5 (rather than spiritual regeneration, Bennet sees Samson attaining true Christian Liberty under the Law). More recent critics to defend one or more versions of the traditional view include Evans, *The Miltonic Moment*, 117–32, and A. Rudrum, 'Discerning the Spirit in *Samson Agonistes*: The Dalila Episode', in Durham and Pruitt, *'All in All'*, 245–58. The political readings of Achinstein, '*Samson Agonistes* and the Drama of Dissent', and Loewenstein, 'The Revenge of the Saint', also build their analysis on the assumption that Milton's Samson is an uncomplicated type of a Puritan saint. In her biography of Milton Lewalski synthesizes several of the 'orthodox' readings. She accepts that the path of regeneration plotted in the poem may not be a straightforward one, but nevertheless concludes with little difficulty that Samson's 'final, miraculous destruction of the Philistine theatre indicates that God has accepted his repentance and has restored his role as judge, that is, as God's agent for the deliverance of his people' (*The Life of John Milton*, 523).

[61] Shawcross, *The Uncertain World of 'Samson Agonistes'*, 102. See also Carey, *Milton*, 138–46; Samuel, '*Samson Agonistes* as Tragedy', in Wittreich, *Calm of Mind*, 235–58; Wittreich, *Interpreting 'Samson Agonistes'* and *Shifting Contexts*; Rushdy, 'According to Samson's Command'; Skulsky, *Justice in the Dock*.

[62] '[Samson] acts in faith, but Milton's fictionalization with its dark emphases presents Samson as a profoundly ambiguous example for Christian imitation ... Against Samson's divinely confirmed faith, Milton sets this questionable moral consciousness, this harshness of human experience under the Law, this state of indirection that creatures suffered as they struggled to find a path to God, this condition of un-Christian savagery acted out in all honesty by human beings ignorant as yet of the living example of Christ's life in time' (Wood, *Exiled From Light*, p. xxii; see esp. Wood's analysis in ch. 7).

the period, at least wears his regenerate heart on his sleeve; Milton's Samson offers us only enigmatic words and a heap of slaughtered bodies.

The dubious resolution of the poem leaves the most central question of whether Samson regains his ability to 'read' God's will wide open. In the poem's pivotal moment Samson addresses the Chorus of his countrymen in the following words, which have confounded critics ever since:

> Be of good courage, I begin to feel
> Some rousing motions in me which dispose
> To something extraordinary my thoughts.
> I with this messenger will go along,
> Nothing to do, be sure, that may dishonour
> Our Law, or stain my vow of Nazarite.
> If there be aught of presage in the mind,
> This day will be remarkable in my life
> By some great act, or of my days the last.
>
> (1381–9)

Unlike the more radically sceptical critics, I do not think there is any real question that a providential God is complicit on some level in Samson's act, if only for the simple reason that God must get the hitherto passive Samson to finally do *something* to serve the Israelite national cause as Judge. The 'Argument' of the poem seems to indicate that Samson himself understands as much when, after the public officer instructs him to go to the Philistine theatre, he was 'at length persuaded inwardly that this was from God, he yields to go along with him, who came now the second time with great threatenings to fetch him'.[63] Samson, whose name was thought to mean 'there the second time', *thinks* he sees the hand of God in unfolding events and so decides—in the silence of inward contemplation—on a course of action which is redemptive but also self-annihilating. However, between the reader appreciating that Samson is an instrument of God in a wider apocalyptic and typological narrative on the one hand, and *knowing* that God is the direct source of Samson's 'rousing motions' on the other, there is still a very large gap of doubt and uncertainty. This gap grows increasingly wider as Samson now begins to distance himself from the reader in ever more abstruse language. There is no moment of declarative clarity, only the unsettling presence of mysterious interiority,

[63] *CSP* 358.

silently propelling Samson towards the final catastrophe. As Fish has shown (before drawing from this evidence an inexplicable conclusion), everything about Samson's 'rousing motions' speech is deliberately vague from the reader's point of view.[64] While the lines 'Masters' commands come with a power resistless | To such as owe them absolute subjection' (1404–5) may indeed suggests that Samson at least believes that his rousing motions are from God, as Fish says, his 'parting words are a forest of qualifications . . . The only prediction Samson will venture is that something will happen; whether this will involve the death he had despairingly invoked is uncertain'.[65] We can never tell what Samson is actually talking about because there is a real sense in which Samson himself seems to be unsure. The point is dramatic, not theological. If Samson is suddenly endowed with the coherence of regenerate vision, why is he being so mysterious? Samson's refusal to reflect his alleged new-found clarity of vision in verbal perspicuity suggests either that he himself is still in the dark, or that he does not trust the Chorus to share this with them. Samson only reassures the Chorus that *whatever* he will now do he will not 'dishonour | Our law', but this too is terribly vague. The tone here is one of veiled resentment; Samson knows that the Chorus, from whom he has been alienated throughout the poem so far, does not care about him as an individual, but only about the integrity of the national Law and the role he plays in that narrative as a heroic, now fallen, Nazarite. He tells the Chorus what they want to hear, indeed what they *need* to hear, as he proceeds to act. Imprisoned on enemy territory, the blind Samson cannot separate friend from foe, truth from falsehood. From here on he will let his actions speak for him, one way or another, and it is this sense of 'one way or another' which has proved so difficult for modern readers.

The confusing ambiguities of Samson's 'rousing motions' speech are only exacerbated as the poem reaches its dramatic climax. The horror-stricken messenger reports that before Samson brings down the Philistine theatre, 'with head a while inclined, | And eyes fast fixed he stood, *as* one who prayed, | *Or* some great matter in his mind revolved' (1636–8, my emphases). As is often remarked, Milton deliberately deletes Samson's actual prayer from the Book of Judges (not merely its reference to revenge, but all of it)—indeed, like the messenger, we cannot be

---

[64] See Fish, *How Milton Works*, 418–19.
[65] Ibid. 419.

sure that he prays at all. At the most crucial moment in the poem, when it would have mattered most, Milton simply bars our access to Samson's mind. Instead, he creates a large gap of silent interpretation between what the messenger sees offstage and what we, as imaginary spectators, are asked to make of it. When the Chorus jubilantly hails Samson's perceived act of sacrificial offering under the Law as 'O dearly-bought revenge, yet glorious!' (1660), the words are those of the Danites and only theirs. The Chorus and Manoa supply their own apocalyptic narrative to Samson's death which has its own interior biblical logic, but which is not necessarily supported by the poem's climactic action as far as the now-dead Samson is concerned. Choruses in Greek tragedy are not always a reliable mouthpiece of the tragedian; in Aeschylus' *Libation Bearers* the Chorus is even complicit in murder. Strangely enough, however, Milton's Chorus *is* reliable, but only from its own, scriptural point of view—it is the voice of typological and scriptural consensus, its proclamations of catharsis looking ahead to Samson's sainthood under the new Christian dispensation. The Chorus is never wrong in the same Protestant sense that the Bible and its typological narratives are never 'wrong' once they yield their desired antitype. But Samson, like an individual reader trapped in a state of scriptural *aphaeresis*, struggles against the silence (both aural and visual) that surrounds him, and there is no telling if he ever breaks free from this maze of uncertainty. By losing touch with his redemptive significance implicit in the biblical riddle, Samson becomes an ambiguous agent of violence and destruction, and it should be obvious, as John Carey continually and rightly reminds us, that violence perpetrated in ambiguity is finally perpetrated in *moral* ambiguity.[66]

---

[66] See Carey's provocative *TLS* piece, 'A Work in Praise of Terrorism?' (*TLS* 6 Sept. 2002). This article is now notorious for its *ad hominem* attack on Fish's reading of *Samson* as immoral, and Carey's charge that Fish's analysis amounts to 'a license for any fanatic to commit atrocity' (p. 15). The fact that Carey made such an accusation in a volume marking the anniversary of the terrorist attacks of September 11 was perhaps unfortunate, because it caused a legitimate literary controversy to devolve into something else entirely and deflected attention from the valid criticism of Fish's assumptions as a literary critic. Indeed, none of the very different replies to Carey by Loewenstein, Lieb, and Fish contained in Lieb and Labriola (eds.), *Milton in the Age of Fish*, resolve the problem that Fish's reading effectively transforms Milton's Samson, an unredeemed type of the Old Law, into an antinomian solipsist which, ironically, renders Samson a very dangerous type of erring criminal even on Milton's Protestant terms, not just Carey's ethical ones.

It seems to me, however, that debates about whether or not *Samson Agonistes* condones or rejects violence miss the point. The dramatic force of the tragedy proceeds from the oppositional clash between two ineffable presences, where the first is the enigmatic character of God in his implicit relationship with his fallen Nazarite, and the second is Samson's equally enigmatic understanding and interpretation of that relationship. If we consider the poem's refusal to yield meaning in the context of ineffable presence as a semantic and religious concept, the absence of definable morality leaves a void of distinct immorality in a very specific soteriological Protestant context. As I have argued in my analysis of *Paradise Lost*, when Milton thinks about the predicament of ineffability in the context of the Protestant religious experience he tends to invest it with an ethical dimension. As we move in *Paradise Lost* from the ineffable plenitude of God to the semiotic disintegration of Satan and the devils, the ineffable, as presence, accrues soteriological and ethical significance. Throughout this process, the Miltonic persona contained within the epic narrator's voice stands aloof to one side, confident in the mimetic grasp of his poetic utterance while the divine source of inspiration which authorizes his utterance is finally mysterious and ineffable. *Paradise Regained* and *Samson Agonistes*, however, contend with the ineffable presence that reveals itself when the inspired agent must turn inwardly and strive not to instruct others but to secure personal salvation. If in *Paradise Regained* the poet immerses himself in the words of the Word and so allows his individual presence to be consumed by the ineffability of divine presence, in *Samson Agonistes* the poet loses himself in the maze of Samson's mind, with the effect that such ineffable presence becomes a symptom of moral abandonment and possible reprobation. It does not follow, then, that Samson *must* be regenerate for God to use him as an agent of destruction. The tragic irony of *Samson Agonistes* depends on the Protestant-Calvinist conceit that God may use even those debarred from grace to bring national salvation to the elect (and no amount of Arminian qualification of the term 'elect' can weaken the menacing force of this conceit). Unlike *Paradise Lost, Samson Agonistes* makes no claims about the will of God. The point is precisely that God's will under the Law is inscrutable and that Samson, the Chorus, and the reader may be making wrong assumptions about it.

When, for example, a bitter Samson complains about the apparent arbitrariness of God's will, the legalistic Chorus reflects revealingly:

> Just are the ways of God,
> And justifiable to men;
> Unless there be who think not God at all,
> If any be, they walk obscure;
> For of such doctrine never was there school,
> But the heart of the fool,
> And no man therein doctor but himself.
>   Yet more there be who doubt his ways not just,
> As to his own edicts, found contradicting,
> Then give the reins to wandering thought,
> Regardless of his glory's diminution;
> Till by their own perplexities involved
> They ravel more, still less resolved,
> But never find self-satisfying solution.
>   As if they would confine the interminable,
> And tie him to his own prescript,
> Who made our laws to bind us, not himself,
> And hath full right to exempt
> Whom so it pleases him by choice
> From national obstriction, without taint
> Of sin, or legal debt;
> For his own laws he can best dispense.

$$(293–314)$$

The word 'justifiable' in line 294 suggests that the execution of God's justice towards Samson and the Philistines is 'justifiable to men' from the Chorus's point of view, but Samson clearly does not gain any discernible comfort from these words. If there is divine justice at play here, the blind Samson cannot see it. These lines, moreover, finally silence the active, Orphic poet shadowed in Samson's persona who has always aspired to perform acts of justification on God's behalf. The oblique reference to the theodicy of *Paradise Lost* is hard to ignore. If Milton, the inspired agent of God, has failed in that project it is because he has been *misread* by an un-'fit' audience; because there will always be men out there 'who doubt his ways not just', or even worse, deny that God actually exists. Even more poignant, perhaps, is the implicit fear that the blind poet-prophet, reduced in *Samson Agonistes* to a type of

Samson, is the one who has vainly sought to 'confine the interminable, | And tie him to his own prescript'. The Chorus's call to finally surrender to the impenetrable will of God, who may 'exempt | Whom so it pleases him by choice | From national obstriction, without taint | Of sin, or legal debt', is also a call to surrender completely to the Law of the hidden God without fear for one's salvation. Far from promoting in the knowing 'fit' Protestant reader an antinomian counter-argument, these lines provide a stark warning against the threat of antinomianism which lurks at the heart of the Protestant principle of justification by faith and Milton's belief in radical Christian liberty from the Law. It is not up to the Protestant individual obliquely addressed here to obtain exemption from 'national obstriction'; only God, acting through Christ—so runs the implied answer—can exempt an individual from the burden of the Law without 'sin, or legal debt'. Arminius is beaten into submission in these lines with a Calvinist hammer, not to retract Milton's belief in free will and Christian liberty, but merely to suggest that man may doubt the point of having free will in such a scheme when all one can do is sit around like the Old Testament Samson and wait to be used. This is not, of course, the first time we encounter such sentiments in Milton's poetry; 'Sonnet XVI', probably occasioned by Milton's total blindness and sense of vocational futility, famously records a similar sense of resignation:

> God doth not need
> Either man's work or his gifts, who best
> Bear his mild yoke, they serve him best, his state
> Is kingly. Thousands at his bidding speed
> And post o'er land and ocean without rest:
> They also serve who only stand and wait.
>
> (9–14)

Samson is denied heroic action in his own right in a conflict where the real *agon* is between Yahweh and Dagon ('all the contest is now | 'Twixt God and Dagon', 461–2). This *agon* takes place mostly offstage in the larger, inferred national narrative, but Samson can no longer participate in this narrative because words—indeed, the proleptic presence of scriptural words and the 'language of Canaan'—have turned into silence, and the ineffable, rather than signifying spiritual succour, now contaminates every aspect of his waking mind with doubt.

Eventually, Samson is used by God to further the Danites' national narrative, but we can never tell if, in using him in this way, God accepts Samson's repentance and offering of self-sacrifice or is merely using and discarding a blunt instrument. Having lost the answer to his own riddle, Samson *becomes* the riddle and effectively removes any hope of ever meaningfully interpreting his death, ambiguously alluded to in the 'Argument' of the poem as potentially unpremeditated: 'what Samson had done to the philistines, and by *accident* to himself.'[67] In Milton's time, like today, the phrase 'by accident' was used adverbially to denote 'anything that happens without foresight or expectation' (*OED* 1*b*). However, the word 'accident' could also denote, in an altogether different context, the medical symptoms—the accidents—of an illness (*OED* 3). The *OED* indeed cites *Samson Agonistes* as an example of this use, when Samson talks of the 'accidents' (612) of what reads like acute depression. I am not suggesting there is a deliberate pun here, but the two words nonetheless echo one another. The 'accident' of Samson's death is indeed a symptom, or accident, of his depression and incurable loss of scriptural identity. Loss of identity was something the post-revolutionary Milton could well relate to: the story of the biblical Samson clearly held deeply personal significance for him, not least because of its scope for an overtly autobiographical meditation on blindness and religious calling. Ironically, however, the resulting poem is in some respects Milton's most de-personalized. The robust presence of the Miltonic bard so familiar from the epic poetry and prose is diffused and scattered among the tragedy's various *dramatis personae*. There is no unifying voice to guide its readers, only a host of discordant dramatic voices plagued by violence, deceit, mistrust, and misinterpretation. *Samson Agonistes* is in one profound sense a poem about the disintegration of personal identity and authority, and by extension about the loss of voice and religious purpose when sacred texts or poems that *ought* to yield supreme 'truths' admit difficult and morally questionable interpretations. At the end of the poem the Chorus of Danites get their catharsis—'All is best' (1745), it proclaims, as God is seen to exact his final vengeance on his enemy Dagon through 'this great event' which dismisses God's servants 'With peace and

---

[67] 'The Argument', *CSP* 358. My emphasis.

consolation . . . And calm of mind all passion spent' (1756–8).[68] But the dead, discarded Samson, doomed now to become a type, melts away with a thinly disguised Miltonic persona into the obscurity of an offstage death reported by a distraught messenger, stunned into incoherence by the unspeakable deeds he has seen, crying: 'O whither shall I run, or which way fly | The sight of this so horrid spectacle | Which erst my eyes beheld and yet behold; | for dire imagination still pursues me' (1541–4). The poem ends by declaring calm and rest, but the 'dire imagination' it provokes can find none.

It might be objected that the foregoing analysis of *Paradise Regained* and *Samson Agonistes* constitutes something of a digression in a book about Milton's treatment of ineffable mystery and apophasis. The dark ambiguities of *Samson Agonistes* especially seem to have little in common with the sort of darkness and ineffable divine presence we encounter in some of Milton's early poems and *Paradise Lost*. However, I believe that far from being a digression, the analysis of silence and interiority in both poems serves as a fitting conclusion to the book as a whole. The principles of negative theology are central to both *Paradise Regained* and *Samson Agonistes*. In both poems gradual apophasis—or the moving away from speech—points to the numinous interior of the texts. Whether we are confronted in the end with the inviolable spiritual sanctity of Jesus' sinless interiority in *Paradise Regained*, or with the impenetrable subjectivity and potentially sinful antinomianism of Samson, the same didactic message emerges: the regaining of Paradise amid the ruins of the fallen world is a fragile affair—it requires complete, self-effacing submission to the Will of God, the strength of spirit to resist temptation, and the certainty—so elusive in *Samson*—that it is God's Spirit, not the fallen will, which works on us inwardly and moves us to action. Such a stark vision is the logical terminus of Milton's

---

[68] See Wilson's thought-provoking analysis of *Samson Agonistes* as a Greek tragedy of 'overliving'. Wilson's analysis also contains one of the more convincing reflections on the role of catharsis in the poem: the Chorus's 'we oft doubt | What the unsearchable dispose | Of highest wisdom brings about' (1745–7) 'is not', argues Wilson, 'an adequate summary of Samson's earlier suffering. The Chorus cannot reduce to just or strict measure the ambiguities of Samson's end and his doubts about God's timing. The end of *Samson Agonistes* achieves a kind of catharsis only at the cost of changing the subject' (*Mocked with Death*, 163).

lifelong poetic struggle with ineffability, and indeed of the Protestant solution to the problem in general: the condition of *aphaeresis* is dislocated from its place in metaphysical speculation, and placed instead at the heart of the Reformed Christian's religious experience, so that life itself and man's ability to make sense of it all by clinging to the Word of God become inscrutable, mysterious, and finally ineffable.

In his early poems the tension between Milton's rational fear of ineffable mystery and his driving ambition to perform as a uniquely elected prophetic poet results in complicated, at times contradictory, poetic expressions, where the young poet both asserts and questions his ability to soar in imaginary, ineffable realms high above the accommodated Word of God. The early poetry allowed Milton to experiment with a poetic strategy that soon became the main driving force behind the imagery and tone of *Paradise Lost*, where he simultaneously pretends to say the unsayable, or asserts his putative ability to do so, but then allows the poetry itself to belie such claims and to suggest that the pretence itself is what counts artistically, not the claims it pretends to. This was viable, however, only so long as the subject of the poetry was God's providence and its action through history, not the poet himself, nor indeed his mysterious powers of ineffable 'inspiration'. When the time came, though, to address deeply personal questions about salvation and redemption and to reflect on the individual burdens of political but finally spiritual liberty, the previous strategy had to be abandoned. The pretence of poetic flight gives way in the 1671 volume to the poetry of introspection, as Milton is finally forced to confront that which is truly ineffable in himself and surrenders to the silence of God working *in* him.

Samson Agonistes, however, and not *Paradise Regained*, is allowed to have the last word in the volume. Here too, as with *Paradise Regained*, the assertive poet who so often intrudes into his poetry to tell us how to read it finally withdraws into the private, ultimately ineffable recesses of personal faith, but in *Samson Agonistes* he also concludes by warning us that we can never presume to know what any human agonist, far removed from the antitype of Christ, actually suffers in the process. At the precise moment, itself unseen, when the Philistine theatre tumbles down, burying its heathen spectators under a pile of rubble, the poet shuts us out as readers from what will be from now on a private *agon* between himself and God. In pretending to speak the unspeakable and allowing that which is ineffable to speak and finally fall silent, the inspired bard also falls silent. His compelling words, however, so often spoken in urgency and always from the deepest conviction, like Raphael's otherworldly voice, linger on after the silence for us to enjoy, puzzle over, and applaud as we sift through the rubble.

Epilogue: Wittgenstein's verdict

I have quoted Wittgenstein twice in this study, in the course of Chapter 2. In the first instance I quoted Wittgenstein's *Tractatus* to illustrate a point about Nicholas Cusanus' mystical theology. The aim there was to make a more general point about negative theology and mysticism, where a deliberate misapplication of Wittgenstein's say–show distinction highlights what is logically unique about mystical rhetorical structures which claim to show the unsayable by failing to say it. In the second instance I quoted a more mysterious aphorism from Wittgenstein's notes (*Culture and Value*), where I felt that what I understood to be the 'inexpressible background against which whatever I say derives its meaning' could illustrate in a profound sense the predicament which Luther and subsequent Reformers found themselves in when they attempted to suppress the inexpressible background of language in the performance of a divinely inspired speech-act. One should always be wary of citing philosophers to make a literary point, and so far I have avoided quoting Wittgenstein a third time in direct relation to Milton. But there is one Wittgenstein quotation which seems to me so apt in terms of the literary questions explored in this study, and which sums up so completely the thrust of my argument about Milton, that quoting it by way of an epilogue now seems to me irresistible, especially given that the context for this quotation is a discussion about poetry. When Wittgenstein's friend Paul Englemann sent him a poem by Uhland, 'Graf Eberhards Weissdorn', Wittgenstein replied in a letter dated 9 April 1917: 'The poem by Uhland is really magnificent. And this is how it is: if only you do not try to utter what is unutterable then *nothing* gets lost. But the unutterable will be—unutterably—*contained* in what has been uttered!'[1] Wittgenstein wrote

---

[1] Engelmann, *Letters from Ludwig Wittgenstein with a Memoir*, trans. L. Furtmüller, 7.

this letter during the last stages of his work on the *Tractatus Logico-Philosophicus*. As explained in his commentary on the letter, Englemann sees in this statement the essence of what we now know to be the early stages of Wittgenstein's philosophical thought, namely, that a proposition cannot state explicitly what is manifest in it. Englemann then applies this idea to Uhland's poem just as Wittgenstein had done, and explains: 'The poet's sentences... achieve their effect not through what they say but through what is manifest in them, and the same holds for music, which also says nothing.'[2]

Uhland's poem tells in twenty-eight lines (seven quatrains) the story of Count Eberhard, who went to fight in the crusades and, while on his journey to the Holy Land, decorated his helmet with a sprig from a hawthorn bush which he cut along the way. When he got back home from the crusades he planted the sprig in the earth of his home, out of which grew a hawthorn tree. As the tree grew taller and the count grew older, the wind blowing through its leaves reminded him of the past and of his part in the crusades. Here is the last quatrain of Uhland's poem:

> Die wolbung, hoch und breit,
> Mit sanftem Rauschen mahnt
> Ihn an die alte Zeit
> Und an das ferne Land.

> The branching arch so high,
> Whose whisper is so bland,
> Reminds him of the past
> And Palestina's strand.[3]

Englemann, who is the closest authority we have on what this poem possibly meant to Wittgenstein, affirms that both he and Wittgenstein were moved by the poem's ineffable power to give a 'picture of a life' in only twenty-eight lines. The poem communicates much more than the total sum of its words, and this, according Engelmann's criterion (and allegedly Wittgenstein's as well), amounts to 'a higher level of poetry'.[4] If the recondite Wittgensteinian philosophy implicit in such an assessment is difficult to comprehend, then the literary sentiment is pleasingly

---

[2] Ibid. 85.
[3] Trans. Alexander Platt. Translation and original quoted in Engelmann, *Letters*, 83–4.
[4] Ibid. 85.

obvious: Wittgenstein admired art that said less and expressed more, and given what we know about Milton's fear of musical harmony without words, and his baroque impulse to leave nothing unsaid, we can speculate that on these terms at least Wittgenstein might not have approved of Milton.

We know, however, that Wittgenstein eventually did read Milton (or was at least casually familiar with him), from a telling comment in his notes made much later in 1946:

It is remarkable how hard we find it to believe something the truth of which we do not see for ourselves. If e.g. I hear expressions of admiration for Shakespeare made by the distinguished men of several centuries, I can never rid myself of a suspicion that praising him has been a matter of convention, even though I have to tell myself that this is not the case. I need the authority of a *Milton* to be really convinced. In his case I take it for granted that he was incorruptible.—But of course I don't mean to deny by this that an enormous amount of praise has been & still is lavished on Shakespeare without understanding & for specious reasons by a thousand professors of literature.[5]

Wittgenstein is commenting here on the mysterious and indeed ineffable quality of Shakespeare's genius—a theme he returns to a number of times in his notes—and Milton (who also admired Shakespeare) is used here not so much for his own sake but as a metaphor for incorruptible conviction. In other words, only a man with a conviction like Milton's could easily believe something, the ineffable truth of which he does not see for himself—in this case, the greatness of Shakespeare which most men appreciate but few really understand (according to Wittgenstein). Wittgenstein rightly saw in Milton a man who was so utterly convinced of the immutable qualities of his personal and transcendental truths that the boundary between what is expressible and inexpressible was nonexistent for him, and this also accords with what I have analysed as the ineffable impasse of Reformation thought more generally. But if we apply Wittgenstein's assessment of Uhland's poem to Milton's poetry in

---

[5] Italics original to the text; Wright, *Culture and Value*, 55e. That Wittgenstein should express this view at a time in his life when he had rejected most of his philosophical insights from the *Tractatus* is irrelevant in the present context simply because the 'say–show' distinction implicit in his earlier admiration for Uhland remains a powerful idea in its own right, and because its place in the later *Philosophical Investigations* is yet to be properly determined.

general, and *Paradise Lost* in particular, where does this leave Milton's poetry? Milton is not a poet who says nothing; he is a poet who is often accused of saying too much about everything. Many readers have felt ill at ease with the violent dislocation of ineffable mystery in Milton's poetry, and especially in *Paradise Lost*, since the unutterable is either not present at all, or is so objectified as to lose its numinous quality. This might be seen as the consequence of Milton's attempts to tyrannize the metaphysical with poetic mimesis, where by attempting to utter the unutterable something indeed gets *lost*. And surely this might be seen as deliberate in a poem which is all about *loss* of one kind or another. With loss of Paradise comes a loss of total meaning, and it would follow that such loss is then manifested in the attempt to say the unsayable without actually saying it.

However, as I have intimated in the Introduction and strived to show throughout, such an assessment of Milton's poetics of ineffability is quite wrong, since Milton only ever *pretends* to say the unsayable, when in fact he does nothing of the kind. He is a poet committed to saying everything that *can* be said, but never what *cannot* be said. When Milton pretends to say the unsayable he does so in an effort to lend what he does say supernatural creditability—and we can either play along with this game of make-believe and accept it for what it is, or denounce Milton as a hypocrite. Either way, the meta-poetic dissonance which allows Milton, for example, to suggest in *Paradise Lost* that what is expressed literally is in fact ineffable never once actually intrudes into the realms of Wittgensteinian nonsense and is dutifully confined to the logic of poetic 'propositions' that make 'sense' (whether we call it mimetic, poetic, or logical sense is beside the point in this case). It is easy to mistake the totality of Milton's vision for a hubristic impulse which seeks to do extreme violence to the truly hidden mysteries of God and his creation, but this violence is merely potential violence which drives much of the poetry's mimetic energy. Milton's poetry always carries with it the potential for such metaphysical violence, and referentially points to it as if to warn against it, even as it draws on this potentiality to assert its artistic singularity. When, in the later poems, Milton finally turned to assess the implications of such potential violence for his 'incorruptible' conviction in his personal authority as an inspired, elect poet, the result was a poetic gesture of self-retraction and even annihilation, as he withdrew inwards away from speech and mimetic intelligibility, finally resting in the transcendental silence which authorizes and sacralizes the Word. Seen in this way, Milton's poetry not only survives Wittgenstein's verdict, but can be seen to triumph precisely on its terms, for here, much more than in any passage of Shakespeare, is a poetic utterance which ineffably *contains* in the sum total of what it utters that which is metaphysically unutterable. In the final analysis it suddenly seems that a book about Milton and the ineffable can only offer an examination of something that only ever takes place ineffably. And at the risk of suggesting this, I may at last hope that what I have nevertheless expressed about Milton's poetry has shown what neither he nor I can actually say about it.

Appendix: Burning Coals

The *Midrash Rabba* on the Book of Exodus (*Midrash Shmot*) narrates the following fable or 'haggada' as a gloss on the words of Moses in Exodus 4: 10: 'I am heavy of mouth and heavy of tongue', translated both in the Geneva and the Authorised Versions of the English Bible as 'slow of speech and slow of tongue'. I have attempted as literal a translation as possible of the Midrashic Hebrew, except where the Hebrew is particularly elliptic and cannot be translated literally:

It was the habit of Pharaoh's daughter to kiss and cuddle the baby Moses as if he was one of her own children, and she would not suffer him to be removed from the king's palace. And since he was a handsome baby, all in the court vied to lay eyes on him, never wishing to part from his presence once they did. And Pharaoh would kiss the baby and cuddle him, and allow him to wear the Pharaoh's crown on his head playfully... The magicians of Egypt who were present then said: we are fearful of him that takes your crown and places it on his head, lest he it is of whom we foretell shall take your kingdom from you. Some of the magicians demanded to have Moses killed, others to have him burned alive. And Jethro, who was among them, then said to the magicians: this baby has no sense, test him and see for yourselves—place before him in a bowl some gold and a burning coal; if he reaches with his hand to the gold then plainly he has sense and you may kill him, but if he reaches for the burning coal then he has none and therefore not to be condemned. Straight away they did as Jethro suggested and Moses reached to take the gold, but the angel Gabriel descended and pushed his hand towards the burning coal instead, and Moses placed the coal in his mouth and burned his tongue—and this is how Moses became heavy of mouth and heavy of tongue.

The *Midrash Rabba* is the largest collection of Midrashim, or rabbinical 'investigations'/'queries' into the biblical text, first published in Constantinople in 1512. It contains exegetical texts from as early as the fifth century AD and as late as the thirteenth century, but much of the exegetical material contained in it, especially the haggadic narratives (that is, exegetical narratives not pertaining to the legal aspects of the Torah), originate from earlier oral traditions, most probably dating from the early Tanaitic and Amoraic periods in Palestine, *c.* second–third centuries AD.[1]

---

[1] See G. Vermes, 'Bible and Midrash: Early Old Testament Exegesis', *CHB* i. 199–231.

Bibliography

PRIMARY SOURCES

Ames, William, *Medulla S.S. theologiae ex sacris literis, earmque interpretibus, extracta, & methodicè disposita per Guilielmum Amesium... In fine adjuncta est disputatio de fidei divinae veritate* (London, 1630).

—— *The marrow of sacred divinity drawne out of the Holy Scriptures, and the interpreters thereof, and brought into method by William Ames... translated out of the Latine...* (London, 1642).

Andrewes, Lancelot, *XCVI Sermons*, ed. William Laud and John Buckeridge (London, 1629).

—— *Lancelot Andrewes: Selected Sermons and Lectures*, ed. Peter McCullough (Oxford: Oxford UP, 2005).

Affinati, Giacomo, *The dumbe divine speaker, or: Dumbe speaker of Divinity. A learned and excellent treatise, in praise of silence: shewing both the dignitie, and defectes of the tongue. Written in Italian, by Fra. Giacomo Affinati d'Acuto Romano. And truelie translated by A. M.* (London, 1605).

Aquinas, Thomas, *Summa Theologiae*, 60 vols., general editor Thomas Gilby (various translators) (London: Blackfriars, 1964–73).

Aristotle, *Metaphysics*, ed. and trans. Hugh Tredennick and G. Cyril Armstrong, 2 vols., Loeb Classical Library (Cambridge, Mass.: Harvard UP, 1935).

—— 'On Interpretation', in *Categories, On Interpretation, Prior Analytics*, ed. and trans. Harold P. Cooke and Hugh Tredennick, Loeb Classical Library (Cambridge, Mass.: Harvard UP, 1938).

Augustine, *Confessions*, trans. William Watts, 2 vols., Loeb Classical Library (Cambridge, Mass.: Harvard UP, 1912).

—— *De Civitate Dei*, trans. David S. Weisen, 8 vols., Loeb Classical Library (Cambridge, Mass.: Harvard UP, 1912).

—— *De Doctrina Christiana*, ed. and trans. R. P. H. Green (Oxford: Clarendon Press, 1995).

—— *The Literal Meaning of Genesis*, trans. John Hammond Taylor, 2 vols., Ancient Christian Writers, 41 (New York: Newman Press, 1982).

—— *The Trinity*, trans. Edmund Hill (New York: New City Press, 1991).

Baxter, Richard, *The saints everlasting rest, or, A treatise of the blessed state of the saints in their enjoyment of God in glory wherein is shewed its excellency and certainty, the misery of those that lose it, the way to attain it, and assurance of it, and how to live in the continual delightful forecasts of it and now published by Richard Baxter*...(London, 1650).

Bunyan, John, *Grace Abounding, with Other Spiritual Autobiographies*, ed. John Stachniewski with Anita Pacheco (Oxford: Oxford UP, 1998).

Burgess, Anthony, *Spiritual refining: or A treatise of grace and assurance Wherein are handled, the doctrine of assurance. The use of signs in self-examination. How true graces may be distinguished from counterfeit. Several true signs of grace, and many false ones* (London, 1652).

Calvin, John, *Commentary on the Epistle to the Hebrews*, trans. William B. Johnston, Calvin's Commentaries, ed. David W. Torrance and Thomas F. Torrance, vol. 5 (Edinburgh: Oliver & Boyd, 1963).

—— *Institutes of the Christian Religion*, ed. T. McNeill, trans. Ford Lewis Battles, 2 vols., Library of Christian Classics, 20–1 (London: SCM Press, 1960).

—— *Ionnis Calvini opera quae supersunt omnia*, ed. G. Baum, E. Cunitz, E. Reuss, and A. Erichson, Corpus Reformatorum, 29–87 (Braunschweig, 1863–1900).

Clement of Alexandria. *Les Stromates*, ed. and trans. Alain Le Boulluec, 7 vols. (Paris: Les Editions du Cerf, 1981).

—— *Stromateis 1–3*, trans. John Ferguson, Fathers of the Church, 85 (Washington, DC: Catholic University of America Press, 1991).

—— *The Writings of Clement of Alexandria*, trans. Revd William Wilson, Ante-Nicene Christian Library: Translations of the Writings of the Fathers, 11–12 (Edinburgh, 1869).

Crashaw, Richard, 'A Hymn of the Nativity, Sung as by the Shepherds', in Colin Burrow (ed.), *Metaphysical Poetry* (London: Penguin, 2006).

Cusanus, Nicholas, *Nicolai De Cusa Opera Omnia: iussu et auctoritate academiae litterarum Heidelbergensis ad codicum fidem edita*, ed. Ernst Hoffman and Raymond Klibansky, 22 vols. (Leipzig: Meiner, 1932–).

—— *Of Learned Ignorance*, trans. Germain Heron (London: Routledge & Kegan Paul, 1954).

Derrida, Jacques, 'How To Avoid Speaking: Denials', trans. Ken Frieden, in Sanford Budick and Wolfgang Iser (eds.), *Languages of the Unsayable: The Play of Negativity in Literature and Literary Theory* (New York: Columbia UP, 1987).

—— *Of Grammatology* (1974), trans. Gayatri Chakravorty Spivak (1976; corrected edn. Baltimore: Johns Hopkins UP, 1997).

—— *Writing and Difference* (1967), trans. Alan Bass (London: Routledge & Kegan Paul, 1978).

Dionysius the pseudo-Areopagite, *The 'Divine Names' and 'Mystical Theology'*, trans. John D. Jones (Milwaukee: Marquette UP, 1980).

Dryden, John, *The Major Works*. ed. Keith Walker (Oxford: Oxford UP, 1987).

Erasmus, Desiderius, *Collected Works*, various editors/translators, 86 vols. (Toronto: Toronto UP, 1974–).

—— *Desiderii Erasmi Roterodami operum omnium*, ed. J. Leclerc, 11 vols. (1703–6; repr. Hildesheim: Olms, 1962).

—— *Opera omnia Desiderii Erasmi Roterodami*, various editors, 12 vols. (Amsterdam: North Holland Publishing, 1969–89).

Ficino, Marsilio, *Platonic Theology*, ed. James Hankins, trans. Michael J. B. Allen, I Tatti Renaissance Library (Cambridge, Mass.: Harvard UP, 2001).

Field, Richard, *Of the Church fiue bookes. By Richard Field Doctor of Diuinity and sometimes Deane of Glocester. Apologie of the Romane Church* (1606, 1610; Oxford, 1628).

Gil, Alexander, *The Sacred Philosophie of the Holy Scripture* (London, 1635).

Gregory of Nyssa, *The Life of Moses*, trans. Abraham J. Malherbe and Everett Ferguson (New York: Paulist Press, 1978).

Herbert, George, *George Herbert and Henry Vaughan: A Critical Edition of the Major Works*, ed. Louis L. Martz, Oxford Authors (Oxford and New York: Oxford UP, 1986).

Hermetica: The Ancient Greek and Latin Writings which Contain Religious or Philosophic Teachings Ascribed to Hermes Trismegistus, ed. Walter Scott, 4 vols. (Oxford: Clarendon Press, 1924).

Hooker, Richard, *The Works of that Learned and Judicious Divine, Mr. Richard Hooker*, ed. John Keble, 3 vols., 7th edn. (Oxford, 1888).

Horace, *Odes and Epodes*, trans. C. E. Bennett, Loeb Classical Library (Cambridge, Mass.: Harvard UP, 1914).

Johnson, Samuel, 'Milton' (1779) in *Samuel Johnson: The Major Works*, ed. Donald Greene (Oxford: Oxford UP, 1984), 698–716.

Lacan, Jacques, *Écrits: A Selection*, trans. Alan Sheridan (New York: Norton, 1977).

Leigh, Edward, *Annotations upon all the New Testament philologicall and theologicall wherein the emphasis and elegancie of the Greeke is observed... sundry passages vindicated from the false glosses of papists and hereticks* (London, 1650).

Luther, Martin, *Collected Works*, 55 vols., general eds. Jaroslav Pelikan and Helmut T. Lehmann, various translators (Saint Louis and Philadelphia: Concordia Publishing House and Fortress Press, 1958–67).

Maimonides, Moses, *The Guide for the Perplexed*, trans. M. Friedlander (1904), 2nd edn. (New York: Dover Publications, 1956).

Marvell, Andrew, *The Poems of Andrew Marvell*, ed. Nigel Smith, rev. edn. (Harlow: Pearson Education Ltd. /Longman, 2007).

Melanchthon, Philipp, *Loci Communes*, ed. and trans. Wilhelm Pauck, Library of Christian Classics, 19 (London: SCM Press, 1969).

Milton, John, *Complete Prose Works of John Milton*, 8 vols., general ed. Don M. Wolfe (New Haven and London: Yale UP, 1953–80).

—— *John Milton Poems: Reproduced in Facsimile from the Manuscript in Trinity College, Cambridge*, ed. W. A. Wright (1899; Menston Ilkley: Scholar Press, 1970).

—— *Milton: Complete Shorter Poems*, 2nd edn., ed. John Carey (London and New York: Longman, 1997).

—— *Milton: Paradise Lost*, 2nd edn., ed. Alastair Fowler (London and New York: Longman, 1998).

—— *Poems of Mr. John Milton Both English and Latin Compos'd at several times* (London, 1645).

—— *Poems, &c. upon Several Occasions by Mr. John Milton: Both English and Latin, &c. Composed at several times* (London, 1673).

—— *The Complete Works of John Milton*, 18 vols., gen. ed. Frank Allen Patterson (New York: Columbia UP, 1931–40).

Nietzsche, Friedrich, *Twilight of the Idols and The Anti-Christ* (1889; 1895), trans. R. J. Hollingdale (London: Penguin, 1968; repr. 1990, 2003).

Perkins, William, *The Works of that Famous and Worthy Minister of Christ...William Perkins*, 3 vols. (London, 1626–35).

Philo, *Philo*, ed. and trans. F. H. Colson and G. H. Whitaker, 13 vols., Loeb Classical Library (London: Heinemann, 1929).

Pico della Mirandola, Giovanni, *De Hominis Dignitate; Heptaplus; De Ente et Uno*, ed. and trans. (Italian) Eugenio Garin (Florence: Vallecchi, 1942).

—— *Pico della Mirandola: On the Dignity of Man*, trans. Charles Glenn Wallis, Paul J. Miller, and Douglas Carmichael (1965; repr. Indianapolis and Cambridge: Hackett, 1998).

Plato, *Cratylus, Parmenides, Greater Hippias, Lesser Hippias*, trans. H. N. Fowler, Loeb Classical Library (Cambridge, Mass.: Harvard UP, 1926).

—— *Euthyphro, Apology, Crito, Phaedo, Phaedrus*, trans. H. N. Fowler, Loeb Classical Library (Cambridge, Mass.: Harvard UP, 1914).

—— *Timaeus, Critias, Cleitophon, Menexenus, Epistles*, trans. R. G. Bury, Loeb Classical Library (Cambridge, Mass.: Harvard UP, 1929).

Plotinus, *The Enneads*, trans. Stephen MacKenna, 4th edn. (London: Faber & Faber, 1969).

—— *The Enneads*, ed. and trans. A. H. Armstrong, 7 vols., Loeb Classical Library (Cambridge, Mass.: Harvard UP, 1984).

Sidney, Philip, *Sir Philip Sidney: A Critical Edition of the Major Works*, ed. Katherine Duncan-Jones (Oxford: Oxford UP, 1989).

Sophocles, *Ajax, Electra, Oedipus Tyrannus*, ed. and trans. Hugh Lloyd-Jones, Loeb Classical Library (Cambridge, Mass.: Harvard UP, 1994).

—— *Ajax, The Women of Trachis, Electra and Philoctetes*, trans. John Moore, Michael Jameson, and David Grene, *The Complete Greek Tragedies*, eds. David Grene and Richmond Lattimore (Chicago and London: Chicago UP, 1957).

Spenser, Edmund, *Edmund Spenser: The Shorter Poems*, ed. Richard A. McCabe (London: Penguin, 1999).

—— *The Faerie Queene*, ed. A. C. Hamilton, Hiroshi Yamashita, and Toshiyuki Suzuki (Harlow: Pearson Education Ltd. /Longman, 2001).

Tertullian, *De Carne Christi: Tertullian's Treatise on the Incarnation*, ed. and trans. Ernest Evans (London: SPCK, 1956).

Virgil, *Works*, trans. H. R. Fairclough, Loeb Classical Library (1916; Cambridge, Mass.: Harvard UP, 1935).

Wittgenstein, Ludwig, *Culture and Value*, trans. Peter Winch, ed. G. H. von Wright (1977; rev. edn., Oxford: Blackwell, 1998).

—— *Paul Engelmann: Letters from Ludwig Wittgenstein with a Memoir*, trans. L. Furtmüller, ed. B. F. McGuinness (Oxford: Blackwell, 1967).

—— *Tractatus Logico-Philosophicus* (1921), trans. D. F. Pears and B. F. McGuinness (rev. edn. 1974; London and New York: Routledge, 2001).

Zwingli, Ulrich, 'On the Lord's Supper', in G. W. Bromiley (ed. and trans.), *Zwingli and Bullinger: Selected Translations with Introductions and Notes*, Library of Christian Classics, 24 (London: SCM Press, 1953).

SECONDARY SOURCES

Achinstein, Sharon, *Milton and the Revolutionary Reader* (Princeton: Princeton UP, 1994).

—— '*Samson Agonistes* and the Drama of Dissent', *MS* 33 (1997), 133–58.

—— and Elizabeth Sauer (eds.), *Milton and Toleration* (Oxford: Oxford UP, 2007).

Ackroyd, P. R., C. F. Evans, G. W. H. Lampe, and S. L. Greenslade (eds.), The *Cambridge History of the Bible*, 3 vols. (Cambridge: Cambridge UP, 1963–70).

Alpers, Paul, *What is Pastoral?* (Chicago and London: Chicago UP, 1996).

Ashworth, E. J., *Language and Logic in the Post-Medieval Period* (Boston and Dordrecht: Springer, 1974).

Bagchi, David and David C. Steinmetz (eds.), *The Cambridge Companion to Reformation Theology* (Cambridge: Cambridge UP, 2004).

Bainton, Ronald H., *Erasmus of Christendom* (London: Collins, 1970).

Barker, Arthur E., *Milton and the Puritan Dilemma 1641–1660* (Toronto: Toronto UP, 1942).

—— (ed.), *Milton: Modern Essays in Criticism* (New York: Oxford UP, 1965).

Bauman, Michael, *Milton's Arianism* (Frankfurt: Peter Lang, 1986).

Belsey, Catherine, *John Milton: Language, Gender, Power* (Oxford: Blackwell, 1988).

Bennet, Joan S., *Reviving Liberty: Radical Christian Humanism in Milton's Great Poems* (Cambridge, Mass., and London: Harvard UP, 1989).

Bentley, Jerry H., *Humanists and Holy Writ: New Testament Scholarship in the Renaissance* (Princeton: Princeton UP, 1983).

Berchman, Robert M., *From Philo to Origen: Middle Platonism in Transition*, Brown Judaic Studies, 69 (Chico, Calif.: Scholars Press, 1984).

Blenkinsopp, Joseph, 'Structure and Style in Judges 13–16', *Journal of Biblical Literature*, 82 (1963), 65–76.

Blodgett, E. D. and H. G. Coward (eds.), *Silence, the Word and the Sacred* (Waterloo, Ontario: Wilfrid Laurier UP, 1989).

Blumenthal, H. J., *Soul and Intellect: Studies in Plotinus and Later Neoplatonism* (Aldershot: Variorum, 1993).

—— and R. A. Markus (eds.), *Neoplatonism and Early Christian Thought: Essays in Honour of A. H. Armstrong* (London: Variorum, 1981).

Blythe, John Heiges, 'The Cloistered Virtue: Rhetorical Posture in *Paradise Regained*', *NM* 89 (1988), 324–32.

Boesky, Amy and Mary Thomas Crane (eds.), *Form and Reform in Renaissance England: Essays in Honor of Barbara Kiefer Lewalski* (Newark: Delaware UP, 2000).

Brewer, Wilmon, 'Two Athenian Models for *Samson Agonistes*', *PMLA* 42: 4 (1927), 910–20.

Broadbent, J. B., *Some Graver Subject: An Essay on Paradise Lost* (London: Chatto & Windus, 1960).

Broek, Roelof Van Den, *Studies in Gnosticism and Alexandrian Christianity* (Leiden: Brill, 1996).

—— and Wouter J. Hanegraaff (eds.), *Gnosis and Hermeticism: From Antiquity to Modern Times* (Albany, NY: New York State UP, 1998).

Budick, Sanfrod, *The Dividing Muse: Images of Sacred Disjunction in Milton's Poetry* (New Haven and London: Yale UP, 1985).

Burbery, Timothy J., *Milton the Dramatist* (Pittsburgh: Duquesne UP, 2007).

Burden, Dennis H., *The Logical Epic: A Study of the Argument of Paradise Lost* (London: Routledge & Kegan Paul, 1967).

Burrell, B. David. *Aquinas: God and Action* (London: Routledge & Kegan Paul, 1979).

Burrell, B. David. *Knowing the Unknowable God: Ibn-Sina, Maimonides, Aquinas* (Notre Dame, Ind.: Notre Dame UP, 1986).

Burrow, Colin, *Epic Romance: Homer to Milton* (Oxford: Clarendon, 1993).

Cable, Lana, *Carnal Rhetoric: Milton's Iconoclasm and the Poetics of Desire* (Durham, NC and London: Duke UP, 1995).

Campbell, Gordon, Thomas N. Corns, John K. Hale, and Fiona J. Tweedie, *Milton and the Manuscript of* De Doctrina Christiana (Oxford: Oxford UP, 2007).

Caputo, John D., *The Prayers and Tears of Jacques Derrida: Religion Without Religion* (Bloomington, Ind.: Indiana UP, 1997).

Carabine, Deirdre, *The Unknown God: Negative Theology in the Platonic Tradition: Plato to Eriugena* (Louvain: Peeters Press, 1995).

Carey, John, *Milton* (London: Evans Bros., 1969).

—— 'A Work in Praise of Terrorism? September 11 and *Samson Agonistes*', *TLS* 6 Sept. 2002, pp. 15–16.

—— 'Milton's Harmonious Sisters', in John Caldwell, Edward Olleson, and Susan Wollenberg (eds.), *The Well Enchanting Skill: Music, Poetry, and Drama in the Culture of the Renaissance* (Oxford: Clarendon Press, 1990), 245–58.

Cassirer, Ernst, *The Platonic Renaissance in England* (1953), trans. James P. Pettegrove (New York: Gordian Press, 1970).

Chadwick, Henry, *Early Christian Thought and the Classical Tradition: Studies in Justin, Clement and Origen* (1966; Oxford: Clarendon Press, 1984).

Christopher, Georgia B., *Milton and the Science of the Saints* (Princeton: Princeton UP, 1982).

Clark, Mary T., *Augustine* (London: Geoffrey Chapman, 1994).

Coffey, John, 'Pacifist, Quietist, or Patient Militant? John Milton and the Restoration', *MS* 42 (2002), 149–74.

Colie, Rosalie Littell, *Paradoxia Epidemica: The Renaissance Tradition of Paradox* (Princeton: Princeton UP, 1966).

Colish, Marcia L., *A Study in Medieval Theory of Knowledge*, 2nd edn. (Lincoln, Nebr.: Nebraska UP, 1983).

Collinson, Patrick, *The Elizabethan Puritan Movement* (1967; Oxford: Clarendon Press, 1990).

Cooper, David. E., *The Measure of Things: Humanism, Humility, and Mystery* (Oxford: Clarendon Press, 2002).

Corns, Thomas N. (ed.), *A Companion to Milton* (Oxford: Blackwell, 2001).

—— *Milton's Language* (Oxford: Blackwell, 1990).

—— 'Milton's Quest for Respectability', *MLR* 77: 4 (1982), 769–79.

—— *Regaining* Paradise Lost (London and New York: Longman, 1994).

Creaser, John, ' "Lycidas": The Power of Art', *E&S* (1981), 123–47.

Crump, Galbraith Miller, *The Mystical Design of* Paradise Lost (Cranbury, NJ: Associated University Presses, 1975).

Culler, Jonathan, *The Pursuit of Signs: Semiotics, Literature, Deconstruction* (London and Henley: Routledge & Kegan Paul, 1981).

Cummings, Brian, *The Literary Culture of the Reformation: Grammar and Grace* (Oxford: Oxford UP, 2002).

Danielson, Dennis R., *Milton's Good God: A Study in Literary Theodicy* (Cambridge and New York: Cambridge UP, 1982).

—— (ed.), *The Cambridge Companion to Milton,* 2nd edn. (Cambridge: Cambridge UP, 1999).

Darbishire, Helen (ed.), *The Early Lives of Milton* (London: Constable, 1932).

Davies, Julian, *The Caroline Captivity of the Church: Charles I and the Remoulding of Anglicanism 1625–1641* (Oxford: Oxford UP, 1992).

Davies, Stevie, *Milton* (Hemel Hampstead: Harvester Wheatsheaf, 1991).

Dickens, A. G. and Whitney R. D. Jones, *Erasmus the Reformer* (London: Methuen, 1994).

Diekhoff, John S., *Milton's* Paradise Lost: *A Commentary on the Argument* (New York: Humanities Press, 1963).

Dietz, Michael, ' "Thus sung the Uncouth Swain": Pastoral, Prophecy, and Historicism in "Lycidas" ', *MS* 35 (1997), 42–72.

Dillon, John, *The Middle Platonists: A Study of Platonism 80 B.C. to A.D. 220* (London: Duckworth, 1977).

Dobranski, Stephen B. and John P. Rumrich (eds.), *Milton and Heresy* (Cambridge: Cambridge UP, 1998).

Durham, Charles W. and Kristin A. Pruitt (eds.), *All in All: Unity, Diversity and the Miltonic Perspective* (Selinsgrove, Pa.: Susquehanna UP, 1999).

DuRocher, Richard J., *Milton and Ovid* (Ithaca and London: Cornell UP, 1985).

Einboden, Jeffrey, 'The Homeric Psalm: Milton's Translation of Psalm 114 and the Problems of "Hellenic Scripture" ', *LT* 17: 3 (2003), 314–23.

Empson, William, *Milton's God* (1961; rev. edn., London: Chatto & Windus, 1965).

Entzminger, Robert L., *Divine Word: Milton and the Redemption of Language* (Pittsburgh: Duquesne UP, 1985).

Evans, G. R., *Problems of Authority in the Reformation Debates* (Cambridge: Cambridge UP, 1992).

Evans, J. Martin, 'The Birth of the Author: Milton's Poetic Self-Construction', *MS* 38 (2000), 47–65.

—— Paradise Lost *and the Genesis Tradition* (Oxford: Clarendon Press, 1968).

—— *The Miltonic Moment* (Lexington, Ky.: Kentucky UP, 1998).

Everson, Stephen (ed.), *Companion to Ancient Thought*, Vol. 3: *Language* (Cambridge: Cambridge UP, 1994).

Fallon, Robert Thomas, *Captain or Colonel: The Soldier in Milton's Life and Art* (Columbia, Miss.: Missouri UP, 1984).

Fallon, Stephen M., *Milton Among the Philosophers: Poetry and Materialism in Seventeenth-Century England* (Ithaca and London: Cornell UP, 1991).

—— *Milton's Peculiar Grace: Self-Representation and Authority* (Ithaca and London: Cornell UP, 2007).

Feinstein, Blossom, 'On the Hymns of John Milton and Gian Francesco Pico', *CL* 20: 3 (1968), 245–53.

Ferry, Anne, *Milton's Epic Voice: The Narrator in* Paradise Lost (Cambridge, Mass.: Harvard UP, 1963).

Fineman, Joel, *The Subjectivity Effect in Western Literary Tradition: Essays Towards the Release of Shakespeare's Will* (Cambridge, Mass., and London: MIT Press, 1991).

Fish, Stanley E., *How Milton Works* (Cambridge, Mass. and London: Belknap Press, 2001).

—— *Surprised by Sin: The Reader in* Paradise Lost (1967; 2nd edn., London: Macmillan, 1997).

—— 'Things and Actions Indifferent: The Temptation of Plot in *Paradise Regained*', *MS* 17 (1983), 163–85.

Fishbane, Michael A., *Biblical Interpretation in Ancient Israel* (Oxford and New York: Clarendon Press, 1985).

Fisher, Alan, 'Why is *Paradise Regained* So Cold?', *MS* 14 (1980), 195–217.

Fixler, Michael, *Milton and the Kingdoms of God* (London: Faber & Faber, 1964).

Fletcher, Harris Francis, *The Intellectual Development of John Milton*, 2 vols. (Urbana, Ill.: Illinois UP, 1956).

Fowler, Alastair, *Time's Purpled Masquers: Stars and the Afterlife in Renaissance English Poetry* (Oxford: Clarendon, 1996).

—— (ed.), *Silent Poetry: Essays in Numerological Analysis* (London: Routledge & Kegan Paul, 1970).

Franke, William, 'Blind Prophecy: Milton's Figurative Mode in *Paradise Lost*', in John C. Hawley (ed.), *Through a Glass Darkly: Essays on the Religious Imagination* (New York: Fordham UP, 1996).

—— (ed.), *On What Cannot Be Said: Apophatic Discourses in Philosophy, Religion, Literature, and the Arts*, 2 vols. (Notre Dame, Ind.: Notre Dame UP, 2007).

Fraser, Russell, 'On Milton's Poetry', *YR* 56 (1967), 182–96.

Frye, Northrop, *Five Essays on Milton's Epics* (London: Routledge & Kegan Paul, 1966).

Frye, Roland M., *God, Man, and Satan: Patterns of Christian Thought and Life in Paradise Lost, Pilgrim's Progress, and the Great Theologians* (Port Washington, NY: Kennikat Press, 1960).

Gerrish, Brian A., *Grace and Gratitude: The Eucharistic Theology of John Calvin* (Edinburgh: T. & T. Clark, 1993).

—— *The Old Protestantism and the New: Essays on the Reformation Heritage* (Edinburgh: T. & T. Clark, 1982).

Gilson, Étienne, *The Christian Philosophy of Saint Augustine* (London: Victor Gollancz, 1961).

Goekjian Gregory F., 'Deference and Silence: Milton's "Nativity Ode"', *MS* 21 (1985), 119–35.

Goldsmith, Steven, 'The Muting of Satan: Language and Redemption in *Paradise Regained*', *SEL* 27 (1987), 125–40.

Goodenough, Erwin R., *An Introduction to Philo Judaeus* (1940; 2nd edn., Oxford: Blackwell, 1962).

—— *By Light, Light: The Mystic Gospel of Hellenistic Judaism* (New Haven and London: Yale UP, 1935).

Graham, Jean E., 'Virgin Ears: Silence, Deafness, and Chastity in Milton's Maske', *MS* 36 (1998), 59–85.

Graves, Neil D. 'Milton and the Theory of Accommodation', *SPH* 98: 2 (2001), 251–72.

Grossman, Marshall, 'Milton's Dialectical Visions', *MPH* 82 (1984), 23–39.

—— '*Authors to Themselves': Milton and the Revelation of History* (Cambridge: Cambridge UP, 1987).

Haan, Estelle, '"Heaven's purest light": Milton's *Paradise Lost 3* and Vida', *CLS* 30 (1993), 115–36.

Hale, John K., 'Milton as a Translator of Poetry', *RS* 1: 2 (1987), 238–56.

Hamilton, Gary D. 'Milton's Defensive God: A Reappraisal', *SPH* 69: 1 (1972), 87–100.

Hanford, James Holly, '"That Shepherd who First Taught the Chosen Seed"', *UTQ* (1939), 403–19.

Haskin, Dayton, *Milton's Burden of Interpretation* (Philadelphia: Pennsylvania UP, 1994).

Hawkins, Peter S. and Anne Howland Schotter (eds.), *Ineffability: Naming the Unnamable from Dante to Beckett* (New York: AMS Press, 1984).

Hill, Christopher, *Milton and the English Revolution* (London: Faber & Faber, 1977).

Hollander, John, *The Figure of Echo: A Mode of Allusion in Milton and After* (Berkeley and London: California UP, 1981).

—— *The Untuning of the Sky: Ideas of Music in English Poetry, 1500–1700* (Princeton: Princeton UP, 1961).

Hughes, Merritt Y., *Ten Perspectives on Milton* (New Haven and London: Yale UP, 1965).

Hyman, Lawrence W., 'The Reader's Attitude in *Paradise Regained*', *PMLA* 85: 3 (1970), 496–503.

Ingram, Randall, 'The Writing Poet: The Descent from Song in *The Poems of Mr. John Milton, Both English and Latin* (1645)', *MS* 34 (1997), 179–97.

Jose, Nicholas, *Ideas of the Restoration in English Literature, 1660–71* (London: Macmillan, 1984).

Kane, Leslie, *The Language of Silence: On the Unspoken and the Unspeakable in Modern Drama* (Cranbury, NJ: Associated University Presses, 1984).

Kelley, Mark R. and Joseph Wittreich (eds.), *Altering Eyes: New Perspectives on Samson Agonistes* (Newark, Del.: Delaware UP, 2002).

—— Michael Lieb and John T. Shawcross (eds.), *Milton and the Grounds of Contention* (Pittsburgh: Duquesne UP, 2003).

Kelley, Maurice, *This Great Argument: A Study of Milton's* De Doctrina Christiana *as a Gloss upon* Paradise Lost (Princeton and London: Princeton UP, 1941).

Kendall, R. T., *Calvin and English Calvinism to 1649* (1979; 2nd edn., Carlisle: Paternoster Press, 1997).

Kenny, Anthony, *Aquinas on Mind* (London: Routledge, 1993).

—— *The God of the Philosophers* (Oxford: Clarendon, 1979).

Kenny, John Peter, *Mystical Monotheism: A Study in Ancient Platonic Theology* (Hanover, NH: Brown UP, 1991).

Kermode, Frank (ed.), *The Living Milton: Essays by Various Hands* (London: Routledge & Kegan Paul, 1960).

Kerrigan, John, 'Milton and the Nightingale', *EC* 42: 2 (1992), 107–22.

Kerrigan, William, *The Prophetic Milton* (Charlottesville, Va.: Virginia UP, 1974).

—— *The Sacred Complex: On the Psychogenesis of* Paradise Lost (Cambridge, Mass. and London: Harvard UP, 1983).

Kessner, Carole S., 'Milton's Hebraic Herculean Hero', *MS* 6 (1974), 243–58.

Kirwan, Christopher, *Augustine* (London: Routledge, 1989).

Knoppers, Laura Lunger, *Historicizing Milton: Spectacle, Power, and Poetry in Restoration England* (Athens and London: Georgia UP, 1994).

Kraye, Jill (ed.), *The Cambridge Companion to Renaissance Humanism* (Cambridge: Cambridge UP, 1996).

Kretzmann, Norman, and Eleonore Stump (eds.), *The Cambridge Companion to Aquinas* (Cambridge: Cambridge UP, 1993).

Kristeller, Paul Oskar, *Renaissance Thought and its Sources*, ed. Michael Mooney (New York: Columbia UP, 1979).

Krouse, Michael F., *Milton's Samson and the Christian Tradition* (1949; New York: Archon Books, 1963).

Kugel, James L. and Rowan A. Greer, *Early Biblical Interpretation* (Philadelphia: Westminster Press, 1986).

Lake, Peter, *Anglicans and Puritans? Presbyterianism and English Conformist Thought from Whitgift to Hooker* (London: Unwin Hyman, 1988).

—— 'Lancelot Andrewes, John Buckeridge, and Avant-Garde Conformity at the Court of James I', in Linda Levy Peck (ed.), *The Mental World of the Jacobean Court* (Cambridge: Cambridge UP, 1991), 113–33.

Landy, Marcia, 'Language and the Seal of Silence in *Samson Agonistes*', *MS* 2 (1970), 175–94.

Lanham, Carol Dana (ed.), *Latin Grammar and Rhetoric: From Classical Theory to Medieval Practice* (London: Continuum, 2002).

Lares, Jameela, *Milton and the Preaching Arts* (Pittsburgh: Duquesne UP, 2001).

Laskowsky, Henry J., 'A Pinnacle of the Sublime: Christ's Victory of Style in *Paradise Regained*', *MQ* 15 (1981), 10–13.

Lawry, John S., *The Shadow of Heaven: Matter and Stance in Milton's Poetry* (Ithaca, NY: Cornell UP, 1968).

Leaman, Oliver, *Moses Maimonides* (1990; 2nd edn., Richmond: Curzon Press, 1997).

Leonard, John, *Naming in Paradise: Milton and the Language of Adam and Eve* (Oxford: Clarendon Press, 1990).

—— '"Trembling Ears": The Historical Moment of "Lycidas"', *JMRS* 21 (1991), 59–81.

Levi, Anthony, *Renaissance and Reformation: the Intellectual Genesis* (New Haven and London: Yale UP, 2002).

Lewalski, Barbara K., *Milton's Brief Epic: The Genre, Meaning, and Art of Paradise Regained* (London: Methuen, 1966).

—— Paradise Lost *and the Rhetoric of Literary Forms* (Princeton: Princeton UP, 1985).

—— *Protestant Poetics and the Seventeenth-Century Religious Lyric* (Princeton: Princeton UP, 1979).

—— '*Samson Agonistes* and the "Tragedy" of the Apocalypse', *PMLA* 85 (1970), 1050–62.

—— *The Life of John Milton: A Critical Biography* (Oxford: Blackwell, 2000).

Lewis, C. S., *A Preface to* Paradise Lost (London: Oxford UP, 1942).

Lieb, Michael, 'Encoding the Occult: Milton and the Traditions of Merkabah Speculation in the Renaissance', *MS* 37 (1999), 42–88.

—— *Milton and the Culture of Violence* (Ithaca and London: Cornell UP, 1994).

Lieb, Michael, 'Milton and the Kenotic Christology: Its Literary Bearing', *ELH* 37 (1970), 342–60.
—— *Poetics of the Holy: A Reading of* Paradise Lost (Chapel Hill, NC: North Carolina UP, 1981).
—— 'Reading God: Milton and the Anthropopathetic Tradition', *MS* 25 (1989), 213–43.
—— *The Sinews of Ulysses: Form and Convention in Milton's Works* (Pittsburgh: Duquesne UP, 1989).
—— *Theological Milton: Deity, Discourse and Heresy in the Miltonic Canon* (Pittsburgh: Duquesne UP, 2007).
—— *The Visionary Mode: Biblical Prophecy, Hermeneutics, and Cultural Change* (Ithaca and London: Cornell UP, 1991).
—— and Albert C. Labriola (eds.), *Milton in the Age of Fish: Essays on Authorship, Text, and Terrorism* (Pittsburgh: Duquesne UP, 2006).
Lilla, Salvatore R. C., *Clement of Alexandria: A Study in Christian Platonism and Gnosticism* (Oxford: Oxford UP, 1971).
Lindberg, Carter (ed.), *The Reformation Theologians: An Introduction to Theology in the Early Modern Period* (Oxford: Blackwell, 2002).
Loewenstein, David, '"Fair offspring nurs't in princely Lore": On the Question of Milton's Early Radicalism', *MS* 28 (1992), 37–48.
—— *Milton and the Drama of History: Historical Vision, Iconoclasm, and the Literary Imagination* (Cambridge: Cambridge UP, 1990).
—— 'Milton Among the Religious Radicals and Sects: Polemical Engagements and Silences', *MS* 40 (2002), 222–47.
—— 'The Revenge of the Saint: Radical Religion and Politics in *Samson Agonistes*', *MS* 33 (1996), 159–80.
—— and James Grantham Turner (eds.), *Politics, Poetics and Hermeneutics in Milton's Prose* (Cambridge: Cambridge UP, 1990).
Louth, Andrew, *The Origins of the Christian Mystical Tradition: From Plato to Denys* (Oxford: Clarendon, 1981).
Low, Anthony, *The Blaze of Noon: A Reading of* Samson Agonistes (New York and London: Columbia UP, 1974).
Lowance, Mason I., *The Language of Canaan: Metaphor and Symbol in New England from the Puritans to the Transcendentalists* (Cambridge, Mass.: Harvard UP, 1980).
Luscombe, David, *Medieval Thought: A History of Western Philosophy II* (Oxford and New York: Oxford UP, 1997).
Luxon, Thomas H., *Literal Figures: Puritan Allegory and the Reformation Crisis in Representation* (Chicago: Chicago UP, 1995).
MacCallum, Hugh R., 'Milton and Figurative Interpretation of the Bible', *UTQ* 31 (1961–2), 397–415.

MacCallum, Hugh R., *Milton and the Sons of God: The Divine Image in Milton's Epic Poetry* (Toronto: Toronto UP, 1986).

MacCulloch, Diarmaid, *Tudor Church Militant: Edward VI and the Protestant Reformation* (London: Penguin, 1999).

McClung, W. A., 'The Pinnacle of the Temple', *MQ* 15: 1 (1981), 13–16.

McGinn, Bernard, *The Foundations of Mysticism*, 4 vols. (London: SCM Press, 1992).

McGrath, Alister E., *The Intellectual Origins of the European Reformation*, 2nd edn. (Oxford: Blackwell, 2003).

—— *Reformation Thought: An Introduction*, 3rd edn. (Oxford: Blackwell, 1999).

McGuire, Maryanne Cale, *Milton's Puritan Masque* (Athens, Ga.: Georgia UP, 1983).

McKim, Donald K., *The Cambridge Companion to Martin Luther* (Cambridge: Cambridge UP, 2003).

Madsen, William G., *From Shadowy Types to Truth: Studies in Milton's Symbolism* (New Haven and London: Yale UP, 1968).

Maleski, Mary A. (ed.), *A Fine Tuning: Studies of the Religious Poetry of Herbert and Milton* (Binghamton, NY: Medieval and Renaissance Texts and Studies, 1989).

Mariani, Paul, *God and the Imagination: On Poets, Poetry, and the Ineffable* (Athens, Ga.: Georgia UP, 2002).

Martin, Catherine Gimelli, *The Ruins of Allegory: Paradise Lost and the Metamorphosis of Epic Convention* (Durham, NC and London: Duke UP, 1998).

Martz, Louis L. (ed.), *Milton: A Collection of Critical Essays* (Englewood Cliffs, NJ: Prentice-Hall, 1966).

—— *Poet of Exile: A Study in Milton's Poetry* (New Haven and London: Yale UP, 1980).

Maxwell, Catherine, *The Female Sublime from Milton to Swinburne: Bearing Blindness* (Manchester: Manchester UP, 2001).

Maxwell, J. C., 'Milton's Samson and Sophocles' Heracles', *PQ* 33 (1954), 90–1.

Moore, A. W., *The Infinite.* (1990), 2nd edn. (London and New York: Routledge, 2001).

—— *Points of View* (Oxford: Oxford UP, 1997).

Moschovakis, Nicholas, 'Great Period: Pointing, Syntax and the Millennium in the Texts of "At a Solemn Musick"', *MQ* 36: 4 (2002), 199–220.

Mueller, Janel M., *The Native Tongue and the Word: Developments in English Prose Style, 1380–1580* (Chicago: Chicago UP, 1984).

Muller, Henri F. and Pauline Taylor, *A Chrestomathy of Vulgar Latin* (Boston: D. C. Heath, 1932).

Mustazza, Leonard, 'Language as Weapon in Milton's *Paradise Regained*', *MS* 18 (1983), 195–216.

—— *'Such Prompt Eloquence': Language as Agency and Character in Milton's Epics* (Lewisburg, Pa.: Bucknell UP, 1988).

—— 'The Verbal Plot of *Samson Agonistes*', *MS* 23 (1987), 241–58.

Norbrook, David, *Poetry and Politics in the English Renaissance* (1984; rev. ed., Oxford: Oxford UP, 2002).

—— 'Republican Occasions in *Paradise Regained* and *Samson Agonistes*', *MS* 42 (2002), 122–48.

—— *Writing the English Republic: Poetry, Rhetoric and Politics, 1627–1660* (Cambridge: Cambridge UP, 2000).

Nuttall, A. D. *The Alternative Trinity: Gnostic Heresy in Marlowe, Milton, and Blake* (Oxford: Clarendon, 1998).

—— *Overheard by God: Fiction and Prayer in Herbert, Milton, Dante and St. John* (London and New York: Methuen, 1980).

Nuttall, Geoffrey F., *The Holy Spirit in Puritan Faith and Experience* (1947; rev. edn., Chicago: Chicago UP, 1992).

Nyquist, Mary, 'The Father's Word/Satan's Wrath', *PMLA* 100: 2 (1985), 187–202.

—— and Margaret W. Ferguson (eds.), *Re-Membering Milton: Essays on the Texts and Traditions* (New York and London: Methuen, 1987).

Oberman, Heiko A., *Forerunners of the Reformation: The Shape of Late Medieval Thought*, trans. Paul L. Nyhus (London: Lutterworth Press, 1967).

—— *The Dawn of the Reformation: Essays in Late Medieval and Early Reformation Thought* (Edinburgh: T. & T. Clark, 1986).

—— *The Reformation: Roots and Ramifications*, trans. Andrew Colin Gow (Edinburgh: T. & T. Clark, 1994).

Ong, Walter J., *The Presence of the Word* (New York: Simon & Schuster, 1967).

O'Rourke Boyle, Marjorie, *Erasmus on Language and Method in Theology* (Toronto: Toronto UP, 1977).

Orr, Warwick, 'Milton and the Defeat of Sacredness', *CQ* 26: 2 (1997), 99–117.

Otto, Rudolf, *The Idea of the Holy: An Inquiry into the Non-rational Factor in the Idea of the Divine and its Relation to the Rational* (1917), trans. John W. Harvey (1923; Oxford: Oxford UP, 1978).

Parker, William Riley, *Milton: A Biography*, 2 vols., 2nd edn., ed. Gordon Campbell (Oxford: Clarendon Press, 1996).

Partee, Charles, *Calvin and Classical Philosophy* (1977; Louisville, Ky.: Westminster John Knox Press, 2005).

Patrides, C. A., *Milton and the Christian Tradition* (Oxford: Clarendon Press, 1966).

—— (ed.), *George Herbert: The Critical Heritage* (London: Routledge, 1983).

—— (ed.), *Milton's Epic Poetry: Essays on Paradise Lost and Paradise Regained* (Harmondsworth: Penguin, 1967).

—— J. H. Adamson, and W. B. Hunter (eds.), *Bright Essence: Studies in Milton's Theology* (Salt Lake City: Utah UP, 1971).

Patterson, Annabel (ed.), *John Milton* (London and New York: Longman, 1992).

Pelikan, Jaroslav, *Christianity and Classical Culture: The Metamorphosis of Natural Theology in the Christian Encounter with Hellenism* (New Haven and London: Yale UP, 1993).

Pope, Elizabeth Marie, *Paradise Regained: The Tradition and the Poem* (Baltimore: Johns Hopkins UP, 1947).

Poole, William, *Milton and the Idea of the Fall* (Cambridge: Cambridge UP, 2005).

Pruitt, Kristin A. and Charles W. Durham (eds.), *Living Texts: Interpreting Milton* (Selinsgrove and London: Susquehanna UP and Associated University Presses, 2000).

Quint, David, 'Expectation and Prematurity in Milton's *Nativity Ode*', *MPH* 97: 2 (1999), 195–219.

—— *Origin and Originality in Renaissance Literature: Versions of the Source* (New Haven and London: Yale UP, 1983).

Radzinowicz, Mary Ann, *Milton's Epics and the Book of Psalms.* (Princeton: Princeton UP, 1989).

—— *Toward Samson Agonistes: The Growth of Milton's Mind* (Princeton: Princeton UP, 1978).

Rajan, Balachandra, '*Paradise Lost*: The Uncertain Epic', *MS* 17 (1983), 105–19.

—— *The Lofty Rhyme: A Study of Milton's Major Poetry* (London: Routledge & Kegan Paul, 1970).

Rapaport, Herman, *Milton and the Postmodern* (Lincoln, Nebr., and London: Nebraska UP, 1983).

Reid, David, *The Humanism of Milton's Paradise Lost* (Edinburgh: Edinburgh UP, 1993).

Reid, J. K. S., *The Authority of Scripture: A Study of the Reformation and Post-Reformation Understanding of the Bible* (London: Methuen, 1957).

Revard, Stella, *Milton and the Tangles of Neaera's Hair: The Making of the 1645 Poems* (Columbia, Miss., and London: Missouri UP, 1997).

Reynolds, Susan, *Medieval Reading: Grammar, Rhetoric, and the Classical Text* (Cambridge: Cambridge UP, 1996).

Ricks, Christopher, *Milton's Grand Style* (Oxford: Clarendon Press, 1963).

Rist, John M. *Augustine: Ancient Thought Baptized* (Cambridge: Cambridge UP, 1994).

Rogers, John, 'The Secret of *Samson Agonistes*', *MS* 33 (1996), 111–32.

Rorem, Paul, *Pseudo-Dionysius: A Commentary on the Texts and an Introduction to their Influence* (Oxford: Oxford UP, 1993).

Rosenblatt, Jason P., *Torah and Law in* Paradise Lost (Princeton: Princeton UP, 1994).

Røstvig, Maren-Sofie, 'Ars Aeterna: Renaissance Poetics and Theories of Divine Creation', *Mosaic*, 3: 2 (1970), 40–61.

Rudrum, Alan (ed.), *Milton*, Modern Judgements Series (Nashville, Tenn.: Aurora Publishers, 1970).

Rumrich, John Peter, 'Milton's *Theanthropos*: The Body of Christ in *Paradise Regained*', *MS* 42 (2003), 50–67.

—— *Milton Unbound: Controversy and Interpretation* (Cambridge: Cambridge UP, 1996).

—— 'Uninventing Milton', *MPH* 87: 3 (1990), 249–65.

Runia, David T., *Exegesis and Philosophy: Studies on Philo of Alexandria* (Aldershot: Variorum, 1990).

—— *Philo of Alexandria and the 'Timaeus' of Plato* (Leiden: Brill, 1986).

Rushdy, Ashraf H. A., 'According to Samson's Command: Some Contexts of Milton's Tragedy', *MQ* (1992), 69–80.

—— *The Empty Garden: The Subject of Late Milton* (Pittsburgh and London: (Pittsburgh UP, 1992).

Said, Edward W., *Beginnings: Intention and Method* (Baltimore and London: Johns Hopkins UP, 1975).

Samuel, Irene, *Dante and Milton: The* Commedia *and* Paradise Lost (Ithaca, NY: Cornell UP, 1966).

—— *Plato and Milton* (Ithaca, NY: Cornell UP, 1947).

—— 'The Dialogue in Heaven: A Reconsideration of *Paradise Lost* III, 1–417', *PMLA* 72: 4 (1957), 601–11.

Samuels, Peggy, 'Duelling Erasers: Milton and Scripture', *SPH* 96: 2 (1999), 180–203.

—— 'Labor in the Chambers: *Paradise Regained* and the Discourse of Quiet', *MS* 36 (1998), 153–76.

Sandmel, Samuel, *Philo of Alexandria: An Introduction* (Oxford: Oxford UP, 1979).

Sauer, Elizabeth, *Barbarous Dissonance and Images of Voice in Milton's Epics* (Montreal and Kingston: McGill-Queen's UP, 1996).

Saurat, Denis, *Milton: Man and Thinker* (London: J. M. Dent & Sons, 1944).

Scharfstein, Ben-Ami, *Ineffability: The Failure of Words in Philosophy and Religion* (Albany, NY: New York UP, 1993).

Scholem, Gershom E., *Elements of the Kabbalah and its Symbolism* (1960; 2nd Hebrew edn., Jerusalem: Shocken Books, 1980).

—— *Jewish Gnosticism, Merkabah Mysticism, and Talmudic Tradition* (New York: Jewish Theological Seminary of America, 1960).

—— *Major Trends in Jewish Mysticism* (New York: Shocken Books, 1946).

Schmitt, Charles B. and Quentin Skinner (eds.), *The Cambridge History of Renaissance Philosophy* (Cambridge: Cambridge UP, 1988).

Schwartz, Regina, 'Redemption and Paradise Regained', *MS* 42 (2003), 26–49.

—— *Remembering and Repeating: On Milton's Theology and Poetics* (1988; Chicago and London: Chicago UP, 1993).

Sharon-Zisser, Shirley (ed.), *Critical Essays on Shakespeare's 'A Lover's Complaint': Suffering Ecstasy* (Aldershot: Ashgate, 2006).

—— 'Silence and Darkness in *Paradise Lost*', *MS* 25 (1989), 191–211.

Shawcross, John T., *John Milton: The Self and the World* (Lexington, Ky.: Kentucky UP, 1993).

—— *Paradise Regain'd: 'Worthy t'Have not Remain'd so Long Unsung'* (Pittsburgh: Duquesne UP, 1988).

—— *The Uncertain World of Samson Agonistes* (Cambridge: D. S. Brewer, 2001).

Shullenberger, William, 'Into the Woods: The Lady's Soliloquy in *Comus*', *MQ* 35: 1 (2001), 33–43.

—— 'Linguistic and Poetic Theory in Milton's De Doctrina Christiana', *ELN* 19 (1982), 262–78.

Simpson, Ken, 'Lingering Voices, Telling Silences: Silence and the Word in *Paradise Regained*', *MS* 35 (1997), 179–95.

Sims, James H. and Leland Ryken (eds.), *Milton and Scriptural Tradition: The Bible into Poetry* (Columbia, Miss.: Missouri UP, 1984).

Skulsky, Harold, *Justice in the Dock: Milton's Experimental Tragedy* (Newark, Del.: Delaware UP, 1995).

—— *Milton and the Death of Man: Humanism on Trial in* Paradise Lost (Newark, Del.: Delaware UP, 2000).

Smith, Nigel, *Literature and Revolution in England, 1640–1660* (New Haven and London: Yale UP, 1994).

—— *Perfection Proclaimed: Language and Literature in English Radical Religion, 1640–1660* (Oxford: Clarendon Press, 1989).

Spaeth, Sigmund, *Milton's Knowledge of Music* (1913; Ann Arbor, Mich.: Michigan UP, 1963).

Spinks, Bryan D. *Two Faces of Elizabethan Anglican Theology: Sacraments and Salvation in the Thought of William Perkins and Richard Hooker* (Lanham, Md.: Scarecrow Press, 1999).

Spitzer, Leo, *Classical and Christian Ideas of World Harmony* (Baltimore: Johns Hopkins UP, 1963).

Stachniewski, John, *The Persecutory Imagination: English Puritanism and the Literature of Religious Despair* (Oxford: Clarendon Press, 1991).

Steadman, John H., '"Faithful Champion": The Theological Basis of Milton's Hero of Faith', *Anglia*, 77 (1959), 12–28.

Stein, Arnold S., *Answerable Style: Essays on* Paradise Lost (Minneapolis: Minnesota UP, 1967).

—— *The Art of Presence: The Poet and* Paradise Lost (Berkeley and London: California UP, 1977).

—— *Heroic Knowledge: An Interpretation of* Paradise Regained *and* Samson Agonistes (Minneapolis: Minnesota UP, 1957).

Stevens, Paul, *Imagination and the Presence of Shakespeare in* Paradise Lost (Madison, Wisc.: University of Wisconsin Press, 1985).

Strier, Richard, 'Milton's Fetters; or, Why is Eden Better than Heaven', *MS* 38 (2000), 169–97.

Sundell, Roger H., 'The Narrator as Interpreter in *Paradise Regained*', *MS* 2 (1970), 83–99.

Swaim, Kathleen M., *Before and After the Fall: Contrasting Modes in* Paradise Lost (Amherst, Mass.: Massachusetts UP, 1986).

—— 'Myself a True Poem: Early Milton and the (Re)Formation of the Subject', *MS* 38 (2000), 66–95.

Teskey, Gordon, *Allegory and Violence* (Ithaca, NY: Cornell UP, 1996).

—— *Delirious Milton: The Fate of the Poet in Modernity* (Cambridge, Mass.: Harvard UP, 2006).

Tillyard, E. M. W., *Milton* (1930; rev. edn., Harmondsworth: Penguin, 1966).

Treip, Mindele Anne, *Allegorical Poetics and the Epic: The Renaissance Tradition to* Paradise Lost (Lexington, Ky.: Kentucky UP, 1994).

Turcan, Robert, *The Cults of the Roman Empire* (1989), trans. Antonia Nevill (Oxford: Blackwell, 1996).

Turner, Denys, *The Darkness of God: Negativity in Christian Mysticism* (Cambridge: Cambridge UP, 1995).

Tuve, Rosemond, *Essays by Rosemond Tuve: Spenser, Herbert, Milton*, ed. T. P. Roche (Princeton: Princeton UP, 1970).

—— *Images and Themes in Five Poems by Milton* (Cambridge, Mass.: Harvard UP, 1962).

Tyacke, Nicholas, *Anti-Calvinists: The Rise of English Arminianism c. 1590–1640* (Oxford: Oxford UP, 1987).

—— 'Lancelot Andrewes and the Myth of Anglicanism', in Peter Lake and Michael Questier (eds.), *Conformity and Orthodoxy in the English Church, c. 1560–1660* (London: Boydell, 2000), 5–33.

Waldock, A. J. A., Paradise Lost *and its Critics* (1947; Gloucester, Mass.: Peter Smith, 1959).

Walker, Julia M. (ed.), *Milton and the Idea of Woman* (Urbana, Ill.: Illinois UP, 1988).

Wallace, Ronald S., *Calvin's Doctrine of the Word and Sacraments* (1953; Edinburgh: Scottish Academic Press, 1995).

Wandel, Lee Palmer, *The Eucharist in the Reformation: Incarnation and Liturgy* (Cambridge: Cambridge UP, 2006).

Waswo, Richard, *Language and Meaning in the Renaissance* (Princeton: Princeton UP, 1987).

Watkins, Owen C., *The Puritan Experience* (London: Routledge & Kegan Paul, 1972).

Webber, Joan, *Milton and his Epic Tradition* (Seattle: Washington UP, 1979).

Weber, Burton Jasper, *Wedges and Wings: The Patterning of* Paradise Regained (Carbondale, Ill.: Southern Illinois UP, 1975).

Weinberg, Bernard, *A History of Literary Criticism in the Italian Renaissance*, 2 vols. (Chicago: Chicago UP, 1961).

Wilding, Michael, *Dragon's Teeth: Literature in the English Revolution* (Oxford: Clarendon Press, 1987).

Williams, Jeni, *Interpreting Nightingales: Gender, Class and Histories* (Sheffield: Sheffield Academic Press, 1997).

Wilson, Emily R., *Mocked with Death: Tragic Overliving from Sophocles to Milton* (Baltimore and London: Johns Hopkins UP, 2004).

Wind, Edgar, *Pagan Mysteries in the Renaissance* (1958; rev. edn., London: Faber & Faber, 1967).

Wittreich, Joseph (ed.), *Calm of Mind: Tercentenary Essays on* Paradise Regained *and* Samson Agonistes *in Honor of John S. Diekhoff* (Cleveland and London: Case Western Reserve UP, 1971).

—— *Interpreting* Samson Agonistes (Princeton: Princeton UP, 1982).

—— (ed.), *Milton and the Line of Vision* (Madison, Wisc.: Wisconsin UP, 1975).

—— '"Reading" Milton: The Death (And Survival) of the Author', *MS* 38 (2000), 10–46.

—— *Shifting Contexts: Reinterpreting* Samson Agonistes (Pittsburgh: Duquesne UP, 2002).

—— *Visionary Poetics: Milton's Tradition and his Legacy* (San Marino, Calif.: Huntington Library, 1979).

Wolosky, Shira, 'An "Other" Negative Theology: On Derrida's "How to Avoid Speaking: Denials"', *PT* 19: 2 (1998), 261–80.

—— *Language Mysticism: The Negative Way of Language in Eliot, Beckett, and Celan* (Stanford: Stanford UP, 1995).

Wood, Derek N. C., '*Exiled From Light': Divine Law, Morality, and Violence in Milton's* Samson Agonistes (Toronto and London: Toronto UP, 2001).

Woodhouse, A. S. P., *The Heavenly Muse: A Preface to Milton,* ed. Hugh MacCallum (Toronto: Toronto UP, 1972).

Worden, Blair, 'Milton, *Samson Agonistes,* and the Restoration', in Gerard MacLean (ed.), *Culture and Society in the Stuart Restoration* (Cambridge: Cambridge UP, 1995), 111–36.

Yates, Frances, *Giordano Bruno and the Hermetic Tradition* (1964; London and New York: Routledge, 2002).

Index

Works are listed under authors' names, except for *Paradise Lost, Paradise Regained, Poems 1645*, and *Samson Agonistes*, which are given separate entries. Authors with more than two works to their name will have those works grouped together under the subheading WORKS.